THE ARABIC LANGUAGE

THE ARABIC LANGUAGE

KEES VERSTEEGH

EDINBURGH UNIVERSITY PRESS

Edinburgh University Press
22 George Square, Edinburgh

Published in Paperback, 2001

Typeset in Linotype Trump Medieval
by Koinonia, Manchester, and
printed and bound in Great Britain
by The University Press, Cambridge

A CIP Record for this book is available
from the British Library

ISBN 0 7486 1436 2 (paperback)

CONTENTS

PREFACE

> 'A legal scholar once said: "Only a prophet is able to have perfect command of the Arabic language". This statement is bound to be true since, as far as we know, no one has ever claimed to have memorised this language in its entirety.' (Ibn Fāris, *aṣ-Ṣāḥibī fī fiqh al-luġa*, ed. by 'Aḥmad Ṣaqr, Cairo, 1977, p. 26)

The aim of this book is to give a sketch of the history of the Arabic language, mother tongue of more than 200 million speakers. Since its earliest appearance as a world language in the seventh century CE, Arabic has been characterised by an opposition between two varieties: a standard language, which occupies a prestige position and is revered as the language of religion, culture and education; and a vernacular language, which serves as the mother tongue for most speakers and is the natural means of communication throughout society. The opposition between these two varieties constitutes the major theme of the present book.

The set-up of the book is basically chronological: after an introduction on the study of the Arabic language in Western Europe, Chapter 2 deals with the position of the Arabic language within the group of the Semitic languages and Chapter 3 with its emergence in historical times. Then, the linguistic situation in the Arabian peninsula in the period immediately preceding the advent of Islam is discussed (Chapter 4).

In the course of the Arab conquests, after the death of the Prophet Muḥammad, the Arabic language was exported together with the religion of the Arabs to a large part of the Mediterranean and Near Eastern world. In the next two chapters, the development of Arabic into a literary standard is analysed. Chapter 5 describes the role of Arabic as the language of literature and administration. Chapter 6 steps outside the chronological framework and discusses the structure of the Arabic language from an unexpected perspective, that of the Arab grammarians, who analysed their own language in a way that differed in many respects from the Western model.

The contact between the speakers of Arabic and the inhabitants of the conquered territories brought about a restructuring of the language, which led to an opposition between standard language and vernacular dialect. Chapter 7 attempts to explain the emergence of vernacular varieties of the Arabic language. In Chapter 8, the influence of the vernacular language in the so-called Middle Arabic texts is analysed.

The next two chapters deal with the study of the modern Arabic dialects: Chapter 9 is a general introduction to the classification and geography of Arabic dialects, and Chapter 10 deals with the characteristics of the major dialects, for which text samples are provided.

In Chapter 11 the development of Modern Standard Arabic in the nineteenth century is discussed, and Chapter 12 deals with the sociolinguistic relationship between standard language and dialect in the contemporary Arabophone world.

Finally, the last two chapters deal with the position of Arabic outside the Arab world, both as a minority language in the so-called linguistic enclaves (Chapter 13), and as a religious language in predominantly Islamic countries (Chapter 14).

Since the present survey is intended as a textbook, I have refrained from giving copious footnotes. Obviously, much of the information is based on the existing literature. The notes on further reading appended to each chapter give information about the main sources used in that chapter; in quoting concrete examples the source is indicated within the text.

I wish to thank those of my colleagues who were willing to read portions of the manuscript and give me their valuable comments: Erik-Jan Zürcher, Harald Motzki, Wim Delsman, Gert Borg. Additional information was kindly given by Louis Boumans and Jan Hoogland.

Knowing from personal experience how much time it takes to read other people's manuscripts, I am ashamed of having taken up so much of the time of my friend and colleague Manfred Woidich. In a way, he himself is responsible for the burden which I imposed on him because of his enthusiasm and never-failing support. His remarks and our subsequent discussions made many things clear to me that I had failed to see for myself.

Special thanks are due to Carole Hillenbrand. Although the completion of this project took many more years than we originally envisaged, she never lost confidence and stimulated me to continue with it. Her critical reading of the entire manuscript was invaluable. In a very real sense, this book would never have appeared without her. I also wish to thank the staff of Edinburgh University Press, and in particular Jane Feore and Ivor Normand, for their encouragement, patience and assistance in bringing this manuscript to press.

In the paperback edition a number of mistakes have been corrected and a few bibliographical items have been added. I have gratefully used the suggestions in some of the reviews of the book by Alan Kaye, Nadia Anghelescu, Clive Holes and Mike Carter.

During the preparation of the present book, I have been very fortunate in receiving the help of Yola de Lusenet. Although being a complete outsider to the field, she took the trouble of going through the pages of the manuscript and pointing out to me with uncanny accuracy every flawed argument and deficient formulation. I am immensely grateful to her for her critical reading and her support.

Nijmegen, February 2000

LIST OF FIGURES AND MAPS

1
The Development of the Study of Arabic

In 632 CE, the Prophet of Islam, Muḥammad, died in the city of Medina. The century of conquests that followed brought both the Islamic religion and the Arabic language to the attention of a world that up until then had possessed only the vaguest notion of what went on in the interior of the Arabian peninsula. Ever since this first confrontation between the Islamic world and Europe, the Arabs and their language have been part of the European experience. At first, the intellectual relationship between the two worlds was unilateral. Greek knowledge and knowledge about Greek filtered through in the Islamic world, while the Byzantines did not show themselves overly interested in things Arabic. Although their military prowess was feared, the Arabs' religion, culture and language were not deemed worthy of study. For the Byzantines, the Greek heritage did not need any contribution from the inhabitants of the desert whose only claim to fame rested on their ability to harass the Byzantine armies and contest Byzantine hegemony in the Eastern Mediterranean.

After the conquest of the Iberian peninsula in 711, however, the perception of the Arabs as a threat to the cultural values of Europe started to change. Through them, Western Europe got in touch with a part of its heritage that it had lost in the turmoil of the fall of the Roman empire. Western medicine and philosophy became dependent on the Arab culture of Islamic Spain for the knowledge of Greek medical and philosophical writings, which were practically unknown in the West. From the eleventh century onwards, after the fall of Toledo in 1085, these writings began to circulate in Latin translations of the Arabic versions. The Arabic language itself was not widely studied, since most scholars relied upon translations that were made by a small group of translators, often Jews, who had familiarised themselves with the language either in Arabic Sicily or in al-'Andalus.

In the twelfth century, during the period of the Crusades, Western Europeans for the first time became acquainted directly with Islamic culture and Arabic. This first-hand contact brought about an ambivalent reaction. On the one hand, Islam was the enemy which threatened Europe and held the keys to the Holy Land. On the other hand, for the time being the Muslims or Saracens were the keepers of the Greek heritage in medicine and philosophy and provided the only available access to these treasures. Thus, while crusaders were busy trying to wrest Jerusalem from the Muslims and to preserve Europe from Islam, at the same time scholars from all over Europe travelled to Islamic Spain in order to study at the famous universities of Cordova and Granada. The study of Arabic served a double purpose. For the medical scholars at the University of Paris, who humbly sat down at the feet of the Arab doctors and called themselves *arabizantes*, the translations of medical writings from Arabic into Latin constituted an indispensable source of knowledge. Others devoted themselves to the translation of what in their eyes was a false religious message, in order to refute the arguments of the 'Mohammedans' or preferably to convert them to the Christian religion. The first translation of the *Qur'ān* appeared in 1143 under the supervision of an abbot of the monastery of Cluny, Peter the Venerable (d. 1157), with the express aim of denouncing the fallacy of the 'Agarenes' (or 'Hagarenes'), as they were often called.

For both purposes, Islamic Spain remained the main gateway to Islam and the only place where people could receive the language training that they needed in order to understand both the Islamic Holy Book and the precious Greek writings. It is, therefore, quite understandable that it was in Spain that the first instruments for the study of Arabic appeared, and it is there that we find the first bilingual glossaries of the language: the *Glossarium latino–arabicum* (twelfth century) and the *Vocabulista in arabico* (thirteenth century).

The end of the *reconquista* of Spain by the Catholic kings of Castile and Navarre changed all this. After the fall of Granada in 1492, the presence of Muslims in the Iberian peninsula was no longer tolerated. In 1502, the choice between emigration or conversion was put to them, and a century later the last remaining *Moriscos* were expelled to North Africa. This removed the last direct link between Europe and Islam. The same period also witnessed the activities of Pedro de Alcalá, who in 1505 published a large dictionary of (Spanish) Arabic (*Vocabulista aravigo en letra castellana*) and a manual of Arabic grammar with a conversation guide for the confessional (*Arte para ligera mente saber la lengua araviga*) intended for those priests who had to deal with newly-converted Muslims. This was the first analysis of Arabic on the basis of a Greco-Latin model.

After the fall of Constantinople in 1453, interest in original Greek materials in the West grew to the point where scholars began to question the trustworthiness of the Latin translations that had been made from Arabic versions of Greek texts. As the familiarity with the Greek sources increased, the new trend became to go back to these sources (*ad fontes*) instead of using the Arabic ones. The resulting altercation between the old-fashioned *arabizantes* and the modernist *neoterici* ended in a victory for the new trend. From now on, the writings of Avicenna became a symbol of the past, and the attitude of Europe towards Islam changed accordingly.

At first, some scholars refused to give up their Arabic connections. In his *Defensio medicorum principis Avicennae, ad Germaniae medicos* ('Defence of the Prince of the medical scholars, Avicenna, to the doctors of Germany', Strasbourg 1530), the Dutch physician Laurentius Frisius states that the study of Arabic is indispensable for those who wish to study medicine. To his opponents, who extolled the virtues of the Greek medical scholars, he concedes that the Arabic language is primitive compared to the Greek language, but he insists that the quality of the language does not matter in the transmission of knowledge. The Arabs, he says, have translated all the essential works of Greek scholars on medicine and philosophy and added their own invaluable commentaries. Frisius' example confirms that at this time some scholars in Western

1143 - 1st Qur'ān translation appears

Europe still regarded Arabic as an important corollary to the study of medicine. But when the Greek sources became known in the West, the Arabic texts were no longer needed, and, what is worse, the comparison between the Greek originals and the Arabic translations (most of which had been made after Syriac translations and had themselves become known in the West through Latin translations) did not work out to the Arabs' advantage. Henceforth, they came to be regarded as defilers of the Greek heritage instead of its guardians. It looked as if the study of Arabic science had become completely unnecessary.

With the change of attitude towards Arabic medicine, the study of Arabic in Western universities took on a new dimension. Throughout the period of the Crusades and in spite of their admiration for the knowledge and wisdom of the Arab doctors, most Christians had regarded Islam as the arch-enemy of Christianity and thus of Europe. Now that the scholarly motive for studies of Arabic had disappeared, the main impetus for such studies became the missionary fervour of the new Europe. Scholars wishing to dedicate themselves to a polemic with the enemy felt the need for didactic materials on the language so that they could understand the original Arabic texts, in the first place of course the text of the Islamic revelation, the Qur'ān. Thus, for instance, Nicolaus Clenardus (1495–1542), in his *Perigrinationum, ac de rebus Machometicis epistolae elegantissimae* ('Most subtle treatises of wanderings and about matters Mohammedan', Louvain 1551), writes that it would be useless to try to convince the 'Mohammedans' in Latin of their errors. He himself had still studied Arabic and medicine in Granada, but he strongly felt that the study of Arabic was needed primarily in order to polemicise against Muslims in their own language. In this connection, a second factor may be mentioned: the wish on the part of the Catholic church to achieve reunification with Eastern Christianity. Contacts with Arabic-speaking Maronites were encouraged, and an increasing number of Levantine Christians came to Rome and Paris in order to help in this campaign. At the same time, the Maronites brought information on Arabic and Islam and became an important source of information on these topics.

Even those scholars whose interest was primarily philological or historical, such as Bedwell (1563–1632) and Erpenius (1584–1624), followed the prevailing views of their contemporaries in regarding Islam as a false religion. Yet, with their grammars and text editions, they laid the foundations for the study of Arabic, and their interest in the language itself was probably genuine. It may well be the case that they sometimes cited religious motives in order to legitimise their preoccupation with the language of the infidels. Erpenius also showed a special interest in the writings of the Arab Christians and was convinced that the study of the Arabic translations of the Bible would make an important contribution to Biblical studies. Since Arabic resembled Hebrew so much, many scholars believed that the study of the Arabic lexicon would be rewarding for the understanding of Biblical Hebrew, and accordingly it became customary to combine the two languages in the curriculum.

In fact, the resemblance between the two languages, especially in the lexicon, is so striking that at a very early date scholars had begun to remark on this relationship. In the Arab world, the general disinterest in other languages did not create an atmosphere in which the relationship could be studied fruitfully, although some of the geographers remarked on it. Hebrew grammarians did devote a lot of attention to the relationship between the two, or, if we count Aramaic as well, the three languages. Since Jews in the Islamic empire lived in a trilingual community, their native tongue being Arabic and the language of their Holy Scripture being Hebrew, with commentary and explanation in Aramaic, they were in an ideal situation to observe similarities across the three languages. Yehuda ibn Qurayš (probably around 900) wrote a *Risāla* in which he stressed the importance of Arabic and Aramaic for the study of the Hebrew Bible. The findings of the Hebrew philologists in comparative linguistics remained, however, restricted to the small circle of the indigenous grammatical tradition and did not affect the development of the study of the Semitic languages in Europe.

In Western Europe, as early as the sixteenth century, philologists working with Hebrew had not been completely unaware of the relationship between Hebrew and other Semitic languages, which is much more transparent than that between the Indo-European languages. They called these collectively 'Oriental languages', a name which at various times included not only Arabic, Hebrew and Aramaic but also Ethiopic, and even unrelated languages such as Armenian and Persian. But this vague awareness of a linguistic connection did not lead to any scientific comparison, and the only practical effect was that the study of Arabic was recommended as an ancillary to the study of the Hebrew Bible. It was generally assumed that Hebrew had been the language of paradise and as such the original language of mankind. The other languages were therefore regarded as its offspring which presented the original language in a degenerated form.

The idea of a relationship between the languages that are now known as Semitic found its Biblical support in the story about the sons of Noah, namely Shem, Cham and Japheth, a division also used by the Hebrew and Arab scholars. The sons of Shem had spread all over the Middle East and North Africa, the sons of Cham were the original speakers of the African languages, and the sons of Japheth were the ancestors of the speakers of a variety of languages in Europe and Asia. In its original form, this classification hardly evoked any diachronic connotation: the languages were seen as equals and the distance between them was a genealogical distance between relatives. Western linguistics in the seventeenth and eighteenth centuries was more interested in the universal structure of human speech, and the ideas of the *Grammaire générale et raisonnée* of Port Royal (1660) about the connections between logic and grammar greatly affected the orientation of Arabic and Semitic linguistics, too, for instance in Silvestre de Sacy's *Grammaire arabe* (1806). The universalist orientation strengthened the ahistorical character of the study of Arabic and Hebrew and did not advance the comparative study of what had become known as the Semitic languages, a term used for the first time in 1781 by A. L. Schlözer.

The two factors that promoted the study of Arabic, the use of Arabic for polemical purposes, and its use for the study of the Hebrew Bible, combined to ensure the continuation of the study of the language, even after the decline of the influence of Arab medical science. It may be added that commercial interests, too, may have played a role in the search for knowledge about Oriental languages. Especially in the Dutch Republic, but also in Germany and France,

2

Arabic as a Semitic Language

2.1 THE CLASSIFICATION OF THE SEMITIC LANGUAGES

Arabic belongs to a group of languages collectively known as the Semitic languages. To this group belong a number of languages in the Middle East, some of them no longer extant. The earliest attested Semitic language is Akkadian, a language spoken in Mesopotamia between 2500 and 600 BCE; from 2000 BCE onwards it was differentiated into Babylonian and Assyrian. As a written language, Neo-Babylonian was probably used until the beginning of the common era. From the Syro-Palestinian area, several Semitic languages are known. Eblaite is the language of the 15,000 inscriptions that were discovered in the city of Ebla, the present-day Tell Mardīḫ, 60 km south of Aleppo; they date from the period between 2500 and 2300 BCE. Ugaritic was used during the fourteenth and thirteenth centuries BCE in Ugarit, the present-day Rās Šamra, 10 km north of Latakia.

While the precise relations between Eblaite and Ugaritic and the rest of the Semitic languages are still disputed (according to some Eblaite belongs to East Semitic), most scholars agree about the other languages in this area, collectively known as the North-west Semitic languages. During the first half of the second millennium BCE, the only traces of North-west Semitic are in the form of proper names in the Akkadian archives, for instance those of Mari. The type of language which these names represent is called Amoritic. At the end of the second millennium BCE, two groups of languages begin to emerge: on the one hand Aramaic, and on the other Canaanite, a collective term for Hebrew, Phoenician and a few other languages, of which little is known. The oldest stage of Hebrew is Biblical Hebrew, the language of the Jewish Bible (1200–200 BCE); later stages are represented by the language of the Dead Sea Scrolls (second and first centuries BCE); the language of the Rabbinical literature known as Mishnaic Hebrew; and Modern Hebrew or Ivrit, one of the two national languages of the state of Israel. Phoenician was the language of the Phoenician cities Sidon and Tyre and their colonies such as Carthage (tenth century BCE to second century CE).

Old Aramaic (first millennium BCE) was spoken at least from the tenth century BCE onwards in Syria. Between the seventh and the fourth centuries BCE, it was used as a *lingua franca* in the Babylonian and Persian empires; it is also the language of some parts of the Jewish Bible. More recent forms of Aramaic are divided into Western and Eastern Aramaic. Western Aramaic was the spoken language of Palestine during the first centuries of the common era, which remained in use as a literary language until the fifth century CE. It was the official language of the Nabataean and Palmyrene kingdoms (cf. below, p. 28).

The most important representatives of Eastern Aramaic were Syriac, the language of Christian religious literature; Mandaean, the language of a large body of gnostic literature between the third and the eighth centuries CE; and the language of the Babylonian Talmud between the third and the thirteenth centuries CE. Syriac was the spoken language of the Syrian Christians until the eighth century CE. Modern varieties of Aramaic survive in a number of linguistic enclaves (cf. below, p. 94).

In the south of the Arabian peninsula and in Ethiopia, a number of Semitic languages were spoken. Epigraphic South Arabian was the language of the Sabaean, Minaean and Qaṭabānian inscriptions (probably between the eighth century BCE and the sixth century CE). The modern South Arabian dialects, such as Mehri, probably go back to spoken varieties of these languages (cf. below, pp. 12, 94). The oldest of the Ethiopian Semitic languages is Classical Ethiopic or Geʿez, the language of the empire of Aksum (first centuries CE). To this group belong a large number of languages spoken in Ethiopia, such as Tigre, Tigriña and the official language of Ethiopia, Amharic.

In the preceding chapter, we have seen how in the nineteenth century the existing ideas about the relationship between the Semitic languages crystallised into a classificatory scheme under the influence of the historical/comparativist paradigm. In this chapter, we shall discuss the implications of this paradigm for the position of Arabic within the Semitic languages. Originally, five languages, Akkadian, Hebrew, Aramaic, Arabic and Ethiopic, had been distinguished and presented more or less as equals. With the growing influence of historical research in the history of the Semitic-speaking peoples, the study of the relations between these languages was approached from a historical perspective, and under the influence of the paradigm of Indo-European linguistics an attempt was made to establish a family tree of the languages involved, supposedly reflecting their genetic relations. Such a genetic interpretation of the classification implied that all Semitic languages eventually derived from a Proto-Semitic language.

In Indo-European studies, it was generally assumed that it was possible to reconstruct a Proto-Indo-European language on the basis of a comparison of the structure of the known Indo-European languages. Similarly, it was thought that a Proto-Semitic language could be reconstructed by comparing Arabic, Hebrew, Akkadian, Aramaic and Ethiopic, and this language was assumed to have the same status with regard to the Semitic languages that Proto-Indo-European had had with regard to the Indo-European languages, namely that of a parental language with its offshoots. The attempts to find a common structure in these languages that could then be assigned to the proto-language led, however, to widely differing results. Unlike the Indo-European languages, spread over a wide area and usually isolated from each other, the Semitic languages tended to be confined to the same geographic area (Syria/Palestine, Mesopotamia and the Arabian desert) and were often spoken in contiguous regions. This led to more or less permanent contacts between the speakers of these languages, so that borrowing between them was always a possibility. Borrowing typically disrupts historical processes of change and makes it difficult to reconstruct the original correspondences between the languages involved.

The affinity between the Semitic languages is generally much more transparent than that between the Indo-European languages, and they share a number of common features that clearly mark them as Semitic. In themselves, none of the features that are usually presented as typical of a Semitic language is conclusive in determining whether a particular language belongs to the Semitic group, but in combination they constitute a reasonably reliable checklist: triradicalism, presence of emphatic/glottalised consonants, special relationship between vowels and consonants, paratactic constructions, verbal system with a prefix and a suffix conjugation, as well as a large number of lexical correspondences.

As long as the presence of common features in a group of languages is interpreted in terms of a typological classification, without implications regarding their genetic relationship, the subgrouping of the languages involved is not problematic. In such a classification, the issue of later borrowing or of independent developments that have led to identical results is left open. A genetic relationship, on the other hand, implies a historical descent from a common origin, a language that is regarded as the common ancestor of all the languages in the group. Since in this framework the ancestor language is presumed to have a historical reality, it must have been the language of a historical people. Semiticists working in the genealogical framework therefore started looking for a Semitic homeland. There has been a lot of controversy about this homeland of the 'Proto-Semites'. Many scholars situated it in the Arabian peninsula, while others mentioned Syria or North Africa. From such a homeland, successive waves of migration were then supposed to have brought various groups to their respective territories, for instance the Amorites between 2000 and 1700 BCE, and the Aramaeans between 1900 and 1400 BCE. Of these waves, the Arab conquests in the seventh century CE were the latest and the last. Such a view of the events leading to the present-day division of the Semitic languages implies that the peoples mentioned in the historical records already spoke the languages associated later with their names and that, once arrived in their new area, these Semitic languages developed independently from each other, either under the influence of languages already being spoken there (substratal influence), or because of internal developments. These factors were held to be responsible for the innovations in each language and for the differences between the various languages.

It is, of course, also possible to view the present distribution of the languages involved not as the result of sudden migrations of peoples, but rather as a gradual infiltration from different centres, which reached out towards the periphery of the area. Such an infiltration could transmit innovations in a wave-like fashion that most strongly affected the central area, whereas in the periphery older forms stood a better chance of maintaining themselves. In Garbini's (1984) view, one area in particular played an essential role in the distribution of innovations, namely the Syrian plain (rather than the coastal region or Palestine), which he regards as the core area of the Semitic languages. The main characteristic of the Syrian region in which these innovations are supposed to have taken place is the contact between sedentary settlements on the fringe of the desert and nomads from the desert. In some cases, the nomads settled and became part of the sedentary population, but in many other cases groups of settlers separated themselves and became isolated as desert-dwelling nomads.

Garbini regards this constant alternation as the origin of the linguistic pattern of innovations spreading from the Syrian area into other areas. Exactly which innovations were brought from Syria into the peninsula depended on the period in which a particular group of people took to the desert.

Garbini cites examples from Akkadian and Eblaite, showing how these languages were not involved in the migratory process and did not share in some of the later innovations in the Syrian area. The common features which Arabic shares with Aramaic and Amorite stem from the period in which the ancestors of the later Arabs still lived in the Syrian region. In his view, Arabic is the nomadic variety of the languages spoken in Syria in the first millennium BCE, which he calls collectively Amorite. He regards the South Arabian and Ethiopian languages as the result of an earlier migration from the same area. According to this theory, those common features between Arabic and South Arabian that are not shared by the languages in the Syrian area are the result of later convergence: the Arabian Bedouin influenced the sedentary languages/dialects in the south, and inversely through the caravan trade the South Arabian languages/dialects became known in the north of the peninsula. The Modern South Arabian languages (Mehri, Soqoṭri) do not derive directly from the Epigraphic South Arabian language. They probably belong to strata that had never been reached by Arabic influence because they were spoken in remote regions. In some respects, their structure is, therefore, more archaic than that of Epigraphic South Arabian.

In the standard model of the classification of the Semitic languages, it is usually assumed that around 3000 BCE a split took place between the North-east Semitic languages (i.e. Akkadian, later separated into Babylonian and Assyrian) and the rest. Around 2000 BCE, a split took place in the West Semitic group between the North-west and the South-west Semitic languages. Finally, around 1000 BCE, North-west Semitic split into Canaanite and Aramaic, whereas the South-west Semitic languages divided into Arabic, South Arabian and Ethiopic. Later discoveries modified this picture considerably, in particular the discovery of Ugaritic in 1929, and the more recent one of Eblaite in 1974. Both are nowadays usually regarded as North-west Semitic languages, but the precise

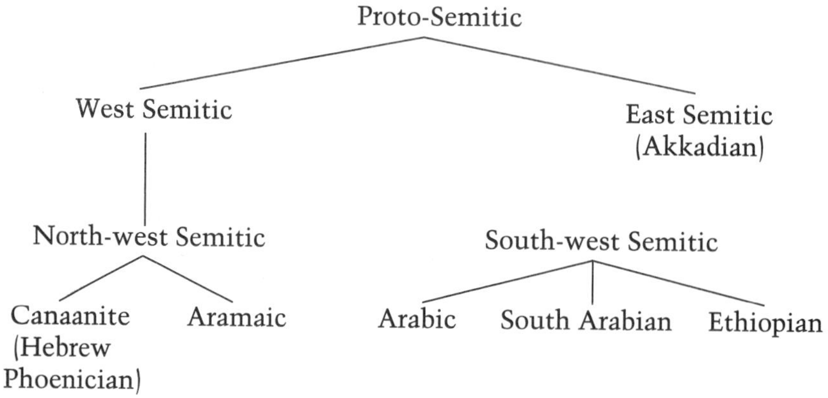

Figure 2.1 The traditional classification of the Semitic languages

relations between the languages of this group are still disputed (see Figure 2.1).

The genealogical paradigm, whether it is framed in terms of the migration of peoples or in terms of the spreading of linguistic innovations, has been severely criticised by some scholars because of its incompatibility with the nature of the linguistic situation in the Near East. Since in this area there are no clear demarcations between the various linguistic groups, they were never completely isolated from each other as in the case of the Indo-European languages. Many of the linguistic communities were contiguous and entertained cultural and political contacts with each other, so that common innovations could spread over large areas and extensive borrowing and interference could take place. Besides, as Blau (1978) has pointed out, several languages served for some time as *lingua franca* in this area, for instance Akkadian and Aramaic. Some of the common features shared by the languages of the region may have been introduced by the presence of such a *lingua franca*. A special problem is the position of Arabic within the Semitic languages. For many Semiticists working within this paradigm, Arabic was the point of departure in their reconstruction of Proto-Semitic. Since the reconstruction of Proto-Semitic was based primarily on Arabic, especially in the phonemic inventory, it is not surprising that Arabic was found to be one of the most archaic Semitic languages.

The most recent attempts at a classification of the Semitic languages usually waver between a historical interpretation of the relationships between the languages involved and a purely typological/geographical approach in which the common features of the languages are recorded without any claim to a historical derivation. Some scholars, such as Ullendorff (1971), reject out of hand the possibility of ever reaching a classificatory scheme reflecting genetic relationship. Others, like Garbini, claim that it is possible to trace the historical development of the Semitic languages, but without any genetic hierarchy, since the pattern of linguistic development in the area is crucially different from that in the Indo-European area.

Some scholars continue to feel that a genetic classification is possible provided that the right principles are used. Thus, for instance, Hetzron (1974, 1976) proposes to base the classification on the principles of archaic heterogeneity and shared morpholexical innovations. The former principle implies that a heterogeneous morphological system is more archaic than a homogeneous one; the latter principle states that morpholexical innovations are unlikely to be subject to borrowing. He illustrates his approach with two examples. The suffixes of the first and second person singular of the past tense of the verb in Arabic are *-tu/-ta*, as in *katabtu/katabta* 'I/you have written'. In Ethiopic they are *-ku/-ka*, but in Akkadian the equivalent suffix form of nouns and verbs (the so-called stative or permansive) has a set of personal suffixes *-(ā)ku/-(ā)ta*. Such a distribution may be explained as the result of a generalisation in Arabic and Ethiopic, which implies that the heterogeneous system of Akkadian is older. The tendency towards homogenisation was realised differently in Arabic (and Canaanite) on the one hand, and in Ethiopic (and South Arabian) on the other. Hebrew has *kātavti/kātavta* and thus shares this innovation with Arabic, setting it apart from the South Semitic languages.

Hetzron's second example has to do with the prefix vowel of the imperfect verb. In Akkadian, the prefixes of the third person singular masculine, the third person plural and the first person plural have *-i-*, while all other persons have *-a-*. In Classical Arabic all persons have *-a-*, while in Ethiopic all persons have *-ə-* (< *-i-*). In this case, too, the heterogeneous system of Akkadian may be regarded as the older one, whereas the prefixes in the other languages are the result of a later generalisation. Actually, the situation in Arabic is somewhat more complicated, since in pre-Islamic Arabic some dialects had *-i-* in all persons, whereas others had *-a-* (cf. below, p. 42). Possibly, there was an intermediate step in which *-i-* was generalised for all persons in verbs with a stem vowel *-a-*, and *-a-* was generalised for all persons in verbs with a stem vowel *-u-/-i-*. The pre-Islamic dialects differed with regard to the further generalisation, in which the correlation with the stem vowel was abandoned.

On the basis of these and similar examples, Hetzron posited a group of Central Semitic languages, separating Arabic from its position in the standard model in which it is grouped together with South Arabian and Ethiopic as South Semitic languages. We shall see below how this affects the classification of the Semitic languages. The main force of Hetzron's arguments is the fact that he does not base his subgrouping of the Semitic languages on common innovations in phonology, syntax or lexicon – in these domains, borrowing is always a distinct possibility – but concentrates instead on morpholexical innovations, which are much less prone to borrowing. We may add that he excludes from his classification arguments based on common retention of features ('negative innovation'), since this may occur independently in several languages and does not imply any sustained contact between the languages involved (see Figure 2.2).

In spite of the hazards of historical/comparative analysis, research in the twentieth century has expanded the scope of Semitic languages even further by including another group of languages, the so-called Hamitic languages. The name itself is derived from the old classificatory scheme of the Book of Genesis (10:1ff.), which divides all mankind among the descendants of the three sons of

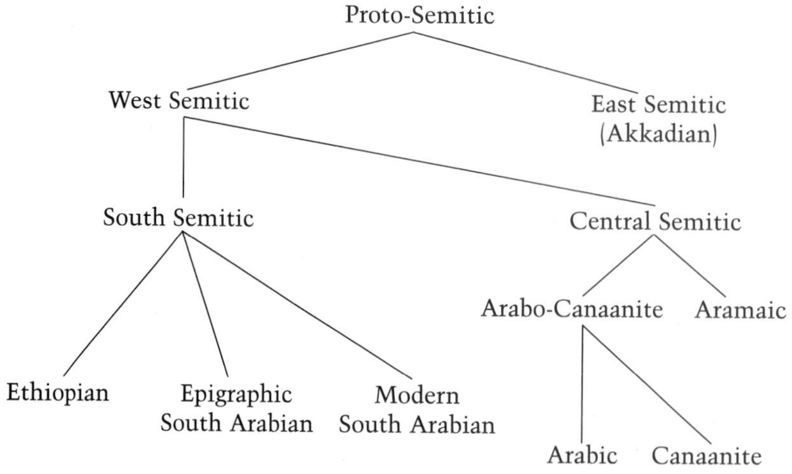

Figure 2.2 The genealogy of the Semitic languages (according to Hetzron 1976)

Noah. This scheme was used by later scholars to divide all languages into those of the descendants of Shem, those of the descendants of Cham and those of the descendants of Japheth. The group of the Hamitic languages originally encompassed all languages of Africa, but in the modern period Hamitic has come to be used collectively for five specific language groups in Africa: the Berber languages of North Africa and their ancestor, Old Libyan; Old Egyptian and its offshoot, Coptic; Hausa; the Cushitic languages; and the Chadic languages. When common links between these language groups and the Semitic languages were discovered, they became collectively known as the Hamito-Semitic languages. Since the 1970s, the current name for this group has become the Afro-Asiatic languages. In the reconstruction of Afro-Asiatic, too, Garbini applies his theory of the innovatory Syrian area. In his view, any attempt to trace the various groups of Semitic and Hamitic (Egyptian, Libyan/Berber, Cushitic and possibly Hausa) back to one ancestor is doomed to failure. It is true that even a cursory comparison of the various groups reveals the presence of related forms, but the fact that there are almost no firm phonetic correlations of the type found in the Indo-European languages shows that we are not dealing here with a language family with sibling languages descending from a common ancestor. In his view, the Hamitic languages are African languages without genetic relationships to the Semitic languages. At one time or another and to different degrees, they were semiticised by groups of people coming from the Syrian area. Old Egyptian, for instance, would have become a Semitic language if the contacts had continued. The basis is diversity; the unity of the later Semitic languages and the varying degrees of resemblance between Hamitic and Semitic languages are the result of later convergence.

Comparative research, however, both in the case of the Afro-Asiatic languages and in that of even higher groupings of languages, has usually persisted in the application of the reconstructive paradigm. The interest in language relationships led to the establishment of progressively higher-level hierarchies, such as the proto-language above the Indo-European and the Afro-Asiatic group. Various attempts have been made to connect the root structure and the phonological inventory of both groups. To some degree, these attempts were facilitated by two developments in Indo-European studies, the laryngal theory and the theory of glottalised consonants in Proto-Indo-European. Both theories brought Indo-European and Afro-Asiatic phonology closer to each other.

Even more audacious conjectures seek to incorporate both Indo-European and Afro-Asiatic languages in such constructs as the Nostratic macro-family, including the Kartvelian languages, Uralo-Altaic and Dravidian. It is hard to say what the value of such conjectures is, since the time-span involved allows for a great deal of speculation about the changes that make it possible to find lexical parallels. Besides, it is debatable whether it is permissible to apply the results of Indo-European linguistics to all linguistic relationships in the world. It could very well be the case that the type of relationship in which a mother language generates daughter languages, as is commonly held to be the case in the Indo-European languages, is an exception.

2.2 THE POSITION OF ARABIC

Within the group of the Semitic languages, Arabic and Hebrew have always been the two most-studied languages. Although the discovery of Akkadian has considerably modified the views on the structure and development of the Semitic languages, and in spite of the fact that the Assyrian/Babylonian material antedates the oldest Arabic materials by more than two millennia, in many respects Arabic still remains the model for the description of the Semitic language type. The reason is not only the familiarity of scholars of Semitic languages with the Arabic language and the relative wealth of data about its history, but also its apparent conservatism, in particular its retention of a declensional system.

The genealogical position of Arabic within the group of the Semitic languages has long been a vexing problem for Semiticists. We have seen above that it was customary to place Arabic in one group with Old South Arabian, Modern South Arabian and the Ethiopian languages, called the South Semitic languages. The main criterion for this classification was the formation of the broken or internal plural, in which the plural of nouns is formed by a restructuring of the singular without any derivational relationship between the two forms. Such broken plurals are current only in South Semitic. In Hebrew, there are several isolated examples of plurals with a different basis from the corresponding singulars, which look like broken plurals, for instance the plural *pəsīlīm* 'idols', which exists alongside the singular *pęsęl* 'idol'. If such plurals are not derived from other singulars, now lost (**pasīl*), they may also be explained as the result of a stress shift. Some of the alleged examples of broken plurals in Hebrew are probably collectives, as in the case of *rōkeb/rękęb* 'rider'. According to Corriente (1971a), the opposition singular/plural as morphological categories is a secondary development in the Semitic languages. Originally, these languages distinguished between two classes of words denoting large, important objects on the one hand, and small, insignificant objects on the other. The latter category also included such words as diminutives, abstract nouns and collectives; words in this category were marked with suffixes such as *-t*, *-ā*, *-ay*, *-ā'u*, which later became the suffixes for the feminine gender.

When the Semitic languages started to develop the opposition between singular and plural, East Semitic and North Semitic languages selected one single morpheme to denote the plural (e.g. Hebrew *-īm*), whereas Arabic and the South Semitic languages distinguished between various kinds of plurality, most of them marked by one of the 'feminine' suffixes to denote plurality, as in Arabic *'aṣdiqā'u* 'friends', broken plural of *ṣadīq*, or *fuqarā'u* 'poor', broken plural of *faqīr*. In the case of human beings, the South Semitic languages, too, used a regular plural morpheme (in Arabic *-ūna/-īna*, feminine *-ātun/-ātin*). According to this theory, the broken plurals in the South Semitic languages were originally external (suffixed) forms that were used for feminine or collective nouns and became fixed as plurals when this category had been developed. Not all broken plurals in Arabic can be explained in this way, but the suffixed forms may have constituted the starting point for the other patterns. Those traces of internal plurals that exist in the North Semitic languages may then be explained as old collectives or abstract nouns. If the origin of the internal plurals really dates back to a common Semitic period, they are not an innovation of the South Semitic languages but a common retention. It was the later development that created the distance between South and North-west Semitic languages in this respect.

The morphological features (the broken plurals and a few others such as the development of a verbal measure *fāʿala* and a passive participle with a prefix *m-*) are accompanied by common phonetic developments in Arabic, South Arabian and Ethiopic, as against the other Semitic languages. In most Semitic languages there is an opposition between *b/p*, but in the South Semitic languages, including Arabic, *f* corresponds to *p* elsewhere (cf., for instance, Hebrew *pāqad* 'to look after, visit'; Akkadian *paqādu* 'to take care of' with Arabic *faqada* 'to lose, look for'; Geʿez *faqada* 'to want, require'). Likewise, South Semitic *ḍ* corresponds to *ẓ* (cf. Akkadian *'erṣetu*, Hebrew *'ęręṣ* with Arabic *'arḍ*, South Arabian *'rḍ*, all meaning 'earth') and *š* corresponds to *s* (cf. below, p. 21).

There are, however, also instances in which Arabic shares innovations with the North-west Semitic languages against South Arabian and Ethiopian languages. One feature has already been mentioned (p. 13), the development of the personal suffixes in the past tense. Arabic and Hebrew generalised the suffixes of the first and second person singular to *-t-*, whereas South Arabian and Ethiopic chose *-k-*. A second feature that differentiates Arabic from South Arabian/Ethiopic concerns the formation of the imperfect. According to most reconstructions, Proto-Semitic had three verbal tenses, an imperfect **yiqattVl*, a perfect **yíqtVl* and a jussive **yiqtV́l*, as well as a suffix form (stative). In all Semitic languages, the suffix form developed into a perfective tense and eventually replaced the old perfect, which had become identical with the jussive because of a stress shift (**yíqtVl* > *yiqtV́l*). The Proto-Semitic perfect originally had past reference, but lost it afterwards. In Ethiopic and South Arabian, the Proto-Semitic imperfect was maintained as *yəqät(t)əl*. This imperfect formed a new verbal system together with the new perfective suffix conjugation and the jussive. In Arabic, Canaanite and Aramaic, the Proto-Semitic imperfect was dropped and the perfect/jussive was adopted as the new form for the durative aspect, together with an indicative morpheme *-u/-na*, retained only in Arabic. This verbal form is usually called 'imperfect'; it has non-past time reference. The original past time reference of the perfect is still visible in the use of the Hebrew imperfect with the so-called *wāw* consecutivum, which indicates a past tense. In Arabic, too, when the imperfect is used with the conditional particle *'in* or the negation *lam*, it refers to the past. The net result of these developments was a verbal system that groups Arabic together with the North-west Semitic languages and sets it apart from the other languages of the South Semitic group.

These are not the only features linking Arabic with the North-west Semitic languages. They are the only languages in which a definite article has developed, in North Arabic (*(h)n-*; cf. below, p. 28), in Arabic (*'l-*) and in Phoenician/Hebrew (*h-*). In all these languages, the article developed out of a demonstrative element that had lost its deictic force; at the same time, new demonstratives were developed from new combinations of deictic elements (e.g. Phoenician *hnd*, *dnk*, *hlk*; Hebrew *hazzē*, *hallazē*; Arabic *hāḏā*, *ḏālika*). An important morpholexical innovation is the presence of a third person pronoun with the element *h* in Arabic (*huwa/hiya*) and the North-west Semitic languages Hebrew *hū*/*hī*) instead of *s* as in the South Arabian personal suffixes *s*, *sw*/*s* (except in Sabaean *hw*, *h*/*h*). Probably this innovation took place, as predicted by Garbini's account, from north to south, since it reached Sabaean but not the other South Arabian languages. Finally, it may be mentioned that in Arabic and in the North-west Semitic languages the feminine ending *-at* developed a new form without the *t*: in Arabic the pausal form is *-ah*, in Hebrew the feminine always ends in *-ā*.

The common features shared by Arabic and the North-west Semitic languages prompted Hetzron (1974, 1976) to propose his new subgrouping of Central Semitic, in which Arabic was to go with Canaanite and Aramaic instead of South Arabian and Ethiopic (cf. above, p. 14). Since the new classification adequately explains the common features between Arabic and North-west Semitic, the question remains of how the common features between Arabic and the South Semitic languages are to be explained. One possible hypothesis is to regard the further development of internal plurals as a phenomenon that affected some of the languages in the West Semitic group, later to become the South Semitic languages. This innovation did not spread to all the languages of the West Semitic group. When the group split, some of them went south, later to become the South-west Semitic languages, while Arabic remained behind and came into closer contact with the other West Semitic languages, Canaanite and Aramaic, together with which it developed a new verbal system, a definite article, a feminine ending and other features.

A further subgrouping within the Central Semitic languages is set up by Hetzron on the basis of another feature, the suffix *-na* in the feminine plural of the verbs. In Arabic, we have *katabū*/*katabna* 'they wrote [masculine/feminine]' and *yaktubūna*/*yaktubna* 'they write [masculine/feminine]' as the third person plural of the perfect and imperfect. This partially matches the endings in the Hebrew imperfect (in the perfect, masculine and feminine have merged) *yiqṭəlū*/*tiqṭolnāh* (without the generalisation of *y* that is found in Arabic), but differs from Aramaic, which marks the feminine plural with *-ān*. Accordingly, Hetzron subdivides his Central Semitic group into Arabic and Hebrew, on the one hand and Aramaic on the other. A further refinement was proposed by Voigt (1987), who emphasises the difference between the Old and the Modern South Arabian languages. According to him, Old South Arabian should be classified as Central Semitic, whereas the Modern South Arabian languages are to be grouped together with the Ethiopian languages in the South Semitic group.

An alternative way of looking at the distribution of common features between Arabic and the other Semitic languages ties in with Garbini's theory. We have seen above that in his view the Arabic type of Semitic language originated when groups of speakers detached themselves from the Syrian area that bordered on the desert and became isolated from the innovative area. The completion of this process of bedouinisation took place at the earliest in the second half of the second millennium BCE. The common features shared by Arabic and North-west Semitic must, therefore, represent innovations that had been introduced in the Syrian area before bedouinisation took place. It appears, indeed, that there are no archaisms in Arabic that do not also occur in the North-west Semitic languages of the second millennium BCE.

As Arabic progressively spread southwards, it reached the domain of the South Arabian language, which had been brought there at a much earlier time. Some of the Arabs settled in the area and established linguistic contacts between the two languages (see below, p. 31). In the first millennium BCE sedentarisation took place in the Syrian region as well, when Arab nomads came from the desert and settled in the more fertile areas; this process led to the arabicisation of the Nabataean empire (see below, p. 28). When the power of the South Arabian empires grew in the first millennium BCE, the influence of the languages of this region on the language of the Arab Bedouin also increased. In Garbini's view, this explains the common features between Arabic and the South Semitic languages. Because of the contacts with Syria and South Arabia, Arabic cannot be said to belong exclusively to either the North-west Semitic or the South Semitic languages. In the course of its history, it was affected by innovations in both groups.

In the past, the tendency to approach the comparative study of the Semitic languages from the perspective of Arabic led to a reconstruction of Proto-Semitic that was remarkably close to the structure of Arabic, which was therefore regarded as archaic compared to the other Semitic languages. Some features of Arabic were indeed present in early stages of other Semitic languages, but were dropped by them at a later stage. Arabic, for instance, has retained the interdentals /ṯ/ and /ḏ/, which were replaced by dentals in Syriac and by sibilants in Akkadian, Hebrew and Ethiopic (cf., for instance, the numeral 'three' in Arabic, *ṯalāṯa*, with Akkadian *šalāšum*; Hebrew *šālоš*; Syriac *təlāt*; Geʿez *šalās*). South Arabian also retained the interdentals in its older stage, and in Old Akkadian and Ugaritic there are still traces of the interdentals.

In the series of the velars (/ẖ/, /ġ/) and the pharyngals (/ḥ/, /ʿ/), only Arabic and Old South Arabian have retained the full set. In most other Semitic languages, the voiceless members of both pairs, /ẖ/ and /ḥ/, have merged into /ḥ/, and the voiced members, /ġ/ and /ʿ/, into /ʿ/ (e.g. cf. Arabic *ġarb* 'sunset'/*ʿayn* 'eye' with Hebrew *ʿfrfb* 'evening'/*ʿēn* 'eye'; Arabic *'aẖ* 'brother'/*'aḥad* 'one' with Hebrew *'āḥ*/*'fḥad*). In Ugaritic, both sets are distinguished in writing. In Akkadian, only /ẖ/ has been preserved, whereas the other velars and pharyngals have merged into /'/ (e.g. *'ẹrēbum* 'to enter', *'ešrum* 'ten', cf. Arabic *ġarb*/*ʿašr*) but there are indications that originally this language, too, contained all four phonemes.

In morphology, the archaic character of Arabic is demonstrated by the existence of a full nominal declension, with three case endings: *-u* (nominative), *-i* (genitive), *-a* (accusative). Old Akkadian has the same declensional endings, but in the later stages of the language (Neo-Babylonian, Neo-Assyrian) the endings are often confused and finally disappear completely. In the older North-west Semitic languages, such as Ugaritic, the declensional endings are still found, but in the later languages of this group, such as Hebrew, they have disappeared. In Old South Arabian there is no declension, but certain orthographic peculiarities seem to point to the original existence of such a system. In Ethiopic there is one oblique ending *-a*, which probably goes back to an original accusative ending.

There are also features in Arabic that as far as we know were never present in any of the other Semitic languages and must, therefore, be innovations that took place independently within Arabic. In morphology, the use of the ending *-n*

	voiceless	voiced	nasal	velarised	lateral	trill
labial	f	b	m			
interdental	ṯ	ḏ		ḏ̣		
dental	s	z	n	ṣ	l	
alveolar	t	d		ṭ	ḍ	r
pre-palatal	š	ğ				
post-palatal	k	q				
velar	ḫ	ġ				
pharyngal	ḥ	ʿ				
laryngal	ʾ	h				

Table 2.1 The Arabic consonantal system.

(nunation) as a marker of indefiniteness is not matched by any of the other Semitic languages. We have seen above that the use of a definite article is a feature shared by Arabic, Canaanite and Aramaic. But Arabic stands alone in the choice of the element *'l-* for this article instead of *h-*, as in North Arabic. In the *fāʿala* form of the verb that Arabic shares with the South Semitic languages, it alone has developed an internal passive *fūʿila*.

The phonemic inventory of Arabic illustrates the combination of archaic and innovative traits in the language (see Table 2.1). We have seen above that the language has retained the interdentals, the velars and the pharyngals that were probably part of the common stock. The following six innovations may be mentioned.

First, a characteristic feature of the Semitic languages is the so-called emphatic consonants. In Arabic, these are articulated by a process of velarisation: the tip of the tongue is lowered, the root of the tongue is raised towards the soft palate, and in the process the timbre of the neighbouring vowels is shifted towards a posterior realisation. The velarised consonants in Arabic correspond to glottalised consonants (consonants accompanied by a glottal stop) in the Ethiopian Semitic languages. This correspondence has led to some speculation as to the original character of the emphatic consonants in Proto-Semitic. According to some scholars, it is easier to imagine a shift from glottalised to velarised consonants than vice versa, so that the velarised realisation in Arabic is to be regarded as a secondary development. It is usually assumed that originally the Semitic languages had five emphatic consonants, **ṭ*, **ṣ*, **ḳ*, **ṯ̣* and **ḍ*; Arabic has only four such consonants, /ṭ/, /ṣ/, /ḍ/, and /ḏ̣/.

Second, the phoneme corresponding in Arabic to Proto-Semitic **ṯ̣* is /ḏ̣/; in other Semitic languages (except Ugaritic and Old South Arabian), this phoneme has lost its interdental character, for instance in Akkadian, Hebrew and Ethiopic /ṣ/ (cf. Hebrew *ṣ*^{e}*bī* 'gazelle', Arabic *ḏ̣aby*). The current transcription with *ẓ* in Arabic is based on the modern pronunciation of this phoneme in loanwords from Classical Arabic in the dialects (e.g. Classical Arabic *ʿaḏ̣īm*, pronounced in Egyptian and Syrian Arabic as *ʿaẓīm*).

Third, the phoneme corresponding in Classical Arabic to Proto-Semitic **ḏ̣* is /ḍ/. There is some evidence in Arabic, based on explanations by the grammarians and Arabic loanwords in other languages (cf. below, p. 89), that /ḍ/ was realised as a lateral or a lateralised /d^l/. Since it exists as an independent phoneme only in the South Semitic languages, it is difficult to say anything about its original realisation. In Akkadian and Hebrew, it has merged with /ṣ/ (cf. Hebrew *ṣāḥaq* 'to laugh' with Arabic *ḍaḥika*). In the modern realisation of Classical Arabic, /ḍ/ has become the voiced counterpart of /ṭ/ and in the modern dialects it has merged with /ḏ̣/.

Fourth, the phoneme corresponding in Classical Arabic to Proto-Semitic **ḳ* was probably a non-emphatic voiced counterpart to /k/, i.e. /g/; this is the phoneme that is nowadays realised in Standard Arabic as a voiceless /q/, but that in earlier stages of Classical Arabic was probably a voiced /g/, as in the modern Bedouin dialects (cf. p. 89). At any rate, /q/ was not emphatic in Classical Arabic, since it did not lead to assimilation of adjacent consonants (cf. *iṣṭabara* < **iṣtabara* with *iqtabara* without assimilation of the *t*).

Fifth, for Proto-Semitic a series of three sibilants, **s*, **š*, and **s̠* (probably a lateralised *s*), is usually posited; the Modern South Arabian dialects still have these three sibilants, but in Arabic **s̠* corresponds to /š/, and **š* and **s* have merged to /s/. In all other Semitic languages, **s* has remained /s/ (e.g. cf. Hebrew *sāʿad* 'to support', *ḥāmęš* 'five' with Arabic *sāʿada* 'to help'/*ḫamsa* 'five').

Sixth, in Arabic the phoneme corresponding to Proto-Semitic **g* was affricated and became /ǧ/ (e.g. cf. Hebrew *gāmāl* with Arabic *ǧamal* 'camel'); this phoneme formed a pre-palatal series with the new /š/.

The debate about the exact position of Arabic within the Semitic languages is still going on. The only conclusion we can draw from the data presented here is that the language exhibits common features with both the Southern (South Arabian, Ethiopic) and the Northern (Canaanite, Aramaic) Semitic languages, and that it also contains innovations not found anywhere else. Because of the uncertainties concerning the chronology of the common features, there is little basis for a genealogical classification of the kind current in Indo-European linguistics, and it may be preferable to stay within the bounds of a descriptive and typological analysis of the relationships between Arabic and its Semitic neighbours.

FURTHER READING

The standard manual of comparative Semitic linguistics is still Brockelmann (1908–13); the most recent manual is Lipiński (1997). A synthesis was published by Bergsträßer (1928). More recent surveys are Moscati (1964) and Hetzron (1997); see also Sáenz-Badillos' (1993) introductory chapter to his history of the Hebrew language. The *Handbuch der Orientalistik* in the volume dedicated to Semitic linguistics has sections on the Semitic language type (Spuler 1964b), the expansion of the Semitic languages (Spuler 1964c) and the history of Semitic linguistics (Fück 1964). These sections are useful as a historical introduction, but must be regarded as outdated. A controversial but highly stimulating view on the relations between the Semitic languages and the value of the comparative paradigm is found in Garbini (1984).

About the problems connected with the genealogical classification of the Semitic languages, see von Soden (1960), Diem (1980b) and Hetzron (1974, 1976). On the typology of the Semitic languages, see Ullendorff (1958). Analysis of individual problems connected with the comparison of the Semitic languages is in the following: root structure, Petráček (1982); internal (broken) plurals, Corriente (1971a), Ratcliffe (1998); declensional system, Rabin (1969).

For an introduction to Afro-Asiatic linguistics, see Diakonoff (1965). A survey of the state of the art in Afro-Asiatic linguistics is in Petráček (1984). Garbini (1974) deals with the position of Semitic within the Afro-Asiatic languages. An etymological dictionary of Afro-Asiatic common roots was produced by Orel and Stolbova (1994).

Because of the highly hypothetical status of recent research in Proto-Nostratic, it is difficult to cite any relevant literature; Bomhard (1984) has introductory chapters on the aims and scope of Proto-Nostratic comparisons.

With regard to the position of Arabic within the group of the Semitic languages, see Petráček (1981), Diem (1980b) and Zaborski (1991). Of special interest are the discussions about the Central Semitic group in Hetzron (1974, 1976) and Voigt (1987). Arguments against the special relationship between Arabic and North-west Semitic are given by Huehnergard (1991); Knauf (1988) argues that Arabic is more related to Aramaic than to Canaanite. Discussion with the emphasis on the parallels between Arabic and North-west Semitic is in Garbini (1984: 97–112).

A classic account of the Arabic phonemic inventory in the light of comparative Semitic linguistics is found in Cantineau (1960).

3
The Earliest Stages of Arabic

3.1 THE ARABS

We do not know when the first nomads came to the Arabian peninsula, and we certainly do not know which language they spoke. It is usually assumed that the settlement of the peninsula took place in the second millennium BCE. In the South, advanced civilisations were established in the period between the thirteenth and the tenth centuries BCE. The languages used in the inscriptions of these civilisations are related to Arabic, but they did not partake in some of the innovations exhibited by Arabic (cf. above, p. 17). The script of the South Arabian civilisations is related to some of the North Semitic scripts, such as Phoenician, and was probably imported from the Syro-Palestine region to the south. It is from the South Arabian script that the later North Arabian scripts are derived. The language of the South Arabian inscriptions is usually called Old (or Epigraphic) South Arabian and is divided into several dialects or languages, the most important of which are Sabaean, Minaean and Qaṭabānian. These languages must have died out soon after the Islamic conquests. The present-day Modern South Arabian languages such as Soqoṭrī and Mehri, that are still spoken in a few linguistic pockets in South Arabia, are related to Epigraphic South Arabian, but do not derive from it directly (cf. below p. 94).

The inhabitants of the South Arabian empires did not call themselves 'Arabs'. Towards the end of the second century BCE, some of the South Arabian inscriptions mention nomads called *ʿrb* (plural *ʾʿrb*), who are contrasted with the sedentary population of the south. The earliest attested use of this name stems, however, from a different region: in a cuneiform inscription dating from 853 BCE, the Assyrian king Salmanassar III mentions as one of his adversaries Gindibu from the land of *Arbi* or *Arbāya*. The name 'Arabs' as a people's name is used somewhat later, for the first time by Tiglatpilesar III (745–727 BCE), and then more frequently by his successors, under the form *Arabu, Aribi*. For the Assyrians and the Babylonians, this term covered all kinds of nomadic tribes, some of them undoubtedly Aramaic-speaking. Probably, it served as a collective name for all people coming from the desert who invaded the lands of the urban civilisations and who were alternately fought by the Assyrians or enlisted by them as allies against other enemies. In 715 BCE, Sargon II attempted to end the opposition from the nomads by settling some tribes in the neighbourhood of Samaria; their names are mentioned in the sources as Tamudi, Ibadidi, Marsimani and Hayapa. Reliefs in the palace of King Assurbanipal in Niniveh show Arab camel-riders being fought and subdued by the Assyrians. The name 'Arabs' is also attested in the Hebrew Bible, for instance in Jeremiah 25:24 (end of the seventh century BCE), where mention is made of all the kings of the ʿ*Arab* and of the ʿ*Ereb* that live in the desert.

The etymology of the name 'Arabs' is unknown. In the Mari inscriptions, mention is made of the Ḫapiru, and according to some scholars these people are identical with the Aribi; their name may be connected with the Sumerian word *gab-bīr* 'desert'. According to another theory, the name 'Arabs' is related to the root ʿ*-b-r* in the sense of 'to cross (the desert)', from which the name of the Hebrews is also derived. Since we do not know which language was spoken by the various tribes indicated with the name *Aribi* and similar names, these early mentions of Arabs do not tell us much about their linguistic prehistory.

The emergence of the Arabs in history is closely connected with the use of the camel. The above-mentioned Gindibu had 1,000 camels at his disposal, and the reliefs show nomads attacking on camels. According to a recent study of the development of camel-breeding, the first domestication of this animal took place in the south of the Arabian peninsula, and from there it became known around 1200 BCE in the north through the incense trade. It may be noted that this is around the time that, according to some scholars, Semitic-speaking groups from the fringes of the Syrian desert detached themselves from the sedentary civilisation and took off into the desert. According to Garbini (1984), the language which we call Arabic was developed in this process of nomadisation or bedouinisation (cf. above, Chapter 2, p. 11).

When the nomads in the Syrian desert invented a new kind of saddle which enabled them to ride the hump of their camels, their range of movement became much larger, they could have herds and, most importantly, they could take over the control of the caravans from the south. This innovation must have taken place in the last centuries BCE, and it marks the beginning of the period of real bedouinisation. The new fashion of riding also enabled the nomads to maintain regular contacts with the urban civilisations in Syria and Iraq. A further refinement was reached in the second and third centuries CE with the invention of the saddle-bow, which led to the development of a society of rider-warriors, represented by the type of Bedouin tribes which we know from the period directly before Islam.

When the land route for the trade between South Arabia and the Fertile Crescent became more important than the sea route, the nomads' role in this trade became a factor to be reckoned with. All along the main route, settlements had been established by the South Arabians; but, when the power of the South Arabian civilisation waned, the nomadic tribes stepped in and began to control the flow of commerce themselves. The first stage of this new development was dominated by the caravan cities of Petra and Palmyra. The Nabataean kingdom of Petra was conquered by the Roman emperor Trajan in 106 CE. After the destruction of Petra, the Palmyrans of the oasis of Tadmūr 200 km to the north-west of Damascus took over.

The conquest of Palmyra by the emperor Aurelian in 272 CE marked the end of the great caravan oases. After the third century, the competition of the three powers of Byzantium, Persia and Ḥimyar, the last of the South Arabian empires, dominated the course of events. Each of these powers had its own ally among the Arab nomads: the Banū Laḫm supported the Persians, the Banū Ġassān the Byzantines, and the kingdom of Kinda was in the service of the Ḥimyarites. In

Map 3.1 North Arabia and the Fertile Crescent before Islam (after Robin 1992: 12, 36)

the fifth and sixth centuries, however, the political scene changed considerably, first after the fall of the Ḥimyaritic kingdom in 525 CE following an Ethiopian invasion, and then after the constant fighting between Persia and Byzantium, which weakened both. With the waning of the power of their patrons, the Arab allies lost their power too. This furthered the emergence of commercial centres inland, in the first place Mecca, which had already become a cultural and religious centre for the nomadic tribes and now saw its chance of dominating the caravan trade. The Banū Qurayš, the dominant tribe of Mecca, became one of the most powerful tribes in the peninsula, and to some extent one could say that thanks to the mission of one of its members, the Prophet Muḥammad, it never lost this position throughout the entire history of the Islamic empire.

3.2 EARLY NORTH ARABIC

For the earliest elements of the Arabic language, we have to turn to inscriptions in other languages. In the South Arabian inscriptions, we find a few proper names of a non-South Arabian type (e.g. *zyd* = *zayd*, *'slm* = *'aslam*, or with the South Arabian mimation ending *slymm* = *sulaymum*, *ʿbydm* = *ʿubaydum*, sometimes even with the Arabic article: *'lḥrṯ* = *al-ḥāriṯ*; cf. *GAP* I, 27). These may refer to North Arabian nomads, whom the South Arabian empires used to protect the caravans along the incense road through the Arabian desert. Of more interest from the linguistic point of view are four groups of inscriptions, first discovered in the nineteenth century and written in a language that seems to be an early stage of the later Arabic language. These inscriptions use scripts derived from Epigraphic South Arabian. The language in which they are written has sometimes been called Proto-Arabic or Early Arabic, but will be referred to here as Early North Arabic, in order to distinguish it from the language of the Arabic inscriptions (Proto-Arabic; see below) and the language of the early Islamic papyri (Early Arabic). Since most of the inscriptions are fragmentary and the vast majority of them contain nothing but proper names, the exact identification of the language involved is difficult. At any rate, the language of these inscriptions is closely related to what we know as Classical Arabic. The four groups of inscriptions are the following:

Thamūdic

The *Qur'ān* mentions the people of Ṯamūd as an example of an earlier community that perished because it did not accept the message of its prophet, in this case the prophet Ṣāliḥ (e.g. Q 7/73ff.). In modern times, the name Thamūdic occurs in a number of historical contexts as well. We have seen above that the Tamudi were mentioned in one of the inscriptions of the Assyrian king Sargon II, who settled them near Samaria (715 BCE). The name Thamūdic has been given to the tens of thousands of mostly short inscriptions in a script derived from the South Arabian script that have been discovered in a string of oases in West and Central North Arabia, along the caravan route to the south, as far as North Yemen. The inscriptions date from the sixth century BCE to the fourth century CE; most of them were found in Dūmat al-Ǧandal and al-Ḥiǧr. One isolated group stems from the oasis of Taymā'. Most of the inscriptions are rather short, containing almost exclusively proper names of the type 'A, son of B'. They do not tell us much about the structure of the language; it is not even clear whether they all belong to the same language. But in any case they all belong to the North Arabic group, characterised by the definite article *h-* (e.g. *h-gml* 'the/this camel').

Liḥyānitic

The earliest examples of these inscriptions, likewise in a South Arabian type of script, probably date from the second half of the first millennium BCE, from the oasis of Didān, modern al-ʿUlā, 300 km north-west of Medina, on the incense route from Yemen to Syria. Originally, this oasis was a Minaean colony, but later it became a protectorate of Ptolemaic Egypt until the second half of the first century BCE. Sometimes a distinction is made between Dedānitic and Liḥyānitic inscriptions on the basis of the royal titles that are used. The oldest are the Dedānitic, which refer to the kings of Didān (*mlk ddn*). The majority of the more than 500 inscriptions from the oasis refer to the kings of Liḥyān; they belong to the period between the fourth and first centuries BCE.

Some of the inscriptions consist only of personal names, often preceded by *l-*, possibly indicating the author of the inscription, or more likely the person for whom the inscription was made. There are, however, also larger texts (votive inscriptions, building inscriptions etc.). The language of the inscriptions belongs to the North Arabic group, with an article *h-* or *hn-* (e.g. *h-gbl hn-'ʿly* 'the highest mountain' and *h-gbl hn-'sfl* 'the lowest mountain'; Robin 1992: 118).

Ṣafā'itic

The Ṣafā'itic inscriptions, also written in a South Arabian type of script, received their name from the Ṣafā' area, south-east of Damascus. In this area and neighbouring regions, as far as the northern parts of Saudi Arabia, more than 15,000 inscriptions have been found. They date from the first century BCE to the third century CE and mostly contain only proper names, almost always preceded by the preposition *l-*. A number of somewhat larger inscriptions refer to Bedouin camp sites, and to mourning for the dead. In some inscriptions, reference is made to political events in the area with the word *snt* 'in the year that'. In this word, we also see the spelling of the feminine ending, *-t*; only in female proper names is the pausal ending *-h* sometimes used. Unlike the later Arabic script, this script does not indicate the long vowels; thus, *dr* stands for *dār* 'camp site'. The diphthongs are very often not written either, so that *mt* usually stands for *mwt* 'death', and *bt* for *byt* 'tent'. Possibly, this vacillation in spelling represents a development in the pronunciation of the diphthongs, *ay* > *ē*, *aw* > *ō*. The article is *h-*, possibly originally *hn-* with gemination of certain following consonants because of assimilation of the *n-*.

In Ṣafā'itic, the sound plural ends in *-n*, which may stand for *-ūn* and *-īn*, since the script does not have a special spelling for the long vowels. Thus, we have for instance *h-ḍlln*, i.e., *haḍ-ḍālilūn/īn* 'those who err' (cf. Arabic *aḍ-ḍāllūn/īn*, with contraction of the two identical consonants). The causative stem is formed with '-, as in the verb *'šrq*, imperfect *yšrq* 'to go east' (cf. Arabic *'ašraqa/yušriqu*). There seem to be some lexical similarities with the North-west Semitic languages, such as in the word *mdbr* 'desert' (cf. Hebrew *midbār*).

Ḥaṣā'itic

To this group belong some forty inscriptions, most of which have been found in the Saudi Arabian province of al-Ḥaṣā' on the Gulf, probably dating from the period between the fifth and the second centuries BCE. They are written in a script that is almost identical with the South Arabian script. The inscriptions are very short and do not tell us much about the structure of the language, but it is clear that the article in these inscriptions, too, is *hn-* in proper names like *hn-'lt*, the name of the goddess 'Ilāt.

If we take only the article as a discriminatory feature, all the inscriptions mentioned here belong to a *h(n)-* group, contrasting with the Classical Arabic *'l-*. Contrary to the situation in the South Arabian languages, which have a postposed article *-n* or *-hn*, the article in North Arabic is preposed, as in Arabic. With Arabic, the language of the inscriptions also shares the reduction of the sibilants to two (*s*, *š*), whereas South Arabian has three sibilants (*s*, *š* and a lateralised *ś*). On the other hand, they usually have a causative prefix *h-* (South Arabian *s-*/*h-*; Arabic *'-*). The pronominal suffix of the third person is formed with *-h-* (South Arabian *-s-*, except Sabaean *-h-*; Arabic *-h-*). These are probably not the only traits that distinguish these languages from Arabic and South Arabian, but at the present stage of research no further conclusions can be drawn.

3.3 NABATAEAN AND PALMYRENE

The inscriptions mentioned in the preceding paragraph were distinguished by their use of the article *h(n)-*. For the earliest testimonies of a type of Arabic that has the article *al-*, we must turn to two other groups of inscriptions, Nabataean and Palmyrene. Both of them are written in Aramaic, but they originated in an environment in which Arabic was the spoken language. In these inscriptions we find many traces of this spoken Arabic, which as far as we can ascertain is closely related to our Classical Arabic.

Nabataean

The Nabataean inscriptions stem from the Nabataean kingdom, with the capital Petra, which flourished until 106 CE. The inscriptions date from the first century BCE to the first century CE; the youngest is from 355/356 CE. Although the texts are in a form of Aramaic script and language, the inhabitants of the Nabataean kingdom must have spoken a colloquial language that was related to later Classical Arabic, as we can see in the form of most proper names and in numerous loanwords. The article in these names and loanwords is *'l-*, although sometimes it is replaced by Aramaic *-ā*, e.g. *'l'bd* (*al-'abd*), alongside *'bd'* (*'abdā*). Most proper names end in *-w*, e.g. *yzydw* (*yazīd*), *ḥrtw* (*ḥāriṯ*, with *t* for Classical Arabic *ṯ*). In theophoric names, one sometimes finds *-y* as an ending, e.g. *'bd'lhy* (*'abdallāhi*). The endings *-w* and *-y* are usually regarded as case endings for the nominative and the genitive. They only occur in proper names and are sometimes omitted. In general, there are many inconsistencies in their use (e.g. *mlk nbṭw* 'the king of the Nabataeans', *šrkt tmwdw* 'the community of the Thamud', where one would have expected a genitive ending). This pattern of use has led to the conclusion that the endings are merely orthographic. In one Classical Arabic proper name, the ending *-w* is still found as an orthographic device, *ʿmrw* (*ʿamr*), to distinguish it from the homographic *ʿmr* (*ʿumar*). In the discussion about the alleged loss of case endings in pre-Islamic Arabic dialects, the testimony of the Nabataean inscriptions has become a crucial element (cf. below, Chapter 4). According to some scholars, the Arabic substratum in these inscriptions belongs to the periphery of the pre-Islamic Arabic-speaking world, in which the language had undergone various changes due to the contact with other languages.

Palmyrene

The group of Palmyrene inscriptions stems from the oasis of Tadmūr (Palmyra), which was destroyed in 273 CE by the Romans. This oasis must have been an Arab settlement, and at one time even the ruling dynasty was of Arab stock. Most of the inscriptions date from the second and third centuries CE, but much earlier inscriptions have also been found. Like the Nabataean inscriptions, the inscriptions from Palmyra are written in the *lingua franca* of this region, Aramaic, in a variety of the Aramaic script. For the history of Arabic they are of less importance, since they do not contain many Arabic words, and most of them are proper names. Sometimes these are spelled with the same ending *-w* as in the Nabataean inscriptions.

The testimony of both the inscriptions from Petra and those of Palmyra with regard to the history of Arabic is indirect, since in both areas Arabic was the colloquial language, whereas the language of prestige and written communication was Aramaic. Consequently, the Arabic elements in the inscriptions remain confined to proper names or loanwords, with occasional interference from the colloquial language in the written language. The information which we can glean from the inscriptions is limited, but we can deduce from them a set of orthographic principles that determined the spelling of Arabic names. According to Diem's (1973a) analysis of the material, these principles formed the basis for the orthographic conventions of the earliest Arabic script.

The influence of the Aramaic script is obvious first of all in the arrangement of the Classical Arabic alphabet, in which pairs of letters are distinguished by a diacritic dot or dots. These pairs go back to the writing system of the Nabataean/Palmyrene inscriptions. Since the Aramaic script did not cover the entire phonemic inventory of Arabic, several letters had to do double duty. Thus, for instance, Aramaic *dalet* transcribed both *d* and *d̲*, *ʿayin* transcribed both *ʿ* and *ġ*, and *ṭet* transcribed both *ḏ̣* and *ṭ*. This principle does not mean that the phonemes in question had merged in the colloquial Arabic of the period, but simply that they were not distinguished in the Nabataean script. In the case of the two phonemes *ḍ* and *ḏ̣*, which soon after the Islamic conquests must have merged in colloquial speech, the inscriptions show different reflexes, *ḏ̣* being transcribed by *ṭet* and *ḍ* by *ṣade*, just like *ṣ*. In the writing system of Classical Arabic, the effect of this distribution is still visible, since the letters *ṭāʾ*/*ḏ̣āʾ* and *ṣād*/*ḍād* form pairs that are distinguished by a diacritic dot. Apparently, *ḏ̣* was perceived as the interdental counterpart of *ṭ*, whereas *ḍ* represented a different category (cf. above, p. 21).

The most important convention that was borrowed from the Aramaic spelling of Arabic proper names concerns the spelling of the long vowels. Long *ā* is spelled defectively within the word, and at the end of the word sometimes with *y* and sometimes with ʾ. This distinction was probably meant as a device to indicate the morphological structure of a word: *ʿalā*, for instance, is spelled with *y*, because with suffixes it becomes *ʿalay-ka*. This device was taken over by the Arabic writing system, hence the large number of words in which final *-ā* is spelled with *yāʾ*. The defective spelling of *ā* within the word is still found in many words in the manuscripts of the *Qurʾān*, e.g. *sulayman, hadā, allah*; later this defective spelling was indicated with the so-called perpendicular *ʾalif* above the word. In one group of words, *ā* within the word is spelled in the Nabataean inscriptions with *w*, e.g. the word *ṣlwh* 'prayer', probably because in Aramaic the long *ā* in these words had developed to ō (Aramaic *ṣlōṯā*). This is the origin of the Qurʾānic spelling of *ṣalāh, zakāh*, etc. with *w*.

We have mentioned above the Nabataean principle of spelling proper names with *-w* or *-y* at the end. In Classical Arabic, this convention is still used in the proper name, *ʿamr*, usually spelled as *ʿmrw*. The situation in the Nabataean inscriptions is as follows (cf. Diem 1981: 336): masculine singular proper names very often end in *-w*, i.e., *-ū*, when they are isolated, e.g. *zydw* (Zayd), *klbw* (Kalb), *ʿmrw* (ʿAmr). In compound names, the second member has either *-y* or *-w*, e.g. *ʿbdmlkw* (ʿAbd Malik or ʿAbd Mālik), *ʿbdʿmrw* (ʿAbd ʿAmr), but *ʿbdʾlhy* (ʿAbd Allāh), *whbʾlhy* (Wahb Allāh). These endings occur independently from the syntactic context and are apparently quoted in their isolated form, which is not surprising since these Arabic names are intrusive elements in Aramaic, which has no case endings.

The most likely explanation for the compound names ending in *-w* is that these are treated as single units following the same convention as the single names by ending in *-w*. If they are indeed names quoted in their isolated form, this means that the endings *-w, -y* could be regarded as the pausal forms of the names. In Classical Arabic, the pausal form of a name such as *ʿamrun* would be *ʿamr*, except in the accusative singular which has *ʿamran* → *ʿamrā*. But the Nabataean evidence suggests that in this earlier period Arabic had pausal endings *ʿamrū, ʿamrī, ʿamrā*, of which only the third remained in Classical Arabic. Feminine names are usually spelled with the ending *-t*, sometimes with *-h*; if this, too, is a pausal ending, it could indicate a change in the pausal form of the feminine nouns, which in Classical Arabic has become *-ah*.

3.4 THE BEGINNINGS OF ARABIC

Thus far, we have looked at texts in languages related to Arabic (the North Arabic inscriptions) and texts in other languages, but with interference from spoken Arabic (the Nabataean and Palmyrene inscriptions). The value of the latter group for the history of Arabic is limited, since they are not written in Arabic but in the official language of that period, Aramaic. It is only because they were written in an environment in which Arabic was the colloquial language of most people that they can tell us something about this spoken language. The same limitation applies to Arabic proper names and loanwords in South Arabian texts.

Some early inscriptions in these scripts, however, are written in a language that contains so many Arabic features that one could perhaps regard them as early forms of Arabic. In South Arabia, a group of inscriptions from Qaryat al-Fa’w (280 km north of Naǧrān), in Sabaean script, contains a language that is closely related to Arabic; they are collectively known as Qaḥṭānic (also called pseudo-Sabaean). The longest of these inscriptions is the tombstone of ʿIǧl (first century BCE). Here we find the ‘Arabic’ article, even with assimilation to some consonants as in Arabic: *w-l-’rḍ* (*wa-l-’arḍ* ‘and the earth’) as against *’-smy* (*as-samā’* ‘the heaven’). According to some scholars, there are a few inscriptions in Liḥyānitic script that have an article in the form *’l-* and must, therefore, be regarded as Arabic, e.g. an inscription from al-H̲urayba. Likewise, a few isolated inscriptions in Nabataean script have been assigned to Arabic by some scholars: two short inscriptions from ’Umm al-Ǧimāl (± 250 CE) and from al-Ḥiǧr (267 CE). They contain some instances of common nouns spelled with the ending *-ū*, e.g. *’lqbrw* (*al-qabrū*) ‘the grave’, *qbrw* (*qabrū*) ‘a grave’.

The most famous Arabic inscription in another script is undoubtedly that from an-Namāra (120 km south-east of Damascus, dating from 328 CE and discovered in 1901). There is a general consensus that this relatively long text in Nabataean script was written in a language that is essentially identical with the Classical Arabic which we know. The inscription was made in honour of Mr’lqys br ʿmrw, i.e. Mar’ulqays bar ʿAmrū (with Aramaic *bar* for Arabic *ibn*). The text of the inscription, tentative vocalisation and translation are given here according to the most recent version of Bellamy (1985):

1. *ty nfs mr ’lqys br ʿmrw mlk ’lʿrb [w]lqbh d̲w ’sd w[m]d̲ḥǧ*
2. *wmlk ’l’sdyn wbhrw wmlwkhm whrb m<d̲>ḥǧw ʿkdy wǧʿ*
3. *yzǧh fy rtǧ nǧrn mdynt šmr wmlk mʿdw wnbl bnbh*
4. *’lšʿwb wwklhm frsw lrwm flm yblġ mlk mblġh*
5. *ʿkdy hlk snt 200 + 20 + 3 ywm 7 bkslwl ylsʿd d̲w wlwh*

1. *Tī nafsu Mri’i l-Qaysi bar ʿAmrin maliki l-ʿArabi wa-laqabuhu D̲ū ’Asadin wa-Mad̲ḥiǧin*
2. *wa-malaka l-’Asadīyīna wa-buhirū wa-mulūkahum wa-harraba Mad̲ḥiǧw ʿakkad̲ā wa-ǧā’a*
3. *yazuǧǧuh(ā) fī rutuǧi Naǧrāna madīnati Šammara wa-malaka Maʿaddw wa-nabala bi-nabahi*
4. *l-šuʿūbi wa-wakkalahum fa-ra’asū li-Rūma fa-lam yablaġ malikun mablaġahu*
5. *ʿakkad̲ā halaka sanata 223 yawma 7 bi-kaslūl yā la-saʿdi d̲ū wālawhu*

1. This is the funerary monument of Imru’u l-Qays, son of ʿAmr, king of the Arabs; and (?) his title of honour was Master of Asad and Mad̲ḥij
2. And he subdued the Asadīs, and they were overwhelmed together with their kings, and he put to flight Ma<d̲>ḥij thereafter, and came
3. driving them into the gates of Najrān, the city of Shammar, and he subdued Maʿadd, and he dealt gently with the nobles
4. of the tribes, and appointed them viceroys, and they became the phylarchs for the Romans. And no king has equalled his achievements.
5. Thereafter he died in the year 223 on the 7th day of Kaslūl. Oh the good fortune of those who were his friends!

Part of the interpretation of this text is clear, but some of the crucial passages are still controversial, in particular the phrase *wa-laqabuhu* in line 1, which in the older literature was read *kullihā*, making Imr'u l-Qays king of all the Arabs. Concerning the text of line 4, long debates have been dedicated to the part which Bellamy reads as *fa-ra'asū*: most older interpreters read here *fārisū* in the sense of either 'cavalry' or 'Persians'. Whatever the interpretation of details, the text is written in recognisably Classical Arabic, with only a few singularities. The female demonstrative *tī* is not unknown in Classical poetry, and the relative *d̲ū* is reported by the grammarians as a pre-Islamic dialecticism (cf. below, p. 45). The word *'kd̲y* (*'akkad̲ā?*) is not attested in Classical Arabic; it is translated as 'thereafter' or 'until then'. Lexically, we note the occurrence of the Nabataean loan *nfs* in the sense of 'funerary monument'.

Rather more difficult to interpret is an even older text, dating from the first century CE and discovered in 1986 in 'En 'Avdat, which possibly represents the oldest example of a text in Arabic. The three lines in Arabic are part of an Aramaic inscription in Nabataean script to the God Obodas, erected by Garm'alahi, son of Taym'alahi. Transliteration and translation are given here after Bellamy (1990):

1. *fyf'l l' fid' wl' 't̲r'*
2. *fkn hn' ybġn' 'lmwtw l' 'bġh*
3. *fkn hn' 'rd ǧrḥw l' yrdn'*

1. *fa-yaf'alu lā fidan wa-lā 'at̲ara*
2. *fa-kāna hunā yabġīnā 'al-mawtu lā 'abġāhū*
3. *fa-kāna hunā 'adāda ǧurḥun lā yurdīnā*

1. For (Obodas) works without reward or favour
2. and he, when death tried to claim us, did not let it claim (us)
3. for when a wound (of ours) festered, he did not let us perish.

Almost no element of this interpretation is uncontested. It seems that in this text the common nouns *'l-mwtw* and *ǧrḥw* contain the Nabataean *-w*, which was later to be used almost only in proper names (as in the an-Namāra inscription). But others deny this and connect the *w* with the next word. The element *kn* is interpreted as a verb *kāna*, or as a conjunction 'if', or as a positive counterpart to Classical *lākin*, i.e. *kin* 'thus'. There can be no doubt, however, that the inscription is in Arabic because of the use of the article *'l-*; and, pending further interpretation, the inscription stands as a fascinating testimony of the oldest form of Arabic.

The most important conclusion to be drawn from the an-Namāra inscription is that the ending *-w* is no longer used for common nouns, as in the inscriptions from 'Umm al-Ǧimāl and al-Ḥiǧr, and not even in all proper names. This would seem to indicate that the pausal ending had become zero, as in Classical Arabic, except in the accusative in *-ā*; the spelling of the proper names would then be a relic of Nabataean/Aramaic spelling that was retained for some time for historical reasons and eventually disappeared in the orthographic system of Classical Arabic, except in the name *'amr*. The pre-Islamic inscriptions do not provide any conclusive evidence for or against the existence of declensional endings in the Arabic of this period. They follow the conventions of Nabataean spelling, among other things in the spelling of the accusative pausal ending. One way or the other, the inscriptions cannot answer the question of whether the distinction of case endings was reintroduced from some kind of poetic language (cf. Chapter 4) or had been retained. The only example that has been adduced of a dual ending, in the an-Namāra inscription, *'l'sdyn*, is controversial: some interpret it indeed as *malaka l-'asadayn* 'he became king of the two tribes 'Asad', but others read *al-'asadīyīna* 'he became king of the 'Asadīs'. In both cases, the syntactic position requires an oblique case anyway, so that we cannot see whether the oblique case would have been used in the subject position as well, as in the new type of Arabic.

With the an-Namāra inscription and the 'En 'Avdat inscription, we have the first documents in unequivocal Arabic, but they are still written in a different script. There are, however, also a few pre-Islamic inscriptions in Arabic in a script that may be called Arabic. The following inscriptions are known:

1. graffiti from Ǧabal Ramm, east of al-'Aqaba (middle of the fourth century CE)
2. the trilingual inscription (Arabic/Syriac/Greek) from Zabad near Aleppo (512 CE)
3. the inscription from Ǧabal 'Usays, ± 100 km south-east of Damascus (528 CE)
4. the inscription from Ḥarrān in the Northern Ḥōrān (568 CE)
5. the inscription from 'Umm al-Ǧimāl in the Southern Ḥōrān from the sixth century CE.

The inscription from Ḥarrān, for instance, reads (Robin 1992: 117) *'n' šrḥyl br ṭlmw bnyt d' 'lmrṭwl šnt 463 b'd mfsd ḫybr b'm*, i.e., in Classical Arabic *'anā Šaraḥīl bin Ẓālim banaytu ḏā l-marṭūla sanata 463 ba'da mafsadi Ḫaybar bi-'āmin* 'I, Šaraḥīl, son of Ẓālim [or: Ṭalmū], built this temple in the year 463 [i.e. 568 CE], one year after the destruction of Ḫaybar'. As these inscriptions are very short and their interpretation controversial, their interest is not so much linguistic as epigraphic, since they show us the early development of the later Arabic script.

The Arabic sources, as long as they do not attribute the invention of the Arabic script to Adam or Ishmael, tell us that the script had been introduced from abroad, either from the South Arabian region by the tribe Ǧurhum, or from Mesopotamia. The latter theory was supported by the people in al-Ḥīra, who claimed that there was some connection with the Syriac script (Ibn an-Nadīm, *Fihrist* 7–8). As a matter of fact, the notation of the short vowels in Arabic script, as well as some other features, were probably borrowed from Syriac in the first century of Islam (cf. below, Chapter 4). In modern times, a theory of Syriac origin was proposed by Starcky (1966). He pointed out that in Nabataean script the letters seem to be suspended from a line, whereas in both Syriac and Arabic script the letters appear to stand on a line. He therefore assumed that in al-Ḥīra, the capital of the Laḫmid dynasty, a form of Syriac cursive script had developed into the Arabic alphabet (see Figure 3.1).

The theory of Syriac origin has now been abandoned by most scholars. It seems much more likely that the Arabic alphabet is derived from a type of cursive Nabataean. In the Aramaic script, from which Nabataean writing

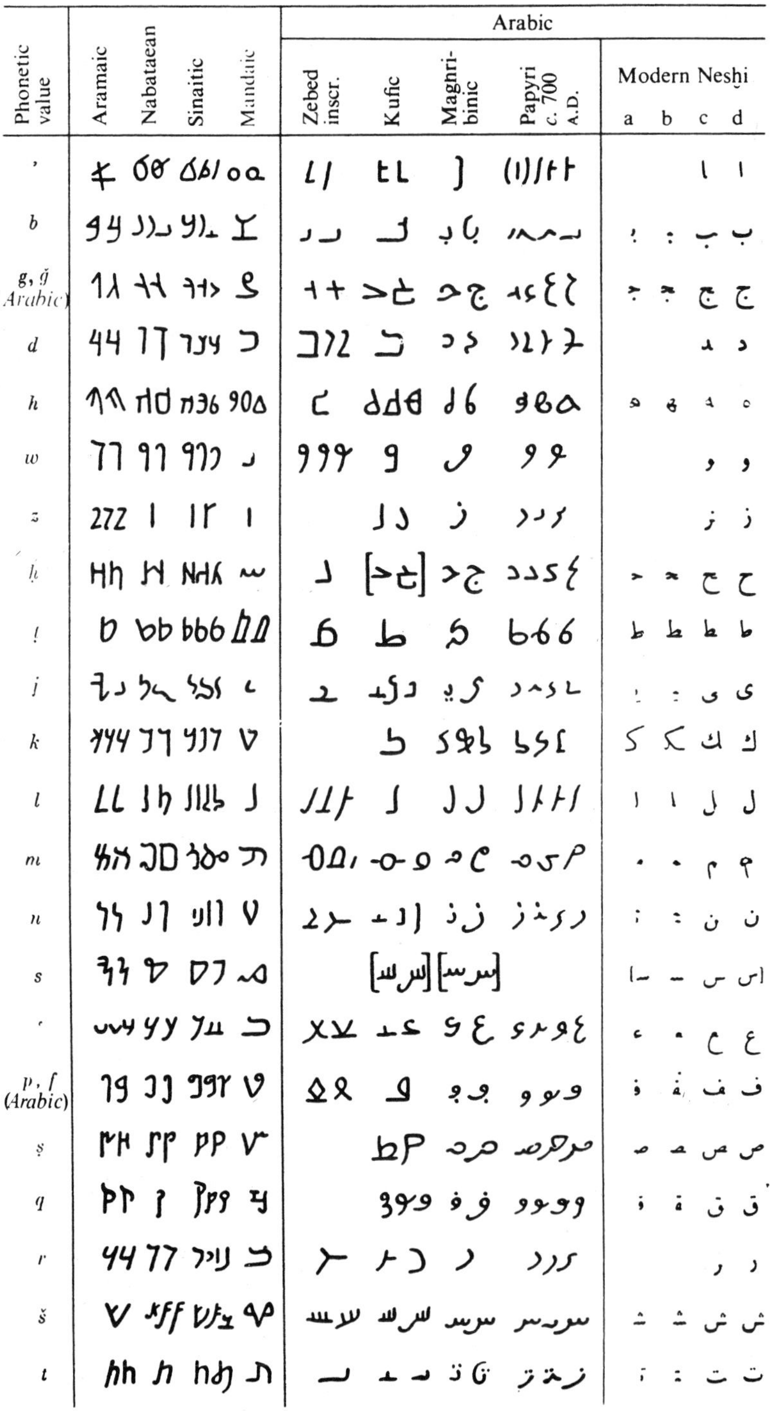
Arabic
Phonetic value
Aramaic
Nabataean
Sinaitic
Mandaic
Zebed inscr.
Kufic
Maghri-binic
Papyri c. 700 A.D.
Modern Neshi
a b c d
'
b
g, ğ (Arabic)
d
h
w
z
ḥ
ṭ
j
k
l
m
n
s
ʿ
p, f (Arabic)
ṣ
q
r
š
t

Figure 3.1 The development of Arabic script (from Hans Jensen, *Sign, Symbol and Script*, 3rd edn, London: George Allen & Unwin, 1970, p. 322)

ultimately derives, there are no ligatures between the letters. But in the cursive forms of the Nabataean script, most of the features that characterise the Arabic script already appear. Even before 200 CE, Nabataean ostraca from the Negev exhibit a cursive script with extensive use of connections, which in epigraphic Nabataean script were not developed until after 400 CE. It is conceivable, therefore, that the elaboration of an Arabic script for texts in Arabic took place as early as the second century CE. This would mean that the development of the Arabic script as it is used in the pre-Islamic inscriptions occurred largely independently from the later developments in Nabataean epigraphic script. The most important internal development in Arabic script is the systematic elaboration of connections between the letters within the word, and the system of different forms of the letters according to their position within the word.

With the inscriptions in (pre-)Arabic script, we are slowly approaching the pre-Islamic period proper, called in Arabic the *Ǧāhiliyya*, the period in which the Bedouin did not yet know the revelation of the *Qur'ān*. This period will be dealt with in Chapter 4. The sum total of the evidence mentioned in this chapter is not large. The number of inscriptions is considerable, but even within the lengthiest ones there is not enough material to enable us to trace the development of the Arabic language in the period preceding the historical period. Still, the stage of the language that we find in the Ṯamūdic, Liḥyānitic, Ṣafā'itic and Ḥaṣā'itic inscriptions, and the Arabic elements that emerge from the Aramaic inscriptions from Petra and Palmyra, give us at least some glimpse of this early development. At the very least, we know that before the earliest written testimonies there was some kind of development, and even though we do not know what the language of the Aribi and the inhabitants of Arbāya was, we know that for a long time nomads calling themselves by a name derived from the radicals *ʿrb* inhabited the desert. We also know that at least from the first century CE onwards some of them used a language that was closely related to Classical Arabic.

FURTHER READING

The standard work on the early history of the Arabs is Altheim and Stiehl (1964–9); the history of the bedouinisation of the peninsula is dealt with in various articles by Dostal (e.g. 1959). A fascinating study of the early development of camel domestication and the history of settlement in the peninsula is Bulliet (1990); on the role of the nomads in Ancient Near Eastern history, see Höfner (1959); see also Klengel (1972) with a section on the occurrence of the Arabs in cuneiform inscriptions (1972: 88–103). On the origin of the name 'Arabs', see Dossin (1959); on ancient Bedouin society, see Henninger (1959). The standard work on the relations between the Arabs and Byzantium is Shahid (1984).

A survey of the various groups of inscriptions mentioned here is given by W. Müller (1982), with further literature. A general survey of the languages in pre-Islamic Arabia is in Beeston (1981) and Robin (1992). For the individual groups of inscriptions, the following sources may be consulted: Thamūdic: van den Branden (1950); Liḥyānitic: publication of most of the inscriptions by Jaussen and Savignac (1909, 1914), new inscriptions in Stiehl (1971); Ṣafā'itic: Littmann

(1943), and the sketch in W. Müller (1982), from which the examples in this chapter were taken; Ḥaṣā'itic: Jamme (1967).

There is an extensive literature on the Nabataean and Palmyran inscriptions. A grammatical description of Nabataean was given by Cantineau (1930–2). On Palmyran, see Cantineau (1935). On the relevance of Nabataean orthography for the history of Arabic, see Diem (1973a).

The pre-Islamic inscriptions are dealt with in Grohmann's (1971: 15–17) handbook of palaeography, as well as in several monographs and articles, e.g. Bellamy (1988); for a survey, see Diem (1976); for the development of the script in these inscriptions and further bibliography, see Gruendler (1993: 12–14).

The most recent publication on the an-Namāra inscription is Bellamy (1985) with further references to older literature. For the inscription of 'En 'Avdat, see Negev (1986), Bellamy (1990), Noja (1989, 1993) and Ambros (1994).

The later development of the Arabic script is treated by Abbott (1939), Grohmann (1967, 1971) and Endreß (1982). For the theory of Syriac origin, see Starcky (1966) and discussion of this theory in Sourdel-Thomine (1966). Gruendler (1993) has detailed charts of the individual letters in both epigraphic and cursive Nabataean and Arabic and a number of tracings of the most important inscriptions from the pre-Islamic and the early Islamic period.

4
Arabic in the Pre-Islamic Period

4.1 THE LANGUAGE OF THE ARABS

When the *Qur'ān* was revealed to the Prophet, it described itself as being *ʿarabiyyun* 'Arabic' and *mubīnun* 'clear'. The two attributes are intimately connected, as for instance in Q 43/2–3 'By the clear Book: We have made it an Arabic recitation in order that you may understand' (*wa-l-kitābi l-mubīni: 'innā ǧaʿalnāhu qur'ānan ʿarabiyyan laʿallakum taʿqilūna*). All later generations have believed that its text was the best example of the *ʿArabiyya*, the language of the Arabs; in fact, that its style and language could not be imitated because of its clarity and correctness (*'iʿǧāz al-Qur'ān*). The *Qur'ān* does not use the word *ʿArab*, only the adjective *ʿarabiyyun*. The plural noun *'Aʿrāb* indicates the Bedouin tribes who lived in the desert and resisted the message of the Prophet, as for instance in Q 9/97 *al-'Aʿrābu 'ašaddu kufran wa-nifāqan* 'the Bedouin are the worst in disbelief and hypocrisy'. In combination with the word *lisān*, the adjective *ʿarabiyyun* indicates a supra-tribal unity, a language that served as the binding factor for all those who lived in the Arabian peninsula, as opposed to the *ʿAǧam*, the non-Arabs who lived outside it and spoke different languages. In pre-Islamic poetry, the term *ʿArab* has this same sense of Arabs as an ethno-cultural group.

In early Islamic terminology, a distinction was made between the *ʿArab*, the sedentary Arabs in cities such as Mecca and Medina, and the *'Aʿrāb* 'Bedouin'. The latter term carried a negative connotation because of its use in the *Qur'ān*. After the period of the conquests, however, the sedentary population began to regard the free-roaming Bedouin, whose language preserved the purity of pre-Islamic times, as the ideal type of Arab, and the term *kalām al-ʿArab* 'language of the Arabs' came to denote the pure, unaffected language of the Bedouin.

It would seem, therefore, that in pre-Islamic nomenclature there was a special term for the nomadic tribes, *'Aʿrāb*, whereas the term *ʿArab* indicated all inhabitants of the peninsula, nomads and sedentary population alike. The matter is complicated by another distinction made in the indigenous historiographical tradition. It was thought that the peninsula had been inhabited from time immemorial by the 'lost Arabs' (*al-ʿArab al-bā'ida*), i.e. those tribes that are mentioned in the *Qur'ān* as having been punished for their disbelief, for instance the tribes of ʿĀd, Ṯamūd and Ǧurhum. The later Arabs all descended from two ancestors, Qaḥṭān and ʿAdnān. Qaḥṭān was related to the 'lost Arabs'; his descendants were identified as the Southern Arabs and they were regarded as the 'real Arabs' (*al-ʿArab al-ʿāriba*). The descendants of ʿAdnān were the Northern Arabs, who were said to have been arabised at a later period (*al-ʿArab al-muta'arriba* or *al-musta'riba*). In the post-Islamic tradition, the descent of the Northern Arabs was traced back through their ancestor 'Adnān to 'Ismā'īl, the son of Abraham. Among the tribes descending from 'Adnān were Huḏayl, Tamīm, Qays, Rabī'a, and the Qurayš of Mecca. Among the offspring of Qaḥṭān were the inhabitants of the South Arabian states, who were said to have descended from Ḥimyar, one of Qaḥṭān's descendants. Some of the tribes in the northern part of the peninsula were of southern provenance, for instance the 'Aws and Ḫazraǧ of Medina and the tribe Ṭayyi'.

It is difficult to say to what degree this distinction between Southern and Northern Arabs goes back to any real memory of a difference between two groups, but it is clear that in the perception of the Prophet's contemporaries they were distinct groups, a distinction that continued to be felt strongly in Islamic times: even as far as Islamic Spain, enmity between representatives of the two groups under the names of Qays for the Northern and Kalb for the Southern group persisted. Linguistically speaking, however, the language of poets from both groups was accepted by the grammarians, and the poems of both groups were used indiscriminately as linguistic primary sources.

A special case is that of the so-called Ḥimyaritic language, about which we have some information from al-Hamdānī's (d. 334/946) description of the Arabian peninsula (*Ǧazīra* 134–6). Since for the Arabs Ḥimyar represented all things South Arabian, one might assume that the language called Ḥimyaritic was the continuation of the Old South Arabian language, but in actual fact it is not. From the features mentioned by al-Hamdānī and others – e.g. the verbal ending *-k-* for the first and the second person, as in South Arabian, e.g. *waladku* 'I bore', *ra'ayku* 'I saw', and the article *am-* – Rabin (1951: 42–53) speculates that Ḥimyaritic was the name that the Arabs gave to the language of those *'rb* who are mentioned in the Old South Arabian sources and who had settled in this region. They were probably immigrants from the north, who spoke a North Arabic dialect, but whose speech was heavily influenced by the South Arabian language (cf. Chapter 3, p. 23). As their speech was comprehensible to a speaker of Arabic, Ḥimyaritic cannot be identical with any of the South Arabian languages, which are characterised by al-Hamdānī as being *ġutm* 'incomprehensible'. It is possible that this language is also reflected in the inscriptions that are sometimes called 'pseudo-Sabaean' (cf. Chapter 3, p. 31). Some of the features mentioned as characteristic of the Ḥimyaritic language still survive in the modern Yemenite dialects (cf. below, p. 150).

Apart from the reports about the Ḥimyarites, the dialects of all tribes were subsumed under the label *kalām al-'Arab*, but the distinctions mentioned above created a difficulty for the later tradition. On the one hand, the idea of one language of the Arabs implies a basic linguistic unity in the peninsula. Moreover, the consensus of the Muslims has always been that the language of the *Qur'ān* was the language of the Prophet and his compatriots, in other words that their everyday speech was identical with the language of the Holy Book, which was the same as the language of the pre-Islamic poems. On the other hand, the grammarians set up a hierarchy of the speech of the various tribes. They held on to the tradition of the sons of Qaḥṭān being the pure Arabs but at the same time believed that the language of the Ḥiǧāz, the region of Mecca, was superior to all other varieties. One way of reconciling both views was to assert that the Qurayš tribe of Mecca had taken over from all other dialects what was best in them. Thus, the hierarchy of Arabic dialects culminated in the language of the Ḥiǧāz, the region where the Prophet was born, and the language of the Qurayš, the tribe in which he was born.

This view implies that there were linguistic differences between the tribes, otherwise no hierarchy would be possible. Indeed, although the general opinion was that in the *Ǧāhiliyya* Arabic (*al-ʿArabiyya*) was the language of all Arabs alike, the grammatical literature records regional differences between the tribes, the so-called *luġāt*. Our information about the linguistic situation in the *Ǧāhiliyya* is largely derived from the Arabic literature on the dialectal differences in pre-Islamic Arabia. Some of these materials were collected in monographs, for instance on the *luġāt* in the *Qur'ān*, while other data are found in the lexica. For the grammarians, the dialectal variants, as long as they were attested in the *Qur'ān* or in poetry, or elicited from a trustworthy Bedouin informant, had to be accepted as correct Arabic. This did not mean, however, that anybody else was entitled to speak in this way, or that such dialectal variants could be used as productive items in the language.

It is difficult to evaluate the testimonies about the geographical distribution of the dialectal differences. Their validity is hard to assess because the grammarians tried to make them fit their scheme. The language of the Southern Arabs – apart from the reports about Ḥimyaritic (see above, p. 38) – was usually indicated as *luġa 'ahl al-Yaman*; one of its best-known features was the use of the definite article *'am-*, still extant in modern Yemenite dialects. The data of the Northern Arabs tended to be systematised into two larger regions, roughly covering the western and the eastern parts of the peninsula: the language of the Ḥiǧāz, often synonymous with that of the Banū Qurayš, or with the language of Mecca and Medina, on the one hand, and the language of the Tamīm, on the other. To a certain extent, this division coincides with that between sedentary Arabs in the pre-Islamic cities and Bedouin tribes in the desert regions.

It seems that the differences between Classical Arabic as we know it and Eastern Arabic were smaller than those existing between Classical Arabic and the language of the Ḥiǧāz. This may partly explain the relative scarcity of data on Eastern Arabic, since the grammarians tended to concentrate on what deviated from the later norm of Classical Arabic, and in this respect the Eastern Arabic variety had much less to offer than the Ḥiǧāzī variety. Since the norm of Classical Arabic was to a large degree derived from the language of the *Qur'ān* and the pre-Islamic poems, the conclusion would seem to be that this language was more related to Eastern than to Western Arabic. In some respects, the language of the Ḥiǧāz differed from the language that we find in the *Qur'ān* and in poetry, and this has led some scholars to assume that the origin of the Classical language, the language of pre-Islamic poetry, lay in the Central or Eastern part of the peninsula, possibly in the Naǧd, where Western and Eastern dialects met. In this area, the kingdom of Kinda and the confederation of the Qays had created larger cultural and political entities, in which there was a fertile environment for the emergence and development of poetry. From here, the poetic language is assumed to have spread to other centres, in the first place to the court of al-Ḥīra, the buffer state in the north between the Bedouin tribes and the Persian empire.

This poetic language must then also have spread to the commercial centres in the peninsula, such as Mecca and Medina. Because of its prestigious and supra-tribal character, it is not surprising that this was the language in which the *Qur'ān* was revealed in Mecca. The text of the *Qur'ān*, in particular its orthography, bears traces of an adaptation to the local pronunciation of the poetic language in the Ḥiğāz. The most obvious adaptation is that of the spelling of the *hamza*, the glottal stop. All sources agree that the Eastern dialects knew a glottal stop, which was absent in the Western dialects, including the dialect of Mecca. In the text of the *Qur'ān* as we have it, the *hamza* is always spelled with a small sign resembling an *ʿayn*, which is usually carried by one of the semi-consonants *w*, *y* or *'alif*. The semi-consonants probably represent the pronunciation of the word in the dialect of Mecca (cf. below).

This example shows that the realisation of Arabic across the peninsula varied, and that the local realisation in Mecca differed from the language of the *Qur'ān* as we have it. This led the German scholar Karl Vollers to go one step further in his theory about the relationship between the text of the *Qur'ān* and the colloquial speech of Mecca. In his book *Volkssprache und Schriftsprache im alten Arabien* ('Vernacular and written language in Ancient Arabia', 1906), Vollers claimed that the revelation had originally taken place in the colloquial language of the Prophet and the Meccans (*Volkssprache*). In his view, this colloquial language was the precursor of the modern Arabic dialects. During the period of the conquests the text was transformed into a language that was identical with the poetic language of the Nağd, called by Vollers *Schriftsprache*. The differences between the two 'languages' included the absence of the glottal stop in Meccan Arabic, as well as the elision of the indefinite ending *-n* (nunation) and the vocalic endings. The motive behind this transformation was, he asserted, the wish to raise the language of the *Qur'ān* to the level of that of the poems. Those who were responsible for the alleged translation were particularly strict in the matter of the *hamza* and the case endings, whereas they allowed some of the other features, sometimes in the official text, and more often in the variants of the text. The literature on the variant readings of the *Qur'ān* in his view preserved many traces of the underlying colloquial language.

It is certainly true, as Vollers says, that the correct declension of the *Qur'ān* was a *topos* in early Islamic literature. But in itself the attention that was given to this phenomenon in post-Islamic times does not tell us anything about the linguistic situation in the pre-Islamic period. It can easily be explained by later linguistic developments in the period of the conquests: many people in the conquered territories did not know Arabic very well and made mistakes when reciting the *Qur'ān*. Therefore, those who cared about the correct transmission of the text were on their guard against mistakes in the use of declensional endings, and instructed people in the correct grammatical rules.

In its extreme form, Vollers' theory has been abandoned nowadays and the concomitant presupposition of a large-scale conspiracy in early Islam concerning the linguistic transformation of the text is no longer held by anyone. The delivery of a revelational document in a 'vulgar' variety of the language is hardly likely in itself. The existence of a poetic register of the language is undisputed, and it is not very likely that for the revelation anything but this prestigious variety of the language would have been chosen. The traces of a transition from Eastern to Western Arabic can also be explained by the activities of the early copyists who were familiar with the Meccan way of speaking and had to devise a way to record the Eastern features such as the glottal stop in an orthographic system that had been invented for the Western way of speaking.

In spite of this rejection of the 'translation theory', the main point of Vollers' theory, the distinction between a *Volkssprache* and a *Schriftsprache*, has remained the leading principle for almost all subsequent attempts by Western Arabists to explain the development of the Arabic language. In modern terms, we could say that the central thought of these theories is that in pre-Islamic there was already diglossia, i.e. a linguistic situation in which the domains of speech are distributed between two varieties of the language (cf. below, Chapter 12). In that case, the division would be approximately the same as it is nowadays in the Arabic-speaking world: a high variety as literary language and a low variety as colloquial language. In theories that take this view, the literary language is usually called 'poetic koine' (cf. below, p. 46).

In itself, it is not unreasonable to assume that there was an essential difference between poetic or literary language and colloquial language. After all, such a situation is found in other oral cultures as well. The question, however, is whether or not such a situation obtained in pre-Islamic Mecca. Contrary to the Arab sources, the theory of a 'literary' language assumes that the case endings (*'i'rāb*) were absent in Bedouin everyday speech. In order to acquire a better idea of the Bedouin language, we shall first look at the data from the literature on the dialectal variants (*luġāt*) of the Arab tribes. Then we shall discuss reports about the language of the Bedouin after the conquests.

4.2 THE PRE-ISLAMIC DIALECTS

Since our data are fragmentary, it is difficult to assess their value, let alone set up a dialect map of the pre-Islamic peninsula (see Map 4.1 for the distribution of our information on the pre-Islamic dialects). The following eight phonological features are frequently mentioned as major differences between the two groups of pre-Islamic dialects.

First, in the Eastern dialects, final consonant clusters did not contain a vowel, whereas in the Western dialects they had an anaptyctic vowel, e.g. (West/East) *ḥusun/ḥusn* 'beauty', *fa<u>h</u>i<u>d</u>/fi<u>hd</u>* 'thigh', *kalima/kilma* 'word', *'unuq/'unq* 'neck'. This difference is probably connected with a difference in stress: it may be surmised that the Eastern dialects had a strong expiratory stress, hence the absence of a vowel. It is difficult to say which of the two variants is original; in Classical Arabic sometimes the one, sometimes the other, sometimes both variants have survived.

Second, the Eastern dialects must have known some form of vowel harmony or assimilation, e.g. (West/East) *ba'īr/bi'īr* 'camel', *minhum/minhim* 'from them'. This feature, too, may be connected with the strong expiratory stress of the Eastern dialects, which encourages assimilation. The Classical language retained the assimilation in those cases where the suffix was preceded by an *i*, e.g. *fīhim* 'in them' (where the Ḥiǧāz had *fīhum* without assimilation).

Third, the long vowel *ā* underwent *'imāla* 'inclination', i.e. a fronted pronunciation of the vowel towards [e], in the Eastern dialects, whereas the Western dialects were characterised by what the grammarians call *tafḫīm*. Usually, this term indicates the centralised pronunciation of a vowel after a velarised consonant, but here it probably indicates the pronunciation as a 'pure' *ā*, or perhaps in some cases even as *ō*, namely in those words which are indicated in Qur'ānic spelling with a *wāw*, e.g. *ṣalāt, zakāt, ḥayāt*, possibly also in other words, e.g. *salām*. Sometimes we find in Nabataean inscriptions a long *ā* spelled with *w*, which may reflect an Aramaic pronunciation with *ō* (cf. above, p. 30).

Fourth, the Western dialects may have known a phoneme *ē*: according to the grammarians verbs such as *ḫāfa* 'to fear', *ṣāra* 'to become' were pronounced with *'imāla*. But since the *'imāla* was otherwise unknown in the Ḥiǧāz and moreover never occurs in the neighbourhood of a guttural, the grammarians' remark may refer to the existence of an independent phoneme *ē*. It is unlikely that this *ē* continues a Proto-Semitic *ē*; perhaps it is an indication for a phonetic development of *-ay-* instead (cf. also above, on Ṣafā'itic diphthongs, Chapter 3, p. 27).

Fifth, the passive of the so-called hollow verbs with a medial *w* was formed differently in the East (*qūla*) and the West (*qīla*). Possibly, both forms are a development from an original /y/, which has disappeared from the phonemic inventory of all Arabic dialects but left some traces; the Classical passive of these verbs is *qīla*.

Sixth, the *qāf* was probably voiceless in the East, voiced in the West; the latter pronunciation became standard practice in early recitation manuals. We have seen above (Chapter 2, p. 21) that the Arabic phoneme *q* possibly evolved from a phoneme **ḳ*, which was neutral with regard to voicing; the Eastern and the Western dialects developed this phoneme in different ways. The Modern Standard Arabic pronunciation of /q/ is voiceless, but in the modern Bedouin dialects it is still realised as a voiced /g/ (cf. below, p. 143).

Seventh, the most remarkable feature of the Ḥiǧāzī dialect has already been mentioned above: the loss of the glottal stop (*hamza*), which was retained in the Eastern dialects (cf. Map 4.2 for the distribution of this feature). In the Western dialects, the loss of the *hamza* was compensated sometimes by the lengthening of a preceding vowel (e.g. *bi'r* 'well' > *bīr*, *ra's* 'head' > *rās*, *lu'lu'* 'pearls' > *lūlū*), or it resulted in contraction of vowels (*sa'ala* 'to ask' > *sāla*) or a change into a corresponding glide (e.g. *sā'irun* 'walking' > *sāyirun*; *yaqra'u* 'he reads' > *yaqrawu*). Since Ḥiǧāzī orthography did not have a glottal stop, the original spelling represented the Ḥiǧāzī pronunciation of the words. The sign for *hamza* is a later addition (cf. below, p. 56).

Eighth, in the Ḥiǧāzī dialect, the prefix of the imperfect contained the vowel *-a-*; all other dialects formed this prefix with *-i-*, the so-called *taltala*, one of the pre-Islamic features that have been preserved in the contemporary dialects, which usually have *-i-*. Both vowels represent a generalisation, since more archaic forms of Semitic have a distribution of the prefix-vowels in which *i* is used for the third person singular masculine and the first person plural, and *a* for the first person singular, the second person, and the third person singular feminine (cf. Hetzron 1976). In this case, Classical Arabic has 'followed' the Western pattern, since all prefixes in Classical Arabic have *-a-*.

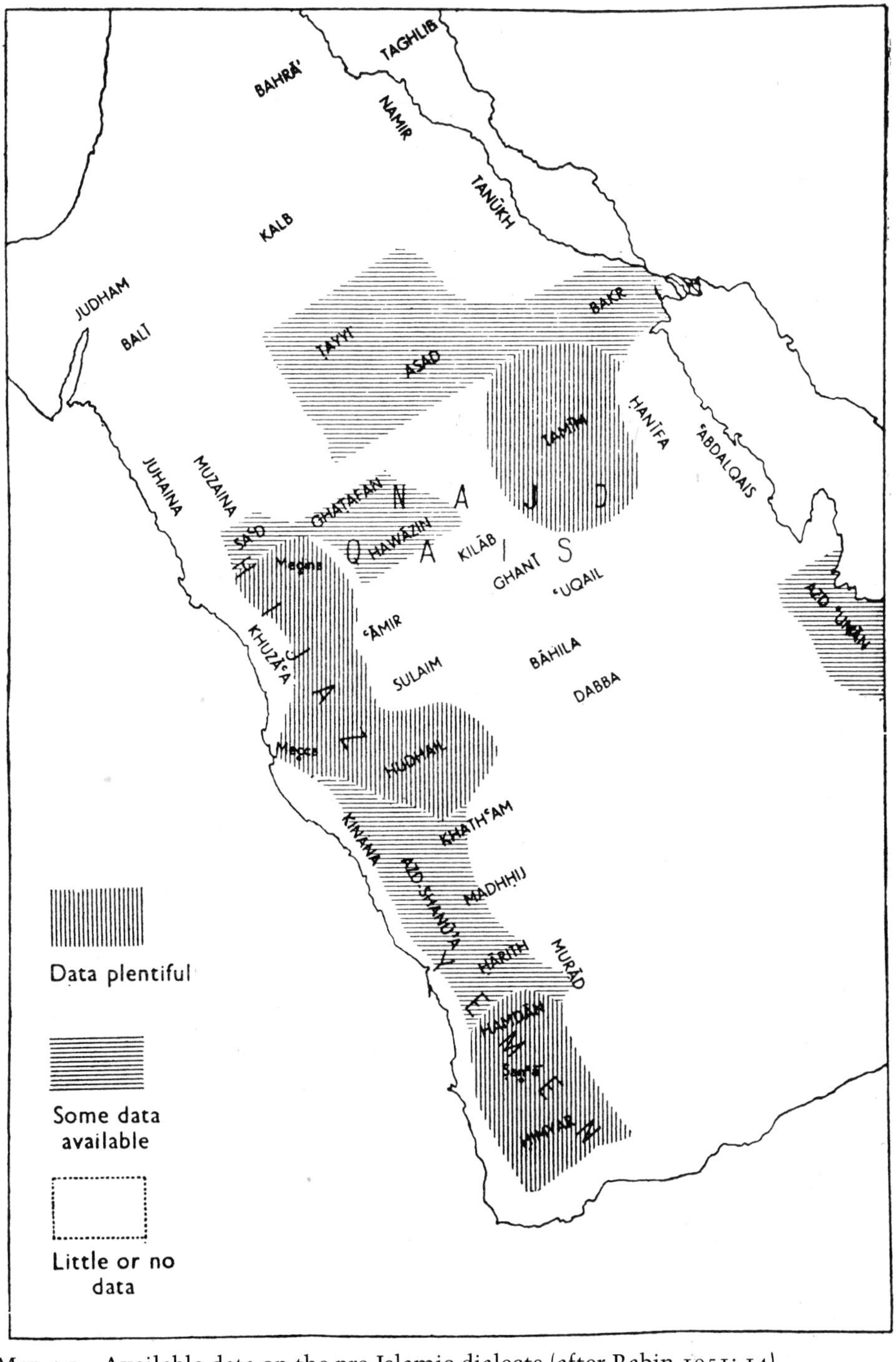

Map 4.1 Available data on the pre-Islamic dialects (after Rabin 1951: 14)

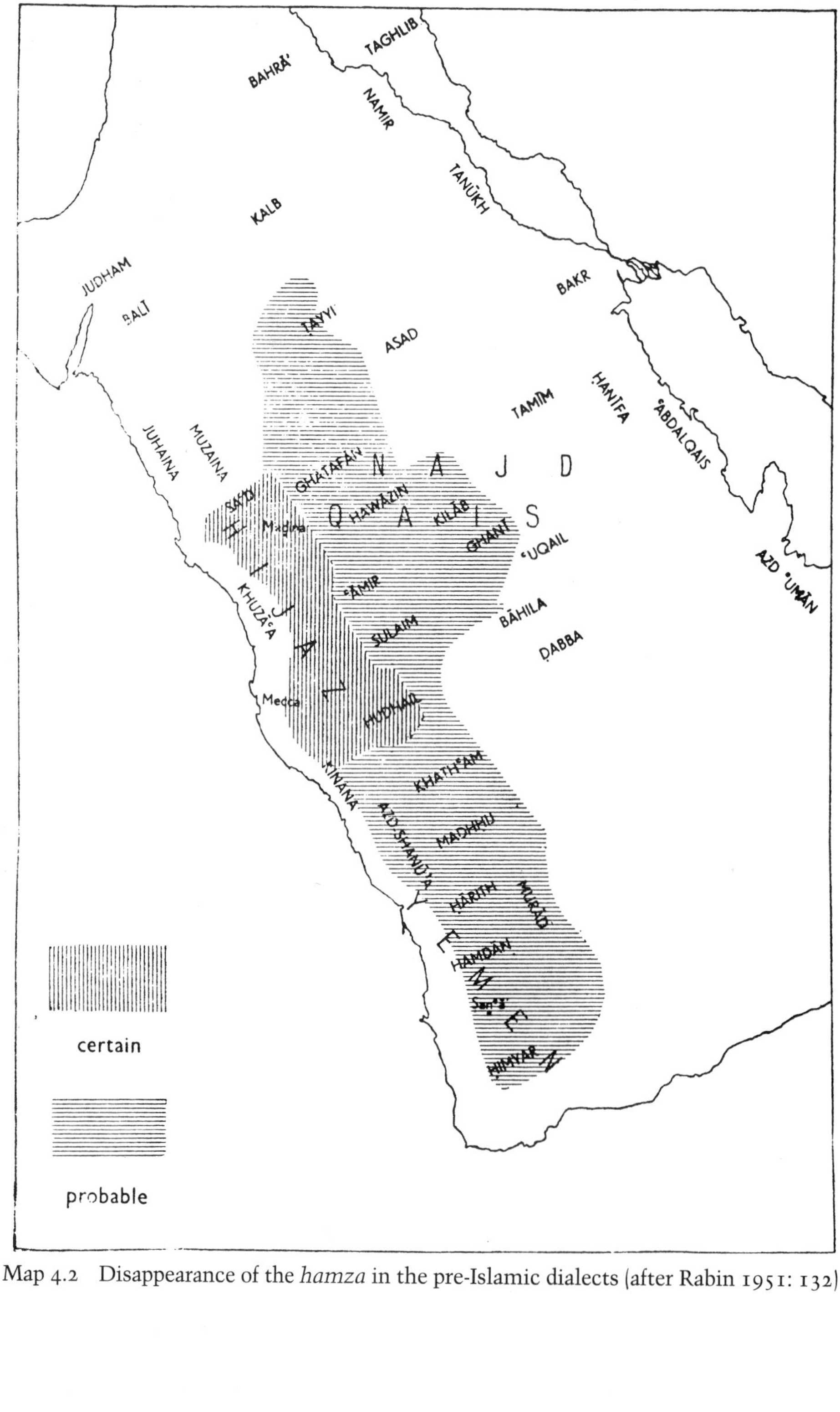

Map 4.2 Disappearance of the *hamza* in the pre-Islamic dialects (after Rabin 1951: 132)

The preceding dialectal differences concerned phonetic or phonological differences between the dialects. There are some testimonies that refer to differences at a higher level of linguistic structure. For instance, there may be some evidence for the existence of an undeclined dual in Ḥiǧāzī Arabic; the most famous example is the Qur'ānic verse 20/63 *'inna hāḏāni la-sāḥirānī* 'these two are sorcerers', in which the particle *'inna* seems to be constructed with a nominative instead of the Classical accusative. This verse caused the commentators a lot of trouble, and we know that in the earliest period of Arabic grammar some of them even suggested regarding this form as a copyists' error, which should be corrected, either by reading the accusative in the following noun, or by changing the particle to *'in* (cf. below, *'in al-muḫaffafa*).

The particles *'in* 'indeed' and *'an* 'that' as abbreviated forms of *'inna* and *'anna* (the so-called *'in, 'an muḫaffafa*) with the following noun in the nominative seem to have been more current in the Ḥiǧāz than in the East. Some examples occur in the *Qur'ān*, e.g. Q 36/32 *wa-'in kullun la-mā ǧamīʿun ladaynā muḥḍarūna* 'verily, all will be brought together before Us'. These forms may even be followed by an accusative, e.g. Q 11/111 *wa-'in kullan la-mā yuwaffiyannahum rabbuka 'aʿmālahum* 'verily, thy Lord will repay everyone their deeds'. Not surprisingly, the grammarians tried to correct such forms, either by changing the case ending of the following word, or by reading the full form *'inna*.

A well-known difference between Ḥiǧāz and Tamīm is the construction of *mā* as a nominal negator. According to the grammarians, *mā* could be construed in the same way as the verb *laysa* 'to be not', with an accusative in the predicate, e.g. *mā huwa kabīran* 'he is not big'. This use of the so-called *mā ḥiǧāziyya* did not occur in the Eastern dialects.

There are some indications that the negation *'in*, which occurs not infrequently in the *Qur'ān*, e.g. Q 11/51 *'in 'aǧriya 'illā ʿalā llaḏī faṭaranī* 'my reward is not due except from Him who created me', is characteristic of Ḥiǧāzī speech.

In some dialects, a relative *ḏī* or *ḏū* (the so-called *ḏū ṭā'iyya*, i.e. of the tribe Ṭayyi') is attested; this relative does not occur in the *Qur'ān*, but it occurs in the an-Namāra inscription (cf. above, p. 31), and it is found in some pre-Islamic poems, e.g. in a line quoted in the *Ḥamāsa*: *li-hāḏā l-mar'i ḏū ǧā'a sāʿiyan* 'to this man who has come to levy tax' (cf. Reckendorf 1921: 431).

Apart from the possible, but unlikely, occurrence of an undeclined dual in one verse in the *Qur'ān* these points concern relatively minor differences. There is, however, one point that touches upon the core of Arabic syntax, the construction of verbal and nominal sentences. In Classical Arabic, when the verb precedes the agent in the so-called verbal sentence (cf. below, Chapter 6, p. 80), there is no agreement in number between verb and agent. According to the grammarians, some dialects in the *Ǧāhiliyya* did allow agreement in this case. Some of the examples they give for this phenomenon – usually called the *'akalūnī l-barāġīṯ* 'the fleas have bitten me' syndrome – stem from Ḥiǧāzī poets, and there are no Eastern examples. This is the only example of a syntactic feature ascribed to a pre-Islamic dialect that is also found in the modern dialects of Arabic, which do not exhibit the difference between verbal and nominal sentences in the Classical sense of the term and always have agreement between verb and agent. In the modern dialects, the canonical word order is subject–verb–object rather than verb–subject–object as in the Classical language. It is, therefore, not clear whether this feature in Ḥiǧāzī Arabic should be interpreted as the first step towards a later development. In the text of the *Qur'ān* as we have it, this feature does not occur.

The conclusion is that in most cases the language of the *Qur'ān* reflects the Eastern usage whenever differences between Eastern and Western Arabic existed. As regards the pronunciation of the glottal stop in the early Islamic period, it was felt to be more prestigious and more fitting for the recitation of the Holy Book, although there seems to have been considerable opposition on the part of the early reciters to such a pronunciation, which they branded as affected. It is equally obvious, however, from the list of differences that the dialects were not very far apart from each other. Most of the features mentioned above concern phonetic or phonological phenomena. Apart from the *'akalūnī l-barāġīṯ* syndrome, the sources mention a few syntactic differences, which we have not listed here, since their status is hard to determine. Some of these almost certainly represent later theorising on the part of the grammarians, for instance, in the case of the various exceptive constructions with *'illā*, for which one dialect is said to have used the nominative and the other the accusative. There is one thing that transpires from such syntactic *luġāt*: if there is any reality to them, both dialect groups must have used case endings. The evidence for an undeclined dual mentioned above is too meagre to warrant any other conclusion. In view of the central role of declension in the various theories about the linguistic situation in the pre-Islamic period, this absence of evidence for declensionless speech in the grammatical literature is crucial for our understanding of the historical development of Arabic.

4.3 THEORIES ABOUT THE LANGUAGE OF THE ǦĀHILIYYA

For the Arabs, the dialects of all tribes belonged to what was basically one language. In spite of the various *luġāt* in the literature, they do not accept a major dichotomy between any 'literary' language and everyday speech. Western scholarship has always been sceptical of this conception of the development of Arabic. Although Vollers' theory with its distinction between a *Volkssprache* and a *Schriftsprache* in pre-Islamic Arabia has been abandoned, most contemporary Arabists still disagree with the Arabs' view on the fundamental unity of the three varieties of everyday speech, the language of the *Qur'ān* and the language of the poetry. In line with Vollers' argumentation, most linguists believe that in the *Ǧāhiliyya* colloquial and 'literary' language already diverged. The colloquial varieties of the tribes are usually called in Western publications 'pre-Islamic dialects'; the language of the *Qur'ān* and the poetry is often designated 'poetico-Qur'ānic koine' or 'poetic koine' (in German publications *Dichtersprache*).

The theory of the poetic koine emphasises the role of the poets, *šu'arā'*, which means 'those who have knowledge, who are aware'. According to Zwettler (1978: 109) they were specialists in an archaic form of the language and the only ones who were still able to handle the complicated declensional endings. In this view, the case system was beyond the reach of the ordinary speakers and could only be acquired by professional poets and their transmitters (*ruwāt*) after a long training.

This view of the linguistic situation before Islam ties in with widely-accepted ideas about the emergence of the new type of Arabic in the period of the Islamic conquests. Most linguists believe that the changes that took place in the transition from Old Arabic to New Arabic, among them the disappearance of the declensional endings, were the continuation of a process that had already begun in the pre-Islamic dialects. Since our information on these dialects is limited, we have to turn to other evidence in order to find out whether the later changes can be traced back to pre-Islamic times; in particular, whether the Bedouin used declensional endings in their colloquial speech.

One source of additional evidence are the pre-Islamic inscriptions. Yet, we have seen above (Chapter 3) that in the pre-Islamic inscriptions no conclusive evidence can be found for or against the existence of declensional endings. In the inscriptions, no declensional endings are used, either because the language which they represent did not have such endings, or because this language distinguished between contextual forms with endings and pausal forms without endings, of which only the latter were used in writing. There is some evidence that the variety of Arabic that is reflected in the Nabataean inscriptions retained fossilised endings in some words. Theophoric compound names very often end in *-y* (*ʿbdʾlhy*), and the element *ʾabū* and *ibnū* in compound names is almost always spelled with *-w* in all syntactic contexts. The usual conclusion is that in this variety of Arabic the declensional endings had been lost before the first century BCE. On the other hand, we should bear in mind that most of the inscriptions stem from a border area where Arabs had been in contact with other peoples for centuries; it may well be possible that the language reflected in these inscriptions underwent changes that were similar to those that affected the language of all Arabs after the conquests, in particular the loss of the case endings. Since the tribes in the North Arabian desert were in touch with an Aramaic-speaking sedentary population, a type of New Arabic may have become current in the small trade settlements of the North Arabian/Syrian desert long before Islam. This may be the type of Arabic that is called by later Arabic sources *nabāṭī*.

A second possibility is to turn to the orthography of the Qurʾānic text. The language of the *Qurʾān* has an operational declensional system, for example in the use of the masculine sound plural endings *-ūna*/*-īna* correlating with the syntactic function of the word, and in the use of the moods of the verb (indicative vs subjunctive/jussive). But the question still remains whether this state of affairs reflects the structure of the language of the Ḥiǧāz. As we have seen above, the orthography of the *Qurʾān* reflects the adaptation of the Ḥiǧāzī dialect to a different phonological system, for instance in the spelling of the *hamza*. For the case endings, there is no such evidence. The only thing that can be said with any certainty is that the Qurʾānic orthography continues the orthographic conventions of the Aramaic/Nabataean script, which were also used in the pre-Islamic Arabic inscriptions. This is clear in the entire system of the rendering of consonants, but it also applies to the representation of endings. The most important principle is that in the consonantal skeleton text the word is always recorded in its isolated (pausal) form. This explains why the nunation is never written, except in the case of the accusative *-an* which sounded in pause *-ā* and was accordingly spelled with *'alif*. The original pausal forms of the nunated endings *-un, -in, -an* were probably *-ū, -ī, -ā*, as we have seen in the inscriptions and in the representation of Arabic names in the Nabataean inscriptions. The same principle also applies to the orthography of the singular feminine noun, with *-at* or *-ah*, where the variation in spelling in the *Qur'ān* – sometimes with *t* and sometimes with *h* – reflects a change in the pausal ending of the feminine words that was already operative in the earlier period. In the later period, when vocalisation had been introduced in order to record both contextual and pausal endings, the pausal *-ah* of the feminine noun was combined with the pronunciation *-t-* of the contextual forms in the orthographic device of the *tā' marbūṭa*, a letter *h* with the two dots of the letter *t*.

Another aspect of the Qur'ānic text mentioned in the discussion about the case endings is that of the rhyming conventions. In pre-Islamic poetry, a system prevails in which short final vowels *-u, -i, -a* are pronounced long and count as part of the rhyme. But in the *Qur'ān* and sometimes in poetry, there is another system of rhyming, in which the final short vowels are dropped and only the rhyming consonant counts. According to Birkeland (1940), this is a new development, reflecting a tendency to drop the declensional endings. The only ending that was spared apocopation is the pausal ending *-an*, pronounced *-ā*. In the view of Birkeland and others, this ending for a long time resisted elision, not because it was a case ending, but because it had a special status (e.g. as an adverbial ending). In some modern Central Arabian dialects, vestiges of this *tanwīn* in the accusative still exist (cf. below, p. 149), and it must have existed in the Ḥiǧāzī dialect, too, because the orthography of the Qur'ānic text consistently notes the final ending *-an* with an *'alif* while ignoring the other nunated endings *-un/-in*. The problem with the rhyming patterns, however, is that it is not clear to what degree pausal phenomena can be used as evidence for the disappearance of case endings. After all, nobody denies that in context both poetry and the *Qur'ān* use case endings as well as modal endings consistently.

The conclusion from pre-Islamic and Qur'ānic orthographical practice is that neither can give a definitive answer to the question about the presence or absence of case endings. This means that the question of whether the Ḥiǧāzī dialect belonged to the Old Arabic or to the New Arabic type cannot be resolved on this basis. Most Western scholars nevertheless continue to believe that the colloquial language of the *Ǧāhiliyya* contrasted with the so-called 'poetic koine' (*Dichtersprache*). In this view, the process of change which the Arabic language underwent in the period of the conquests was so radical that some of the changes must have been latently present in the pre-Islamic period. One typical argument for this view points out that the functional load of the declensional endings in Classical Arabic was already low, so that these endings could disappear without the risk of ambiguity. This is the view advanced by Corriente (1971b) in a discussion with Blau, in which Corriente maintains that Old Arabic did not have the synthetic character often attributed to it. He concedes that the daily speech of the Bedouin, perhaps even that of some city-dwellers, contained declensional endings, but points out that this was of little importance since the functional yield was almost zero. In this view, the functional yield of the declensional endings is determined by their indispensability.

In other words, if it can be shown that in many cases the declensional endings can be omitted without the sentence losing its meaning, this demonstrates that declension is just an 'idle tool' (Corriente 1971b: 39) and that the morphs expressing the declension are redundant.

In his response to this criticism of the traditionally-accepted synthetic character of Old Arabic, Blau (1972–3) states that redundancy is a normal phenomenon in any language. The shift from synthetic to analytic devices in the language involves the introduction of a whole new set of morphs, for instance, the introduction of a genitive exponent in New Arabic to denote a possessive relationship between words (cf. below, p. 107). There is no indication at all in any Old Arabic text that such a device was used. The use of the synthetic genitive in Old Arabic in the construct state is, of course, highly redundant because of the fact that the head noun of the construction loses its article, thereby marking the construction as a possessive one and rendering the genitive ending of the second member dispensable. Yet in Old Arabic this did not lead to the use of an analytic possessive device as in the modern dialects. Something else must, therefore, have happened in the shift from Old to New Arabic, and this new development had nothing to do with the functional yield of the declensional endings, although their redundance may have facilitated their disappearance. It is sometimes thought that synthetic declensional endings are introduced in order to enable the speakers to utilise a free word order. But usually free word order is only a stylistic phenomenon. It is true that in Old Arabic some things were possible that would lead to ambiguity in New Arabic, for instance the fronting of a direct object, or the right dislocation of a co-subject, as in the Qur'ānic verse Q 9/3 *'inna llāha barī'un min al-mušrikīna wa-rasūluhu* (see below, p. 50). But this flexibility in word order is a consequence of the presence of declensional endings rather than its cause.

A similar reasoning ascribes the loss of the declensional endings to a phonetic phenomenon: since there was a tendency to elide word-final short vowels, so the argument goes, the declensional endings were dropped, at least in the singular. In this line of reasoning, the loss of the plural endings is then explained as a case of analogy. But a tendency to drop word-final short vowels, if it really existed, is part of an allegro style of discourse and belongs to the normal range of stylistic registers of a language. In a normal process of language acquisition, children learn the full range of styles and get acquainted with both the short and the long forms. By itself, a tendency to drop final vowels in fluent speech can never lead to their disappearance as case markers. Only when there is a break in the normal transmission process may we expect to find any correlation between the coexistence of various stylistic registers and a change in the structure of the language. Discourse phenomena such as the slurring or dropping of unstressed vowels may at best reinforce the development of innovations that find their origin somewhere else.

From another angle, the phonetic explanation has been rejected because of the relative chronology. According to Diem (1991), in the modern Arabic dialects, forms with the pronominal suffix such as *bint-ak, bint-ik* 'your [masculine/feminine] daughter' may be explained as cases of vowel harmony from older **bint-a-ka, *bint-i-ki*. The vowel between noun and suffix is a generalised case ending which was selected on the basis of correspondence with the final vowel of the suffix. Therefore, the case endings must already have become inoperative at a time when the short end vowels were still pronounced, otherwise a form such as *bint-ak* could not have arisen. Besides, the survival of fossilised case endings in some Bedouin dialects (cf. p. 149) is inexplicable if one assumes that the short vowel endings disappeared before the collapse of the case system.

The debate about the colloquial varieties in the *Ǧāhiliyya* may be approached from yet another angle if we turn to the speech of the Bedouin in post-Islamic times. The Arab grammarians believe that the Bedouin spoke 'pure Arabic' (*faṣīḥ*) and continued to do so after the conquests, at least for some time. In the words of Ibn Ḫaldūn (d. 757/1356), the Bedouin spoke according to their linguistic intuition and did not need any grammarians to tell them how to use the declensional endings. He clearly thought that in the first centuries of Islam, before Bedouin speech had become affected and corrupted by sedentary speech, it still contained correct declensional endings. The force of this argument partly depends on the value which we attach to reports about Bedouin purity of speech. According to these reports, it was fashionable among caliphs and noble families to send their sons into the desert, not only to learn how to shoot and hunt, but also to practise speaking pure Arabic. Other reports come from professional grammarians who stayed for some time with a Bedouin tribe and studied their speech because it was more correct (*faṣīḥ*) than that of the towns and the cities.

Of course, these reports may also be regarded as symptomatic of the generally nostalgic attitude towards the Bedouin past and the desert. Besides, the Bedouin could have preserved certain forms of poetry with a Classical type of *'i'rāb*, just as they do nowadays in Central Arabia, while using a form of New Arabic in their everyday speech. Since the grammarians were looking for traces of *'Arabiyya* and often used transmitters of poetry as informants, they got exactly what they were asking for, which was not necessarily the colloquial speech of the Bedouin tribes involved. If one takes this view, the linguistic purity of the Bedouin became a mere *topos*, along with stories about their chivalry, manliness and generosity. On the other hand, if we believe the reports by professional grammarians, we also have to believe that in the *Ǧāhiliyya* Bedouin more or less spoke the same language as that of their poems, which in its turn was the language in which God revealed His last message to the world.

In the literature about the linguistic situation in the *Ǧāhiliyya*, much importance has been attached to reports about linguistic mistakes in early Islam. There is, indeed, a vast amount of anecdotes concerning the linguistic mistakes made by the *mawālī*, the non-Arabs who had converted to Islam. It is commonly believed that these anecdotes document a state of confusion and corruption of the Classical language. Yet such reports do not necessarily support the view that the system of declension had become redundant. If anything, the point in the anecdotes is precisely that the target language of the newly converted, the language of the Arabs which they wished to imitate, still contained declensional endings. In the most frequently-quoted instances of such mistakes, a connection is suggested between faulty Arabic and the 'invention' of grammar by 'Abū l-'Aswad ad-Du'alī (d. 69/688?; cf. below, p. 56).

In one story, someone makes a mistake in the Qur'ānic verse 9/3 *'inna llāha barī'un min al-mušrikīna wa-rasūluhu* 'God keeps aloof from the polytheists, and so does His Prophet' and recites *'inna llāha barī'un min al-mušrikīna wa-rasūlihi* with an incorrect genitive ending, thus uttering a blasphemous 'God keeps aloof from the polytheists and from His Prophet'. In another example, a recent convert is reported to have said *tuwuffiya 'abānā wa-taraka banūna* 'our father [accusative] has died and left sons [nominative]' (Ibn al-'Anbārī, *Nuzha* 6–7). While the first example may have been fabricated, the second one clearly shows a tendency on the part of the non-Arab client to use hypercorrect endings (otherwise he would have said *banīna* in the accusative as well). In both Ibn al-'Anbārī's and Ibn Ḫaldūn's account of the history of the Arabic language, a link is made between the corruption of speech and the beginnings of the grammatical tradition (cf. below, Chapter 7).

The first written examples of wrong case endings stem from the first half of the first century of the Hiğra. In two Egyptian papyri that have been examined by Diem (1984) dating from year 22 of the Hiğra, we find the proper name *'Abū Qīr* in a genitive position and the hypercorrect expression *niṣfu dīnāran* 'half a dinar'. Many more mistakes may be cited from later papyri (cf. below, p. 118). These papyri were written in a bilingual context, and, as the scribes may have been bilingual, such early mistakes cannot be taken as proof for the disappearance of the case endings before the period of the conquests. On the contrary, the occurrence of hypercorrect forms suggests that the target language still contained a case system.

What, then, may we conclude about the presence or absence of diglossia in the pre-Islamic period? One point is certain: there are no traces of pseudo-corrections in the poems preserved from the pre-Islamic period. Such forms are usually a corollary of a sharp divergence between a literary norm and a colloquial variety (cf. below, p. 115), and their absence would seem to point to a more widespread usage of the case endings than the limited one advocated by the proponents of the 'poetic koine'. One could, of course, object that any errors would have been weeded out by later collectors of poetry and copyists anyway. The general conclusion is that even when some of the changes which Arabic underwent in the post-Islamic period may have been present in pre-Islamic speech, the fundamental structural differences between the Old Arabic of the pre-Islamic period and the New Arabic represented by the contemporary dialects still need an explanation. The emergence of this new type of Arabic in the period of the conquests is characterised not only by the disappearance of the declensional system but also by a complex of other features (cf. the discussion in Chapter 7).

FURTHER READING

The best introduction to the pre-Islamic dialects is still Rabin (1951), who gives several maps to show the distribution of certain phenomena in the *Ǧāhiliyya*; also Kofler (1940–2), 'Anīs (1952) and al-Ǧindī (1983); see also Rabin's article (1955) on the origin of Classical Arabic, and his article in *EI(2)* *'Arabiyya* (1960). On the difference between *'Arab/'A'rāb*, see Marbach (1992); and on Sībawayhi's use of Bedouin informants, see Levin (1994). On the genealogy of the Arabs and their provenance, see *EI(2)* (*'Arab*, *Djazīrat al-'Arab*) and Dagorn (1981).

The discussion about diglossia in the pre-Islamic period is a complicated one, and it is hardly possible to expect an impartial account, since most authors have taken a strong position in this debate. For a survey of the different points of view, see Zwettler (1978). The controversy concerning the functional yield of the declensional endings in Old Arabic is found in Corriente (1971b) and Blau (1972–3). Arguments against diglossia include Fück (1950), Blau (1977), Versteegh (1984: 1–15) and to a certain extent Nöldeke (1904). For arguments for diglossia, see Vollers (1906), and also the arguments given by Wehr (1952) and Spitaler (1953) in their reviews of Fück (1950); see also Diem (1978, 1991) and Corriente (1971b, 1975). The first occurrences of wrong case endings are discussed by Diem (1984: 268–73).

The speech of the Bedouin in the Islamic empire and its relationship with the standard Classical language is dealt with by Fleisch (1964); and cf. also below, Chapter 5, p. 59.

For the textual history of the *Qur'ān*, see Nöldeke and Schwally (1961). The relevance of Qur'ānic orthography, the pre-Islamic Arabic inscriptions and the Aramaic/Nabataean inscriptions for the question of the case endings was discussed by Diem in a series of articles (1973a, 1976, 1979b, 1980a, 1981). For the evidence of the pausal forms in poetry and the *Qur'ān*, see Birkeland (1940).

5
The Development of Classical Arabic

5.1 INTRODUCTION

At the beginning of the Islamic period, only two sources of literary Arabic were available, the *Qur'ān* and the pre-Islamic poems. It is not surprising, then, that these two sources were to play a crucial role in the standardisation and development of the Arabic language. It is not surprising, either, that the first scholarly activities in Islam concentrated on the text of the *Qur'ān*, which had to be transmitted and explained, both on the level of the text and on that of the contents. At the same time, when the direct ties with the desert were broken, the living practice of poetry was very soon replaced by scholarly interest in the pre-Islamic poems. The transmission of both 'texts' had taken place orally and informally, but in the rapidly-expanding empire such a form of transmission could no longer be trusted.

The language itself, too, underwent a process of standardisation. While in pre-Islamic times the Bedouin regarded themselves as members of one speech community, they had no single linguistic norm, and even in the language of poetry, which was supposed to be supra-tribal, a great deal of variation was accepted. After the conquests, when Arabic became the language of an empire, there was an urgent need to standardise the language for three reasons. First, the divergence between the language of the Bedouin and the various colloquial varieties that emerged became a real threat to communication in the empire. Second, the policy of the central government, first in Damascus and later in Baghdad, aimed at the control of the subjects, not only in economical and religious but also in linguistic matters. Obviously, if Arabic was to be used as the language of the central administration, it had to be standardised. Third, the changed situation called forth a rapid expansion of the lexicon, which had to be regulated in order to achieve some measure of uniformity.

This chapter deals with three topics connected with the process of standardisation. The most important prerequisite for the written codification of the language was the invention of an orthography, or rather the adaptation of existing scribal practices to the new situation. Then a standardised norm for the language was elaborated, and the lexicon was inventoried and expanded. Subsequently, when these requirements had been met, a stylistic standard was developed. The existing Bedouin model was instrumental in the development of a stylistic standard for poetry, but the emergence of an Arabic prose style marked the real beginning of Classical Arabic as we know it. In the final section of this chapter, we shall deal with the official status of the Arabic language.

5.2 THE DEVELOPMENT OF ORTHOGRAPHY

The first concern of Islamic scholars was to codify the texts with which they worked. Even though oral transmission continued to remain an essential component of Islamic culture, the risk of major discrepancies in the transmission became too large to ignore. The need for an authoritative text was imperative above all in the case of the Revealed Book. Clearly, the central government had a major stake in the acceptance of a uniform Book throughout the empire as the basis for all religious and political activities.

The codification of the *Qur'ān* was a crucial moment in the development of a written standard for the Arabic language. On a practical level, the writing-down of the text involved all kinds of decisions concerning the orthography of the Arabic script and the elaboration of a number of conventions to make writing less ambiguous and more manageable than it had been in the *Ǧāhiliyya*. We have seen above (Chapter 3) that writing was not unknown in the peninsula in the pre-Islamic period. But, for religious reasons, early Islamic sources emphasised, perhaps even exaggerated, the illiteracy of the Prophet and, by extension, of the entire Ǧāhilī society. The Prophet had been an *'ummī*, someone who could not read nor write, and this was what made the revelation of the *Qur'ān* and his recitation of the text a miracle.

There are clear indications that as early as the sixth century writing was fairly common in the urban centres of the peninsula, in Mecca and to a lesser degree in Medina. In the commercial society that was Mecca, businessmen must have had at their disposal various means of recording their transactions. There are references to treaties being written down and preserved in the Kaʿba in Mecca. Even the *rāwī*s, the transmitters of poetry, sometimes relied on written notes, although they recited the poems entrusted to them orally. In the *Qur'ān*, we find the reflection of a society in which writing for commercial purposes was well established. In the second sura we find, for instance, detailed stipulations on the settlement of debts that include the exact writing-down of the terms (*Q* 2/282):

> O you believers, when you take a loan among you for a certain period of time, write it down and let a scribe write it down fairly between you, and let no scribe refuse to write as God has taught him and let him write and the creditor dictate (*yā 'ayyuhā lladīna 'āmanū 'idā tadāyantum bi-daynin 'ilā 'aǧalin musamman fa-ktubūhu wa-l-yaktub baynakum kātibun bi-l-ʿadli wa-lā ya'ba kātibun 'an yaktuba kamā ʿallamahu llāhu fa-l-yaktub wa-l-yumlili lladī ʿalayhi l-ḥaqqu*)

In the biography of the Prophet, there are many references to his using scribes for his correspondence with the Arab tribes and for the writing of treaties, for instance the famous treaty with the settlements in North Arabia. This treaty, which was signed in the course of the expedition to Tabūk in year 9 of the Hiǧra, laid down for the first time the relations between Muslims and people of other religions. In the account preserved by the historians, the scribe and the witnesses are mentioned, as well as the fact that the Prophet signed it with his fingernail (cf. al-Wāqidī, *Maġāzī* III, 1,025ff.). This last detail is probably added to underscore the fact that the Prophet himself could not write.

The Prophet may well have been illiterate himself, but there were scribes on whom he could rely, just as his fellow Meccans used scribes in the management of their affairs. In the beginning, the revelation consisted of short messages which the Prophet brought to the believers and which could easily be committed to memory. But very soon, the messages grew longer and longer, and it became essential to have a written aid to memory, while the recitation of the text continued to take place orally. Tradition has preserved the names of several scribes to whom Muḥammad dictated the messages, chief among them being Zayd ibn T̠ābit (d. 45/665). The text of the *Qur'ān* itself documents this shift from recitation to collected text. The current term *qur'ān* in the early suras (possibly borrowed from Syriac *qeryānā* 'recitation') is replaced increasingly often in the later suras with the term *kitāb* 'book'.

Both Islamic tradition and Western scholars agree that there was no complete collection of the revelation during the Prophet's lifetime, but there were fragments of all kinds of material, on which parts of the messages were recorded. The actual collection of all these fragments took place after the death of the Prophet. According to the tradition, the third caliph, 'Ut̠mān (r. 25/644–35/656), ordered the establishment of an authoritative codex of the *Qur'ān*. He entrusted this edition to Muḥammad's scribe Zayd, who had already been involved in the recording of the text during the Prophet's lifetime. When the work was finished, the codex was sent to the important centres of the Islamic empire, where it was to replace all existing alternative readings. Acceptance of this text, usually called *al-muṣḥaf*, was slow, and non-canonical variants continued to be transmitted; but eventually, by the end of the second century of the Hiǧra, the 'Ut̠mānic text had become the basis for religious teaching and recitation almost everywhere. In the first grammatical treatise of Arabic, Sībawayhi's (d. 177/793) *Kitāb*, all deviations from the consonantal text of the codex are rejected and only some divergence in the vocalisation of the text is allowed. Around the variant readings (*qirā'āt*), a massive literature arose which at the same time contributed to the linguistic study of the text and the language of the *Qur'ān*.

Apart from the problems of unification encountered during the codification of the text, the main problem confronting Zayd ibn T̠ābit and his committee of text-editors was the ambiguity of the Arabic script. The type of script which the Meccan traders had at their disposal was still a primitive one. Basically, there were two problems connected with this primitive form of the Arabic alphabet. In the first place, there were as yet no diacritic dots to distinguish between certain phonemes, and many of the letters of the alphabet indicated two or even more phonemes, in the case of *sīn/šīn, ṣād/ḍād, bā'/tā'/t̠ā'/nūn/yā', fā'/qāf, dāl/d̠āl, rā'/zāy, ṭā'/ẓā'*. This was the heritage of the Nabataean script that had been the model for the earliest form of Arabic script and that did not contain all of the Arabic phonemes. The second problem was connected with a general trait of all Semitic scripts, namely the fact that these scripts do not indicate the short vowels. In the case of the Nabataean model, even many of the long vowels were written defectively (cf. above, p. 30). The former problem may already have been solved in pre-Islamic times. There are some indications that, very early on, scribes had used diacritic dots to distinguish between homographs. They may have borrowed this device from a Syriac model, since in the Syriac script dots are used to distinguish between allophonic variants of phonemes. According to some scholars, there are even examples of the use of dots in the Nabataean script.

The notation of the short vowels was an altogether more complicated problem. During the first century of Islam, when people started to collect and record the fragments of the Qur'ānic revelation, the need for a uniform and unambiguous system for the short vowels made itself felt. Various grammarians, among them the legendary 'inventor' of grammar, 'Abū l-'Aswad ad-Du'alī (d. 69/688?), are credited with the introduction of a system of (coloured) dots below and above the letters to indicate the three short vowels. In the version of the tradition that is reported by Ibn al-'Anbārī, 'Abū l-'Aswad gives a scribe the following instruction:

> When I open my lips, put one dot above the letter, and when I press them together put a dot next to the letter, and when I draw them apart put a dot beneath the letter, and when I make a humming sound after one of these vowels, put two dots. (*fa-'iḏā fataḥtu šafatayya fa-nquṭ wāḥidatan fawqa l-ḥarf, wa-'iḏā ḍamamtuhumā fa-ǧ'al an-nuqṭa 'ilā ǧānibi l-ḥarf, wa-'iḏā kasartuhumā fa-ǧ'al an-nuqṭa min 'asfalihi, fa-'iḏā 'atba'tu šay'an min hāḏihi l-ḥarakāt ġunnatan fa-nquṭ nuqṭatayn*; Ibn al-'Anbārī, *Nuzha*, ed. Attia Amer, Stockholm, 1963, pp. 6–7)

In this story, the origin of the dot notation of the three vowels and the nunation is ascribed to 'Abū l-'Aswad, and the names of the vowels (*fatḥa, ḍamma, kasra*) are connected with their articulation. We know from the Islamic sources that at first there was considerable opposition to the use of vowel dots in Qur'ānic manuscripts, and as a matter of fact this system is absent in the oldest manuscripts in Kūfic script as well as in the inscriptions. In some manuscripts, the dots have been added by a later hand.

Two other innovations attributed to 'Abū l-'Aswad concern the notation of the *hamza* (glottal stop) and the *šadda* (gemination). Both signs are absent in the Nabataean script. We have seen in Chapter 4 (p. 42) that in the Ḥiǧāz the *hamza* had probably disappeared, but in the variety of the language in which the *Qur'ān* was revealed and the pre-Islamic poems were composed, the *hamza* was pronounced. Because of the prestige of the language of poetry and the *Qur'ān*, the Ḥiǧāzī scribes had to devise a way of recording the glottal stop. Since in their own speech the *hamza* had been replaced in many cases by a long vowel, they spelled words containing a *hamza* with a long vowel, indicated by a semi-consonant *w*, *y* or *'alif*. According to the tradition, 'Abū l-'Aswad improved this system by using a small letter *'ayn* above the semi-consonant; this *'ayn* indicated the presence of a guttural sound, namely the glottal stop. The gemination of a consonant was noted by a diacritic dot.

A substantial improvement in the system of short-vowel notation is usually attributed to the first lexicographer of the Arabic language, al-H̱alīl ibn 'Aḥmad (d. 175/791). He replaced the system of dots with specific shapes for the three short vowels, a small *wāw* for the vowel *u*, a small *'alif* for the vowel *a*, and a (part of a) small *yā'* for the vowel *i*. He also changed the sign for the *šadda*, using a small *sīn* (short for *šadīd* 'geminated') instead. When a single consonant was intended, a small *ẖā'* (short for *ẖafīf* 'light') could be used. Originally, this system had been devised for writing down poetry, which also went through a period of codification, but gradually it spread to Qur'ānic manuscripts written in cursive script as well. It was considerably less ambiguous than the old system, in which the dots had to perform various functions.

With al-Ḫalīl's reform, the system of Arabic orthography was almost completed and, apart from a very few additional signs, it has remained essentially the same ever since. The frequency of diacritic dots and vowel signs varies considerably, however, and alongside fully-vowelled manuscripts one finds texts in which even the diacritic dots are left out. After the establishment of the orthography, a large variety of writing styles were developed, each with its own special domains. Apart from the epigraphic script (called Kūfic), which was also used in early Qur'ānic manuscripts, a cursive script was developed for use in the chancellery, after ʿAbd al-Malik's reform (cf. below). The script itself became an essential component of Islamic art. Because of the general aversion to pictorial art, calligraphy was one of the most important means of decoration. This development of Arabic script will not be dealt with here.

Having an orthography is one thing, but elaborating a standardised language for official – commercial and administrative – purposes is another. As far as we know, the Meccan traders did not have any archives, and we must assume that they did not have at their disposal an elaborate legal terminology or conventions for book-keeping, either. In the first period of the establishment of the Islamic empire, the government, therefore, opted to use Greek-speaking clerks in Syria and Egypt and Persian-speaking clerks in the East for purposes of administration and taxation. In the sources, the shift from Greek to Arabic in the tax register (*dīwān*) is traditionally connected with the name of the caliph ʿAbd al-Malik. According to this story, the caliph ordered the clerks to shift to Arabic in the year 81/700, allegedly because one of the Greek clerks was caught urinating in an inkwell (al-Balāḏurī, *Futūḥ* 196–7). Whatever the truth of that story, the shift is a sign of the growing self-confidence of the Arabs and their increased familiarity with a practical writing system.

5.3 THE STANDARDISATION OF THE LANGUAGE

Even before the language shift of the *dīwān*, Arabic was used as a written language: the earliest papyri date from year 22 of the Hiǧra, and at the end of the first century of the Hiǧra quite a number of papyrus texts must have been circulating. The language of these papyri is highly irregular from the point of view of the codified grammar of Classical Arabic, but the fact that they contain a large number of hypercorrections demonstrates that the scribes tried to emulate a linguistic ideal. In Chapter 8, on the so-called Middle Arabic texts, we shall deal with the linguistic features of the corpus of papyri. In this chapter, our main purpose is to sketch the process of standardisation that was soon under way.

The Qur'ānic language, though virtually identical with the language of pre-Islamic poetry, has a typically religious flavour, manifesting itself in peculiarities of style and language that must have been absent in other registers. Likewise, the language of the poems was marked by poetic licences that did not occur in ordinary language. Although both sources constituted a model for correct Arabic, they could hardly serve as a model for ordinary prose. The arbiters of linguistic correctness, the Bedouin, were frequently called in for help in linguistic matters, but they were in no position to enforce a standard language, if only because of their own linguistic differences. We have seen above (Chapter 4) that in the period of the *Ǧāhiliyya* the language of the various tribes varied to a certain extent; and, even though it is reasonable to assume that there were no real problems of communication, there was no general standard either. On the other hand, the growing sedentary population with a more or less complete command of the language was very much in need of such a standard, but could hardly be expected to devote themselves to decisions about linguistic correctness. As a matter of fact, their slipshod use of the language for practical purposes, as in the texts which we find in the papyri, was one of the reasons for a growing concern on the part of those who regarded themselves as the true heirs of Bedouin civilisation, the pure Arabs. Even if we do not believe the account of Muslim historians such as Ibn Ḫaldūn about the corruption of speech as the main motive behind the 'invention' of grammar (cf. p. 102), it can hardly be denied that in the early decades of Islam there was an increasing call for specialists who could provide adequate teaching in Arabic.

According to most of our sources, the fourth caliph ʿAlī (r. 35/656–40/661) was the first to insist that something be done about the growing number of mistakes in speech (other sources mention the governor of the two Iraqs, Ziyād ibn ʾAbīhi). The person whose name has become connected with the first efforts to standardise and codify the language was the same ʾAbū l-ʾAswad whom we met above as the reformer of the writing system. Several stories are told about his reluctance to accept this job; according to some historians, he was finally persuaded when his own daughter made a terrible mistake in the use of the declensional endings, by confusing the expressions *mā ʾaḥsana s-samāʾa* 'how beautiful is the sky!' and *mā ʾaḥsanu s-samāʾi* 'what is the most beautiful thing in the sky?' (as-Sīrāfī, *ʾAḫbār*, ed. F. Krenkow, Beirut, 1936, p. 19). Another version of this story, in which the mistakes occur in the recitation of the *Qurʾān*, has been mentioned above (Chapter 4, p. 50).

The historicity of these anecdotes is, of course, doubtful, and Talmon (1985) has shown that the figure of ʾAbū l-ʾAswad was used by later grammarians as some kind of eponym for their own grammatical school. But the point remains that grammarians must have played an important role in the standardisation of the language. The earliest scholarly efforts concerned the exegesis of the Revealed Book, but since study of the language of the *Qurʾān* could hardly ignore that other source of pre-Islamic Arabic, the poems, very soon the two main components of the corpus of texts that was to become canonical for the linguistic study of Arabic were combined in the writings of the grammarians.

The first grammarian to give an account of the entire language in what was probably the first publication in book form in Arabic prose, Sībawayhi, was not of Arab stock himself, but a Persian from Hamadhan. His example set the trend for all subsequent generations of grammarians. The grammarians believed that their main task was to provide an explanation for every single phenomenon in Arabic, rather than a mere description, let alone a set of precepts on how to talk Arabic correctly. Consequently, they distinguished between what was transmitted and what was theoretically possible in language. In principle, they accepted everything that was transmitted from a reliable source: in the first place the language of the *Qurʾān*, which was sacrosanct anyway, in the second place everything that had been preserved from pre-Islamic poetry, and in the third place testimonies from trustworthy Bedouin informants. In this framework, even singularities or deviant forms were incorporated without, however, being accepted as productive forms that could constitute the basis for a theoretical linguistic reasoning. Such a distinction is characteristic of Islamic science as a whole, where *ʿaql* 'logical reasoning' is always carefully distinguished from *naql* 'transmitted knowledge'. In this way, a separation was realised between the study of attested forms and the theories of the grammarians, and without being prescriptive the grammarians could still impose a canonical norm of the language.

The codification of grammatical structure went hand in hand with the exploration of the lexicon and its necessary expansion. These two aspects of the process of standardisation are connected. Just as the grammarians were needed because of the perceived 'corruption' of the language, the first aim of the lexicographers seems to have been the preservation of the old Bedouin lexicon, which was at risk. There are several reasons for the lexicographers' worries. In the first place, the sedentary civilisation of early Islam was markedly different from that of the desert tribes, who had been the guardians of the special vocabulary of the pre-Islamic poems. No city-dweller could be expected to know all the subtle nuances of a vocabulary connected with camels and animal wildlife and tents. There are several anecdotes about grammarians that stress this component of a grammarian's activities. Thus, the grammarian 'Abū ʿAmr ibn al-ʿAlā' (d. 154/770), when he started lecturing about language and poetry, was confronted by a real Bedouin, who interrogated him about the explanation of obscure words. When the grammarian passed the test, the Bedouin said *ḫuḏū ʿanhu fa-'innahu dābba munkara* 'transmit from him, because he is an extraordinary beast of burden [i.e. a depository of knowledge]!' (az-Zağğāğī, *Mağālis*, ed. Hārūn, Kuwait, 1962, p. 262). This anecdote shows how grammarians had to prove their worth by their knowledge of the Bedouin lexicon.

For the ordinary speaker, who had grown up in an Islamic city and knew nothing about the Bedouin milieu, even ordinary Arabic words had become unfamiliar. From one of the earliest commentaries on the *Qur'ān*, we can get an idea about which words had fallen into disuse. Muqātil ibn Sulaymān's (d. 150/767) *Tafsīr* contains a large number of paraphrases of Qur'ānic words that he felt to be in need of explanation, e.g. *'alīm* 'painful' (replaced by *wağīʿ*), *mubīn* 'clear' (replaced by *bayyin*), *naba'un* 'news' (replaced by *ḥadīṯun*), *nasīb* 'share' (replaced by *ḥaẓẓ*), the verb *'ātā* 'to give' (replaced by *'aʿṭā*) and the interrogative adverb *'ayyān* 'when?' (replaced by *matā*).

The second threat to the lexicon had to do with the contact with other languages. When the Arabs became acquainted with the sedentary culture of the conquered territories, they encountered new things and notions for which there did not yet exist Arabic words. The most obvious sources for terms to indicate the new notions were, of course, the languages spoken in the new Islamic empire. And this was precisely what some of the Arab scholars feared. They were convinced that the influx of words from other cultures would corrupt the Arabic language, which had been chosen by God for His last revelation to mankind.

In the first century of the Hiğra, this attitude did not yet make itself felt, as the comments by the earliest exegetes on the vocabulary of the *Qur'ān* demonstrate. In pre-Islamic times, the Arabs had taken over a considerable number of words from the surrounding cultures. Most of them were borrowed either through the Jewish/Aramaic language of Syria, or through the Christian/Syriac language in Mesopotamia, where al-Ḥīra was the most important centre for cultural and linguistic contacts. Examples of early borrowings that occur both in pre-Islamic poetry and in the *Qur'ān* are the following:

from Middle Persian (Pahlavi) through Syriac/Aramaic:
zanǧabīl 'well in paradise' < Syriac *zangabīl* < Pahlavi *singaḇēr* 'ginger'
warda 'rose' < Aramaic *wardā* < Avestan *varəḏa*.

Some words must have been borrowed directly from Middle Persian, such as:

istabraq 'brocade' < Pahlavi *staḇr* 'thick (of clothing)' + suffix *-ak*
ǧund 'army' < Pahlavi *gund* 'army, troop'
kanz 'treasure' < Pahlavi *ganǰ* 'treasure'
dirham 'silver coin' < Pahlavi *draxm* < Greek *drachmè*.

or from Greek/Latin through Syriac/Aramaic:

burǧ 'tower' < Syriac *būrgā* < Greek *púrgos*
zawǧ 'pair, married couple' < Syriac *zūgā* 'yoke', *bar zūgā* 'husband, wife' < Greek *zeũgos* 'yoke'
dīnār 'gold coin' < Syriac *dīnarā* < Greek *dènárion* < Latin *denarius*
qaṣr 'castle' < Aramaic *qaṣrā* < Greek *kástron* < Latin *castrum, castra*
ṣirāṭ 'path' < Aramaic *isṭrātiyā* < Greek *stráta* < Latin *strata*
yāqūt 'sapphire' < Syriac *yaqūnṭā* < Greek *huákinthos* 'hyacinth'
qirṭās 'scroll of paper' < Syriac *qarṭīsā, karṭīsā* < Greek *chartès*.

And, of course, there was a large number of words that came in straight from Syriac/Aramaic, such as:

ṣalāt 'prayer' < Aramaic *ṣlōṯā*
tīn 'fig' < Aramaic *tīnā*
sifr 'large book' < Aramaic *sifrā*
masǧid 'place of worship' < Aramaic/Nabataean *msgd'*.

A special category of loanwords is constituted by those words that came in by a southern route, from languages such as South Arabian or Ethiopic, e.g.:

ṣanam 'idol' < South Arabian *ṣnm*, Ṣafā'itic *ṣnmt*.

The oldest commentaries on the *Qur'ān*, such as the one by Muǧāhid (d. 104/722), had no qualms in assigning words in the *Qur'ān* to a foreign origin. Muǧāhid stated, for instance, that the word *ṭūr* 'mountain' came from Syriac, the word *siǧǧīl* 'baked clay' from Persian or Nabataean, and the word *qisṭās* 'balance' from Greek. In the cases mentioned here, he was not that far off, since *ṭūr* comes indeed from Syriac *ṭūr*, *siǧǧīl* from Pahlavi *sang* 'stone' + *gīl* 'clay', and *qisṭās* perhaps ultimately derives from Greek *dikastès* 'judge', through Syriac *dīqasṭūs*. Some of the etymologies quoted by the commentators may be fanciful, but the important thing is that they looked upon the enrichment of the vocabulary as an advantage and as a sign of the superiority of the creative genius evidenced in the *Qur'ān*. By the end of the second century of the Hiğra, however, some philologists had started to attack the notion that the *Qur'ān* could contain foreign loanwords, and attempted to connect the vocabulary of the *Qur'ān* with a Bedouin etymology. Thus, for instance, 'Abū ʿUbayda (d. 210/825) says that 'the *Qur'ān* was revealed in clear Arabic language, and whosoever claims that the word *ṭāhā* is Nabataean makes a big mistake' (*nazala l-Qur'ānu bi-lisānin ʿarabiyyin mubīnin fa-man zaʿama 'anna ṭāhā bi-n-Nabaṭiyyati fa-qad 'akbara, Mağāz* I, ed. F. Sezgin, Cairo, 1954, p. 17). Although most Arab lexicographers, such as as-Suyūṭī (d. 911/1505), continued to assign a foreign origin to many Arabic words, the idea of the purity of the Arabic language remained the prevalent attitude among some Islamic scholars, and attempts by Western scholars to find traces of other languages in the *Qur'ān* were and still are vehemently rejected.

The real problem arises in the case of Qur'ānic words that have developed a new technical meaning not supported by the semantics of the Arabic root. In such cases, the exegetes go out of their way to find a connection. Thus, for instance, for the expression *yawm al-qiyāma* 'the day of resurrection', the standard explanation in the commentaries is that it is connected with the root *q-w-m* 'to stand up', but most likely the Christian Syriac term *qiyāmeṯā* as a translation of the Greek *anástasis* 'resurrection' prompted the semantic extension of the Arabic word. Similar examples are those of *zakāt* 'alms', *masğid* 'mosque', *ṣuḥuf* 'scriptures', *sabt* 'Saturday', *sūra* 'portion of the *Qur'ān*', and such central notions in the Qur'ānic message as *kitāb* 'book', *sāʿa* 'hour' etc. The term *ṣuḥuf* 'scriptures', plural of *ṣaḥīfa*, is connected by the Arab commentators with a root *ṣḥf*, which occurs only as a denominative in the second measure with the meaning of 'making a mistake in reading'. In pre-Islamic poetry, *ṣaḥīfa* (plural *ṣaḥā'if*) is used in the sense of 'page of writing'. The Qur'ānic use of the word in the sense of 'scriptures' (e.g. Q 20/133 *aṣ-ṣuḥuf al-'ūlā* 'the first scriptures') is difficult to explain from this, which is why Western commentaries often connect it with an Old South Arabian word *ṣḥft* or with the common Ethiopic root *s'-ḥ-f* 'to write'.

In line with the idea of the purity of the language, the semantic extension of an existing word was regarded as the most appropriate device for the expansion of the lexicon. The model for this procedure was believed to have been given by the language of the *Qur'ān* itself. Since the grammarians analysed many religious terms such as *ṣalāt* 'prayer', *zakāt* 'alms', and the term *'islām* itself, as old Bedouin words which had received a specialised meaning in the religious context, semantic extension became an accepted method of creating new terminology. They were doubtless right in the sense that part of the religious vocabulary of the *Qur'ān* is the result of an internal development without external influence. A case in point is the word *'islām*, which meant in general 'to surrender oneself', but came to mean 'to surrender oneself to God, to convert to the new religion brought by the Prophet'. Besides, even when the new meanings of existing words were calqued on cognate words in other languages, their occurrence in the *Qur'ān* canonised the new meaning.

The large-scale influx of new notions and ideas in the early Islamic period could not be handled by giving new meanings to existing words alone. In spite of the purists' opposition, many words from other languages were simply taken over, either in their original form or with some slight adaptation to Arabic phonology or morphology. Loanwords from Persian abound in the domains of pharmacology, mineralogy and botany, for instance in the name of plants: *banafsağ* 'violet'; *sanḫār* 'gladiolus'; *bāḏinğān* 'eggplant'; *bābūniğ* 'camomile'; *banğ* 'henbane'; *fustuq* 'pistachio'; *ḫašḫāš* 'poppy'; *narğis* 'narcissus'.

In the earliest translations of Greek logical, medical and philosophical writings, some of the technical terms are simply transliterations of a Greek word for which the translators were unable to find an Arabic equivalent. Thus we have, for instance, *hayūlā* 'substance' (< Greek *hulē*), *bulġum* 'phlegm' (< Greek *phlégma*) and *'usṭuquss* 'element' (< Greek *stoicheîon*). The next best solution was to create a new word on the basis of an existing root by the application of one of the numerous morphological patterns of Arabic. In the beginning, each translator created in this way his own set of terms. The ensuing confusion was more or less ended with the establishment of the *Bayt al-Ḥikma* 'House of Wisdom', the translators' academy founded by the Caliph al-Ma'mūn in 215/830. The Greek term *katègoroúmenon* 'predicate', for instance, had been variably translated as *maḥmūl, maqūl, ṣifa* or *naʿt*, until it was standardised as *maḥmūl*. The Greek term *apóphansis* 'proposition' had been translated by as many as five different terms (*ḥukm, ḫabar, qawl ğāzim, qawl qāṭiʿ, qaḍiyya*), until *qaḍiyya* became the usual term.

The use of patterns to create neologisms from existing roots was particularly useful in the translation of Greek medical terminology. A few examples may suffice to illustrate this method of inventing new vocabulary items. In his terminology of the skins of the eye, Ḥunayn ibn 'Isḥāq translated Greek words in *-eidès* with abstract adjectives, e.g. *qarniyya* (Greek *keratoeidès*) 'cornea', *zuğāğiyya* (Greek *hualoeidès*) 'corpus vitreum', *ʿinabiyya* (Greek *rhagoeidès*) 'uvea', *šabakiyya* (Greek *amphiblèstroeidès*) 'retina'. The pattern *fuʿāl* was used to systematise the names of illnesses, e.g. *zukām* 'catarrh', *ṣudāʿ* 'headache', *ṣufār* 'jaundice', *duwār* 'dizziness', *ṭuḥāl* 'infection of the spleen', and even *ḫumār* 'hangover'.

A prerequisite for the creative use of the existing lexicon was its codification. The first complete dictionary of the Arabic language was composed by Sībawayhi's teacher, al-Ḫalīl ibn 'Aḥmad, who had also been involved in the reform of the Arabic script (cf. above, p. 56) and who is generally acclaimed as the inventor of Arabic metrical theory. The professed aim of the *Kitāb al-ʿayn*, which goes under his name, was the inclusion of all Arabic roots. In the introduction, a sketch is given of the phonetic structure of Arabic, and the dictionary fully uses the available corpus of Arabic by including quotations from the *Qur'ān* and from the numerous pre-Islamic poems, which had both undergone a process of codification and written transmission by the hands of the grammarians.

The arrangement of al-Ḫalīl's dictionary, which seems to have been completed by his pupils, set the trend for many subsequent lexicographical writings. The dictionary is divided into books, one for each letter, starting with that of the letter *ʿayn*, hence the name of the dictionary. Each book is divided into chapters, each dedicated to one set of radicals and containing all the permutations of these radicals. Thus, for instance, the chapter on the radical *ʿ-q-z* contains the roots *ʿ-z-q, q-z-ʿ, z-ʿ-q*, and *z-q-ʿ*, which are the ones actually used in the language (*musta'malāt*). Perhaps this reflects some idea of a higher semantic connection between the permutations of radicals, although al-Ḫalīl does not mention such a connection. The system of the *Kitāb al-'ayn* remained in use for a long time, even after a new system had been introduced by the grammarian al-Ǧawharī (d. 393/1003) in his *Ṣiḥāḥ*. He arranged all roots in a kind of rhyming order, that is, alphabetically according to the last radical, then the first, then the second. This system became the current dictionary arrangement with the *Lisān al-'Arab* by Ibn Manẓūr (d. 711/1311), the most popular dictionary ever written in the Arab world.

In the *Kitāb al-'ayn*, the emphasis had been on those words that were in common use in Arabic writing, but later compilers aimed at complete coverage of all Arabic words, both common and rare. This sometimes led to the inclusion of ghost-words that had never existed as such, or the recording of several meanings for a word on the basis of just one particular context. A rich source of lexical items is constituted by the vocabulary of *rağaz* poetry in the slightly informal iambic trimeter, which often had an improvised character. The poets in this genre stretched the potential of Arabic word-building to its limits. Ullmann (1966) has shown that the many words in the dictionaries that are quoted from *rağaz* poetry are very often neologisms on the basis of existing roots, rather than separate roots. Triliteral words may be expanded more or less at will with prefixes, infixes and suffixes. Thus, for instance, from the existing word *'adlamu* 'very black' the verb *idlahamma* was created, from *kadaḥa* 'to make an effort' the verb *kardaḥa*, from the root *ğ-l-b* 'to bring' the verb *iğla'abba*. New verbs were made with the infixes *-ran-*, *-lan-*, *-'an-* or *-ḥan-*, e.g. *islanṭaḥa* 'to be wide' from *saṭaḥa* 'to expand', *iq'anṣara*, with verbal adjective *qinṣa'run*, from *qaṣura* 'to be short', and many more examples. New nouns were made with the suffix *-m*, e.g. *baldamun*, *balandamun* with the same meaning as *balīdun* 'stupid', *šağ'amun* with the same meaning as *šuğā'un* 'courageous'. The point is that the lexicographers took such invented words, which never gained any currency, for existing roots, which were then duly entered in the dictionary.

The early beginnings of grammar and lexicography began at a time when Bedouin informants were still around and could be consulted. There can be no doubt that the grammarians and lexicographers regarded the Bedouin as the true speakers (*fuṣaḥā'*) of Arabic. As late as the fourth/tenth century, the lexicographer al-'Azhari (d. 370/980) extolled the purity of their language. He had been kidnapped by Bedouin and forced to stay with them for a considerable period of time. On the basis of this 'fieldwork' he wrote his dictionary *Tahḏīb al-luġa* 'The reparation of speech', in the introduction to which he says: 'They speak according to their desert nature and their ingrained instincts. In their speech you hardly ever hear a linguistic error or a terrible mistake' (*yatakallamūna bi-ṭibā'ihim al-badawiyyati wa-qarā'iḥihim allatī 'tādūhā wa-lā yakādu yaqa'u fī manṭiqihim laḥnun 'aw ḫaṭa'un fāḥiš*, *Tahḏīb* I, ed. Hārūn, Cairo, 1964–7, p. 7). Other grammarians, too, collected materials from the nomad tribes, and it is often reported that caliphs or other dignitaries sent their sons into the desert in order to learn flawless Arabic.

In the course of the centuries, the Bedouin tribes increasingly came into the sphere of influence of the sedentary civilisation, and their speech became contaminated by sedentary speech. In his description of the Arabian peninsula, al-Hamdānī (d. 334/945) sets up a hierarchy of the Arab tribes according to the perfection of their speech. He explains that those Arabs who live in or near a town have very mediocre Arabic and cannot be trusted; this applies even to the Arabs who live near the Holy Cities of Mecca and Medina. The grammarian Ibn Ǧinnī (d. 392/1002) includes in his *Ḫaṣā'iṣ* a chapter about the errors made by Bedouin and he states that in his time it is almost impossible to find a Bedouin speaking pure Arabic (*li-'annā lā nakādu narā badawiyyan faṣīḥan*, *Ḫaṣā'iṣ* II, ed. an-Naǧǧār, Cairo, 1952–6, p. 5). At the same time, Ibn Ǧinnī advises his students always to check their linguistic facts with Bedouin informants.

Even in the early period of Arabic grammar, our sources record examples of Bedouin who sold their expertise in matters of language to the highest bidder, as in the case of the famous *mas'ala zunbūriyya*. In this controversy between Sībawayhi and a rival grammarian, a question was raised about the expression *kuntu 'aẓunnu 'anna l-ʿaqraba 'ašaddu lasʿatan min az-zunbūri fa-'iḏā huwa 'iyyāhā* 'I thought that the scorpion had a stronger bite than the hornet, but it was the other way round'. Sībawayhi gave the correct answer – the last clause has to be *fa-'iḏā huwa hiya* – but was defeated by the judgment of a Bedouin arbiter, who had been bribed by his adversary (Ibn al-'Anbārī, *'Inṣāf*, ed. G. Weil, Leiden, 1913, pp. 292–5).

Modern critics of the attitude of the grammarians towards the alleged perfection of Bedouin speech often point out that the idealisation of their speech may have been part of a general trend to extol the virtues of desert life, and that even nowadays one sometimes hears stories about Bedouin speaking perfect Classical Arabic. Usually this means that they use words that have become obsolete elsewhere, or it refers to their poetical tradition, which often uses a classicising style of language. We are not concerned here with the question of whether the Bedouin had still preserved declensional endings in the third/ninth century (for which see above, Chapter 4). What is important for our present discussion is the fact that in the fourth/tenth century linguistic experts could apparently still find informants whom they trusted. From the fourth century onwards, however, this tradition disappeared. In the story about Sībawayhi and the Bedouin informant, there is already an element of corruption, and later the general image of the Bedouin became that of a thieving and lying creature whose culture was inferior to the sophisticated sedentary civilisation. For the practice of grammar, this meant that the process of standardisation had come to a standstill. Since there were no longer living informants to provide fresh information, the corpus of the language was closed, and 'fieldwork' could no longer produce reliable results. References to the *kalām al-ʿArab* 'language of the Bedouin' still abounded in the books of the grammarians, but these were no longer connected with any living speech.

5.4 THE DEVELOPMENT OF AN ARABIC LITERARY STYLE

The history of literary style in Arabic went hand in hand with the standardisation of the language. The development of such a style did not have to start from scratch. The same two sources that had been available for the standardisation of the language, the *Qur'ān* and the pre-Islamic poems, became the initial models for a literary style. As in other cultures, the structured composition of poetry in

Arabic preceded the emergence of a literary prose style. But here, too, the desert type of poetry did not satisfy all the needs of a new, elegant sedentary civilisation. New forms of poetry developed under the dynasty of the 'Umayyads, at whose court love poems became a new fashion (e.g. the poems of ʿUmar ibn 'Abī Rabīʿa, d. 43/712). Inevitably, this led to a looser use of language and to the development of new, often strophic types of poetry, that were not as heavily dependent on the Bedouin model. In such forms of poetry, there was easier access for popular expressions reflecting the new environment of Arabic culture. Some deviations in morphology, syntax and lexicon became gradually accepted, e.g. the use of contracted forms such as *nasīhi* (< *nasiyahu*), *baqī* (< *baqiya*), or the confusion of the fourth and the first verbal form (cf. Fück 1950: 73ff.). In *rağaz*, poets could experiment with the creation of new words and word forms to a much higher degree than was permitted in official poetry. In general, the *muwalladūn*, the new Arabs, who had never seen the desert, could not be expected to be as excellent connoisseurs of Arabic as the pre-Islamic poets. Although for a long time the Bedouin model continued to serve as a strict canon, in Sībawayhi's *Kitāb* the poems of the *muwalladūn* are not excluded as evidence: the 1,000-plus quotations from poetry in the *Kitāb* include both Ğāhilī poets and those from the urban milieu of the 'Umayyad period, such as ʿUmar ibn 'Abī Rabīʿa; he even quotes from *rağaz* poetry.

Gradually, a distinction came into being between the official brand of poetry that clung to the old models and took pleasure in using obsolete vocabulary and avoiding any adaptation to the new modes of speaking, on the one hand, and a new, 'faster' kind of poetry, often improvised, often in strophic form, and very often containing vulgarisms, on the other. In the course of time, these two kinds of poetry grew further apart. Official poetry became more and more erudite, until it could no longer be understood without explanation. The poet al-Mutanabbī (d. 355/965), for instance, published his poems together with a learned commentary. The more popular form of poetry, on the other hand, went through a different development. In its most developed form, the strophic *muwaššaḥ* and the *zağal*, it included the use of colloquial forms in a refrain. This kind of poetry became especially popular in the Islamic West (cf. below, p. 227).

Because of its idiosyncrasies, poetry is of lesser importance in the standardisation of language than prose. We have seen above that for commercial and administrative purposes Arabic was used from the beginning of the Islamic empire. Such written documents had no literary pretensions whatsoever, although their scribes did try to maintain a Classical norm, which means that already at this time there was a standard (on the language of the papyri see below, Chapter 8). But there were other forms of speech, some of them with roots in the *Ğāhiliyya*. In the first place, Arabic culture had a reputation of long standing for its ability to put speech to rhetorical use. The Bedouin admired verbal prowess, and the tradition of delivering public speeches was continued in early Islam. The earliest preserved speeches already exhibit the use of various literary devices and conventions, in particular that of parallelism. A famous example is the speech given by al-Ḥağğāğ (d. 95/714) on the occasion of his inauguration as governor of Kufa:

> The Commander of the Believers has emptied his quiver and tested its arrows. He found me to be of the firmest wood and of the strongest shaft and shot me at you. As long as you gallop in rebellion and recline in the beds of error and follow the stray path, by God, I shall skin you like a new stick and bind your leaves like a thorn bush and whip you like wandering camels. (*'inna 'amīra l-mu'minīna kabba kinānatahu ṯumma ʿağama ʿīdānahā fa-wağadanī 'amarrahā ʿūdan wa-'aṣlabahā ʿamūdan fa-wağğahanī 'ilaykum fa-'innakum ṭālamā 'awḍaʿtum fī l-fitani wa-ḍṭağaʿtum fī marāqidi ḍ-ḍalāli wa-sanantum sunana l-ġayyi 'ammā wa-llāhi la-'alḥawannakum laḥwa l-ʿaṣā wa-la-'aʿṣibannakum ʿaṣba s-salamati wa-la-'aḍribannakum ḍarba ġarā'ibi l-'ibil*, al-Ğāḥiẓ, *Bayān* II, ed. as-Sandūbī, Beirut, n.d., p. 349)

A second genre of texts with roots in the pre-Islamic period is the art of story-telling. From early times onwards, storytellers (*quṣṣāṣ*) had played an important role in the life of the tribe by transmitting the stories about the exploits of the tribes (*'ayyām al-ʿArab*), and this tradition was continued in a modified form in early Islam when storytellers went around to tell about the events in the life of the Prophet, the early Islamic expeditions and the conquests of foreign countries. These stories were meant for the general public and they were no doubt told in a lively style, full of fictitious conversations and without any literary embellishments. The topics dealt with by the professional storytellers were also studied by scholars. They had in common with the storytellers a certain aversion to writing down their reports: only the *Qur'ān* could be a written Book. They did use written notes for recording their own memories and those of their informants, but these were intended for private use only. The earliest efforts to put down in writing systematically the traditions about Muḥammad and the early period of the conquests did not start until the end of the first century of the Hiğra, at a time when the last people who had actually met the Prophet were old men and women who were bound to die soon. This period witnessed a feverish activity on the part of scholars to collect all they could from the last witnesses still alive. Scholars such as az-Zuhrī (d. 124/742) compiled collections of *ḥadīṯs*, that were eagerly sought by the caliphal court and were probably deposited in the palace.

The best-documented genre in early Islam is the epistolary one. The earliest examples of epistolary texts are found in the accounts of the correspondence between the Prophet and the tribal chieftains. During the period of the conquests, there must have been a constant stream of letters between the central authorities in Medina and the commanders in the field. The contents of these letters were mostly commercial, but no doubt some epistolary conventions existed even then. It is impossible to determine to what degree the texts of those letters that have been preserved by later historians are authentic. Some historians refer to actual documents, for instance the treaty between the Prophet and the community of Dūmat al-Ğandal, which al-Wāqidī (*Maġāzī* III, 1,030) claims to have seen personally. But in general we have no guarantee about the authenticity of the exact wording, although the historians may well have preserved the gist of the contents. The same conclusion applies to such texts as the letters of the early *rāšidūn* or the arbitration pact of Ṣiffīn.

Since most of the scribes (*kuttāb*) in the early period were Syrians or Persians, or perhaps even Christian Arabs from the tribes outside the peninsula, some foreign examples and conventions may have found their way into Arabic literary products at this period. The reform of the caliph ʿAbd al-Malik (r. 65/685–86/705), who as we have seen was responsible for the shift of language in the *dīwān*, must have been the starting point for a new fashion in writing Arabic for official purposes. Since the secretaries were responsible for the composition of official documents and letters, their role in the development of a chancellery style was essential. Under ʿAbd al-Malik's successor Hišām (r. 105/724–125/743), the foundation was laid for the administrative system that was later taken over and perfected by the ʿAbbāsid caliphs.

From the beginning of the 'Umayyad dynasty, the sponsorship of the caliphs was an important factor in the production of texts, both literary and administrative. According to some sources as early as Muʿāwiya's (r. 41/661–60/680) reign, the caliph had some kind of library in which he deposited written versions of *ḥadīṯ*s, some of which had been collected at his request. His grandson H̱ālid ibn Yazīd ibn Muʿāwiya had a keen interest in alchemy and may have commissioned the first translations from Greek into Arabic. Certainly there are enough reports about the later 'Umayyads requesting translations of Greek or Syriac books, mostly on medicine, to warrant the conclusion that a depository (*ẖizāna*) of books belonged to the normal appurtenances of the caliphal court. Although the ʿAbbāsids did their best to suppress any favourable report about the 'Umayyads, it is fairly certain that the 'Umayyad caliphs actively supported the activities of scholars such as az-Zuhrī in the field of *ḥadīṯ*-collecting.

The development of a written Arabic style went hand in hand with the development of a literary prose corpus consisting of translations from Persian, including the *Kitāb fī s-siyāsa al-ʿāmmiyya mufaṣṣalan* 'Treatise on general administration, with full particulars' that is sometimes attributed to Hišām's secretary 'Abū l-ʿAlā' Sālim. The epistolary style was perfected by his successor ʿAbd al-Ḥamīd ibn Yaḥyā (d. after 132/750), secretary of Marwān II (r. 127/744–132/750), who used this style in treatises, some of which have been preserved, such as his *Risāla 'ilā l-kuttāb* 'Letter to the scribes'. He used an ornate style, with an extensive eulogy at the beginning of the treatise, ample use of parallelism, in a quantitative rhythm, sometimes in rhymed prose (*sağʿ*), sometimes in a loose parallel structure of patterns. On the other hand, his style does not include the use of intricate rhetorical figures or rare vocabulary.

The first sermons and epistles such as those by al-Ḥasan al-Baṣrī (d. 110/728) adopted the form of the epistolary genre by addressing them to the caliph, but adapted the epistolary style to the topic at hand. Because of their religious contents, these texts borrow much more from the *Qur'ān* than ʿAbd al-Ḥamīd did.

> For the Book of God Almighty is life amid all death and light amid all darkness and knowledge amid all ignorance. God has left for his servants after the Book and the Messenger no other proof and He has said 'so that those who perished, perished after a clear sign, and so that those who lived, lived after a clear sign, for God is all-hearing and all-knowing' [*Qur'ān* 8/42]. Reflect, Commander of the Believers on the word of God Almighty 'To each of you who wishes to go forward or go backwards, his soul is a pawn for what it has earned' [*Qur'ān* 74/38]. (*fa-kitābu llāhi taʿālā ḥayātun*

ʿinda kulli mawtin wa-nūrun ʿinda kulli ẓulmatin wa-ʿilmun ʿinda kulli ǧahlin, fa-mā taraka llāhu li-l-ʿibādi baʿda l-kitābi wa-r-rasūli ḥuǧǧatan wa-qāla ʿazza wa-ǧalla 'li-yahlika man halaka ʿan bayyinatin, wa-yaḥyā man ḥayya ʿan bayyinatin wa-'inna llāha la-samīʿun ʿalīm' fa-fakkir 'amīra l-mu'minīna fī qawli llāhi taʿālā 'fa-man šā'a minkum 'an yataqaddama 'aw yata'aḫḫara kullu nafsin bi-mā kasabat rahīna', Ḥasan al-Baṣrī, *Risāla fī l-qadar*, ed. ʿAmāra, Beirut, 1987, p. 113.5–9)

The tradition of caliphal sponsorship of book-writing that was initiated by the 'Umayyad caliphs was continued under the ʿAbbāsid dynasty. At the request of some of the caliphs, books were composed, mostly by foreigners, that were to acquaint the intellectual elite with the achievements of other cultures. Scholars such as the Persian Ibn al-Muqaffaʿ (d. ±142/759), a near-contemporary of ʿAbd al-Ḥamīd, produced literary translations from Pahlavi. His most famous translation was that of the Indian fables of *Kalīla wa-Dimna*, but he also composed new original treatises, such as the *Kitāb al-'adab al-kabīr* and the *Risāla fī ṣ-ṣaḥāba*. These treatises were mostly concerned with court etiquette and the behavioural code in the relations between rulers and ruled.

Because of the scarcity of preserved texts from the 'Umayyad period, it is difficult to pinpoint the exact model for the style of early ʿAbbāsid writings. The language of the *Qur'ān* gained in influence during the ʿAbbāsid period, but it cannot be regarded as a direct model for the prose style. Ibn al-Muqaffaʿ's work abounds with antithetic statements and parallelisms formulated in a syntactically complicated language, full of participles and infinitives, which, however, always remains lucid and easy to follow, as in the following fragment:

> Know that the receiver of praise is as someone who praises himself. It is fitting that a man's love of praise should induce him to reject it, since the one who rejects it is praised, but the one who accepts it is blamed. (*wa-ʿlam 'anna qābila l-madḥi ka-mādiḥi nafsihi, wa-l-mar'u ǧadīrun 'an yakūna ḥubbuhu l-madḥa huwa llaḏī yaḥmiluhu ʿalā raddihi, fa-'inna r-rādda lahu maḥmūdun, wa-l-qābila lahu maʿībun*, Ibn al-Muqaffaʿ, *'Adab*, ed. Beirut, 1964, p. 69)

The 'Umayyad trend of commissioning translations of scientific writings reached its apogee under the ʿAbbāsid caliphs. The Arabic translations of (Syriac versions of) Greek writings that were produced before al-Ma'mūn's establishment of the translators' academy, the *Bayt al-ḥikma*, were written in a clumsy style that betrays its Greek origin in every line. One example from a translation of Hippocrates' *On the Nature of Man* should suffice (an attempt has been made to imitate the style in English!):

> When spring comes, it is necessary to add to the drinking, and it must be broken with water, and you must cut down bit by bit on food, and you must choose of it that which is less nourishing and fresher and you must adopt instead of the use of much bread the use of much barley meal. (*wa-'iḏā ǧā'a r-rabīʿ fa-yanbaġī 'an yuzād fī š-šarāb wa-yuksar bi-l-mā' wa-tanquṣ min aṭ-ṭaʿām qalīlan qalīlan wa-taḫtār minhu mā huwa 'aqall ġaḏā' wa-'arṭab wa-tastaʿmil makāna l-istikṯār min al-ḫubz al-istikṯār min as-sawīq, Kitāb Buqrāṭ fī ṭabīʿat al-'insān*, ed. J. N. Mattock and M. C. Lyons, Cambridge, 1968, pp. 27–8)

The thoughtless reference to the Greek custom of mixing wine with water is as inappropriate in an Islamic context as the style of the entire text. In the writings of the greatest of all translators, Ḥunayn ibn 'Isḥāq (d. 260/873), there is no trace of such translated language. He explicitly rejects the literal translations of his predecessors and uses a businesslike, terse style that makes full use of the syntactic possibilities of Arabic and shuns the ornate epistolary style. His preference for complicated infinitival and participial constructions may reflect the structure of the Greek original:

> I wrote for him a book in Syriac, in which I took the direction he had indicated to me when he requested me to write it [lit.: in his requesting its composition from me]. (*fa-katabtu lahu kitāban bi-s-Suryāniyya naḥawtu fīhi n-naḥwa lla<u>d</u>ī qaṣada 'ilayhi fī mas'alatihi 'iyyāya waḍ'ahu*, Ḥunayn ibn 'Isḥāq, *Risāla Ḥunayn ibn 'Isḥāq 'ilā 'Alī ibn Yaḥyā fī <u>d</u>ikr mā turǧima min kutub Ǧālīnūs bi-'ilmihi wa-ba'ḍ mā lam yutarǧam*, ed. G. Bergsträßer, Leipzig, 1925, p. 1)

Both Ibn al-Muqaffa''s treatises and the translations of Greek logical, medical and philosophical writings were publications in the real sense of the word. They were public books, not restricted to the court, but intended to be read by individuals. With respect to Islamic writing, i.e. writing on legal matters (*fiqh*), traditions of the Prophet (*ḥadī<u>t</u>*), history, Islamic campaigns (*maġāzī*) and Qur'ānic exegesis (*tafsīr*), things were different. When the 'Abbāsid caliphs requested scholars to write down their information in the form of actual books for the benefit of the heirs to the throne, who needed such information for their education, they did so partially in reaction to the 'Umayyads. The 'Umayyad caliphs did support the scholarly work of individual *ḥadī<u>t</u>*-collectors, but the 'Abbāsid propaganda emphasised their worldly interests and minimised their role in the collection of Islamic writing. One of the earliest court scholars was Ibn 'Isḥāq (d. 150/767). He had collected materials about the history of the Arabs and Islam in order to use them in his instruction. At the special request of the Caliph al-Manṣūr (r. 136/754–158/775), he presented them in a structured form at court and deposited them as a permanent text in the caliphal library (<u>H</u>aṭīb al-Baġdādī, *Ta'rī<u>h</u> Baġdād* I, 220f.).

Although there are no copies of this or similar limited publications, Ibn 'Isḥāq's activities mark the beginning of historical writing and to a large degree determined its literary form and style. We may assume that the accounts of what happened during the Prophet's life and the early conquests were written in the kind of narrative prose that we find in all early (and even later) historians, all of which grew out of the simple contextless *'a<u>h</u>bār* of the storytellers. The emphasis is on the liveliness of the story, which does not depend on literary decoration and uses simple words in a preponderantly paratactic construction, preferably in dialogue form. The following example illustrates this style and shows the division of the story into two parts, a chain of informants (*'isnād*) and the actual contents (*matn*):

> Ibn 'Isḥāq said: 'Āṣim ibn 'Umar ibn Qatāda told me on the authority of 'Anas ibn Mālik. He said: I saw the cloak of 'Ukaydir when it was brought to the Messenger of God – may God bless him and protect him! – and the Muslims started to touch it with their hands and they admired it. The

Messenger of God – may God bless him and protect him! – said: 'Do you admire this? In the name of Him in whose hands my soul is, the kerchiefs of Sa'd ibn Mu'ā\d{} in paradise are more beautiful than this!' (*qāla Ibn Mālik: fa-ḥaddaṯanī 'Āṣim ibn 'Umar ibn Qatāda 'an 'Anas ibn Mālik, qāla: ra'aytu qubā'a 'Ukaydir ḥīna qudima bihi 'alā rasūli llāh – ṣallā llāhu 'alayhi wa-sallam – fa-ǧa'ala l-Muslimūna yalmisūnahu bi-'aydīhim wa-yata'aǧǧabūna minhu, fa-qāla rasūlu llāh – ṣallā llāhu 'alayhi wa-sallam – 'a-ta'ǧibūna min hāḏā? fa-wa-llaḏī nafsī bi-yadihi, la-manādīlu Sa'd ibn Mu'āḏ fī l-ǧannati 'aḥsanu min hāḏā!*, Ibn Hišām, *as-Sīra an-Nabawiyya* IV, ed. as-Saqā, al-'Ibyārī and Šalabī, Cairo, 1936, pp. 169–70)

By their nature, texts of this type did not have the same kind of literary pretensions as, for instance, poetry. Doubtless, later historians such as aṭ-Ṭabarī (d. 310/923) did not content themselves always with simply copying the stories which they transmitted from their predecessors, but they attempted to structure and stylise them. Compared to poetry, however, there was so much freedom in this kind of prose and so few restrictions with regard to the form that the Arab literary critics could not be expected to devote much time to them, except perhaps to deplore the many 'mistakes' against grammar that crept in. The literary critic Qudāma ibn Ǧa'far (d. 337/958) in his *Naqd an-naṯr* 'Criticism of prose' distinguishes between two styles, the one low (*saḫīf*), the other elevated (*ǧazl*), and he gives precise instructions on when to use the one and when the other.

What Qudāma designates 'elevated style' is the kind of Arabic prose which we find in official correspondence, which is written in a florid style with a heavy emphasis on the form. In this kind of writing, we find the rhymed sequences that became so characteristic of Arabic style. Even non-literary works traditionally begin with an introduction in which this kind of prose is used. In the debate among literary critics on the question of whether 'expression' (*lafẓ*) or 'meaning' (*ma'nā*) is more important in a literary work, the prevalent opinion was that a literary work should be evaluated according to its expression, its form, since the meaning expressed by the writer is universal and accessible to everyone, whereas the form is something that only an accomplished writer can handle. Such an attitude could and did easily lead to a formulaic style. Form came to be seen as the most important dimension of style, whereas content was of secondary importance. In the literary genre of the *maqāmāt*, this tendency reached its apogee, and the production of writers such as al-Ḥarīrī (d. 516/1122) contains pieces that are pure exercises in form.

There is another kind of writing in Arabic, corresponding to what Qudāma calls the 'lower style'. It is found in private letters and in non-literary writing, such as geographical works, historiography, biographical dictionaries, handbooks of Islamic law and theology, and even in grammatical treatises. In such writings, we find a relaxation of the strict standards, the introduction of colloquialisms and a businesslike style. Some of these authors went even further and used a kind of prose language that had freed itself from the bonds of Classical Arabic and came a long way down to the vernacular of their time. But even when these authors used vernacular constructions or lexical items, they never stopped writing within the framework of Classical Arabic. From the point of view of historical linguistics, texts like the memoirs of 'Usāma ibn Munqiḏ (d.

584/1188), or Ibn 'Abī 'Uṣaybiʿa's (d. 668/1270) biographical dictionary, belong to the category of 'Middle Arabic' (cf. below, p. 120). There is a vast difference between this genre, in which intellectuals strove after a simple style, and the large quantity of documents written in faulty language that are normally subsumed under the same label of 'Middle Arabic'.

The coexistence of and the conflict between a high and a low variety of the language in Islamic culture made its presence felt from the time of the earliest papyri. Through the Middle Arabic texts, this diglossia was introduced in the domain of literary and semi-literary products. We shall see below (Chapter 12) that this conflict has never disappeared since. In Modern Arabic literature, just like in that of the Classical age, authors have to choose the level of speech in which they wish to write. But the main constraint for all written production in Arabic is the position of Classical Arabic as the language of prestige. Whether in an 'elevated' or in a 'lower' style, the ultimate model remains the standard language, and even when an author deliberately sets out to write in the vernacular, in the end he can never escape the framework of the written language.

5.5 THE OFFICIAL STATUS OF ARABIC

Throughout the classical period of Islam, Arabic remained the language of prestige that was used for all religious, cultural, administrative and scholarly purposes. In none of these functions was it ever seriously threatened in the first centuries of Islam. In their attitude towards other languages, the speakers of Arabic took it for granted that there could be no alternative to the Arabic language. This explains the disappearance of all other cultural languages in the Islamic empire, such as Coptic, Greek, Syriac and even Persian. With very few exceptions, the Arab grammarians showed no inclination to study other languages, and speakers of these languages only very seldom found anything to boast of in their own language, preferring to speak and write in Arabic instead. During the first centuries of the Hiğra, speakers of Persian tended to regard their own language as inferior to Arabic. We have already seen that the author of the first linguistic description of Arabic, Sībawayhi, was himself a speaker of Persian, but there are absolutely no traces in his *Kitāb* of any interest in the Persian language. Another famous grammarian, al-Fārisī (d. 377/987), on being asked by his pupil Ibn Ǧinnī about his mother tongue, Persian, stated unequivocally that there could be no comparison between the two languages, since Arabic was far superior to Persian (*Ḫaṣā'iṣ* I, 243). Eventually, a counter-movement of Persian ethnic feeling (*šuʿūbiyya*) arose which opposed the monopoly of the Arabs but did not challenge the position of Arabic.

From the ninth century onwards, however, Persian became increasingly used as a literary language, first of all in Eastern Iran, where Arabic culture had never gained a foothold. At the court of the more or less independent dynasties in the East, New Persian or Farsī was used in poetry. Under the dynasty of the Samānids (tenth century), it replaced Arabic as the language of culture. After the fall of Baghdad (657/1258) during the Mongol invasion, Arabic lost its position as the prestigious language in the entire Islamic East to Persian, except in matters of religion. In Iran itself, the Safavid dynasty under Shah 'Ismāʿīl (906/1501) adopted Farsī and the Shiʿite form of Islam as the national language and religion.

In all other regions, Arabic kept its position for a long time. A case in point is Mamluk Egypt. The Arabs had always looked down on the Turks, whom they regarded as good soldiers and therefore useful as protectors of Islam, but without any gift for culture. Their Arabic, if they spoke it at all, was deficient. Yet, Mamluk trainees received intensive instruction in Arabic, and most Mamluks must at least have understood the language. In the biographical sources about the Mamluks (e.g. aṣ-Ṣafadī's *al-Wāfī bi-l-wafayāt*), mention is made of many Mamluk scholars who occupied themselves with the religious and grammatical literature in Arabic, and even when in the fourteenth century they started to produce scholarly writings in Qipčaq and Oğuz Turkic, Arabic remained in use in Egypt as the main literary language.

When the Seljuks conquered Anatolia, Turkish became the official language of their empire, with Persian as the literary language; but even then, Arabic remained important, in the first place as a source of loanwords in Turkic (cf. below, Chapter 13, p. 234), and in the second place as the language of religion. It lost, however, its place as administrative language of the empire to Turkish. At the end of the nineteenth century, during the Renaissance (*Nahḍa*) of Arabic (cf. below, Chapter 11), attempts were made to reintroduce Arabic as the language of administration, but with the advent of the colonial period these attempts turned out to be short-lived, and it was not until the independence of the Arab countries as political entities in the twentieth century that it became once again the language in which matters of state and administration could be expressed.

FURTHER READING

A classic work on the development of Classical Arabic is Fück (1950); in a series of thirteen essays he discusses more or less chronologically the development of Classical Arabic style and lexicon, not by closely-reasoned argumentation, but with the help of selected items from the sources. Fück strongly believed in the survival of the declensional endings in Bedouin speech for centuries after the Islamic conquests (cf. above, Chapter 4). For more recent opinions about this controversy, see Fleisch (1964), Zwettler (1978) and Versteegh (1984: 10–13).

The development of Arabic orthography is dealt with by Abbott (1939, 1972); a study on the development of the diacritic dots is Revell (1975); a short survey of the traditional Arabic accounts of the invention of the orthographic system is in Semaan (1968). The most recent synthetic account of the development of orthography is by Endreß (1982). On the earliest examples of Qur'ānic writing, see Grohmann (1958); on the development of chancellery writing, see Abbott (1941). The later history of the Arabic script has not been treated here; for further references, see Schimmel (1982).

The history of the development of Arabic orthography is closely related to the textual history of the *Qur'ān*, for which Nöldeke and Schwally (1961) remains the standard handbook. On the shift from recitation to book, see Nagel (1983) and Schoeler (1992); on the reception of the Qur'ānic codex by the grammarians, see Beck (1946).

Both grammar-writing and lexicography played a crucial role in the standardisation of the Arabic language. The emergence of the discipline of grammar is treated by Abbott (1972); for further literature about the two disciplines, see below, Chapter 6, p. 91. The role of 'Abū l-'Aswad is discussed by Talmon (1985).

Schall (1982) gives a general introduction to the study of the history of the Arabic lexicon. For the question of foreign words in the *Qur'ān*, see Fraenkel (1886) and Jeffery (1938); for the commentators' attitude towards foreign words, see Versteegh (1993a: 88–91). The examples from Muqātil's *Tafsīr* are taken from Versteegh (1990). The controversy about foreign words in the *Qur'ān* and in Arabic is dealt with by Kopf (1956). The foreign vocabulary in Ibn Hišām's *Sīra* is listed by Hebbo (1970), who discusses more than 200 loanwords, of which more than 50 per cent derive from Aramaic/Syriac, while approximately 40 per cent derive from Persian and 10 per cent from Greek. On Persian borrowings in Arabic, see Asbaghi (1988). Bielawski (1956) compares the various methods used to expand the lexicon in the old and the modern period (cf. also below, Chapter 11) and provides many examples of loanwords. The examples of translations of logical terms are taken from Zimmermann (1972). A dictionary of the Arabic equivalents that were used for Greek words by the translators is being compiled by Endreß and Gutas (1992–).

On the language of *rağaz* poetry and the special lexicon used by these poets, see Ullmann (1966), from which the examples quoted above were taken. For the development of prose style in Arabic literature, see the programmatic article by Leder and Kilpatrick (1992) and the surveys in *CHAL* by Latham (1983) and Serjeant (1983). The development of Islamic writing and the dichotomy between oral and written in early Islam is the subject of a series of articles by Schoeler (1985, 1989a, 1989b, 1992). Information about the development of a library system in Islam is in Eche (1967). The activities of az-Zuhrī are dealt with by Motzki (1991). For history-writing and the development from *'aẖbār* to annalistic writing, see Rosenthal (1968). The issue of authenticity of historical documents in the historians is discussed at length by Noth (1973). For the language of writers such as 'Usāma and Ibn 'Abī 'Uṣaybiʿa, see below, Chapter 8, p. 120.

The relationship between Arabic and Turkic in Mamluk Egypt is analysed by Haarmann (1988); on the influence of Arabic in Turkish, see below, Chapter 14, p. 234. On the emergence of New Persian as a literary language, see Lazard (1975); on Arabic influence in Persian, see below, Chapter 14, p. 232.

6
The Structure of Classical Arabic in the Linguistic Tradition

6.1 INTRODUCTION

Western descriptions of the structure of Classical Arabic, almost without exception, use a Greco-Latin grammatical model and hardly ever mention the differences between this model and that of the Arabic grammarians. The choice of the Greco-Latin model serves a didactic purpose, because these grammars are intended for the teaching of Arabic to non-Arabophones, who are usually more familiar with the Greco-Latin model of school grammar. Either may be assumed to give an adequate description of the structure of Classical Arabic, but the framework of the Arabic grammarians served exclusively for the analysis of Arabic and therefore has a special relevance for the study of that language. From the period between 750 and 1500 we know the names of more than 4,000 grammarians who elaborated a comprehensive body of knowledge on their own language. In this chapter, we shall present some examples of their theories, which in spite of their unfamiliarity may provide a novel way of looking at the language from the privileged point of view of its own scholars. Most Arabic grammars of Arabic follow the order established by the first grammarian, Sībawayhi (d. 177/793?), in his *Kitāb* and start with syntax, followed by morphology, with phonology added as an appendix. The Western terms used here correspond roughly to the two traditional components of Arabic linguistics: *taṣrīf*, usually translated as 'morphology', and *naḥw*, usually translated as 'syntax'. But whereas we assign to morphology the study of all alterations of words, the Arabic grammarians assign the study of declensional endings to *naḥw* and all remaining changes in the form of words, e.g. plural endings and derivational patterns, to *taṣrīf*.

A remark is in order here concerning the practice of translating Arabic technical terms with technical terms from the Western model. The names of the parts of grammar illustrate the lack of correspondence between the two sets of terms. Another example is that of the term *rafʿ*, usually equated with 'nominative', which introduces the concept of 'case endings' that is foreign to the indigenous framework. The term *ʿamal* in Arabic grammar indicates the syntactic effect of one word on another; this term is often translated as 'rection', which suggests a parallel with Greco-Latin grammar, or as 'governing', which inevitably suggests a parallel with modern linguistic theories. On the other hand, using only the Arabic terms makes it difficult to follow the discussion. For the sake of convenience, we have chosen in this chapter to provide the Arabic terms with English equivalents, on the understanding that these will not be taken as exact equivalents. Where necessary, the difference between the concepts involved will be mentioned.

The aim of linguistics in the Arabic tradition differed from ours. The grammarian had a fixed corpus of language at his disposal, consisting of the text of the *Qur'ān*, pre-Islamic poetry, and the idealised speech of the Bedouin (cf. above, Chapter 5). Since by definition the native speakers knew how to speak Arabic, the grammarians did not have to give instructions: their grammar was not a prescriptive discipline. It was not a mere description, either. Since (the Arabic) language was a part of God's creation, its structure was perfect to the tiniest detail, and the task of the grammarian was to account for every single phenomenon of the language, i.e. to determine its status within the system of rules. Language was regarded as a hierarchically-ordered whole, in which each component had its own function. Explanations often took the form of a comparison or analogy (*qiyās*). Structural similarity between two components implied a similarity in status, or, in the terminology of the grammarians, equality in rights. Apparent deviations from the perfect harmony of the language were explained by assuming that these belonged to the surface structure of speech, but that on an underlying level (*'aṣl, ma'nā*) the deviations were in line with the system of the language.

In the syntactic part of linguistics, the grammarians' main preoccupation was the explanation of the case endings of the words in the sentence, called *'i'rāb*, a term that originally meant the correct use of Arabic according to the language of the Bedouin (*'Arab*) but came to mean the declension. The case endings were assumed to be the result of the action of an *'āmil*, a word in the sentence affecting or governing another word. This influence manifested itself in what we would call 'case endings', i.e. in the definition of the grammarians 'a difference in the ending of the words caused by a difference in the governing word' (*iḫtilāf 'awāḫir al-kalim bi-ḫtilāf al-'awāmil*). Explaining a case ending was tantamount to identifying the word responsible for this ending (*'āmil*). When no such word could be identified in the surface sentence, the grammarian had to reconstruct (*taqdīr*) the underlying level on which the governing word could be seen to operate.

In morphology (*taṣrīf*), the focus was on the structure of words and the explanation of the non-syntactically-motivated changes which they underwent. These changes could be derivational, i.e. entailing a change in meaning, or non-derivational, i.e. morphonological in nature. Examples of these changes will be given below (pp. 83, 85). Phonology did not count as an independent discipline and was therefore relegated to a position at the end of the treatise. Only insofar as the phonological rules interacted with the form of the word did they draw the grammarians' attention. Purely phonetic issues were only dealt with as a kind of appendix to the grammatical treatises, although a considerable body of phonetic knowledge was transmitted in introductions to dictionaries and in treatises on the recitation of the *Qur'ān* (*tağwīd*).

Arabic grammatical treatises are full of references to the *ma'nā* 'meaning'. By this they refer either to the intention of the speaker, or to the functional meaning of linguistic categories, but not to the lexical meaning of the words, which was reserved for lexicography. In both cases, the semantic aspect of speech was taken for granted but, at least in early grammar, hardly ever thoroughly discussed. The meaning of grammatical categories was thought to be expressed by the pattern of a word, the lexical meaning being inherent in the radicals from which it was derived. The derivational system of the Arabic grammarians operated with a chain of combinations of an *'aṣl* and a *ma'nā*. At the highest level, the *'aṣl* is the consonantal skeleton (root), e.g. Ḍ-R-B carrying the meaning of 'hitting'; to this root a pattern is applied, e.g. Fa'aLa, which has a meaning of its own (transitive verb). The result is a morphological form |ḍaraba|, which in its turn functions as the *'aṣl* for further derivations, e.g. with the pattern yaFa'iL (imperfect), which produces |yaḍarib|. The morphological forms serve as the point of departure for further extensions, e.g. with a pronoun of the first person in |ḍaraba-tu|, or a declensional ending in |yaḍarib-u|. Finally, the morphological forms are affected by phonological rules, producing the phonological forms /ḍarabtu/, /yaḍribu/ (cf. below, p. 84). In the system of segmentation, one of the most important axioms was the strict correlation between morphemes and grammatical functions: each function was represented by one morpheme, and each morpheme could represent only one function.

Normally, Arabic grammatical writings do not take into account the lexical meaning of words and roots. The grammarians left the semantic analysis to lexicography (*'ilm al-luġa*) and concentrated instead on the morphological function. Still, they did not ignore completely the relationship between lexical meaning and the radicals. Very early on, the idea of a relationship between roots differing in only one consonant seems to have existed in the Arabic tradition. Lexicographers formalised this principle under the name of *al-ištiqāq al-'akbar* 'greater etymology', stating that words with two similar radicals are semantically related to each other. The grammarian Ibn Ǧinnī (d. 392/1002), in his Ḫaṣā'iṣ (II, ed. an-Naǧǧār, Cairo, 1952–6, pp. 133–9), went one step further. Already in the earliest dictionary, the *Kitāb al-'ayn* (cf. above, Chapter 5) the arrangement of the roots had suggested a semantic relationship between the permutations of a root. Ibn Ǧinnī formalised this principle by stating that there existed an *ištiqāq kabīr* 'great etymology', a higher semantic level on which all permutations of three radicals had a common meaning. From the set of radicals *'-b-r*, for instance, Ibn Ǧinnī derived the following words: *'ibāra* 'expression', *'abra* 'tear', *'arab* 'nomads', *bara'a* 'to excel', *ba'r* 'dung', *rab'* 'spring camping site', *ru'b* 'fear'. He asserted that all these words expressed a common meaning, that of 'transfer'. The general idea of a semantic relationship between words with similar consonants seems to have been accepted by most scholars in the Arabic tradition, although most of them hesitated to go as far as Ibn Ǧinnī did.

In modern comparative linguistics, it has been speculated that originally all words in Semitic were biradical, the third consonant acting as some kind of suffix or prefix. This theory is supported by the fact that there are both within Arabic and between the Semitic languages triradical words that differ only in one (usually weak) consonant, e.g. in Arabic *f-r-r* 'to flee', *f-r-q* 'to tear apart', *f-r-z* 'to separate', *f-r-d* 'to be alone', *f-r-ṣ* 'to slit, pierce'. Similarly, in Hebrew we have *p-r-d* 'to separate', *p-r-m* 'to tear', *p-r-q* 'to pull apart', *p-r-r* 'to dissolve'. On the basis of such word groups, a Proto-Semitic root *p-r* with the general meaning 'to divide' might be posited. The added consonants are assumed to have served to specify the semantic range of the derived words.

Recently, Bohas (1993, 1995, 1997) has proposed a modern version of this theory and to a certain degree revindicated Ibn Ǧinnī's ideas. He starts by referring to roots that differ only in one glide (*w*, *y*) and that have the same semantic load, either within Arabic (e.g. *bahha*, *bāha*, *bahā*, all meaning 'to calm down') or across Semitic languages. A similar phenomenon is observable with other sonants (*n*, *r*, *l*, *m*, etc.) and gutturals, e.g. *ǧazza* 'to cut, shear', *ǧazara* 'to slaughter, cut off', *ǧazala* 'to cut a stick in two pieces', *ǧazama* 'to cut off, trim', *ǧazaʿa* 'to cut, cross a river'. He concludes that all triradical verbal roots ultimately go back to biradical types with a similar semantic load. He then further extends this principle to radicals from the same articulatory class, which may occur in either order. These constitute matrices, for instance the matrix consisting of a uvulovelar and a dental with the general meaning of 'cutting', to which in addition to the roots above there also belong: *ǧadda* 'to cut', *ǧadara* 'to eradicate', *ǧadama* 'to cut off a hand'; *qadda* 'to cut lengthwise', *qatala* 'to kill', *qaṣara* 'to shorten', *qaṭaʿa* 'to cut', and so on. It is difficult to see in what way Bohas' theory could be verified, but even in a weaker form it may tell us much about the organisation of the Arabic lexicon and explain a number of phenomena which up until now have had to be regarded as coincidental.

6.2 SYNTAX

Traditionally, Arabic grammatical treatises start with a series of definitions in which the main categories of language are introduced. The first chapter in Sībawayhi's *Kitāb*, for instance, reads as follows:

> Chapter of the knowledge of words in the Arabic language. Words are noun, verb, or particle intended for a meaning which is neither noun nor verb. Nouns are *raǧul* 'man', *faras* 'horse', *ḥā'iṭ* 'wall'. Verbs are patterns taken from the expression of the events of the nouns; they are construed for what is past; for what is going to be, but has not yet happened; and for what is being without interruption ... As for that which is intended for a meaning, without being a noun or a verb, this is like *ṯumma* 'then', *sawfa* [particle of the future], *wa-* in oaths, *li-* to indicate possession, and so on. (*hāḏā bāb ʿilm al-kalim min al-ʿarabiyya, fa-l-kalim ism wa-fiʿl wa-ḥarf ǧā'a li-maʿnan laysa bi-sm wa-lā fiʿl, fa-l-ism raǧul wa-faras wa-ḥā'iṭ wa-'ammā l-fiʿl fa-'amṯila 'uḫiḏat min lafẓ 'aḥdāṯ al-'asmā' wa-buniyat limā maḍā wa-limā yakūnu wa-lam yaqaʿ wa-mā huwa kā'in lam yanqaṭiʿ ... wa-'ammā mā ǧā'a li-maʿnan wa-laysa bi-sm wa-lā fiʿl fa-naḥwa ṯumma wa-sawfa wa-wāw al-qasam wa-lām al-'iḍāfa wa-naḥwa hāḏā, Kitāb* I, ed. Bulaq, n.d., p. 2.1–3)

This division into what we would call three parts of speech remained intact throughout the history of the Arabic grammatical tradition. The category of the noun (*ism*) was defined either as a word with certain syntactic characteristics, such as its combinability with an article, or as a word denoting an essence. It included not only what we call nouns, but also our adjectives, pronouns and even a number of prepositions and adverbs, such as *'amāma* 'in front of', *kayfa* 'how?'. The category of the verb (*fiʿl*) was defined either as a word that may be combined with the future particle *sawfa*, or as a word denoting an action. It included some words which we would call interjections such as *hayhāt* 'come on!', *ṣah* 'hush!'. In the Arabic system, the category of the particle (*ḥarf*) included the remaining words; they could not be declined and acted only as governing words, for instance *li-* 'for', governing nouns and verbs, and *'an* 'that', governing verbs alone. Their main function was to assist other words in their function in the sentence.

The basic difference between the three parts of speech is the declension (*'i'rāb*). In principle, only nouns have case endings to indicate their function in the sentence. Western grammars usually call the three endings *-u*, *-i*, *-a* 'nominative', 'genitive', 'accusative', respectively; in Arabic grammar they are called *raf'*, *ğarr*, *naṣb*. The case endings refer to syntactic functions; they may be followed by an ending *-n* to indicate that the word is indefinite (*tanwīn*, nunation). Unlike the Greco-Latin grammarians, the Arabic grammarians do not assign to them any independent semantic content. The nominative case indicates that a noun's function is that of agent (*fā'il*), topic (*mubtada'*), or predicate (*ḫabar*) of the sentence (about these sentential constituents, see below, p. 80).

The two main functions of the genitive case are to mark the effect of particles on nouns and to indicate the second noun in possessive constructions. Particles governing nouns are called in the Western tradition 'prepositions', e.g. *ma'a r-rağuli* 'with the man', *'ilā l-madīnati* 'to the city'. In the possessive construction (*'iḍāfa*), the first noun (*al-muḍāf 'ilayhi*) has neither article nor nunation, and the second noun (*al-muḍāf*) is put in the genitive case, e.g. *baytu l-maliki* 'the king's house'. The governance relationship between the two nouns in the *'iḍāfa* construction is a controversial issue. Since in principle nouns do not govern, later grammarians objected to Sībawayhi's view that the first noun governs the second. Instead they attributed the genitive ending to a particle *li-* 'for, belonging to' which was inserted on an underlying level, i.e. **baytu li-l-maliki* 'house for-the-king [genitive]'.

The accusative case is used for the direct object (*maf'ūl*), e.g. *ḍarabtu zaydan* 'I hit Zayd', and for a large variety of other objects of time, place, intensity and reason, as well as for the so-called *ḥāl* 'circumstantial', the *tamyīz* 'specifier' and the internal object (*maf'ūl muṭlaq*). In Arabic grammar, the verb in a sentence such as *ḍaraba zaydun 'amran* 'Zayd hit 'Amr' is said to 'transcend the agent towards the object' (*yata'addā l-fā'il 'ilā l-maf'ūl*). This means that such a verb, which we would call 'transitive', not only causes the accusative of the object but also the nominative of the agent. A verb, moreover, implies not only an agent and, when it is transitive, an object, but also the time and the place of the action. Therefore, expressions of time and place (*ẓurūf*) also receive the accusative case ending, as in *ḍarabtu-hu l-yawma* 'I hit him today' and in *ḍarabtu-hu 'amāmaka* 'I hit him in front of you'. In addition, the verb implies its own action as an internal object, as in *ḍarabtu-hu ḍarban* 'I hit him a hitting, I hit him hard'. As in English, some Arabic verbs govern through a preposition, for instance in *marartu bi-hi* 'I passed by him'. Later grammarians regarded *bi-hi* in such a sentence as a real object, the particle (preposition) *bi-* serving as a link between the verb and its object.

Although in principle verbs are not declined, there is one category of verbs that do receive declension. In Arabic grammar these are called *muḍāri'* 'resembling', since they owe their declension to their resemblance to the nouns. This resemblance manifests itself in the fact that in some constructions a verb may be used as a substitute for a noun, e.g. *'inna zaydan la-ḍāribun* 'Zayd is hitting', which is equivalent to *'inna zaydan la-yaḍribu* 'Zayd hits'. The resembling verbs correspond to what the Western tradition calls 'imperfect verbs', because they are used for incompleted actions, e.g. *yaḍribu* 'he is hitting, he will hit'. The terminological difference demonstrates a difference in approach: Greco-Latin grammar names after the semantic content, whereas Arabic grammar names after formal characteristics, in this case the fact that this category of verbs exhibits the same endings as the noun. In Greco-Latin grammar, these are called modal endings: indicative (*yaḍrib-u*), subjunctive (*yaḍrib-a*), and jussive or apocopate (*yaḍrib*). In the Arabic tradition, the endings *-u*, *-a* and *-Ø* are regarded as having the same status as the endings of the nouns, and accordingly such verbs are said to be declined (*mu'rab*). The endings *-u* and *-a* are identical with those of the noun and, like these, are called *raf'* 'nominative' and *naṣb* 'accusative'; the zero-ending is called *ǧazm*, literally 'cutting off'.

	nouns	imperfect verbs
raf'	*zayd-u-n*	*yaḍrib-u*
ǧarr (ḫafḍ)	*zayd-i-n*	
naṣb	*zayd-a-n*	*yaḍrib-a*
ǧazm		*yaḍrib*

Table 6.1 The endings of nouns and imperfect verbs.

When words are combined, they constitute an utterance (*qawl*). When this utterance conveys a meaningful message, it becomes *kalām*, a semantically complete message. The closest equivalent in Arabic grammar to our notion of 'sentence' is that of *ǧumla*, a syntactically complete string of words. In a sentence, there is always one head word that relays or determines the sentential functions resulting in markers in the form of case endings. In their analysis of the sentential constructions, the Arabic grammarians differ most from our analysis. According to the Western analysis of Arabic sentence structure, there are two types of sentences: nominal and verbal sentences. When the sentence does not contain a verb, it is called a nominal sentence with two constituents, a subject and a nominal predicate, e.g. *zaydun ṭabībun* 'Zayd is a doctor'. The verbal sentence always contains a verb, and its constituents are either verb–subject–object or subject–verb–object. Examples of this structure are *ḍaraba zaydun 'amran* or *zaydun ḍaraba 'amran* 'Zayd hit 'Amr', which under this analysis are regarded as stylistic alternatives of the same verbal sentence. In these two examples, the agreement relations between verb and subject are identical, both being singular, but when the subject becomes plural there is only agreement in number when the subject precedes the verb: *ar-riǧālu ḍarabū* 'the men hit', with both verb and noun in the plural, but *ḍaraba r-riǧālu* 'the men hit', with singular verb and plural noun. In both word orders, there is gender agreement between verb and subject in singular and plural, e.g. *al-fatayātu ḍarabna* and *ḍarabat* [singular!] *al-fatayātu* 'the girls hit'.

In their analysis of the sentence, the Arabic grammarians focused on the fundamental difference in agreement between the two word orders. According to them, there is a distinction between a nominal sentence (*ğumla ismiyya*), i.e. a sentence which in its underlying structure starts with a noun, and a verbal sentence (*ğumla fiʿliyya*), i.e. a sentence which in its underlying structure starts with a verb. These represent not just alternative word orders, but basically different sentence types. In the verbal sentence, the two constituents are the verb (*fiʿl*) and the agent (*fāʿil*). Thus, we have:

ḍaraba zaydun ʿamran
fiʿl fāʿil mafʿūl
'Zayd hit ʿAmr'

In this sentence, the verb is responsible for the nominative of the agent *zaydun* and the accusative of the object *ʿamran*. In the nominal sentence, which in Western analysis is simply a sentence without a verb, two basic constituents are distinguished by the Arabic grammarians, the one with which the sentence starts (*mubtada'*) and the one that tells something about it (*ẖabar*), e.g.:

muḥammadun 'aẖūka
mubtada' ẖabar
'Muḥammad is your brother'

The grammarians found it difficult to account for the nominative of the first constituent in such a sentence: by definition, no other word preceding it could be held responsible for its ending. The standard theory found the solution in an abstract principle called *ibtidā'*, i.e. the initial position in the sentence, which caused the nominative ending. The second constituent in its turn was assumed to be governed by the first.

In the example given here, the *ẖabar* is a noun, but it may also be a sentence, as in the following two examples:

muḥammadun 'aẖūhu zaydun
mubtada' ẖabar
mubtada' ẖabar
'Muḥammad, his brother is Zayd'

muḥammadun ḍaraba 'abūhu ʿamran
mubtada' ẖabar
fiʿl fāʿil mafʿūl
'Muḥammad, his father hit ʿAmr'

Most Western analyses call this phenomenon 'topicalisation': it consists in the fronting of a constituent from the sentence for special emphasis. In these sentences, the Arabic term *mubtada'* is, therefore, the exact equivalent of the Western term 'topic'. The novelty of the grammarians' approach becomes evident when it is applied to sentences of the following type:

muḥammadun ḍaraba ʿamran
mubtada' fiʿl-fāʿil mafʿūl

In such a sentence, the grammarians analyse *ḍaraba* as a combination of a verb with a zero agent, which is not visible on the surface level but must be posited on an underlying level. When the agent is plural, it does appear:

ar-riǧālu *ḍarabū* |ḍaraba-w|
mubtada' *ḫabar*
fi'l-fā'il
'the men hit'

The verbal form *ḍaraba* is combined here with the agent pronoun of the plural *-w*; at a morphological level, this becomes |ḍaraba-w|, at a phonological level /ḍarabu-w/ with assimilation of the vowel to the glide, which is realised as [ḍarabū]. Similarly, in *ḍarabta* 'you have hit', what we call the ending *-ta* is regarded by the Arabic grammarians as a bound pronoun (/ḍaraba-ta/ → *ḍarabta* because of a phonological rule which prohibits the occurrence of the sequence CvCvCvCv). In the case of a feminine noun, the analysis is somewhat more complicated. In the sentence

al-fatātu kataba-t
'the girl wrote'

the ending *-t* cannot be analysed as an agent pronoun, since it also appears when the noun follows:

kataba-t al-fatātu

Since two agents cannot occur in one sentence, the *-t* cannot be an agent. Consequently, it is analysed by the grammarians as a feminine marker, essentially identical with the feminine marker *-t* of the noun. In *al-fatātu katabat*, the agent of *katabat* must then be a zero pronoun, just as in the masculine form.

In this way, the Arabic analysis provides an explanation for the agreement between noun and verb in sentences where the noun is initial, and at the same time it brings together all noun-initial sentences into one category of topicalised sentences. The latter seems to be supported by the semantics of the construction: later grammarians pointed out that in a sentence such as *zaydun ḍaraba* the focus is on *zaydun*, about whom something is predicated, rather than on the action. On both syntactic and semantic grounds, the Arabic analysis of the linguistic material is certainly preferable to the Western analysis, which applies the notion of 'subject' to both sentence types in Arabic.

6.3 MORPHOLOGY

The most characteristic feature of all Semitic languages is the peculiar relationship between form and meaning. In the majority of words, the lexical meaning is represented by three radicals and the morphological meaning is added to these radicals in the form of a vowel pattern, sometimes with auxiliary consonants (*zawā'id*). The radicals *k-t-b*, for instance, represent the general meaning of 'writing', and from these radicals we get: *kātib* 'writing [participle]', plural *kuttāb*; *yaktubu* 'he writes', perfect *kataba*; *kitāb* 'book', plural *kutub*; *maktab* 'desk, office', plural *makātib*; *maktaba* 'library', plural *maktabāt*; *takātaba* 'to correspond', etc. At a very early date, the grammarians invented a notation for the morphological patterns, which represented the three radicals with the consonants *f-ʿ-l*, in which the vowels and the auxiliary consonants were inserted. The pattern of the word *kātib*, for instance, is represented as *fāʿil*, and the pattern of *maktab* as *mafʿal*.

For the Arabic grammarians, the primary task of morphology (*taṣrīf*) was the breakdown of words into radical consonants and auxiliary consonants (*zawā'id*). There are ten consonants that may serve as augments (/"/, /w/, /y/, /'/, /m/, /t/, /n/, /h/, /s/, /l/, contained in the mnemonic phrase *'al-yawma tansāhu* 'today you will forget him'). Since all ten consonants (except the abstract element /"/; cf. below, p. 90) may serve either as augment or as radical, it is not always obvious which of the consonants in a given form are radicals and which are *zā'id*. The grammarians set up methods to identify the radicals, of which the most important was the *ištiqāq* (lit. 'splitting', sometimes translated with the Western term 'etymology'), the comparison of the form under scrutiny with morphologically-related words with the same semantic content. When *'aktaba* 'he caused to write' is compared with *kataba* 'he wrote', they turn out to have the same semantic load, so that the /'/ must be regarded as an augment. Likewise in *manǧanīq* 'ballista', the first /n/ does not recur in the plural *maǧānīq* and must therefore be regarded as an augment. Since not all words are triradical, this analysis is not as simple as it may sound. Apart from the triradical words, there are four-radical verbs, and nouns consisting of four or maximally five radicals. The small group of biradical nouns such as *yad* 'hand', *ibn* 'son', *fam* 'mouth' were incorporated in the system by deriving them from triradical roots (*y-d-y*, *b-n-w*, *f-w-h*). In a word such as *ʿankabūt* /ʿankabuwt/ 'spider' there are six consonants (counting the 'lengthening' *w* as a consonant; cf. below), any of which may be a radical. The form of the plural, *ʿanākib*, shows that only four of them, *ʿ-n-k-b*, are really radicals, since these are the only ones to be preserved in inflectional processes.

6.3.1 The Noun

The first part of speech is the noun (*ism*). We have seen above that nouns receive case endings (nominative, genitive, accusative) and, when they are indefinite, the nunation. However, there is a category of nouns with only two endings, one for the nominative, and one for the genitive and the accusative, which is identical with the accusative ending of other nouns (called in Western grammars the diptotic declension). Nouns belonging to this category, when they are indefinite, do not have nunation and lose the genitive ending. When they become definite, they return to the triptotic declension. Western grammars usually do not go beyond a listing of the groups of words that are diptotic; but, for the Arabic grammarians, explaining why some nouns lose part of their declension was one of the most important tasks of morphology. Diptotic nouns are called in Arabic *ġayr munṣarif* 'not free to move', since they lack part of the alterability that is inherent in nouns. According to the Arabic grammarians, the main principle is that if a noun deviates from the unmarked (i.e. singular, masculine, indefinite) state in more than one way, it resembles a verb and therefore loses part of its declensional rights. These deviations are the so-called *mawāniʿ aṣ-ṣarf* 'the preventing factors of complete declension', for instance, when a noun is definite, plural, feminine, a proper name, of foreign origin, an epithet, or when it has a verbal pattern. On this basis, words like *yazīdu* 'Yazīd' [name, verbal pattern], *'ibrāhīmu* 'Abraham' [name, foreign origin] and the comparative *'afʿalu* [epithet, verbal pattern] are assigned to the category of the diptotic nouns.

In Arabic grammatical theory, diptotic nouns are fundamentally different from nouns that in their surface form do not exhibit all case endings. This occurs in the so-called weak nouns, i.e. nouns containing one of the glides *w*, *y* or *'alif*. In these nouns, morphonological rules may produce a merger of case endings, e.g. *qāḍin* 'judge', with genitive *qāḍin*, accusative *qāḍiyan*; or *'afʿan* 'viper', with genitive and accusative both *'afʿan*. The grammarians derive these surface forms from an underlying form, on which all three case endings are visible: /qa"ḍiyun/, /qa"ḍiyin/, /qa"ḍiyan/; /'afʿayun/, /'afʿayin/, /'afʿayan/. According to them, the reason for these specific changes is that the speakers of Arabic dislike combinations of the vowels *i* and *u* or of two *a*'s with the glide *y*, which they find too 'heavy' to pronounce.

Apart from the case endings and the nunation, nouns may undergo morphological alterations, i.e. changes in their form that are not caused by a governing word. The most frequent alteration consists in the category of number: nouns may become dual or plural. The dual number of nouns is formed with suffixes, in the masculine *-āni* for the nominative, *-ayni* for the genitive/accusative; in the feminine *-atāni/-atayni*. In the plural, we have to distinguish between a declension with suffixes (the so-called sound plural) and a declension by pattern modification (the so-called broken plural). The sound plural suffixes are *-ūna* for the nominative, *-īna* for the genitive/accusative; in the feminine nouns, the suffixes are *-ātun/-ātin*. The sound plural is used almost exclusively for animate plurals and certain adjectives, as well as for the participles.

Because of the above-mentioned principle (p. 76) of one-morph-one-meaning, the segmentation of the dual and plural endings constituted a major problem for the Arabic grammarians. Take, for instance, the form *zaydūna* 'Zayds', genitive/accusative *zaydīna*: in the morph-by-morph segmentation of the Arabic grammarians, this becomes |zayd-u-w-n-a|, |zayd-i-y-n-a|. The /n/ is analysed as a compensation for the fact that plural nouns do not have nunation, which is why they receive an /n/ that disappears as soon as the word is followed by a genitive (*zaydū l-madīnati* 'the Zayds of the city'). The vowel /a/ at the end is necessitated by the consonant cluster that arises with /-w-n/ at the end of the word. The real problems are the vowels /u/, /i/ and the glides /w/, /y/: they share between them the double function of indicating plurality and nominative case, but it is impossible to assign either function to one of them alone. The linguistic model followed by the grammarians did not allow them to posit combined morphs |-uw-|, |-iy-| with a double function. They resorted, therefore, to other solutions, for instance, by assigning the function of plural morph to the glides /w/, /y/ and positing an underlying, virtual case ending that was deleted in the surface form (for instance, /zayd-uw-u-na/ → [zayd-ū-na]). Another solution was to deny the existence of case endings in the dual and the plural by calling the glides *dalā'il ʿalā l-'iʿrāb* 'markers of the declension', rather than real declensional endings. Either solution led to new complications within the framework of Arabic morphological theory.

The second type of plural is that of the broken or internal plural. The term 'broken plural' stems from the Arabic tradition, which calls these plurals *ǧamʿ mukassar*, referring to the breaking-up of the consonant pattern by different vowels. Of all Semitic languages, Arabic exhibits the largest expansion of the system of broken plurals (cf. above, Chapter 2, p. 16). There are more than thirty-six patterns for plurals, and, while it is sometimes possible to guess which plural pattern belongs to which singular pattern, one is as often wrong as right. In this domain, the grammarians did not proceed beyond an inventory of the patterns without making an attempt to formulate rules for the plural formation of classes of singular nouns.

6.3.2 The Verb

The second part of speech is the verb (*fiʿl*). The verbal system of Arabic has a two-way distinction of a prefix and a suffix conjugation, traditionally called in Western grammars the imperfect and the perfect. The opposition between these two verbal forms has been interpreted in different ways: past/non-past, perfective/imperfective, completed/uncompleted. Since the suffix conjugation usually denotes both past tense and perfective aspect, some scholars propose a mixed aspectual/temporal opposition. Others point out that for the prefix conjugation to denote the imperfective aspect in the past it needs a past marker (*kuntu ʾafʿalu*), so that the basic opposition must be aspectual.

For the Arabic grammarians, the verb's main feature was the indication of time: already in Sībawayhi's definition (see above, p. 77), three tenses are distinguished, namely past, present and future, which are expressed by only two verbal forms, called by him *māḍī* 'past' and *muḍāriʿ* 'resembling'. The latter term refers to the resemblance of the imperfect verb to the noun, which is the cause of its declension. Later grammarians called the prefix conjugation *mustaqbal* 'future' and denied the existence of a special form for the physical present. It remains surprising that with only two verbal forms the grammarians thought in terms of a temporal tripartition; and foreign influence, for instance from Greek philosophy, is not to be excluded in this case. In Western grammars, verbs are said to be conjugated, and the conjugation of the Arabic verb is represented in the same way as that of the Greek and Latin verb, as in Table 6.2.

We have seen above that the analysis of verbal forms by the Arabic grammarians was quite different: they regarded the forms in Tables 6.2 and 6.3 as combinations of a verb and a pronoun. A form such as *ḍarabtu* 'I have hit' is analysed by them as the verb *ḍaraba* with the bound pronoun of the first person singular *-tu*; *ḍarabū* is the same verb *ḍaraba* with the pronoun of the third person masculine plural *-w*. The form *ḍaraba* itself is ambiguous: in a verbal sentence it is the verbal form, but in a nominal sentence it is the verbal form with the zero pronoun for the third person masculine singular (cf. above, p. 81); likewise, the form *ḍarabat* is either the verb with a feminine marker *-t*, or the verb with the feminine marker and a zero pronoun.

There are three morphological types of the perfect, *faʿala, faʿila, faʿula*. These correlate with three patterns of the imperfect verb, *yafʿalu, yafʿilu, yafʿulu*. The imperfect patterns are derived from the perfect; they consist of a prefix, the verbal stem and an ending. The verbal stem in the imperfect has the form

CCvC, in which the first radical is vowelless and the second radical has a vowel that correlates with the vowel of the perfect. The underlying form is CvCvC like the perfect, but in combination with the prefix and the ending this would produce a non-allowed form with a sequence of four Cv's, hence the deletion of the first vowel (**ya-ḍa-ri-bu* > *yaḍribu*). According to the grammarians, the derivation of the imperfect from *faʿila* and *faʿula* perfects is rule-bound: they always have an imperfect *yafʿalu* and *yafʿulu*, respectively. In the case of *faʿala*, the vowel of the imperfect is either *u* or *i*: here the correlation is *samāʿī* 'based on hearing', in other words, it has to be learnt from the speakers and cannot be predicted. Those *faʿala* verbs that have a guttural as second or third radical, e.g. *zaraʿa* 'to sow', have a regular (*qiyāsī*) imperfect with *a*, *yazraʿu*. The endings *-u*/*-a*/*-o* of the imperfect verb are case endings (cf. above, p. 79). Finally, the prefixes of the imperfect cannot be pronouns, since they co-occur with nominal agents, as in *yaḍribu zaydun* 'Zayd hits'. Consequently, they are to be regarded as some kind of markers (*dalāʾil*) that have no independent status like the pronouns.

When a verb contains one of the glides *w* or *y*, it is commonly known as a weak verb (*muʿtall*). For this class of verbs, the grammarians set up a number of

'to hit'		singular	dual	plural
perfect	1st	*ḍarabtu*		*ḍarabnā*
	2nd masc.	*ḍarabta*		*ḍarabtum*
			ḍarabtumā	
	2nd fem.	*ḍarabti*	*ḍarabtunna*	
	3rd masc.	*ḍaraba*	*ḍarabā*	*ḍarabū*
	3rd fem.	*ḍarabat*	*ḍarabatā*	*ḍarabna*

Table 6.2 The conjugation of the perfect verb.

		indicative	subjunctive	jussive
singular	1	*ʾaḍribu*	*ʾaḍriba*	*ʾaḍrib*
	2m	*taḍribu*	*taḍriba*	*taḍrib*
	2f	*taḍribīna*	*taḍribī*	*taḍribī*
	3m	*yaḍribu*	*yaḍriba*	*yaḍrib*
	3f	*taḍribu*	*taḍriba*	*taḍrib*
dual	2	*taḍribāni*	*taḍribā*	*taḍribā*
	3m	*yaḍribāni*	*yaḍribā*	*yaḍribā*
	3f	*taḍribāni*	*taḍribā*	*taḍribā*
plural	1	*naḍribu*	*naḍriba*	*naḍrib*
	2m	*taḍribūna*	*taḍribū*	*taḍribū*
	2f	*taḍribna*	*taḍribna*	*taḍribna*
	3m	*yaḍribūna*	*yaḍribū*	*yaḍribū*
	3f	*yaḍribna*	*yaḍribna*	*yaḍribna*

Table 6.3 The conjugation of the imperfect verb.

morphological and phonological rules to explain the various changes that affect them. Morphologically, they patterned weak verbs on the sound verbs, and by reconstructing underlying forms they managed to achieve greater symmetry. For the hollow verbs (verbs in which the medial radical is *w* or *y*), for instance, they reconstructed the medial radical by referring to morphologically-related words: *qāla* 'to say' is related to *qawl* 'speech', *sāra* 'to go' to *sayr* 'journey', and *ẖāfa* 'to fear' to *ẖawf* 'fear', therefore their radicals are *q-w-l, s-y-r* and *ẖ-w-f* respectively. Their next step was to determine to which perfect pattern these verbs belonged on the basis of the underlying forms of the imperfect **yaqwulu*, **yasyiru*, and **yaẖwafu*. The first two must come from a perfect *faʿala* (*yaqwulu* cannot come from *faʿila*, for then it would have an imperfect *yafʿalu*, and it cannot come from *faʿula*, since that pattern is reserved for intransitive verbs; for **yasyiru* the only possibility is *faʿala*). But **yaẖwafu* must come from **ẖawifa*, since otherwise the imperfect pattern *yafʿalu* would be inexplicable.

The next step was the explanation of the phonological changes: how do we come from **yaqwulu* and so on to *yaqūlu* and so on? We cannot go into all the details of the intricate system of rules set up by the grammarians and will have to limit ourselves to some examples (an extensive analysis of all weak forms, including the perfect forms such as *qultu, sirtu, ẖiftu*, will be found in Bohas and Guillaume 1984). One of the first rules states that a combination of /a/ followed by /w/ or /y/ plus a vowel is changed into *'alif* /"/, an abstract element on the underlying level, thus /qawama/ → /qa"ma/, which is realised phonetically as [qāma] (cf. below, p. 90), likewise /sayara/ → /sa"ra/ and /ẖawifa/ → /ẖa"fa/.

A second rule changes the order of the vowels and the glides for ease of pronunciation, so that, for instance, /yaqwulu/ becomes /yaquwlu/, and /yasyiru/ becomes /yasiyru/. A third rule states that there is a special relationship between /i/ and /y/, /u/ and /w/, and /a/ and /"/; therefore, after a vowel, glides often change into the related glide of the vowel, e.g. /iw/ → /iy/, /uy/ → /uw/, as in the words /miwqa"t/ → /miyqa"t/ and /muysir/ → /muwsir/. In the case of the weak verbs, this rule is invoked to explain derivations such as the imperfect of *ẖāfa*: /yaẖwafu/ → /yaẖawfu/ → /yaẖa"fu/.

In the system of phonological rules with which the Arabic grammarians operated, one of the most important principles was that of the relative weight of

	underlying	3rd person perfect	3rd person imperfect	1st person imperfect
Iw	*waʿada*	*waʿada*	*yaʿidu*	*waʿadtu*
IIw	*qawama*	*qāma*	*yaqūmu*	*qumtu*
	ẖawifa	*ẖāfa*	*yaẖāfu*	*ẖiftu*
IIy	*sayara*	*sāra*	*yasīru*	*sirtu*
IIIw	*daʿawa*	*daʿā*	*yadʿū*	*daʿawtu*
IIIy	*mašaya*	*mašā*	*yamšī*	*mašaytu*
	laqiya	*laqiya*	*yalqā*	*laqītu*

Table 6.4 The classes of weak verbs.

the phonemes of the language. They set up a hierarchy that went from the lightest elements, the vowels, via the glides to the consonants. Within the class of the vowels, they determined the following order: /a/ < /i/ < /u/. In the explanation of phonological changes, this relative order of the phonemes played an important role, since the speakers of the language were credited with an aversion to combinations that were too heavy. Thus, for instance, the combination /-iya-/ is possible, because it goes from heavy to light, whereas the combination /-iyu-/ is regarded as too heavy and therefore impermissible because it contains a passage from a heavy to a heavier element (e.g. in /qa"ḍiyu/ 'judge', which therefore becomes /qa"ḍiy/).

Among the derivational alterations of the verb are the so-called verbal measures. These involve additions to the verbal stem, with a concomitant modification of the lexical meaning of the verb. In some cases the modification is productive, but in the majority of cases it has become lexically fixed. As examples, we may quote *kataba* 'to write', *’aktaba* 'to force someone to write' [causative], *takātaba* 'to correspond' [reciprocal]; *kasara* 'to break', *kassara* 'to shatter' [intensive], *inkasara* 'to break' [intransitive]; *ḥarraka* 'to move' [transitive], *taḥarraka* 'to move' [intransitive]; *ġafara* 'to forgive', *istaġfara* 'to ask forgiveness'; *ǧamaʿa* 'to collect', *iǧtamaʿa* 'to assemble' [reflexive]. Traditionally, Western grammars distinguish ten measures; infrequently one finds other measures as well, up to sixteen. The distinction of numbered measures is a Western innovation, probably introduced by Erpenius. The Arabic grammarians regarded the verbal measures as part of the derivational morphology. They distinguished between three primary augmented verbal measures, *’afʿala*, *faʿʿala* and *fāʿala*, each with its own concomitant meaning. Each of these measures could receive an additional augment *t* or *n* in order to express the meaning of *muṭāwaʿa*, reflexivity or medial voice: *faʿʿala* → *tafaʿʿala*; *fāʿala* → *tafāʿala*; *faʿala* → *iftaʿala*; *faʿala*/*’afʿala* → *infaʿala*. What mattered to them was the fact that the augment (*ziyāda*) correlated with an additional meaning, e.g. intensivity; they were not concerned with the precise analysis of this meaning.

6.4 PHONOLOGY

Although Arabic grammarians were not concerned with phonetic analysis as such, they usually included an elementary description of the speech-sounds in their treatises. In the introduction to the first Arabic dictionary, al-H̲alīl's *Kitāb al-ʿayn*, the consonants are classified according to their place of articulation (*maẖraǧ*). Al-H̲alīl identifies each group of consonants with a collective term, but he does not differentiate between the active and the passive articulator (*Kitāb al-ʿayn* I, ed. Mahdī al-Maẖzūmī and ’Ibrāhīm as-Sāmarrā’ī, Beirut, 1988, p. 58):

ḥalqiyya 'consonants of the throat': *h*, *ʿ*, *ḥ*, *ẖ*, *ġ*
lahawiyya 'consonants of the velum': *q*, *k*
šaǧriyya 'consonants of the palate': *ǧ*, *š*, *ḍ*
’asaliyya 'consonants of the tongue-tip': *ṣ*, *s*, *z*
niṭʿiyya 'consonants of the prepalate': *ṭ*, *t*, *d*
liṯawiyya 'consonants of the gums': *ḏ̣*, *ḏ*, *ṯ*

> *d̲alaqiyya* 'consonants of the tongue-apex': *r, l, n*
> *šafawiyya* 'consonants of the lips': *f, b, m*
> *hawā'iyya* 'consonants of the air': *y, w,* " (*'alif*), '

In Sībawayhi's *Kitāb* (II, p. 405), a more detailed description of the various places of articulation is given, in which Sībawayhi corrects al-H̲alīl's classification in some points and identifies the active and the passive articulator of each group of consonants. In most respects, this classification is remarkably similar to our own classification of the phonemic inventory of Arabic (see above, p. 20).

One of the reasons why the Arabic grammarians concerned themselves with the classification of the consonants is that this classification played an important role in the analysis of roots. In Semitic languages, certain constraints operate in verbal root-formation to avoid the co-occurrence of similar consonants. A general principle states that the first two radicals of the triliteral root may not be identical, nor homorganic (belonging to the same articulatory class), while the last two radicals may be identical, but not homorganic; the first and the third radical usually obey the same principle. Thus, for instance, there are no roots in Arabic beginning with *b-m-* (two bilabials) or *ǧ-k-* (two velars; *ǧ* deriving from **g*, cf. above, p. 21); likewise, there are roots like *m-d-d*, but no roots like *m-d-t* (two dentals). In their formulation of these constraints, the Arabic grammarians set up articulatory classes which extended over adjacent places of articulation. Thus, for instance, a root like *h̲-ḥ-q* is inadmissible because the three consonants belong to the same 'articulatory class'. Obviously, for the formulation of the constraints on root-building, the Arabic grammarians needed articulatory terms to describe the nature of consonants. In the analysis of loanwords, the grammarians formulated similar constraints. One of their most interesting observations is that there are no quadriliteral Arabic roots that do not contain at least one of the consonants *b, f, m, r, n, l*, which are called by al-H̲alīl collectively *d̲alaqiyya*.

In some respects, the classification of the consonants by the Arabic grammarians differs from the Western standard account. Their main classification of the consonants according to manner of articulation was that between *mahmūsa* 'whispered' (*h, ḥ, h̲, k, š, t, ṣ, s, t̲, f*) and *mağhūra* 'spoken aloud' (*b, ǧ, d, r, l, m, n, w, y, ḍ, ḏ̣, ṭ, q,* ʿ, "). In describing these two categories, Sībawayhi (*Kitāb* II, p. 405) says that in the *mağhūra* consonants

> the pressure is fully applied at the place of articulation and the breath is impeded from flowing through till the pressure is completed and the sound goes on. (*'ušbiʿa l-iʿtimād fī mawḍiʿihi wa-muniʿa n-nafas 'an yağriya maʿahu ḥattā yanqaḍiya l-iʿtimād ʿalayhi wa-yağriya ṣ-ṣawt*)

The *mahmūsa* consonants are described as follows:

> the pressure is weakly applied at the place of articulation so that the breath flows freely with it. (*'uḍʿifa l-iʿtimād fī mawḍiʿihi ḥattā ğarā n-nafas maʿahu*)

Elsewhere, he adds that in the case of the *mağhūra* consonants the articulation is accompanied by a *ṣawt fī ṣ-ṣadr* 'sound in the breast', apparently in an effort to account for the difference in sound between voiced and voiceless consonants. He could not refer to the action of the vocal cords as such, since their function was unknown at the time (they were not discovered until the sixteenth century). The inclusion of the *ṭ* and the *q* in the category of the *mağhūra* may seem surprising, since these are usually classified as voiceless consonants, which is how they are realised in Modern Standard Arabic. On the basis of historical data (cf. above, p. 21) it is not unreasonable, however, to suppose that in Sībawayhi's time these two consonants were indeed voiced. In most of the modern Bedouin dialects, the *q* is still realised as [g] (cf. below, Chapter 9, p. 143).

A third consonant whose description by Sībawayhi differs from the modern pronunciation is the *ḍād*. The unique character of this consonant is borne out by the fact that the grammarians called the Arabic language 'the language of the *ḍād*' (*luġat aḍ-ḍād*), apparently believing that only an Arab would be able to pronounce this sound. The modern realisation of the *ḍād* is that of an emphatic *ḍ*, yet there is reason to believe that in Classical Arabic it was a lateral consonant $ḍ^l$ (cf. above, p. 21). In Akkadian, the name of the Arabic god *Ruḍā'* was transcribed as *Ruldā'u* or *Rulṭā'*, and early loans from Arabic in Spanish (e.g. *alcalde* 'mayor' < *al-qāḍī*) and in Malaysian languages (e.g. in Bahasa Indonesia, *ridla* as a spelling variant of *ridha, ridza* 'God's blessing' < *riḍā*) also exhibit traces of this lateral character of the *ḍād*. In itself the evidence of loans can never be conclusive, but it is supported by Sībawayhi's description (*Kitāb* II, p. 405) of the place of articulation of the *ḍād*, which he says is 'between the first part of the side of the tongue and the adjoining molars' (*min bayna 'awwal ḥāfat al-lisān wa-mā yalīhi min al-'aḍrās*).

Although the Arabic grammarians were not interested in phonetics as such, they did distinguish a number of allophones, some of them permissible variants, others incorrect realisations of the phonemes of Arabic. In Classical Arabic, in certain contexts, the consonants *r* and *l*, for instance, could have an emphatic allophone (e.g. in the name of God after a back vowel: *waḷḷāhi* as against *billāhi*). Such emphatic realisations are called by the Arabic grammarians *mufaḫḫam*. Impermissible allophones refer to deviations in the pronunciation of Arabic by non-native speakers, for instance 'the *kāf* between the *ğīm* and the *kāf*' (i.e. [č]), 'the *ğīm* that is as the *šīn*' (i.e. [ž]) and 'the *bā'* that is as the *fā'*' (i.e. [v]).

Arabic script, like most Semitic scripts, does not represent the vowels in writing. In Classical Arabic, there are only three vowels, *a*, *i* and *u*. The descriptions of the grammarians indicate, however, that there were various allophones, as in the Modern Standard realisation. The *a* has the allophone [æ] in emphatic, non-pharyngal contexts; this pronunciation is usually called *'imāla* 'leaning [towards an anterior realisation]'; in emphatic contexts the allophone is [ɐ] (*tafḫīm*). The *i* has an allophone in emphatic contexts that was probably a centralised high [y]. It is not entirely clear why the grammarians occupied themselves with the allophones of the vowels, which are irrelevant for the morphological structure of the words. One possible explanation may be that the rules for *'imāla* are not entirely phonological in nature, but depend at least in part on the morphological context.

With regard to the long vowels, the relevance of phonological analysis for morphology is much more obvious. Arabic script indicates what we call 'long vowels' with an orthographic device, by writing the short vowels together with one of the so-called *matres lectionis*, i.e. the three letters *wāw*, *yā'* and *'alif* (cf. above, p. 30). According to the Arabic grammarians, the long vowels are to be analysed as combinations of a short vowel and a glide (*ḥarf al-līn wa-l-madd*). The three glides which they distinguish are *w*, *y* and an abstract element called *'alif*, indicated here with the sign /"/. Thus, for instance, *sūdun* 'black [plural]' is represented as /suwdun/, *bīḍun* 'white [plural]' as /biyḍun/, *dārun* 'house' as /da"run/. In this analysis, the glide *'alif* is a purely abstract element, which does not have any phonetic status but serves purely as an element in the underlying phonological structure. Since the names of the phonemic glides are identical with those of the letter signs that are used to indicate the long vowels in the script, it has sometimes been assumed that the analysis of the Arabic grammarians was based on a confusion between letters and phonemes; but this is certainly wrong. The main argument for their analysis was its advantage in the analysis of word structure: compare, for instance, /suwdun/ with the word /ḥumrun/ 'red [plural]', which has the same structure. This analysis forms the basis for their explanation of the changes in the weak verbs (cf. above, p. 85).

Finally, there is one topic that is completely missing in Arabic linguistic treatises, that of stress. In Classical Arabic, stress is not phonemic: there are no two words that are distinguished solely by a difference in stress. It is, therefore, understandable that the Arabic grammarians did not feel the need to discuss stress as a feature of Arabic. Stress must have existed as a prosodic feature in speech, but it is difficult to say where it fell in the word. Usually it is assumed that in Arabic stress always falls on the first closed syllable from the end, barring the final, and never before the antepenultimate: *ḥúblā*, *ḍa'ífun*, *qátala*, *ḍā́ribun*, but *madrásatun* (the so-called *Dreisilbengesetz* 'law of three syllables'). This is the practice that is generally followed in Western manuals of Arabic. In the modern realisation of Classical Arabic, stress rules vary according to the rules of the local vernacular.

FURTHER READING

There is a whole range of grammars of Classical Arabic in the Western philological tradition, although a complete, modern reference grammar of the Classical language is still sorely missed. A classic is Howell (1883–1911); on this grammar, Caspari (1887; this is the fifth edition, revised by A. Müller) is based, which in its turn formed the basis for the best available grammar, W. Wright (1859–62), usually consulted in the revised third edition by Robertson Smith and de Goeje (1896–8, numerous re-editions). In French, the best grammar is Blachère and Gaudefroy-Demombynes (1952). Shorter (teaching) grammars are Brockelmann, revised by Fleischhammer (1965), and Blachère (1961); the best modern grammar of this type is Fischer (1972). Detailed treatment of the morphology and phonology of Classical Arabic with numerous references to the grammatical tradition is in Fleisch (1961, 1979) and Roman (1983). A sketch of the Classical language is given in Beeston (1968), Fleisch (1968) and Denz (1982). For grammatical descriptions of Modern Standard Arabic and for course books, see Chapter 11, p. 187.

The lexicon of Classical Arabic still remains to a large extent unexplored. For detailed information, research depends on the indigenous Arabic dictionaries, in particular the *Lisān al-ʿarab* of Ibn Manẓūr (d. 711/1311). About the development of lexicography in Islam, see Haywood (1965) and Wild (1965; about al-Ḫalīl ibn ʾAḥmad); handbook treatment is in Sezgin (1982). The beginnings of modern lexicography in the Middle East are described by Sawaie (1987, 1990). The Western Orientalist dictionaries of the Classical Arabic language that were written in the seventeenth and eighteenth centuries were superseded by Lane (1863–93); his dictionary included all the available information from the Arabic sources, but remained incomplete (up to the letter *qāf*). Dozy (1881) was intended as a supplement, with special emphasis on the vocabulary of the North African and Andalusian sources. In 1957, the *Deutsche Morgenländische Gesellschaft* began to work on a new dictionary of the Classical Arabic language (*WKAS*), starting with the letter *kāf*; in the meantime, this dictionary has reached the letter *mīm* (on the *WKAS*, see Gätje 1985). In France, Blachère, Chouémi and Denizeau (1964–) started their large Arabic–English–French dictionary with the letter *ʾalif*. The lexicon of the *ḥadīṯ* literature may be studied with the help of the index that was started by Wensinck (*Concordances*). The only dictionary of the Qurʾānic lexicon is the outdated Penrice (1873). For the lexicon of the translation literature, see Endreß and Gutas (1992–), in course of publication. Of the smaller dictionaries of the Classical language, Hava's (1964) Arabic–English dictionary deserves to be mentioned.

For the phonetic and phonological structure of Classical Arabic, Cantineau (1960) is still one of the best studies. Fleisch's *Traité de philologie arabe* in two volumes (1961, 1979) analyses the morphological structure of the language, with observations about its Semitic setting and the indigenous system of grammar. Reckendorff's manuals of Arabic syntax (1895–8, 1921) are still valuable research tools. Nöldeke's studies on Arabic grammar (1897) contain important additions to the existing grammars; they were re-edited by Spitaler together with Nöldeke's marginal notes (1963).

For the indigenous grammatical system, Carter (1981) is recommended as a first introduction. This book is a commentary on a late grammatical treatise, the *ʾĀǧurrūmiyya*, and its notes touch on virtually every aspect of Arabic grammar. A general survey of the history of the Arabic grammatical tradition is Ḍayf (1968); handbook treatment is in Sezgin (1984); for shorter accounts see Versteegh (1987) and Carter (1990). A synthetic view of the theories of the grammarians is given by Bohas, Guillaume and Kouloughli (1990). A lucid analysis of the phonological and (mor)phonological principles of the Arabic grammarians is Bohas and Guillaume (1984), one of the best studies of the Arabic theory of grammar. For the grammarians' methodological presuppositions, see the commentary on az-Zaǧǧāǧī's *ʾĪḍāḥ* (Versteegh 1995). The thorny question of the comparison between Arabic grammar and modern Western linguistics is dealt with admirably by Owens (1988). On the notion of 'underlying level' in Arabic grammar, see Versteegh (1994).

On Sībawayhi's theory of grammar, there is a large literature. The text of the *Kitāb* was published by Derenbourg (2 vols, Paris, 1881–9, repr. Hildesheim, 1970), which formed the basis for both the Bulaq edition (2 vols, AH 1316, repr. Baghdad, n.d.) and the edition by ʿAbd as-Salām Muḥammad Hārūn (5 vols, Cairo, 1966–77). There is an older German translation by Jahn (2 vols, Berlin, 1895–1900, repr. Hildesheim, 1961). Sībawayhi's grammatical system is analysed by Mosel (1975). An index of his grammatical terminology was compiled by Troupeau (1976). For the status of the *Kitāb* as a book, see Schoeler (1989a). The early textual history of the *Kitāb* and its reception are dealt with by Humbert (1995) and Bernards (1997).

Special mention should be made of a few studies on methodological issues: Bohas (1981, 1985) deals with the phonological argumentation of the Arabic grammarians; Ayoub and Bohas (1983) treat the Arabic grammarians' analysis of sentence structure; in Versteegh (1985) the structure of morphological segmentation is analysed; the nature of the case endings in Arabic linguistic theory is discussed by Ermers (1995). On the epistemology of the Arabic grammarians see Suleiman (1999).

The literature on the Arabic verbal system is extensive: see, for example, Aartun (1963), Fleisch (1979: 169–206) and Nebes (1982). An interesting treatment of aspect and tense in Arabic in the framework of functional grammar is in Cuvalay (1996). On the problem of the weak roots in Semitic and in Arabic, see Voigt (1988). On the system of the verbal measures, see Leemhuis (1977); Saad (1982) discusses the relations between transitivity and the causative measure and the passive.

On the phonetic/phonological theories of Sībawayhi, see Al-Nassir (1993); on Arabic phonetics in general, see Bravmann (1934); on the interpretation of the notions *mağhūra*/*mahmūsa*, see Blanc (1967) and Fleisch (1958). Ibn Ğinnī's theories are dealt with by Bakalla (1982); a modern version of this theory is found in Bohas' publications on the Arabic lexicon (1993, 1995). There is an extensive literature on the nature of Arabic *ḍād*: see, for example, Cantineau (1960: 54–6), Versteegh (1999). On the pronunciation of the *qāf* and the split between /q/ and /g/, see Blanc (1969). The incompatibility of phonemes within Semitic roots is analysed by Greenberg (1950), with comprehensive tables of all existing verbal roots in Arabic. On the problem of stress in Classical Arabic, see Birkeland (1954) and Janssens (1972).

7
The Emergence of New Arabic

7.1 THE LINGUISTIC SITUATION IN THE ISLAMIC EMPIRE

The period of the Islamic conquests immediately after the death of the Prophet in 10/632 constituted a drastic change in the history of the Arabic language. Within a few decades, speakers of Arabic spread over an enormous territory and imposed their language on the inhabitants of the conquered countries. Even though speakers of Arabic had been resident in Syria and Egypt before Islam (see above, Chapter 3), their language had never been a language of prestige outside the peninsula, and consequently there had never been an incentive for non-Arabs in these countries to learn their language. In this chapter, we shall look at the consequences of the process of arabicisation after the conquests for the structure of the language. First, we shall describe the linguistic situation in the conquered territories, then the changes in the language will be discussed. Finally, we shall look into the explanations that have been advanced for these changes.

The historical details of the conquests are known from the detailed accounts of the Muslim historians, but much less is known about the process of arabicisation. In the earliest stages of the conquests, the military efforts of the Islamic authorities in Medina were aimed at the political control of the Arabic-speaking tribes, first within the peninsula during the so-called *ridda*-wars, and then outside the peninsula, where since time immemorial Arabic-speaking tribes had roamed the Syrian desert and in Iraq. The initial motive behind the conquests may have been the idea that all Arabic-speaking peoples should be united under Islamic domination, while the conquest of the neighbouring sedentary areas occurred more or less as an afterthought.

Because of the lack of relevant documents, it is hard to tell what the rate of arabicisation was, and in most cases we can only make a guess as to the period of time that was needed for the adoption of Arabic as the main language of the empire. We do know that arabicisation was much more complete and possibly even progressed at a faster rate than the process of islamisation. There were probably material advantages in conversion to Islam, for instance, the dispensation of the poll-tax (*ǧizya*) and the loss of the minority status as *ḏimmī*, but on the whole the prevailing tolerance on the part of the Muslims towards Christians and Jews did not generate an urgent need to convert to Islam. As a result, language became a binding factor for the Islamic empire to a far greater degree than religion. Even nowadays there are large groups of Christians, and to a lesser degree Jews, in the Arabic-speaking countries whose mother tongue is Arabic just like that of their Muslim neighbours.

The linguistic situation in the incipient Islamic empire is relatively well known. In the Arabian peninsula, the only 'foreign' language which the Arabs encountered was South Arabian. The language was no longer used in its epigraphic form, but some varieties must have remained in use as a colloquial language, since in a few linguistic pockets South Arabian languages are still spoken today by some tens of thousands of speakers, in the provinces of Mahra (Yemen) and Ẓafār (Oman) and on the island of Suquṭra. Six different languages have been identified so far (Mehri, Ḥarsūsī, Baṭḥarī, Ǧibbālī, Soqoṭrī and Hobyōt), all of them incomprehensible for a speaker of Arabic. We have seen above (p. 38) that in al-Hamdānī's (d. 334/946) description of the linguistic situation in the peninsula they are characterised as *ġutm* 'incorrect, indistinct' and distinguished from varieties of Arabic that had been influenced by South Arabian. The modern South Arabian languages probably do not derive directly from the Old South Arabian language, but represent isolated forms that were never touched by Arabic influence until the modern period.

In Iraq, most of the population spoke Aramaic, the *lingua franca* of the area. Middle Persian (Pahlavi) was used as an administrative language in the regions under Sasanian control. Arabic was spoken by a sizeable portion of the population, most of them nomadic tribes who roamed the desert areas of Iraq. Some of the Arabic tribes had become sedentary, such as the Banū Tanūẖ, who inhabited an entire quarter of the city of Aleppo at the eve of the conquest. The majority of these tribes had converted to Christianity a long time ago, in particular those tribes who formed the state of al-Ḥīra, which the Persian kings used as a buffer between themselves and the Bedouin tribes of Arabia. Some of the tribes of North and East Arabia, even though their core area lay within the peninsula, had frequent contacts with the Mesopotamian tribes.

In Syria, Greek remained in use for some time as the language of administration, but was replaced by Arabic at the end of the first century of the Hiǧra. Syriac continued to be used by the Christians as a spoken language until the eighth century CE, and as a literary language until the fourteenth century. In its spoken form, it has remained in use in a few isolated linguistic pockets: Western Aramaic in the village of Ma'lūla in the mountains of the Antilebanon; Central Aramaic or Ṭurōyo in Ṭūr 'Abdīn in Western Kurdistan. Eastern Aramaic, usually called Assyrian or Neo-Syriac, is still spoken by approximately 300,000 speakers in Iran, Turkey and Iraq, and by immigrants from Iraq in Syria and the Caucasus. Almost all of them belong to a Christian community.

The history of Persian is a special case. During the first century of Islamic rule, the Middle Persian language (Pahlavi) was still used as an administrative language, but after the reforms of 'Abd al-Malik it was replaced by Arabic, in H̲urāsān at a somewhat later date, 124/741, than in Western Iran. After that, it remained in use only as a written language in the circles of the Mazdaean priests, and Arabic reigned supreme as the administrative, literary and religious language. By the third/ninth century, Arabic had become the language of culture and literature. A large part of the relevant Iranian literature had been translated into Arabic, and Persian intellectuals, even when they proclaimed their ethnic distinctness in the movement of the *Šu'ūbiyya*, accepted Arabic as the natural language of Iranian culture.

The spoken language of the Iranian provinces was a different matter, however.

Arabic had been the language of the Arab settlers in some of the towns and the language of the Arab tribes that came to live in Ḫurāsān. But, by the eighth century, these Arabic-speaking immigrants had taken over the colloquial language of the majority of the population, the dialect that was known as Darī or Parsī-i darī that had been in use as the spoken language of the court in Sasanian Iran and that represented the colloquial register of Middle Persian. With the spread of Islam, Darī was adopted by an increasing number of people and eventually ousted all the other local dialects. By the ninth century, most inhabitants of the Iranian provinces spoke Darī, albeit with a measure of regional variation. We shall see below that, starting at the courts of some of the independent Eastern dynasties, Persian in its colloquial form regained its position as a language of literature during the ninth and tenth centuries (cf. Chapter 14, p. 232).

In Egypt, as in Syria, Greek was the language of a small, hellenised elite, and besides it served as the language of administration. The mass of the population spoke Coptic, which had become a literary language by the ninth century, when the Bible was translated into the Sahidic dialect of Coptic in Upper Egypt. It served as a religious language for the common believer, who certainly did not understand Greek. When ʿAmr ibn al-ʿĀṣ started the conquest of Egypt in 640 with a small group of 4,000 soldiers – later reinforced with an additional 12,000 – he followed the pattern of the settlement policy in Iraq and made the military camp of al-Fusṭāṭ his centre of administration. Very soon, Copts came to live here, too, and the contacts between Coptic-speaking inhabitants and Arabic-speaking garrisons all over the country increased. Once the country had been incorporated into the Islamic empire, further migration of Arabian tribes took place on an irregular basis.

During the early centuries of Islamic domination of the country, Coptic patriarchs had to communicate with the Arab conquerors through interpreters, but by the tenth century the Coptic bishop Severus of Eshmunein, author of a history of the patriarchs, complained that most of the Copts no longer understood Greek or Coptic and were only able to communicate in Arabic. This probably means that in Lower Egypt all Christians had switched from Coptic to Arabic. In Upper Egypt, Coptic may have survived somewhat longer, but by the fourteenth century Coptic had become limited to a few small pockets in the countryside and to the clergy in the monasteries. Although there are some references to Coptic being spoken in a few villages up to the sixteenth century, it is generally believed that by this time the use of the language had become restricted to the liturgy in the Coptic church, as it is now. The period of Coptic/Arabic bilingualism in Lower Egypt, which lasted about two centuries, was shorter than the period of bilingualism in Syria; this may be responsible for the limited influence of the language in the Egyptian Arabic dialect (cf. pp. 106, 162). Even the number of loans from Coptic is surprisingly low.

The arabicisation of North Africa is a special case, since it took place in two distinct waves which were centuries apart in time. During the first Arab invasion of North Africa, the few urban centres which were left after the wandering of the peoples in the fourth and fifth centuries CE were occupied by the Arab armies. But the most important centre for the dissemination of Arabic culture and language became a new city, the military camp of Qayrawān, which soon grew into the most important city of North Africa. In Qayrawān, as in other urban centres, Arabic soon became the language of communication, although there are some reports according to which as late as the twelfth century there were still speakers of Romance in Gafsa and Gabes. Most of the countryside and the nomadic population of North Africa remained Berber-speaking until the second invasion in the eleventh century, when the Bedouin tribes of the Banū Sulaym and Banū Hilāl entered the Maghreb. These tribes originally came from Syria and North Arabia; they were joined by a third tribe, that of the Maʿqil, of Southern Arabian origin. They had migrated first to Egypt, but had been sent away by the Fāṭimid caliphs, no doubt because the presence of so many nomads had become a threat to Egyptian society.

The total number of Bedouin coming to North Africa was estimated by contemporary sources at one million (out of a total population of six million), but their invasion was not a single event. It took the Bedouin two years to reach Tunisia, but about 100 years to come to Algiers, and eighty more years to reach Oran. Morocco had been invaded by them somewhat earlier. Parts of the Maʿqil confederation conquered Mauritania, where their dialect is still spoken nowadays under the name of Ḥassāniyya (cf. below, p. 167). Wherever they went, the Bedouin tribes became an important military factor. They themselves were not interested in political power, but the political landscape in North Africa with its numerous dynastic quarrels enabled them to switch alliances all the time.

The result of the invasion of the Bedouin tribes was that a large part of the Berber population in the countryside took over the Arabic language. Nowadays the Berber languages are found almost exclusively in mountainous areas where, even after the second wave of arabicisation, many people continued to speak Berber. A considerable percentage of the population still speak Berber as their only or as their first language. No exact figures about the number of speakers is available, partly because of the lingering taboo on Berber language and culture (cf. below, Chapter 12, p. 205), but the usual estimates are for Morocco 40–45 per cent, for Algeria 30 per cent, for Tunisia 5 per cent and for Libya 25 per cent. In Egypt, Berber is spoken only in the small oasis of Siwa.

The conquest of North Africa was the starting point of the conquest of the Iberian peninsula and the subsequent attempt to penetrate Europe. From 711 onwards, the Arab presence in al-'Andalus, as the peninsula was called in the Arabic sources, was uninterrupted until 1492, and Arabic very soon became the administrative, religious, cultural and even colloquial language of most of Spain (cf. below Chapter 14, p. 227). The island of Malta was conquered by the Aghlabid empire in present-day Tunisia in 256/870; the further history of the Arabic language on this island will be dealt with below (Chapter 13, p. 209).

In the early stages of the conquests, Arabic was disseminated primarily from the cities, either existing ones like Damascus, or the military centres that were established all over the empire. Most contacts with the indigenous population took place in these camps, which soon grew into new cities and towns, such as Baṣra, Kūfa, al-Fusṭāṭ and Qayrawān. In these centres, the necessary contacts between conquered and conquerors in matters of taxation, trading and administration led to some kind of linguistic accommodation on the part of the conquered. In Arabic geographical literature, the difference between the speech of the sedentary population and that of the Bedouin is mentioned frequently (cf.

below, p. 131), but the only linguistic sources that we have about the kind of Arabic that was spoken between non-Arabs and Arabs are the numerous anecdotes about the speech of the early converts. The standard form of an anecdote is that a client (*mawlā*), i.e. a recently-converted non-Arab, comes to the caliph and attempts to speak in correct Arabic, without success (cf. above, p. 50). What these anecdotes document is not the actual colloquial speech of the new converts, but their efforts to adopt the standard language in certain situations. They confirm that, for the newly converted, the standard language with the declensional system was still available as a model: mistakes in the use of case endings only occur when people attempt to imitate a model in which the endings occur.

Throughout the history of Arabic philology, treatises were written about the linguistic mistakes of the common people (*laḥn al-ʿāmma*). But in spite of what the titles of these treatises might lead us to believe, they are not concerned with the colloquial language as such. Their aim is to preserve the purity of the standard language; and, while some of the mistakes which they criticise may have been caused by interference of the colloquial language, it would be wrong to assume that we can reconstruct the vernacular on the basis of this material. A few examples from a sixth/twelfth-century Andalusian treatise of this genre may suffice to demonstrate this. In his *Madḫal 'ilā taqwīm al-lisān wa-taʿlīm al-bayān* ('Introduction to the correction of speech and the teaching of eloquence'), Ibn Hišām al-Laḫmī (d. 577/1182) mentions a large number of 'mistakes' that the common people make (*yaqūlūna* ... 'they say ...') and gives the form which he regards as correct (*wa-ṣ-ṣawāb* ...): wrong vowels (*muqāmāt* instead of *maqāmāt*; *ḏihāb* instead of *ḏahāb*), wrong consonants (*mirkās* instead of *mirqās*; *mutadaʿdiʿ* instead of *mutaḍaʿḍiʿ*), inappropriate assimilations (*muštahid* instead of *muǧtahid*), wrong form of the verb (*'arsā* instead of *rasā*), noun of place instead of noun of instrument (*maġsal* instead of *miġsal*), dropping of glottal stop (*ṯār* instead of *ṯa'r*; *riyya* instead of *ri'a*), wrong construction of the numerals (*ṯalāṯ šuhūr* instead of *ṯalāṯat 'ašhur*). Some of these mistakes may have been inspired by the spoken language, but the author's main concern is with mistakes that are made in writing. Thus he also mentions cases such as *ḥalwa* (with *tā' marbūṭa*) instead of *ḥalwā* (with *'alif maqṣūra*), which in his time must have been purely a matter of orthography. The sum total of the mistakes may tell us something about the interference of the colloquial language in the use of Classical Arabic, but it does not provide a complete view of the structure of the vernacular of the time, let alone of the relative chronology of the changes.

An important source for our reconstruction of the colloquial in the early Islamic period is the so-called Middle Arabic texts, in the first place the papyri, and in the second place the more or less literary texts which contain many 'mistakes' and deviations from Classical grammar. Some of these mistakes can indeed be explained as interference by colloquial speech, but since the written medium remained the domain of the Classical language, Middle Arabic texts cannot provide us with material to study the chronology of the development of spoken Arabic. What the written texts document are changes in the norms for the standard language. A striking illustration is the use of colloquial personal suffixes in North African Middle Arabic texts. While these texts exhibit fairly often the use of the first person singular of the imperfect with *n-* (in writing *nqtl* 'I kill'), the use of *n-...-ū* (in writing *nqtlw* 'we kill') for the first person plural is much less common. It is reasonable to assume that the avoidance of the plural form is connected with the fact that in Classical Arabic such a form cannot occur in writing, whereas the singular form is at least a possible word, even though it has a different meaning in Classical Arabic. When in later texts the plural form does occur, this cannot be taken to imply that it has recently been introduced in the colloquial language, but it simply means that the norms for the written language have changed, and the form has become less stigmatised (for more details about Middle Arabic, see below, Chapter 8).

7.2 THE NEW TYPE OF ARABIC

Our main sources for the reconstruction of the historical process of emergence of a colloquial type of Arabic are the modern dialects. Terminologically, there is some confusion about the name for the new type of Arabic. The name 'New Arabic' (or 'Neo-Arabic') will be used here for the colloquial type of Arabic that was current in the early stages of the conquests and that developed into the Arabic dialects as we know them nowadays. In this terminology, the new type of Arabic is contrasted with Old Arabic, i.e. the Arabic that was used in the *Ǧāhiliyya*. As we have seen in Chapter 6, there is no general consensus about the linguistic situation in the pre-Islamic period, so that the term 'Old Arabic' is used both for the *ʿArabiyya* as the uniform language of the Bedouin tribes, the *Qur'ān* and pre-Islamic poetry, and alternatively, for the poetico-Qur'ānic koine that was used as an artificial language transcending the dialects of the Bedouin tribes. In either case, Old Arabic represents the type of Arabic that in its codified form by the grammarians became the literary and cultural language of the Arabo-Islamic empire and is usually called Classical Arabic. After the period of the conquests, Old and New Arabic coexisted in a sociolinguistic relationship that is usually called 'diglossia' (see below, Chapter 12).

Whatever our views on the linguistic situation in the pre-Islamic period, we still need an explanation for the emergence of the new type of Arabic, since even if some of the traits of this new type of Arabic were already found in the pre-Islamic dialects – such as the subject/verb agreement or the undeclined dual in the Ḥiǧāz (cf. above, Chapter 4, p. 45), or the possible disappearance of the declensional endings in the peripheral dialects in North Arabia (cf. above, p. 47) – no-one maintains that all features of the modern dialects can be traced back to the pre-Islamic period. Any theory about the emergence of the dialects must therefore account for the changes that took place after the conquests and that demarcate the new type of Arabic from the old type. At the same time, such a theory must not only explain the common features of the dialects as against the Classical standard but also provide an explanation for the numerous differences among the dialects. In the pre-Islamic period, Arabs from all over the peninsula could with relative ease communicate with each other. Nowadays, Moroccans and Iraqis, each speaking their own dialect, would find it extremely difficult to understand each other, and it is fair to say that the linguistic distance between the dialects is as large as that between the Germanic languages and the Romance languages, including Romanian, if not larger.

Before we go into the theories that have been advanced for the present-day situation of Arabic, we shall first survey the common features that characterise the dialects vis-à-vis the Classical language. No single dialect exhibits all of these features, but they may be regarded as a common denominator of the most innovative dialects in the Arab world. Generally speaking, the innovations are much more frequent in the sedentary dialects, for which Syrian Arabic has been used here in most examples, whereas the Bedouin dialects tend to be more conservative (cf. below, Chapter 9).

In the phonological system of the dialects, a number of changes have taken place:

- the glottal stop, which was already absent in West Arabic (cf. above, pp. 40, 42), has disappeared in all dialects (e.g. Classical Arabic *ra's* 'head', Syrian Arabic *rās*; Classical Arabic *mi'a* 'hundred', Syrian Arabic *mīya*).
- in the sedentary dialects, the interdental spirants have been replaced by dental occlusives (e.g. Classical Arabic *t̲alāt̲a* 'three', Syrian Arabic *tlāte*; Classical Arabic *d̲anab* 'tail', Syrian Arabic *danab*); most Bedouin dialects have preserved the interdentals.
- the two Classical Arabic phonemes /ḍ/ and /ḏ̣/ have merged into /ḍ/ in the sedentary dialects, and /ḏ̣/ in the Bedouin dialects (e.g. Classical *ḏ̣uhr* 'afternoon', Syrian Arabic *ḍəhr*).
- final short vowels have been dropped in the dialects; final long vowels have become short (e.g. *kataba/katabū* 'he wrote/they wrote', Syrian Arabic *katab/katabu*).
- stress in the Arabic dialects has become more expiratory, as shown by the frequent reduction of short vowels in open syllables (e.g. Classical Arabic *kat̲īr* 'many' > *kit̲īr* > Syrian Arabic *ktīr*; Classical Arabic *kātiba* 'writing [feminine]' > Syrian Arabic *kātbe*); in the dialects of North Africa, only stressed short vowels have been retained.
- the opposition of the two short vowels /i/ and /u/ has been reduced in many of the sedentary dialects; often they merge into one phoneme, usually transcribed with /ə/, e.g. in Syrian Arabic *'əṣṣa* 'story' < Classical Arabic *qiṣṣa*, and *mərr* 'bitter' < Classical Arabic *murr*.

Partly as the result of phonological changes, there are a number of morphonological differences between the dialects and Classical Arabic:

- the use of the vowel *-i-* instead of *-a-* in the prefixes of the imperfect verb, which already occurred in some of the pre-Islamic dialects (cf. above, p. 42), e.g. Classical Arabic *yaḥmilu* 'he carries' > *yiḥmil* > Syrian Arabic *yəḥmel*).
- the use of the pattern *fuʿāl* instead of *fiʿāl* in the plural of adjectives (Classical Arabic *kibār* 'large [plural]' > *kubār* > Syrian Arabic *kbāṛ*).
- the absence of the consonant *-h-* in the pronominal suffix of the third person masculine after consonants (Classical Arabic *qatala-hu* > Syrian Arabic *'atalo*).
- the use of the pattern *fʿālil* instead of *faʿālīl* in quadriliteral plural patterns (Classical Arabic *sikkīn*, plural *sakākīn* 'knife', Syrian Arabic *səkkīn*, plural *sakakīn*).

- the use of the ending *-i* in *nisba* adjectives instead of *-iyy* or *-īy* (Classical Arabic *masīḥiyyun* 'Christian' > Syrian Arabic *masīḥi*).

The morphology of the dialects is characterised by a considerable reduction of morphological categories:

- the sedentary dialects have lost the gender distinction in the second and the third person plural of pronouns and verbs, whereas the Bedouin dialects have retained this distinction.
- in the verbs and pronouns the category of the dual has disappeared; in the nouns the names for parts of the body have retained the historical dual ending, which came to be used for the plural as well (pseudo-dual, cf. below); most dialects have developed a new dual ending with strictly dual meaning, which may be used with many nouns.
- the internal passive (Classical Arabic *fuʿila, yufʿalu*) has been replaced by either an *n*-form or a *t*-form, e.g. in Syrian Arabic *nḍarab* 'to be hit'; Moroccan Arabic *ttəḍrəb* 'to be hit'; in some of the Bedouin dialects, the internal passive is still productive.
- the causative of the verb (*'afʿala*) has been replaced in most dialects by analytical expressions with the help of verbs meaning 'to make, to let'; only in some Bedouin dialects does the causative pattern remain productive (cf. below, p. 149).
- of the three patterns of the perfect verb in Classical Arabic, *faʿula* has disappeared; verbs of this pattern, which in Classical Arabic was used for permanent qualities, have merged with *faʿila*, or been replaced with other forms, e.g. Classical Arabic *ḥamuḍa* 'to be sour', Syrian Arabic *ḥammaḍ*.
- the three feminine endings of Classical Arabic, *-ah*, *-ā* and *-ā'*, have merged into one ending, *-a*, as for instance in the feminine adjective *ḥamrā'u* 'red' > Syrian Arabic *ḥamra*.
- the relative pronoun (Classical Arabic *allaḏī*, feminine *allatī*, plural *allaḏīna, allawātī, allātī*) has lost its inflection, for instance in Syrian Arabic *(y)əlli*.

The working of analogy has eliminated a large number of anomalous or irregular forms. In Classical Arabic, weak verbs with a third radical *w* were still distinct from verbs with a third radical *y* in the basic pattern of the verb; in the dialects, both categories have merged into those with a third radical *y*; thus we find, for instance, in Syrian Arabic *rama/ramēt* 'he/I threw' and *šaka/šakēt* 'he/I complained', against Classical Arabic *ramā/ramaytu* and *šakā/šakawtu*. Likewise, the reduplicated verbs (Classical Arabic *radda* 'to repeat', first person singular of the perfect *radadtu*) have been reanalysed as verbs with a third radical *y* in the second measure, e.g. in Syrian Arabic *radd*, first person singular *raddēt*.

Individual dialects have gone a long way towards a general levelling of the endings of the weak and the strong verbs. In many dialects, some of the endings of the weak verbs have been replaced by those of the strong verbs, for instance in Syrian Arabic *ramu* 'they threw' like *katabu* 'they wrote', as against Classical Arabic *katabū/ramaw*. Inversely, in Muslim Baġdādī Arabic, weak endings have substituted for some of the endings of the strong verbs (e.g. *kitbaw* 'they wrote', like *mašaw*). In the Jewish dialect of Baghdad, this tendency is also manifest in the endings of the imperfect verb, e.g. *ykətbōn* 'they write'/*tkətbēn* 'you [feminine singular] write', like *yənsōn* 'they forget'/*tənsēn* 'you forget' (cf. Classical Arabic *yaktubūna*/*taktubīna* and *yansayna*/*tansayna*). In the Sunnī dialect of Bahrain, the first person singular of the perfect of all verbal classes has taken the weak ending: *kitbēt* 'I wrote', *nāmēt* 'I slept', *ligēt* 'I found' (Classical Arabic *katabtu, nimtu, laqītu*).

In some syntactic constructions, the Arabic dialects developed towards a more analytical type of language, in which syntactic functions were expressed by independent words rather than by morphological means. Often, these independent words were subsequently grammaticalised and became new morphological markers. In the nominal system, the declensional endings have disappeared, and in the place of the Classical Arabic possessive construction with a genitive an analytical possessive construction has developed, in which a genitive exponent expresses the meaning of possessivity (see below). In the verbal system, the distinction between three moods in the imperfect verb has disappeared. The imperfect verb without modal endings has taken over most modal functions. In most dialects, a new morphological contrast has developed in the imperfect by means of a set of markers to express tenses and aspects (see below).

The sentence structure of Classical Arabic has changed drastically in the modern dialects. The distinction between two types of sentence, one with topic/comment and one with verb/agent (cf. above, Chapter 6), has disappeared. In its place, one canonical word order has emerged, which seems to be in most dialects subject–verb–object, although verb–subject occurs in many dialects as a stylistic variant. But even in those cases in which the verb precedes the subject, there is full number agreement between them. This proves that such constructions are not simply a translation of a Classical Arabic pattern, but belong to the structure of the dialect (on the occurrence of variable agreement patterns in some dialects, see below, p. 111).

In Classical Arabic, the pronominal indirect object had a relatively free syntactic position: both *'urīdu 'an 'aktuba lakum risālatan* 'I want to write you a letter' and *'urīdu 'an 'aktuba risālatan lakum* 'I want to write a letter to you' were allowed. In the modern dialects, the pronominal indirect object is connected clitically with the verbal form: Syrian Arabic *bəddi 'əktob-lkon* 'I want to write you'. The dialects differ with regard to the extent of this construction: some dialects allow almost any combination of direct and indirect object suffixes on the verb, others make a more restricted use of clitics. In combination with the negative circumfix *mā-...-š*, the aspectual particles of future and continuous, and the clitics, verbal forms in some dialects can become quite complex, as for instance in Moroccan Arabic

> *ma-ġa-nekteb-o-lek-š*
> [negation]-[future]-I write-it-to you-[negation]
> 'I won't write it to you'

or in Egyptian Arabic

> *ma-bi-tgib-ha-lnā-š*
> [negation]-[continuous]-you bring-her-to us-[negation]
> 'you're not bringing her to us'.

In modal expressions such as 'want to, must, can', Classical Arabic made use of a hypotactic construction with the conjunction *'an* governing the following verb in the subjunctive form of the imperfect, e.g. *yurīdu 'an yaqtul-a-nī* 'he wants to kill me'. In the modern dialects, this construction was replaced by an asyndetic construction of the imperfect without modal endings, e.g. in Syrian Arabic *bəddo yə'təlni* 'he wants to kill me' (from Classical Arabic *bi-wuddihi* 'it is in his wish'), in Egyptian Arabic *lāzim tiʿmil da* 'you must do this', in Moroccan Arabic *ẖəṣṣni nəktəb* 'I must write' (from Classical Arabic *ẖaṣṣa* 'to concern specially').

There is a set of lexical items that is found in almost all dialects, e.g. the verbs *ğāb* (< *ğā'a bi-*) 'to bring', *šāf* 'to see', *sawwa* (*sāwa*) 'to do, make', and *rāḥ* 'to go away'. Some of these items were used in Classical Arabic in a less general sense, which was expanded by a process of semantic bleaching; *šāf*, for instance, originally meant 'to observe from above' (cf. *šayyifa* 'scout'), *sawwā* 'to render equal, to arrange', *rāḥ* 'to go away in the evening'. Characteristic of the dialects is the nominal periphrasis of some interrogative words: they all have a variant of the expression *'ayyu šay'in* 'which thing?' instead of Classical Arabic *mā*, e.g. Egyptian *'ēh*, Moroccan *āš*, Syrian *šnu*. For *kayfa* 'how?', such periphrases as Syrian Arabic *šlōn* (< *'ēš lōn*, literally 'what colour?', Classical Arabic *lawn*) and Egyptian Arabic *izzayy* (< *'ēš zayy*, literally 'what appearance?', Classical Arabic *ziyy*) are found.

7.3 THEORIES ABOUT THE EMERGENCE OF NEW ARABIC

The current opinion about the linguistic situation in the *Ğāhiliyya* is that the shift from Old to New Arabic took place as early as the pre-Islamic period in the colloquial language of the Arab tribes. The Arabic sources view the development of their language quite differently. According to them, as long as the tribes lived in the peninsula the language was basically uniform, with only marginal differences. But after the conquests, when the Arabs came in contact with people who spoke other languages, they transmitted their language to these people, who then started to speak Arabic with lots of mistakes. As a result, the language became corrupted (*fasād al-luġa*), and the grammarians had to intervene because the text of the Revealed Book threatened to become incomprehensible. This view is summed up by the famous historian Ibn H̱aldūn (d. 757/1356) as follows:

> When Islam came and they [the Arabs] left the Ḥiğāz ... and started to mingle with the non-Arabs, their [linguistic] habits began to change as the result of the different ways of speaking they heard from those who tried to learn Arabic, for hearing is the source of linguistic habits. As a result of this influence, Arabic became corrupt ... Their scholars began to fear lest the [linguistic] habit become completely corrupted, and lest people grow used to it, so that the *Qur'ān* and the Tradition would become incomprehensible. Consequently, they deduced laws from their [the Arabs'] ways of speaking, that were universally valid for this habit ... and that could be used as a canon for the rest of their speech. (*fa-lammā ğā'a l-'Islām wa-fāraqū l-Ḥiğāz ... wa-ẖālaṭū l-ʿAğam taġayyarat tilka l-malaka bimā 'alqā 'ilayhā s-samʿ min al-mustaʿribīn wa-s-samʿ 'abū l-malakāt al-*

lisāniyya wa-fasadat bimā 'ulqiya 'ilayhā ... wa-ḫašiya 'ahl al-ʿulūm minhum 'an tafsuda tilka l-malaka ra'san wa-yaṭūla l-ʿahd bihā fa-yanğaliqa l-Qur'ān wa-l-Ḥadīṯ ʿalā l-mafhūm fa-stanbaṭū min mağārī kalāmihim qawānīn li-tilka l-malaka muṭṭaridatan ... yaqīsūna ʿalayhā sā'ir 'anwāʿ al-kalām, Muqaddima, ed. Beirut, n.d., p. 546)

This quotation shows clearly that in the mind of the Arabs the changes in the language and the emergence of the colloquial varieties were linked with the polyglot composition of the Islamic empire and the introduction of Arabic as the new *lingua franca.*

Some scholars have attempted to explain the presence of numerous common features in the Arabic dialects as against the Classical language with a theory of monogenesis, which posits a single point of origin for the present-day dialects. According to Ferguson (1959), for instance, the common ancestor of the dialects originated in the military camps in Iraq, where the speakers of the various pre-Islamic dialects mingled. The coalescence of these dialects led to the emergence of a military koine in which the common features developed. Specifically, Ferguson bases his theory on a list of fourteen features, which in his view cannot be attributed to an independent, general trend in the development of the dialects, but must be assigned to a common ancestor, for instance the use of the lexical items *šāf* and *ğāb*, the disappearance of the dual in the verb and the pronoun, the merger of /ḍ/ and /ḏ̣/, and the merger of verbs with a third radical *w* and *y*.

A theory of monogenesis, such as Ferguson's, proposes a common origin for the modern dialects in order to explain the features which they have in common against the standard language. Differences between the dialects are then explained as the result of a later process of divergence, possibly because of the substratal influence of the languages that were spoken in the various regions into which Arabic was imported. Critics of the theory of a common origin have objected to Ferguson's theory that the resemblances could also be explained as either the product of a general trend, or as the result of a later process of convergence which homogenised the dialects in the various areas. Proponents of the idea of a general trend point out, for instance, that languages not related to Arabic have also lost their dual, just like the Arabic dialects, so that it is entirely possible that the dialects lost this category independently from each other. The main problem with the theory of a general trend is that the explanatory power of such a principle is minimal since the mere fact that similar phenomena occur in different languages does not provide us with an explanation of the causes behind them.

Other critics of a theory of common origin emphasise the role of convergence in the development of the language. According to Cohen (1970), the Arab armies consisted of a mixture of different tribes, so that the existing differences between the pre-Islamic dialects were levelled out. The new dialects in the conquered territories must have resulted from local, independent evolution. Later convergence resulted from the pervasive influence of Classical Arabic and the spreading of linguistic innovations from one or several cultural or political centres. These innovations were taken over by speakers accommodating to the language of prestige. Theories of convergence look upon the origin of the dialects as a polygenetic process: colloquial varieties sprang up independently in each region where the Arab armies came and gradually became more similar to each other as the result of later contact. While some of the similarities between the dialects within one region can undoubtedly be regarded as convergence from one cultural centre, it would be difficult to explain in this way the common features that exist between remote regions of the Arabophone world that were never in contact with each other.

Whether the similarities between the dialects are the result of a common origin or a secondary process of convergence, there are many differences between the dialects, too. In the theory of polygenesis, these are regarded as the natural outcome of the independent development of colloquial varieties. The linguistic input in all regions outside the original tribal area was more or less the same (the type of speech spoken by the Arab armies), but the local circumstances differed because of the presence of other languages in the region into which Arabic was introduced. When the speakers of these languages came into contact with the speakers of Arabic, they started speaking the new language in their own special way, introducing the kind of interference that takes place in any process of second-language-learning. In the course of time, these special ways of speaking developed into local features, even after the speakers of the original language had shifted to Arabic.

In the case of Berber, the original language triggering off the deviations is still spoken in approximately the same area, even though some Berber speakers have now given up their own language. In such a case, it is customary to speak of an adstratal language, whose interference in the realisation of Arabic both in bilingual and in monolingual speakers is to be expected. Thus, for the Algerian dialect of Djidjelli, Ph. Marçais (n.d.) traces a number of phenomena to the surrounding Berber dialects. Berber influence is first of all demonstrated by the presence of more than 150 words of Berber origin with the prefix *a-*, e.g. *agméz* 'thumb', *arīsek* 'blackbird', *aġrūm* 'bread'. The use of this prefix has spread to words of Arabic origin as well, e.g. *asdér* 'breast' (Classical Arabic *ṣadr*), *ažnéḥ* 'wing' (Classical Arabic *ğanāḥ*), *aqṭōṭ* 'cat' (Classical Arabic *qiṭṭ*), *aḥmír* 'donkey' (Classical Arabic *ḥimār*, plural *ḥamīr*). In most words the prefix may be omitted, so that both *asdér* and *sdér* are heard. The origin of the Berber prefix is obscure, but contemporary speakers seem to regard it as a definite article: when it is used in a word, it cannot be combined with the Arabic article. Marçais also mentions a few syntactic phenomena. Certain nouns change their gender under the influence of the Berber equivalents: *lḥém* 'meat', for instance, is feminine (like Berber *tifi*), and *ržél* 'foot, leg' is masculine (like Berber *aḍar*). The word *má* 'water' is plural in Djidjelli Arabic like its Berber equivalent *aman*. In possessive constructions with kinship names, the first word carries a pronominal suffix, e.g. *ḫtú ddə-mḥəmmed* 'sister-his of-Muḥammad [Muḥammad's sister]'. Djidjelli Arabic also uses a presentative particle *d-* in sentences such as *d-āna* 'it's me', *d-buk w-úll* 'is it your father or not?', *húma d-el-ḫāwa* 'they are brothers'. This particle may have its origin in a Berber particle *ḏ-*, although some of its uses are paralleled in Egyptian Arabic.

In the examples mentioned from Djidjelli Arabic, the Berber connection is obvious, since most of the speakers of the dialect speak Berber as well, and the phenomena concerned do not occur elsewhere. In many cases, however, the original language has disappeared completely, as in the case of Syriac or Coptic.

When interference of such a language in the development of Arabic is claimed, one speaks of substratal influence. This influence is much harder to prove than that of an adstratal language. Phenomena that appear in a certain region and could in principle be attributed to substratal influence sometimes appear in other regions as well, where the substratal language concerned was never spoken. In Egyptian dialects, for instance, the interdentals have shifted to dentals, and it has sometimes been claimed that this was caused by the substratal influence of Coptic. But the disappearance of the interdentals is a widespread phenomenon in all sedentary dialects of Arabic, even in places where Coptic was never spoken. The shift from interdentals to dentals can, therefore, not be attributed to substratal influence alone, but must be regarded as an instance of a more general process of second-language acquisition, in which marked phonemes like the interdentals were replaced by unmarked ones, just as the emphatic or pharyngal consonants disappeared in some of the Arabic linguistic enclaves (cf. below, pp. 210, 212).

A similar situation of bilingualism to that in North Africa must have existed in the Syrian area between Aramaic and Arabic, and still exists in the linguistic enclaves in the Qalamūn mountains north of Damascus where Western Neo-Aramaic is spoken in three villages around Maʿlūla. The Arabic dialects in the neighbourhood of these villages exhibit several traces of Aramaic influence. According to Arnold and Behnstedt (1993), isoglosses of possible Aramaic traits in these dialects increase in frequency as one approaches the area where Aramaic is still spoken. They conclude that for a long time, possibly until the fourteenth century, Aramaic remained the language of the entire region and that it was gradually forced back towards its present small area. Some of the phenomena in the Arabic dialects in this region may help clarify the question of Aramaic substratal influence in Syrian dialects. Arnold and Behnstedt show, for instance, how the personal pronoun of the third person plural *hinne*, suffix *-hun* (Damascus *hənne*, suffix *-hon*) could have originated in a bilingual environment, in which the Aramaic forms *hinn*, suffix *-hun* were current.

Other phenomena in Syrian dialects that have been attributed to Aramaic substratal influence include the voiceless realisation of /q/, the elision of short /u/ and /i/, and the shift from interdentals to dentals. But the general occurrence of these phenomena in many other areas of the Arabic-speaking world obviates the need for such an explanation. This is not to say that the presence of substratal languages was completely immaterial. Obviously, when speakers of a language having interdentals started learning Arabic, they had no reason to shift to dentals. But for speakers of languages like Coptic or Syriac, which had no interdentals, there was nothing in their own language to prevent them from following the general tendency of simplifying the articulation of the interdentals. In this sense, we may say that the structure of Coptic and Aramaic reinforced a change that was already taking place.

In general, substratal influence on the Arabic dialects has been invoked in many cases without much justification. In an article that appeared in 1979, Diem follows up on all the alleged cases of substratal influence in the Arabic dialects. He allows the attribution to substratal influence only on two conditions: in the first place, the presence of a certain phenomenon in the modern dialect as well as in the original language spoken in the region; in the second place, the absence of this phenomenon in any other region. His conclusion is that in most of the alleged instances similar developments can be attested in other dialects as well, where the same substratal language was not present, so that the explanatory power of a theory of substratal influence is minimal. Only in a few cases does he concede that the structure of the language of the conquered population may have affected the development of the local dialect, e.g. the split of the phoneme /ā/ into /å/ and /ä/ (or /ō/ and /ē/) in North Lebanese dialects; cf. pp. 153–4), and perhaps the elision of /a/ in open unstressed syllables in these dialects, which may have been influenced by the phonemic structure of the Aramaic dialects spoken in this area. In the case of Berber influence in North Africa, Diem mentions cases such as the affrication of /t/ and the loan pattern *tafəʿʿalət*, but adds that it is difficult to decide whether this is an instance of substratal influence or of interference as the result of prolonged bilingualism.

Of special interest are those phenomena in Yemenite Arabic dialects that are attributed to substratal influence from South Arabian. In this region, the evidence of the Modern South Arabian languages makes it relatively easy to determine substratal influence. Among the phenomena mentioned by Diem are the use of the *k*- perfect and the plural patterns *faʿawwil/faʿāwil* and *fiʿwal/fuʿwal* (*fiʿyal/fuʿyal*). In some of the Yemenite dialects, the first and the second person singular of the perfect verb have a suffix -*k*-, instead of Classical Arabic -*t*-, e.g. *katab-k* 'I have written'. This feature, which they share with the South Semitic languages (cf. above, Chapter 2), occurs in the Western mountains, where according to Classical sources the Ḥimyaritic language was spoken, i.e. the area of the pre-Islamic immigrants in the South Arabian region (cf. above, Chapter 4, and below, p. 150; see also Map 10.1).

The plural patterns *faʿawwil* and *fiʿwal* are used exclusively in some regions in Yemen: for *faʿawwil*, Diem cites cases such as *bilād/belawwid, kalām/kalawwim, kitāb/kutawwib*. These are related to a plural pattern that exists in Mehri (*qetōwel* < **qetawwel*), and it may reasonably be assumed that in this case the Arabic dialect borrowed the plural pattern from South Arabian during the early stages of settlement, perhaps even before the Islamic conquests. Likewise, the pattern *fiʿwal* occurs in the mountainous regions of Yemen where the first settlement of Arab tribes took place; the dialects in this region present forms such as *ṭarīg/ṭirwag* 'street', *šarīṭ/širwaṭ* 'rope' that are related to Modern South Arabian plurals *qetwōl/qetyōl*.

In the majority of cases, the interference that resulted from language contact may have consisted not in the emergence of new phenomena but in the tipping of the balance towards one of two existing alternatives. In such cases, the learners of Arabic may have been influenced by their first language in the selection of one alternative. An interesting example is that of the position of the interrogatives in Egyptian dialects. In Egyptian Arabic, there is no fronting of interrogative words, which remain at their structural position in the sentence, as for instance in the following two sentences:

'ult^{i} da li-l-muʿallim 'you told the teacher this'
'ult^{i} 'ēh li-l-muʿallim 'what did you tell the teacher?'

In other Arabic dialects, such a word order is also possible, but then it is highly marked (corresponding to English 'you told the teacher whát!?'). Likewise, in Egyptian it is possible to say *'ēh 'ult*^{i} *li-l-muʿallim*, meaning something like 'what was it you told the teacher?' Such alternatives exist in all spoken languages as discourse phenomena that have to do with emphasis, highlighting, topicalisation and so on. Speakers of Coptic were used to a language in which there was no fronting of interrogatives, for instance *ekdo de u* 'what are you saying?', in which the interrogative pronoun *u* remains at the normal position of the object instead of being fronted. When they became acquainted with the two alternatives of Arabic, they were likely to choose the alternative that was more similar to their own language, even though in Arabic this was the marked option (for a similar explanation of word order in Uzbekistan Arabic, see below, p. 217).

Substratal influence is not a sufficient explanation for the differences between the dialects, but neither is convergence for the common features. Good examples of structural changes that took place in virtually all dialects, but with a different realisation, are the possessive construction and the aspectual particles. New Arabic was characterised by the disappearance of the case endings, often quoted as the most characteristic difference between colloquial and standard language. We have seen above (Chapter 4, p. 49) that there are several reasons why this process cannot be explained by purely phonetic reasons. In all dialects, the genitive case in the possessive construction was replaced by an analytical possessive construction:

> Classical Arabic *baytu l-maliki*
> house the-king [genitive]
> 'the house of the king'
>
> Egyptian Arabic *il-bēt bitāʿ il-malik*
> the-house [possessive particle] the-king
> 'the house of the king'

In the analytical construction, the meaning of possessivity is indicated with a possessive marker, *bitāʿ* (also called 'genitive exponent'), which replaces the Classical Arabic possessive construction with a genitive case ending. This construction is found in all dialects, but they differ with regard to the form of the possessive marker, as shown in Table 7.1.

Egyptian Arabic (Cairo)	*bitāʿ*
Syrian Arabic (Damascus)	*tabaʿ*
Moroccan Arabic (Rabat)	*dyal, d-*
Maltese	*ta'*
Sudanese Arabic	*ḥaqq*
Chad Arabic	*hana*
Cypriot Arabic	*šáyt*
Baghdad Muslim Arabic	*māl*
qəltu Arabic	*līl*

Table 7.1 Genitive exponents in Arabic dialects.

The second phenomenon of pluriform development of a common feature is connected with the loss of the modal endings. In Classical Arabic, there is a distinction in the imperfect verb between *yaktubu* (indicative), *yaktuba* (subjunctive) and *yaktub* (jussive). In the dialects, the morphological category of mood has disappeared, and in the singular the form is always *yaktub*. In most dialects, this form has acquired a modal meaning. In Egyptian Arabic, for instance, *tišrab 'ahwa?* means 'would you like to drink coffee?' For non-modal, aspects the dialects have developed a new system of aspectual markers, originally auxiliary verbs or temporal adverbs, which became fossilised as part of the morphology of the verbal form. In Egyptian Arabic, for instance, we find *bi-* for the continuous aspect, *ḥa-* for the future.

b-tišrab 'you are drinking, you habitually drink'
ḥa-tišrab 'you will drink'

In this respect, too, all dialects have gone through the same development, but again they differ with regard to the form of the markers. Most dialects have a system of two markers: continuous/habitual and future. The exact distribution of semantic functions differs in the various dialects. In Syrian Arabic, strict continuity is expressed by *ʿam-*, while *bi-* is used for actions that are intended in the future and for habitual actions. In Iraqi Arabic, *da-* is used for continuous/habitual actions, but the imperfect without marker is used for statements that are generally valid. In many cases, the exact etymology of the markers is unknown, but it seems to be the case that future markers often derive from verbs meaning 'to go' (e.g. Egyptian Arabic *ḥa-*, Syrian Arabic *raḥ-*, Tunisian Jewish Arabic *maši-*, Maltese *sejjer*), whereas continuous markers derive from the verb *kāna*, or from participial forms meaning 'sitting', 'doing', 'standing' (Syrian Arabic *ʿam* < *ʿammāl*, Anatolian Arabic *qa-* < *qāʿid*, Moroccan Arabic *ka-*, Maltese *'aed* < *qāʿid*, Uzbekistan Arabic *wōqif*).

In both the analytical genitive and the system of aspectual markers, we find a similar pattern: a general trend that has occurred in all Arabic dialects, and an individual translation of this trend in each area. Any theory about the emergence of the new type of Arabic must take into account this development. The difference in realisation precludes an explanation in terms of later convergence, because typically dialect contact leads to the borrowing of another dialect's markers, not to the borrowing of a structure which is then filled independently.

One possible scenario connects the origin of the changes in the language with the acquisitional process. During the first centuries of Islam, Arabic was learnt

	continuous/habitual	future
Syrian Arabic (Damascus)	*ʿam-, bi-*	*raḥ(a)-, laḥ(a)-*
Egyptian Arabic (Cairo)	*bi-*	*ḥa-*
Moroccan Arabic (Rabat)	*ka-*	*ġa-*
Iraqi Arabic (Baghdad)	*da-*	*raḥ-*
Yemeni Arabic (Ṣanʿāʾ)	*bi-* (1st person *bayn-*)	*ʿa-* (1st person *šā-*)

Table 7.2 Aspectual markers in Arabic dialects.

by the local population as a second language in a highly unstructured way, with no formal teaching and with minimal attention to correctness and maximal attention to communicational value. During the period of bilingualism, most speakers used Arabic as a second language, whereas only a minority spoke it as their mother tongue. In such a situation, redundant forms disappear, leading to a greater degree of regularity; preference is given to analytical constructions (as in the case of the genitive exponent), and various categories are conflated in order to increase learnability. Besides, the lexicon is partially restructured, as items of lesser transparency are replaced by items that are more transparent.

In such a scenario, most of the 'initiative' in the changes is assigned to the inhabitants of the conquered territories. Most theories about the emergence of the new dialects, however, tend to look for the cause of the innovations in natural tendencies that already existed latently in the pre-Islamic language. Generally speaking, scholars agree that in the beginning of the Islamic era simplified varieties of the language were current, but the consensus seems to be that these disappeared without leaving any traces. This issue hinges on the development of the standard language. If at first the acquisition process of Arabic led to a drastic restructuring of the language and to the emergence of simplified varieties, one must assume that at a later stage the influence of the Classical standard and in particular the language of the *Qur'ān* reintroduced many of the features of standard Arabic that are found in the modern dialects, such as the inflection of the verb and the existence of two verbal forms. In this scenario, the population of the urban centres of the Islamic empire originally communicated with the Arab conquerors in a simplified variety of Arabic. In the linguistic melting-pot of the cities, such varieties became the mother tongue of children in mixed marriages between Arabs and indigenous women, or between speakers of different languages whose common second language was Arabic.

The dissemination of Classical Arabic as the prestige language of culture and religion introduced a model that affected the linguistic situation to such a degree that between colloquial speech and standard language a linguistic continuum arose that paralleled the present-day diglossia of the Arabophone world. In this continuum, the lower (basilectal) speech levels were stigmatised and ultimately abandoned by the speakers in favour of higher (acrolectal) features. In principle, the replacement of basilectal features by acrolectal features is not uncommon. There is no direct evidence for such a large-scale restructuring in historical times, but to some extent the process may be compared to contemporary Classical interference, which leads to shifts in the language used by dialect-speakers. For many literate speakers of Arabic, for instance, the use of the Classical genitive construction alongside the dialectal construction has become a normal part of their linguistic competence, and this use filters down to the speech of illiterate speakers. A major difference with the situation in the first centuries of Islam is, of course, the influence of the language of the mass media.

A similar process takes place between dialects. In Cairene Arabic, the massive influx of dialect speakers from the countryside led to a stigmatisation of those features that Cairene Arabic at that time had in common with the countryside dialects. As a result, some of these forms have become restricted to the lower classes, and eventually they may even disappear completely. As an example, we may mention the ending of the third person plural of the perfect verb, which was probably *-um* in all registers in the nineteenth century, but which is now predominantly heard in the poor quarters of the city (cf. below, Chapter 10). Another example is the introduction of the *b-* imperfect in Bedouin dialects of the Negev and the Sinai. According to Palva (1991), these Bedouin dialects belong to a group of dialects that in general do not have the *b-* prefix, and he ascribes its occurrence in them as the result of levelling to sedentary speech. In some cases, variation may still be observed in which the *b-* imperfect is used in polite conversation with sedentary speakers, whereas the *y-* imperfect is used with fellow tribesmen.

The possibility of disappearance of basilectal speech is illustrated dramatically by recent developments in Sudan, where the pidginised and creolised variety of Arabic that goes by the name of Juba Arabic seems to be recovering some of the categories of 'normal' Arabic under the influence of the prestige dialect of Khartoum (cf. below, p. 218). Juba Arabic has only one verbal form that is used in combination with aspectual markers. When speakers of Juba Arabic are exposed to Standard Arabic and Khartoum Arabic in the media and become acquainted with both the prefix and the suffix conjugation of Arabic, they at first reanalyse the personal prefixes of Arabic imperfect verbs *ya-*, *ta-*, *na-* as aspectual markers and start using them instead of or in combination with the aspectual markers in Juba Arabic, without regard to personal agreement. At a later stage, they become aware of the real function of the personal prefixes and learn to use them correctly. Diachronically, this means that in their speech they have introduced a new opposition between perfect and imperfect verbs, thus making their dialect structurally similar to the 'normal' dialects of Arabic.

The development in Juba Arabic only took place in the speech of some speakers, but the present variation in the language shows at the very least that it is possible for an Arabic dialect to lose the distinction between perfect/imperfect and then recover it later through the interference of a prestige variety. If we had no knowledge of the previous structure of the language of these speakers, we would probably regard their speech as just another regional variety of Arabic. Since our only information about the vernacular in the early centuries of Islam derives from written sources that were highly classicised, we must at least allow for the possibility that this vernacular resembled the uncontaminated form of such varieties as Juba Arabic and was later classicised to such a degree that the original structure was erased.

Against the scenario of interference from Classical Arabic, various arguments have been adduced. Contrary evidence consists, first of all, of Classical features in dialects that cannot be attributed to Classical interference. Ferguson (1989) cites the case of the dual in modern dialects. Most dialects distinguish between a pseudo-dual and a 'real' dual. The pseudo-dual is used for paired parts of the body (hands, feet, eyes, ears) and also for the countable plurals of these words; it loses the *-n-* before a personal suffix. The 'real' dual almost always has the same ending as the pseudo-dual, but it is never used for a plural and cannot be combined with personal suffixes. In Egyptian Arabic, for instance, we have *riglēn* 'feet' as plural and pseudo-dual (with personal suffixes *riglēhum*, *riglēki* etc.), and *waladēn* 'two boys' as a real dual. In some dialects the two duals are distinguished, for instance in Moroccan Arabic *wədnin* 'ears', *rəžlin* 'feet' as against *yumayn* 'two days'. The point of this argument is that the 'real' dual always takes plural agreement and thus cannot have been introduced from Classical Arabic. The evidence of Middle Arabic shows that when a dual is used as a classicising device it sometimes takes feminine singular and sometimes plural agreement. Therefore, in Ferguson's view the distinction of two duals must be an old dialectal distinction; since they were both used for countable entities, they took plural agreement.

Ferguson also signals the existence of an equivocal agreement pattern as an alternative for plural agreement. In Damascene Arabic, for instance, instead of using plural agreement between subject and predicate it is possible to say *'əžānā makatīb ktīr/'əžətna makatīb ktīr* 'many letters reached us'. This pattern may seem to conform to the Classical Arabic pattern, and one might, therefore, be tempted to attribute it to interference from the standard language. Yet, Ferguson believes that it cannot be regarded as a reintroduction of the standard pattern, since contrary to expectation the dialect pattern of plural agreement, *'əžūna makatīb ktīr*, instead of disappearing, is gaining in popularity over the Classical pattern. In the absence of a reliable corpus of dialect speech, which would allow frequency counts, it is hard to judge the validity of this particular argument. The point of the argument is that it should not be taken for granted that all movement on the continuum between dialect and standard is upwards. In some contexts, it is perfectly possible that there is a movement towards the dialect pattern. In other cases, interference from the standard language leads to a redistribution of grammatical functions. In the case of the agreement in Syrian Arabic, there probably is a semantic difference in that the plural is used for countable entities, whereas the feminine singular is used for non-countable or collective plurals.

A second argument against the interference of Classical Arabic calls into question the capacity of the standard language to affect the structure of the colloquial language. Diem (1978) points out that historically in most dialect areas there are two layers. The first wave of conquests led to the emergence of urban dialects with a high rate of innovation. These spread in the form of urban koines over the area immediately adjacent to the cities. The urban dialects were superseded by a second wave that was much more gradual: the steady migration of Arabian tribesmen to areas outside the Arabian peninsula. In Mesopotamia, for instance, the older layer of sedentary *qəltu* dialects was partially covered by a second layer of Bedouin *gilit* dialects. In Lower Egypt, a sedentary dialect was introduced during the first conquests, but the countryside and Upper Egypt were arabicised by later migrations of Bedouin tribes from the peninsula. In North Africa, the arabicisation of most of the countryside was not accomplished until the invasion of the Banū Hilāl in the eleventh century. In Diem's view, this second wave of arabicisation achieved a measure of homogeneity of Arabic dialects within each area that was absent before the Bedouin immigration. Compared to the development of the Aramaic dialects, which produced widely differing Eastern and Western varieties, Arabic dialects in spite of their differences are remarkably uniform typologically. In Diem's view, this is the result of convergence during the formative period, which prevented too large a deviation from the target. In this process, the Bedouin dialects that broke up the sedentary koines played a much more important role than the Classical language.

Others, for instance Holes (1995a), add to these objections considerations of a sociopolitical nature: the situation in the early Islamic empire was such that simplified varieties of Arabic did not get a chance to develop into full-blown vernaculars. He assumes that in the early stages of the conquests linguistic accommodation did take place, but neither the linguistic data nor the historical record supports the existence of an environment in which the simplified varieties could be maintained over time. According to Holes, the early papyri (cf. below, p. 118) document a transitional phase on the road to standardisation, in which the linguistic norms were still unstable. In his view, the language of the papyri does not document any drastic breakdown of the language, and accordingly he opts for a gradual evolution of the language towards the present colloquial type for most speakers, while only a few professionals among the population learnt the standard language. Most people, he maintains, were not in contact with any model of the Classical language. In short, Arabic, when it was learnt, was learnt as a foreign language rather than a makeshift variety.

One way of reconciling the two views on the possibility of influence by the standard language could be to speculate that it was the second wave of arabicisation that was responsible for the reintroduction of Classical features. The Bedouin speakers involved in the second wave of migration had not yet been affected by sedentary speech patterns and were able to impose their own dialects' patterns. Secondary bedouinisation is not an uncommon feature even in more recent times, when Muslim urban populations shifted to a bedouinised dialect, whereas the Christians and Jews stuck to their urban dialect. As for the Bedouin speakers themselves, even today some of them have managed to escape sedentary interference to a certain degree (cf. p. 143). Besides, in the course of time the scale of prestige has changed. In the early period of the Islamic conquests, the urban dialects almost certainly did not have the kind of prestige that they enjoy nowadays, so that they were not likely to affect the way of speaking of the Bedouin. At a later stage, the urban centres became the focus of Islamic civilisation and the seat of power, so that the Bedouin could hardly avoid the interference of urban speech.

In general, we must conclude that too little is known about the process of classicisation to determine the extent to which it may have influenced the growth of the dialects. Since we know only the output of the process of change which Arabic underwent after it was exported from the Arabian peninsula, namely the modern dialects, the question of interference on the part of the Classical standard is crucial if we wish to extrapolate from the structure of the modern dialects to the early vernacular varieties of the language during the first centuries of the Islamic era. On the other hand, none of the existing theories about the emergence of the new dialects – monogenesis, substratal influence, convergence, natural development, general trends – offers a comprehensive explanation of the evolution of the dialects, although each of them explains a subset of the phenomena in this process. In the present state of affairs, we have to conclude that the study of the history of the Arabic language alone cannot provide a satisfactory answer. Much more information is needed about the sociolinguistic context of the early Islamic empire and the pattern of settlement in each particular area. Even more help may be expected from general diachronic linguistics in the form of better models to explain the evolution of language in general.

FURTHER READING

Many details of the Islamic conquests are still unknown, if we wish to go beyond the military account (for which see Donner 1981). There is no comprehensive account, for instance, of the process of arabicisation. For individual areas, we may refer to Poliak (1938, the arabicisation of Syria), W. Marçais (1961, the arabicisation of North Africa), Anawati (1975, the arabicisation of Egypt), ʿUmar (1992, history of Arabic in Egypt) and Zarrinkūb (1975, the conquest of Persia). For the role of the Bedouin in the process of arabicisation, see Singer (1994). For the history of Persian in the Islamic empire, see Lazard (1975).

An extensive survey of the common features in the modern Arabic dialects is given in Fischer and Jastrow (1980: 39–48); most of the examples from Syrian Arabic quoted above have been taken from Grotzfeld's (1965) analysis of the dialect of Damascus.

In view of the many conflicting theories about the emergence of the new type of Arabic, it is hardly possible to refer to an authoritative account. For a general overview, see A. Miller (1986). The original theory of a monogenetic development was advanced by Ferguson (1959a) and repeated by him (1989); for a discussion of the fourteen features, see Kaye (1976: 137–70). D. Cohen's article (1970) on convergence has already been referred to in this chapter (see also Diem 1978), as was Diem's survey of possible substratal changes (1979a). Some publications deal with the Coptic influence on Egyptian Arabic, e.g. Bishai (1960, 1961, 1962), Sobhy (1950) and Palva (1969b); on the word order in interrogative questions, see Nishio (1996). Aramaic influence in Syrian Arabic is discussed by Arnold and Behnstedt (1993); for the issue of substratal influence in the personal pronouns in Syrian Arabic, see also Diem (1971). On Berber influence in the Arabic of Djidjelli, see Ph. Marçais (n.d.: 607–11). Versteegh's proposal to interpret the development of the new dialects in terms of a process of pidginisation/creolisation (1984) has met with considerable scepticism (e.g. Ferguson 1989; Diem 1991; Holes 1995a: 19–24; Fischer 1995).

For special topics dealt with in this chapter, we may refer to the following publications: the *laḥn al-ʿāmma* treatises: Molan (1978); Pérez Lázaro (1990, edition and critical study of Ibn Hišām al-Laẖmī's treatise); for the anecdotes about the *mawālī*, see above, Chapter 4, p. 50; the possessive construction in the Arabic dialects: Eksell Harning (1980; partly based on written texts that contain classicisms); the aspectual particles: Czapkiewicz (1975); pseudo-dual: Blanc (1970a); agreement rules: Ferguson (1989).

The data about Juba Arabic derive from Mahmud's (1979) study on variation in this dialect; cf. also Versteegh (1993b). On classicisation in Arabic dialects, see Palva (1969a).

8
Middle Arabic

8.1 THE DEFINITION OF 'MIDDLE ARABIC'

In the preceding chapters, both the development of literary Arabic and the emergence of colloquial Arabic have been discussed. A principal question that we should now address concerns the relationship between these two varieties of the language in the written production, both literary and non-literary, in early Islam. The language of many of the preserved written sources does not correspond to the form of Arabic as it was codified by the grammatical tradition. This applies both to the formal literary language of the later period and to the language of the early papyri. No grammarian, for instance, would ever use a form such as *yaktubū* instead of *yaktubūna* for the indicative of the verb, but this form regularly turns up both in the papyri and in some written texts. Since this is the form that the contemporary dialects use, the obvious conclusion is that this usage reflects the vernacular of the writer. In this chapter, we shall look at the source of the deviations from the Classical norm in written texts.

In modern studies of Arabic, the collective name for all texts with deviations from Classical grammar is Middle Arabic. The term in itself has led to a lot of ambiguity, and it is essential to explain first what it does not mean. In the history of English, Old English, Middle English and Modern English are distinguished as chronological periods, and it is tempting to take the term Middle Arabic to mean a stage of the language between the Classical period and the modern period, say between 800 and 1800. As a matter of fact, some writers use the term 'Middle Arabic' in this way. In his handbook of Christian Middle Arabic (1966–7: I, 36), Blau stated that 'M[iddle] A[rabic] constitutes the missing link between C[lassical] A[rabic] and modern dialects'. In later publications, however, he has modified his use of the term, in order to avoid the misunderstandings that arise when Middle Arabic is treated as a historically intermediate stage. In contemporary Arabic texts, mistakes may occur just as easily as in the Classical period, and it would therefore be a mistake to assign any chronological connotation to the term 'Middle Arabic'. We shall see below that when we analyse mistakes in contemporary texts, these turn out to be very much like those in Middle Arabic texts from the 'Classical' period.

Some people regard Middle Arabic as a discrete variety of the language, a special brand of Arabic, situated between the Classical language and the colloquial language. This is not in accordance with the true nature of these texts. Anyone wishing to write in Arabic does so with the Classical norm in mind. The amount of deviation or the distance from the colloquial varies with the degree of education of the author of the text. Thus, some Middle Arabic texts exhibit only an occasional mistake, whereas in other texts the entire structure of the language is almost colloquial. But even in the most extreme cases of colloquial interference the texts still cannot be regarded as truly dialectal, because they continue to be approximations of Classical Arabic, albeit with a lot of colloquial features thrown in. When in 1888 Landberg edited one of the first Middle Arabic texts to be published, he was convinced that he had found in the story of Bāsim a true specimen of Egyptian dialect. In reality, it is easy to see that although some of the passages of the story really sound Egyptian, in most cases its author was not able to escape, and probably did not even want to, the norms of written Arabic. But the novelty of finding dialectal expressions in a written text was still such that it is easy to understand why Landberg believed that this story had been recorded in 'real' dialect.

In every linguistic community, there is a certain distance between the colloquial language and the written norm, in spelling, lexicon and even in structure. But in those communities in which there is an institutionalised relationship between a high and a low variety (called 'diglossia': see below, Chapter 12), the distance between the written standard and normal everyday speech is very large. If in such a community the average level of education is low, access to the written language remains severely restricted. At the same time, the use of the written medium is automatically linked with the acceptance of the written norm: if one wishes to write in Arabic, one has no choice but to submit to the written norm. The problem is, of course, that the level of the written standard language is beyond the reach of most people. As soon as they start writing in Arabic, they make mistakes, which in many cases originate in their spoken language. An example is the merger of the two Classical phonemes /ḍ/ and /ḏ̣/ into colloquial /ḍ/, which leads to spelling errors such as *ʿaḍīm* instead of *ʿaḏ̣īm* or *ḍabyun* instead of *ḏ̣abyun*. An example from the domain of morphology is the disappearance of the modal endings of the imperfect verb in dialect, which makes it difficult for people to know when to use the indicative *yaktubūna* and when the subjunctive *yaktubū*. This induces them to use the colloquial form *yaktubū* in all contexts.

It would be wrong to suppose that every deviation in a written text is colloquial. Since people know that there is a difference between written and spoken language, they make a conscious attempt to write correctly but in doing so sometimes overreact using forms that are neither colloquial nor standard. In the case of the modal endings just cited, for instance, the correct form in the jussive is *lam yaktubū*, but in their fear of colloquial interference people sometimes use *lam yaktubūna* in order to show that they are not illiterate. Such errors are called 'pseudo-corrections'. Usually two categories are distinguished: hypercorrections and hypocorrections. In the example given above, we have an instance of a hypercorrection: in correcting the dialectal forms, the writer exaggerates and ends up using a form that is 'too Classical'. In hypocorrections, on the other hand, the correction is incomplete. In Middle Arabic texts, the usual verbal form to refer to a dual subject is the plural, e.g. *ar-rağulāni yadḫulū* 'the two men [dual] enter [plural]'. When this form is corrected incompletely, it becomes *yadḫulā*, which is neither colloquial nor Classical Arabic (*yadḫulāni*). A further example of incomplete correction occurs when the writer inverts the order of the sentence to make it more Classical, but leaves the dual form instead of changing it into a singular as in Classical Arabic *yadẖulu r-rağulāni.*

The use of pseudo-corrections is not limited to written speech. Since the written standard also serves as the model for formal elevated speech, in modern times one finds many examples of pseudo-corrections in speech. Egyptian speakers, for instance, are very much aware of the correlation of Classical /q/ with colloquial /ʾ/ (glottal stop). When they wish to appear educated, they tend to replace every glottal stop with /q/, not only in those words that in Classical Arabic contain /q/, but also in those words that never had /q/ in the first place. Thus, one occasionally even hears forms such as *qurqān* for *qurʾān.*

Apart from deficient knowledge of the standard, manifesting itself in plain errors and pseudo-corrections, deviations in written language from the standard norm may have another source. Because of the large distance between spoken and written language, it is difficult to represent in written language a lively dialogue between real people. In modern Arabic literature, this is a much-debated problem, and it must have existed in the Classical period as well, in particular in stories that were intended to be read to a larger audience. As a result, in such text types there was always a tendency to enliven the dialogue with dialect words or even dialect constructions. In the aforementioned story of Bāsim (Landberg 1888), for instance, we find in a conversation between the Caliph Hārūn, his vizier Ğaʿfar and his eunuch Masrūr the following expressions, that add to the *couleur locale.* First the vizier says to the caliph:

> *yā ʾamīr al-muʾminīn masrūr ʿammāl yaqūlu lī rubbamā ʾanna l-malika ğāʿa isʾalhu r-ruğūʿ li-s-sarāya* 'O, Prince of the Believers, Masrūr keeps telling me "perhaps the Caliph is hungry, ask him to return to the palace!"'

To this Masrūr says:

> *ʾanā qultu laka wallā ʾanta bi-taqūlu lī qūl lahu* 'Did I say that or were you saying that to me? Tell him!'

And the Caliph says:

> *mānīš ğīʿān ẖallūnā natafarrağ* 'I am not hungry; let's have a look!'

All participants in the conversation use colloquial expressions: continuous imperfects with an aspectual prefix (*ʿammāl yaqūlu, bi-taqūlu*), *li-* instead of *ʾilā, wallā* for Classical *ʾam,* nominal negation *mānīš.* In telling the story, the narrator doubtless adapted to the colloquial pronunciation even more (*bi-tʾul, ʾultíllak,* etc.). Obviously, the writer knew very well what the correct Classical expressions were, but he chose to use the colloquial ones in order to amuse his audience. In some cases, one has the impression that he deliberately has someone deliver a sentence in Classical Arabic ending with a colloquial word in order to increase the humorous effect. One may be sure that the audience had to laugh when such lofty personages were speaking in what they recognised as Egyptian colloquial. In the Syrian version of the same story, the Egyptian colloquialisms were dutifully replaced by Syrian forms.

In another story of the same type, that of the Doctor and the Cook (Nöldeke 1891), the deviations are clearly not intentional.

> *wa-hāḏihi l-ğasūra marākib murabbaṭīn fī baʿḍihim al-baʿḍ wa-tamšī n-nās ʿalayhim li-yaqḍūna ʾašğālahum ... wa-baynamā huwa fī ḏāt yawm*

> *yatafarraǧ fī l-'aswāq fa-ǧtāza ʿalā dukkān ṭabbāḫ* 'These bridges were ships that had been tied together and the people crossed them in order to go about their business ... and one day when he was looking through the markets, he came upon a cook's shop'

In this story, it is apparent that the author attempts to write in Classical Arabic, but is unable to observe the rules of the standard language consistently. Thus, for instance, he refers to the plural *ǧasūra* sometimes with a feminine singular and sometimes with a masculine plural, he uses the indicative instead of the subjunctive of the verb after the conjunction *li-*, and gets into trouble with the complicated reciprocal expression *baʿḍuhā fī baʿḍ*. In the temporal sentence with *baynamā*, he tries to enhance the Classical character of his language by introducing the main clause with *fa-*. The author of this text does not bother to insert dialecticisms for humorous reasons.

There may be a third reason for the presence of deviations in a Middle Arabic text, connected with the use of Middle Arabic as a written in-group language in the Classical period. Since for Christians and Jews the model of the language of the *Qur'ān* was not as powerful or authoritative as it was for Muslims, they felt much freer than Muslims did to use colloquial forms in their written language. In this sense, it is legitimate to speak of Jewish Middle Arabic (or Judaeo-Arabic) and Christian Middle Arabic as a special language, in much the same way that the in-group language of the early Christians in the Roman empire may be called Christian Latin or Christian Greek.

While it is true that the term 'Middle Arabic' may be used for texts that are found as early as the seventh and as late as the twentieth century, it is also true that most studies of Middle Arabic concentrate on texts from the Classical period. This is because these texts are often used in attempts to reconstruct the emergence of the dialects. The presupposition here is that the use of colloquialisms in the texts reflects a diachronic development in the spoken language. However, because of their nature, the Middle Arabic texts have only limited value for historical linguistic research. The mixture of spoken/written language depends on the individual author's abilities and inclinations, so that the presence or absence of a certain feature does not tell us anything about the actual situation in the vernacular. Because of this individual character, the increased frequency of a feature over time does not necessarily correlate with a development in the vernacular, but only signals a change in the linguistic norms. The fact that the analytical genitive does not occur in early texts but is used increasingly often in later texts does not reflect an increased use of this construction in the vernacular, but an erosion of the norm that proscribed the use of such a form in writing.

Besides, as we have seen, some of the deviations in the texts stem from a different source: pseudo-corrections, forms that never existed in either variety of the language. This is not to say that we cannot use the evidence of Middle Arabic texts, but it should be done with care. From the confusion of *ḍ* and *ḏ̣* in Middle Arabic texts, we may draw the conclusion that these two phonemes had merged in the vernacular, but the texts provide us only with a *terminus ante quem*, i.e. we know that this feature existed at the time of writing the text, but we do not know for how long it had been present in the vernacular.

This conclusion even applies to the very few examples of vocalised transcriptions of Arabic into other scripts, of which the best-known example is that of the psalm translation in Greek letters that was edited by Violet. The text, a translation into Arabic of Psalm 78 probably dating from the beginning of the ninth century, is unique in that it provides us with some clues about the pronunciation of the vowels in this period. It exhibits, for instance, the loss of short vowels at the ends of words, e.g. *oamithl raml elbou.chour* (*wa-mi<u>t</u>l raml al-buḥūr* 'and like the sand of the seas'). The *'imāla* of the *a/ā* in certain environments is clearly visible, e.g. *fá.dat* (*fāḍat*) as against *fasélet* (*fa-sālat*), *ken* (*kāna*), *geb* (*ǧāba*) as against *sak* (*sāqa*). There are some indications that the Arabic represented here had *taltala*, i.e. the prefix vowel *-i-* in the imperfect instead of Classical *-a-*, e.g. in the form *iechfa.dou* (*yaḥfaẓū*), in which the *e* probably does not represent *'imāla*, because of the following *ḥ*, but *i* > *e*. The form *semig* (*samiʿa*) possibly indicates a change *faʿila* > *fiʿil*. But the language of the translation itself is not particularly colloquial, and the author of the transcription must have had a written example, since the article is transcribed in an unassimilated form, e.g. *elturáb* (*at-turāb*), and the vowel of the *hamzat al-waṣl*, which is dropped in pronunciation, is retained in the transcription, e.g. *fa.ankalebu* (*fa-nqalabū*).

There were also transcriptions in other scripts, for instance in Coptic, Syriac, Iranian, Latin, Hebrew, Armenian and South Arabian, but most of these transcriptions date from later periods and are therefore not very helpful in any reconstruction of the pronunciation of Arabic in the earliest period. In section 8.3 below, on Jewish Middle Arabic, we shall mention the transcription of Arabic into Hebrew, and in section 8.4, on Christian Middle Arabic, Arabic texts in Coptic letters will be discussed.

8.2 MUSLIM MIDDLE ARABIC

There is one category of texts that stands apart from all other categories to be mentioned here, namely the large corpus of papyri. The earliest manuscript copies of Classical Arabic texts, literary and non-literary alike, date from the third century of the Hiǧra. Since they may contain adaptations and corrections by scribes or copyists, it is hazardous to draw any conclusions from them about the state of the language at the time the texts were composed. The papyri, however, are original documents. It has been estimated that more than 16,000 papyri have been preserved and a total of more than 33,000 items written on paper; there is, moreover, a very large collection of texts written on other materials (leather, wood, coins, glass and so on), as well as a corpus of inscriptions.

The earliest papyri date from year 22 of the Hiǧra (two papyri and a Greek–Arabic bilingual; cf. above, p. 51). From the period between years 54 and 70 of the Hiǧra, there are the archives of Nessana, and from years 90–91 of the Hiǧra the archives of Aphrodito. From the end of the first century of the Hiǧra, there is a steady increase of papyri, the largest number dating from the third century of the Hiǧra, after which they gradually disappeared. Most of the papyri stem from Egypt, most of them were written by Muslims, and most of them contain non-literary (administrative or commercial) texts.

The significance of the papyri lies in the fact that their language exhibits more or less the same traits as later Middle Arabic texts, which confirms the fact that from the very beginning these changes had been present in colloquial language. On the other hand, the colloquial interference should not be exaggerated, since the language of the papyri is never free from influence of the Classical norms. In view of the purpose of most of these documents, this is not surprising: they were written by official scribes (i.e. people who had had some kind of education) for official purposes, and their bureaucratic language contains many stereotyped formulae. Thus, for instance, when we find that in the papyri the internal passive is used rather frequently or that the negative *lam* is quite common, this does not mean that people used the passive in everyday speech. Such forms are typical examples of Classical markers (not only then but still today!). This is also confirmed by the abundant occurrence of pseudo-corrections in the papyri, for instance, the use of the accusative *'alif* in nominative position, the ending *-ūna* after *lam*, etc. There are no instances of analytical genitives or aspectual particles, but this is not unexpected, since such forms belonged to the most informal register of speech.

Apart from the papyri, various categories of pre-modern Middle Arabic texts may be distinguished. Among the best known are fairytales of the Arabian Nights (*ʿAlf layla wa-layla*) type. Most of these stories originated in the period from the twelfth to the sixteenth centuries, and the manuscripts date from the thirteenth to the nineteenth centuries. In the form in which we have them, they have undergone a literary adaptation, and the colloquial elements represent a conscious attempt to enliven the narrative. Most printed editions have 'corrected' the text in the manuscripts according to the standard norm, but the most important collection, that of the Arabian Nights, is now available in a critical edition by Muḥsin Mahdī (1984), based entirely on the manuscripts. As an example of this style, we quote from another collection of similar stories the following passage, illustrating the dialogue style with a number of colloquial traits (use of the negation *mā*, imperatives *imḍī*, *ǧī*; feminine gender of *ḫātim*; asyndetic use of a hypotactic clause with *'aṣlaḥ*):

> *fa-qāla r-Rašīd: ḏālika l-Malīḥ man huwa? 'aḫbirnī bihi! fa-qāla: yā mawlānā mā yanfahim kalām Masrūr? fa-qāla: imḍī izʿaq bihi! fa-qāla Masrūr: mā 'amḍī 'ilayhi, fa-qāla r-Rašīd: yā Ǧaʿfar, udḫul bi-llāh wa-'abṣir man huwa llaḏī qad ḍaraba Masrūr wa-hāḏihi ḫātimī imḍī bihā 'ilayhi wa-ǧī bihi! fa-qāla Ǧaʿfar: yā mawlānā Masrūr yaǧī 'aṣlaḥ!* 'Ar-Rašīd said: "Who is this Malīḥ? Tell me about him!". He said: "My Lord, are Masrūr's words not understood?" He said: "Go and frighten him!" Masrūr said: "By God, I'm not going!" Ar-Rašīd said: "Ǧaʿfar, by God, go in and see who it is that hit Masrūr; here is my ring, take it to him and bring him!" Ǧaʿfar said: "My Lord, it is better for Masrūr to go".' (Wehr 1956: 386.12–15)

The Arabian Nights differ from real folktales in that the latter stem from an oral tradition of folk poetry and folktales, told by professional storytellers wherever people were gathered in the marketplace. Presumably these stories were originally told in the vernacular. When they were written down later by interested collectors, they did not escape the influence of the standard norm, so that in their present form they cannot be regarded as examples of pure colloquial speech. Many of these stories are still extant in manuscript form, especially in the libraries in Moscow and Cambridge.

Throughout history, poets have sometimes used the medium of colloquial Arabic to express their feelings. This led to some kind of literary vernacular rather than a true reflection of the colloquial as it was spoken by the poet and his audience. Such poems have been preserved from the Syrian poet ʿUmar al-Maḥḥār (thirteenth century), the Egyptian poet ʿAlī ibn Sūdūn (fifteenth century) and the Ḥaḍramawtī poet as-Saʿd ibn Suwaynī (fifteenth century). This kind of poetry was particularly popular in the Maghreb, where it even infiltrated Classical poems. In the genre known as *muwaššaḥ*, it became customary to add a refrain in the colloquial language, either the Arabic colloquial or in some cases the Romance language spoken in Andalusia (the so-called *jarchas*; cf. below, Chapter 14, p. 227).

In the types of texts mentioned thus far, the colloquial elements were connected with their literary or narrative function. In Arabic scientific treatises, however, when the topic is exclusively technical and of no interest to the general intellectual elite, the colloquial elements are more or less accidental. In the field of medicine or pharmacology, or in the field of the technical sciences such as mathematics, astronomy or mechanics, the author was less constricted by the norms of the Classical language, and, if he preferred to follow the rules of his colloquial speech instead, nobody blamed him. In such texts, as in those texts whose author deliberately chose a more informal medium of expression, deviations from the Classical norm are widespread, but pseudo-corrections are seldom found.

As an example of 'educated' Muslim Middle Arabic, we quote here a passage from the memoirs of 'Usāma ibn Munqiḏ (d. 584/1188).

> *fa-lammā waṣalnā ʿAsqalān saḥaran wa-waḍaʿnā 'aṯqālanā ʿinda l-muṣallā ṣabaḥūnā l-'Ifranǧ ʿinda ṭulūʿ aš-šams fa-ẖaraǧa 'ilaynā Nāṣir ad-Dawla Yāqūt wālī ʿAsqalān fa-qāla: irfaʿū, irfaʿū 'aṯqālakum, qultu: taẖāfu lā yaġlibūnā l-'Ifranǧ ʿalayhā? qāla: naʿam, qultu: lā taẖāfu, hum yarawnā fī l-barriyya wa-yuʿāriḍūnā 'ilā 'an waṣalnā 'ilā ʿAsqalān, mā ẖifnāhum; naẖāfuhum l-'ān wa-naḥnu ʿinda madīnatinā?* 'When we came to Asqalon at daybreak and we put down our luggage at the prayer site, the Franks came on us at sunrise. Nāṣir ad-Dawla Yāqūt, the governor of Asqalon, came to us and said: "Take up, take up your luggage!" I said: "You're afraid the Franks will take them away from us?" He said: "Yes!" I said: "Don't be afraid! They saw us in the desert and kept up with us until we came to Asqalon. We didn't fear them, so shall we fear them now that we are near our city?"' ('Usāma ibn Munqiḏ, *Kitāb al-iʿtibār*, ed. Qāsim as-Sāmarrā'ī, Riyadh, 1987, pp. 38–9)

In this fragment, we find the kind of language that could be expected from an 'Arab gentleman' like 'Usāma, who had studied grammar without becoming a purist. He had no qualms about leaving out accusative endings, using verb/subject agreement, using *'ayy šay'* (i.e. *'êš*) instead of *mā*, connecting verbs with hypotactic clauses asyndetically, and using the imperfect verb ending *-ū* instead of *ūna*. In his writing, he maintained a colloquial flavour without losing touch with the standard language, and felt free to bend the grammatical rules without appearing illiterate. The common feature between this kind of Middle Arabic and the texts mentioned above is the presence of deviations from standard grammar. But pseudo-corrections are completely absent from the prose of 'Usāma and other writers like him.

8.3 JUDAEO-ARABIC

As we have seen above, Middle Arabic is not a special variety of the language but the name for a category of texts with deviations from the Classical standard language. When Jews and Christians write in Arabic, however, it is legitimate to regard their language as a special variety, since their brand of written Arabic became a special in-group form of the language, a new norm. The Jewish variety of Middle Arabic is often indicated with the special name of 'Judaeo-Arabic'. At the beginning of the Islamic conquests, the language of the Jews in the conquered territories was Aramaic; Hebrew was their language of religion and poetry, but was not used as a spoken language. We do not know when the colloquial language of the Jews became Arabic, but it must have been rather early. The first literary works written in Arabic by Jews date from the ninth century, and most of the non-literary documents date from the period after the year 1000; the majority of them have been found in the Cairo Geniza. Since for Jewish speakers of Arabic the Classical standard served less as a constraint, their written version of the language exhibited more colloquial features. These are not to be regarded as mistakes or signs of deficient knowledge. Maimonides (d. 1204), for instance, uses a flawless type of Classical Arabic in letters to Muslims, but when he writes to his co-religionists his language contains many of the features found in other Middle Arabic texts.

The written Arabic of Jewish authors is characterised by two special features: the fact that it is written in Hebrew script, and the presence of a large number of Hebrew loans. The representation of the Arabic phonemes by Hebrew letters is strictly a system of transliteration, i.e. every character of the Arabic text is represented by a Hebrew character on a strict one-to-one basis. Since the Hebrew alphabet has fewer letters than the Arabic, some adjustments were needed. The most ingenious invention of the Jewish scribes is their use of Hebrew allophones for Arabic phonemes. In Hebrew, most occlusives have a spirant allophone in certain environments, indicated by a dot in the letter (the so-called *dageš*), e.g. the Hebrew *dalet* indicates the *d*, and with a dot its allophone *d̠*; similarly, *tav* indicates *t*/*t̠*, *kaf* indicates *k*/*h̠*, and so on. In transcribing Arabic words, the scribes used these letters with dots to represent Arabic *d̠*, *t̠*, *h̠* (in the manuscripts the dot is often omitted, so that the script retains a certain ambiguity). For those letters with which this device did not work, they used the letters for Hebrew voiceless sounds, and provided them with a dot: in this way, *ṣade* with a dot was used for Arabic *ḍ*, and *ṭet* was used for *ḏā'*. The fact that the scribes distinguished between *ḍād* and *ḏā'* already indicates that we are dealing here with a strictly written tradition, since in pronunciation both phonemes had merged. Likewise, the scribes faithfully rendered the Arabic article, even when it was assimilated, as well as the otiose *'alif* in Arabic verb forms.

There are traces of an earlier stage in which the transliteration of Arabic into Hebrew took place on the basis of the spoken language. Although most Judaeo-

Arabic texts date from the period after the year 1000, we have a few ninth-century Judaeo-Arabic papyri from Egypt, written in a transcription not influenced by the orthography of Classical Arabic. The most significant feature is that both Arabic *ḍ* and *ḍ̣* are transcribed with Hebrew *dalet*, which for the scribes must have been the closest phonetic equivalent available. Moreover, the Arabic article when assimilated is always represented in its assimilated form. This means that originally the scribes used a transcription system that was based on the conventions of their own Hebrew/Aramaic script applied to an oral form of Arabic. After the year 1000, this system was replaced by a system based entirely on the Arabic script, possibly because of the influential position held by the Arabic translation of the *Pentateuch* by Saadya Gaon (882–942 CE), in which these conventions are used. There are a few early texts in which the Arabic vowels are consistently transcribed with Hebrew Tiberian vowel signs. In a fragment of Saadya's translation of the Bible (Levy 1936: 18), the declensional endings are indicated, as befits a Bible translation, but other short final vowels have been elided. Noteworthy are the strong *'imāla* (e.g. *mūsē* for *Mūsā*, *allēhi* for *Allāhi*) as well as the *-i-* in the relative pronoun *illaḏī* (*allaḏī*), the conjunction *wi-*, and the article *il*.

The reason behind the use of Hebrew letters is the special position of the Jews in the Islamic empire. Although generally speaking they were emancipated, and as *ḏimmī*s lived under the protection of the caliph and could freely exercise their religion, the social barriers between Jews and Muslims were considerable, and no doubt they remained a special group. The use of their own alphabet reinforced this in-group feeling. Many Arabic texts were either transcribed by them in Hebrew letters or translated into Hebrew.

The second feature that sets the Judaeo-Arabic texts apart from the rest of Arabic literature is the extensive use of Hebrew loans. Through the use of these loans, the language of Jewish literary and scientific writings became in fact incomprehensible or unfamiliar to Muslims. Thus, although structurally Judaeo-Arabic is quite similar to Muslim Middle Arabic or to Christian Arabic, the presence of Hebrew words immediately marks a text as having been written by a Jewish author. The use of Hebrew words is not restricted to the written language only, as we know from the evidence of the modern Judaeo-Arabic dialects, for instance the Arabic of the Jews of Tunis, or that of the Jews who emigrated from Iraq to Israel. In their colloquial speech, one finds many Hebrew words, especially in typically Jewish domains such as religion and worship.

In some Judaeo-Arabic texts, Hebrew passages alternate with Arabic ones, for instance in explanations of the *Talmud*, where first the Hebrew (or Aramaic) text is quoted and then explained in Arabic. But exclusively Arabic passages also abound in Hebrew words. When Hebrew words are used in their Hebrew form, i.e. not as loans but as instances of code-switching, they are integrated syntactically; in most cases, however, the Hebrew words are also integrated phonologically and morphologically, thus showing that they have become part of an Arabic vocabulary. The writers of Judaeo-Arabic were aware of equivalences between Hebrew and Arabic, and this enabled them to arabicise Hebrew words, for instance by shifting them from the Hebrew *hitpa'el* measure to the Arabic *tafa''ala*, or from the Hebrew *hif'il* to the Arabic *'af'ala*: *hit'abel* becomes *ta'abbala* 'to mourn', *hisdīr* becomes *'asdara* 'to organise a prayer'.

Hebrew verbs may be inflected as Arabic verbs, e.g. *naḥūšū* 'we fear' (< Hebrew *ḥōš* 'to fear' with the Maghrebi Arabic prefix of the first person plural *n-...-ū*).

Hebrew substantives may receive an Arabic broken plural, e.g. *rewaḥ*, plural *'arwāḥ* 'profits' instead of the Hebrew plural *rewaḥot*; *seder* 'prayer', Hebrew plural *s^edarīm*, receives an Arabic plural *'asdār*; *maḫzōr* 'prayer book for the festival', Hebrew plural *maḫzōrīm*, receives an Arabic plural *maḫāzīr*. The Arabic article replaces the Hebrew article sometimes even when the entire context is Hebrew, thus demonstrating the fact that *al-* was regarded as an integral part of the Hebrew words, e.g. *bet al-kneset* 'the synagogue', or *al-berit qodeš* 'the holy covenant'. There is one text from the Cairo Geniza in which the Arabic components are written in Arabic and the Hebrew ones in Hebrew, so that it is easy to see which elements were regarded as Hebrew. In this text, the combination of Arabic article with Hebrew noun is written in Hebrew characters. As an example illustrating the mixed character of Judaeo-Arabic, we may quote from Blau (1965: 152; Hebrew written words underlined) the phrase *al-ʿiqār* <u>*we-'afʿal gab*</u> *'in lam yuktab* <u>*š^eṭār*</u> 'the immovable property, in spite of the fact that no note was written'.

The *ad hoc* character of the use of Hebrew words instead of Arabic words is demonstrated in texts in which both alternatives are used in an arbitrary pattern; thus we may find in one line *zawǧ ṯānī* 'a second husband' and in the next *baʿluhā ṯ-ṯānī* 'her second husband', or *dīney goyim* 'laws of the Gentiles' alternating with *maḏhab al-goyim*. This happens even with proper names, so that the same person may be indicated within one text alternatingly as *Šelomoh ben Dawid* and *Sulaymān ibn Dā'ūd*. Most of the integrated loanwords, but by no means all of them, belong to the sphere of religion and religious practice, for which there were sometimes no corresponding Arabic words.

It is difficult to distinguish regionally-defined categories within the group of Judaeo-Arabic texts. In the first place, the use of written Arabic by Jews tended to become conventionalised, and a kind of standard Judaeo-Arabic developed all over the empire. In the second place, the patterns of migration among the Jews in the Islamic empire often disturbed the picture, so that, for instance, Egyptian Jews wrote in a markedly more Maghrebi Arabic than their Muslim compatriots. Finally, as in all varieties of Middle Arabic, even Judaeo-Arabic could not escape entirely the attraction of the Classical standard.

8.4 CHRISTIAN MIDDLE ARABIC

Just as was the case for Judaeo-Arabic, texts in Arabic written by Christians were much less influenced by the Classical standard than those written by Muslim writers. The majority of the texts stem from the Southern Palestinian area, including the Sinai. Many of the texts are preserved nowadays in the Monastery of Saint Catherine in the Sinai. A special characteristic of Christian Arabic literature is the fact that most of the texts are translations from either Greek or Syriac and only a very few were written originally in Arabic. This adds, of course, to the peculiar quality of the language of these texts and makes it at times difficult to distinguish between regular phenomena of interference by the vernacular of the writer, on the one hand, and interference due to the translation, on the other. The translations were often rather literal, using loan constructions from the Greek or Syriac original. Such constructions no doubt sounded awkward in Arabic, but they could become productive in the idiom of Christian Arabic writers in the same way that the Bible translations in European languages to a large extent influenced the stylistic and idiomatic development of these languages in spite of the fact that they contained calques from the original Greek or Hebrew text.

Christian Arabic documents go back to an earlier date than the Jewish Arabic documents, sometimes even to the eighth century. In this period, Aramaic was still a living language, and many of the Christian writers were bilingual in Aramaic/Syriac and Arabic, so that their use of Arabic may even reflect direct interference from their first language. Some of the texts are written in Syriac characters, known as Kharšūnī texts, and there is one in Greek characters, the famous psalm fragment mentioned above (p. 118). There are even a few texts that have been preserved in Coptic characters (cf. below).

Among the Christian Middle Arabic texts, translations of hagiographic texts, for instance *vitae* of Christian saints, homilies and sermons, and patristic texts constitute the most important category. A considerable number of Bible translations existed, both of the Old Testament and of the New Testament, but it is doubtful that these go back to pre-Islamic times, as has sometimes been maintained, since they contain the type of pseudo-corrections that belong to the period in which there was a codified linguistic norm. A number of texts have originally been written in Arabic and are not a translation of a Greek or Syriac original; most of these concern christological treatises by Arab Christians, for instance the treatises by Theodore 'Abū Qurra (d. ± 820). Non-literary texts by Christians include historical texts, for instance the chronicle of Agapius (tenth century) and that of Yaḥyā ibn Sa'īd al-'Anṭākī (tenth/eleventh century).

In the South Palestinian texts from the eighth century onwards that were used by Blau in his grammar of Christian Arabic, some features are conspicuously absent. Blau specifically mentions the near-absence of the genitive exponent in these texts. In these older texts, the norm of the standard language was still more or less adhered to, and some features do not make their appearance until much later, when the norm had been eroded. In a Christian Arabic text written in Coptic script and dating from the thirteenth century, we find clear traces of colloquial pronunciation, but in spite of the fact that it was written in a foreign orthography the syntax and part of the morphology are still Classical, and the presence of several pseudo-corrections shows the inclination of the author towards the standard language.

Although this Coptic text, possibly a *vita* of Saint Pachomius, does not exhibit many deviations from Classical Arabic, it is a fascinating document of thirteenth-century Arabic because of the spelling of the vowels. The *'imāla* is very pronounced, *a*/*ā* are consistently transliterated as *e*, except after an emphatic or guttural consonant, e.g. *wekefeh* (*wāqifa*) 'standing', *seha* (*sā'a*) 'hour', *bemexafet* (*bi-maḫāfa*) 'in fear'. Since the article is written with *e* even before emphatic consonants (*essora* = *aṣ-ṣūra* 'the picture'), we may assume that it transliterates colloquial *il* rather than Classical *al* with *'imāla*. The vowel *e* is also used for unstressed *i*/*u*, which were probably elided and reduced as in the modern dialects, e.g. *ešševeyoux* (*aš-šuyūḫ* 'the old men'). A striking feature of the text is the use of a suffix *en*, sometimes written as an independent word, which is used after indefinite nouns, regardless of its syntactic function in the sentence, to indicate that they are connected with an attribute, as in *k'en mehellemen ǵarib* (*kāna mu'allim ġarīb* 'there was a strange teacher'), *be mesk'enet'en hazimeh* (*bi-maskana 'aẓīma* 'in awful poverty'), *rojol en kaddis ebsar* (*rağul qaddīs 'abṣara* 'a holy man saw'). This suffix is probably derived from the Classical nunation, but it has become a new marker that serves as the connection between indefinite noun and attribute. In this function, it resembles the *tanwīn* markers in modern Arabic Bedouin dialects in the Arabian peninsula (cf. below, Chapter 10, p. 149).

As we go to later Christian texts, we find phenomena that demonstrate a clear neglect of the Classical norm. For an example of an analytical genitive in a manuscript, we may refer to a *vita* of Saint Menas dating from the eighteenth century: *bi-l-ḥaqīqa lā budd hādihi l-'a'ḍā min aš-šuhadā' bitā'inā* 'indeed, these bones must belong to our martyrs' (Jaritz 1993: 452.6). The *vita* of Saint Menas is preserved in many versions, most of which contain an abundance of pseudo-corrections, e.g.:

> *fa-lammā mašayat fī l-barriyya waḥdahā wa-hiya bi-l-qurb min bay'at al-qiddīsa Tikla naḥwa mayl wa-lam yakūn 'aḥadan min an-nās yamšī ma'ahā wa-'idā bi-ğundī min ḥurrās aṭ-ṭarīq qad daẖala fīhi š-šayṭān ğamī' 'a'ṭāhu fa-masakahā wa-qāla lahā: 'ilā 'ayna māḍiya? fa-ḍannat 'annahu yaḥmil alladī 'aẖadathu ma'ahā fa-qālat lahu: 'anā māḍiya yā sayyidī 'ilā bay'at aš-šahīd al-'aẓīm 'Abū Mīnā* 'When she was going in the desert all alone and came near the church of Saint Thecla, approximately one mile, and nobody was walking with her, and lo, there was a soldier from the guardians of the road, in all whose limbs the devil had gone, and he grabbed her and said to her: "Where are you going?" She thought that he was going to carry away the things she had taken with her and said to him: "I am going to the church of the great martyr 'Abū Mīnā".' (Jaritz 1993: 416)

In this text, we find several instances of pseudo-correct accusatives, incorrect verbal forms (*mašayat, lam yakūn*), use of *'anna* instead of *'an*, colloquial construction of the participle without subject (*māḍiya*), and a real jumble in the orthography (sometimes *ḍ* for *ẓ*, sometimes *ṭ*: *ḍannat*, *'a'ṭāhu* = *'a'ḍā'ihi*, and a fairly consistent replacement of all *ta' marbūṭa*s with *tā'* (on the other hand, *ḍannat* is spelled with *ṭā' marbūṭa*!).

These examples show on the one hand that Christian writers did feel restricted by the Classical standard (otherwise they would not have been tempted to use pseudo-corrections), and on the other hand, that in some respects the standard had become more lenient than before (otherwise there would not occur any analytical genitives in these texts). In the explanatory texts on Coptic icons from the eighteenth and nineteenth centuries, although these belong to the religious domain, one finds elements that are conspicuously absent from contemporaneous Muslim Arabic texts, for instance the use of the *bi-* imperfect.

8.5 CONTEMPORARY MIDDLE ARABIC?

Depending on the definition of 'Middle Arabic', contemporary texts in a mixed style may be regarded as a special category, or they may be included in the category of texts that has been discussed so far. Paradoxically enough, with the spreading of education the number of people with some degree of schooling in Standard Arabic has increased immensely. There is a large number of semi-literates, people who are able to write simple messages but lack the skills to write the language correctly according to the strict rules of grammar. When these people write Arabic, they tend to make the very same mistakes which one finds in the Middle Arabic texts of the Classical period.

The most obvious feature of both Classical and contemporary texts is their variation and inconsistency, which underscores the fact that these texts are not written in a discrete variety of the language. An incorrect form in one sentence may be repeated correctly in the next, the word order may vary between the colloquial and the standard order, the agreement rules of Classical Arabic are applied in one sentence and neglected in another, within one and the same sentence reference to two persons may be made in the dual and in the plural, and so on.

In the usual definition, the term 'Middle Arabic' also includes literary texts with dialectal elements, such as the memoirs of 'Usāma ibn Munqiḏ. There is a large difference, however, between the mixed literary texts of the Classical period and examples from modern literature. After the period of the *Nahḍa* (cf. below, Chapter 11), the use of colloquial elements in literary texts became a permanent issue in any discussion between intellectuals in the Arab world. In Egypt, the emphasis on 'egyptianisation' stimulated some writers to experiment with the diglossic reality of their language. Some writers felt that the use of dialect in dialogues was unavoidable when reporting the speech of illiterate people, and started using a combination of standard and colloquial. Although educated people, too, use dialect in their everyday speech, there was a general feeling that it would be improper to have them speak like that on paper.

After the initial attempts to integrate dialect and standard in literary texts in the early part of the twentieth century, the shift towards pan-Arabic nationalism in most Arab countries turned the use of colloquial elements in literature into a controversial option. Even those writers who had used dialect in earlier publications, such as Tawfīq al-Ḥakīm, publicly regretted their transgressions and reverted to the use of a pure standard. Two points are to be noted here. In the first place, even those writers who were determined to write in colloquial Arabic could never escape completely the influence of the written language. Thus, the language of their writings is hardly ever an example of 'pure' colloquial speech. Very often, the use of dialect amounts to no more than the insertion of colloquial markers (cf. also below, Chapter 12).

In the second place, literary writers have an intimate knowledge of Classical Arabic and their use of colloquial language is always intentional. Thus, in their writings there are no examples of pseudo-correction due to lack of grammatical education. This kind of Middle Arabic is therefore much more akin to those Middle Arabic texts in which colloquial elements are used for the purpose of *couleur locale*. Some contemporary Arab authors pride themselves on being able to write theatre plays in 'pure' colloquial speech, whereas in reality they have adopted a literary form of the dialect. Admittedly, contemporary Egypt is farthest in this direction, since the position of the dialect in Egypt is different from that in other Arab countries. But even in Egypt, written dialect is not identical with spoken dialect, and theatre plays have to be 'translated' before they can actually be staged.

An interesting parallel is the use of colloquial colouring in formal radio speech. Sometimes the speaker in a radio programme, in order to create an intimate atmosphere, tries to transform the (written) text serving as the basis for the broadcast into a dialect text with the help of dialect markers. Take the following example from the beginning of a programme for housewives.

> *fī 'akbar magalla nisā'iyya fī 'urubba 'arêt dirāsa ʿan il-mar'a; dirāsa ġarība wi-mufīda, wa-'ayḍan musīra; li-'annáha tikallim ʿan is-sirr 'allaḏī yagʿal il-mar'a šaẖṣiyya lā tunsa, šaẖṣiyya mā ḥaddiš 'abadan yi'dar yinsāha* 'In the largest women's weekly in Europe I read an article about women; a strange and useful article, and also touching; because it talks about the secret that makes a woman into an unforgettable personality, a personality that nobody can ever forget' (Diem 1974: 71)

In this example, the speaker tries to use dialect – and apparently feels that she is actually speaking dialect – but at the same time it is clear that the original of her speech is Classical Arabic: the construction with *'akbar*, the use of *'ayḍan*, the use of the conjunction *li-'annahā*, and the phrase with an internal passive (*lā tunsā*), which is paraphrased in its entirety. This example shows the strength of the standard model in formal settings: even when speakers deliberately attempt to speak dialect, they will always unconsciously revert to Classical patterns.

An interesting parallel may be found in official Dutch brochures for the Moroccan minority. For ideological reasons, the policy in the Netherlands has become to use the Moroccan dialect. In actual practice, this leads to the insertion of a few markers, whereas the structure of the text remains decidedly Standard Arabic. As an example, we quote the following sentence from a brochure about taxes in the Netherlands.

> *kamā taʿrifūna 'inna l-'ağnabī ka-yitlaqqā kaṯīr aṣ-ṣuʿūbāt wa-t-taġayyurāt fī l-ḥayāt dyālo wa-bi-l-ẖuṣūs maʿa l-'awlād 'illī ka-yimšiw li-l-madrasa; wa-li-hāḏā fa-min al-wāğib ʿalaykum bāš taʿrifū n-niẓām wa-kayfiyyat at-taʿlīm fī hūlandā* 'As you know, a foreigner encounters many difficulties and changes in his life and in particular with the children that go to school; therefore, it is necessary for you to know the system and the nature of education in Holland'

In spite of the obvious attempts at writing Moroccan dialect (aspectual prefix *ka-*; genitive exponent *dyāl*; conjunction *bāš*; the verbal form *ka-yimšiw*, spelled *k-y-m-š-i-w*), the translator of this originally Dutch text obviously could not escape Standard Arabic phraseology and structure of the sentence (although, of course, the transcription used here masks some of the dialectal features that would come out in pronouncing the text). In the rest of the text, there is a constant variation between dialectal and standard forms that shows the inability of the translator to avoid classicisms.

It is certainly not current usage to call a text such as the one just quoted 'Middle Arabic'. Yet, there is an unmistakable similarity between these contemporary examples and the texts discussed in the preceding sections of this chapter. The common denominator in all instances of mixed language and at all levels of written production is the centripetal force of the standard language. Whether authors deliberately use colloquial features or simply fail to attain the level of grammatically correct speech, they always remain within the framework of the standard language. In Chapter 12, we shall see that something similar happens even in the production of spoken speech.

FURTHER READING

The best general introduction to Middle Arabic is still Blau (1965); see also Lebedev (1977). In numerous articles, Blau has defined the character of Middle Arabic (e.g. 1972–3, 1981); especially worth reading is his terminological discussion of the term 'Middle Arabic' (1982), in which he admits that the earlier use of the term erroneously assumed that Middle Arabic is a speech variety rather than a sociolinguistic label to indicate a category of texts. The important subject of hyper- and hypocorrections is dealt with by Blau (1965: 27–34, 1970). A reprint of Blau's most important articles on the subject of Middle Arabic was published in Blau (1988).

On Muslim Middle Arabic, an introduction to the study of the papyri is in Grohmann (1966); see also analysis of the language of the papyri by Hopkins (1984) with details on the publication of the material. Studies on texts in Muslim Middle Arabic include Schen (the memoirs of 'Usāma ibn Munqiḏ, 1972–3) and A. Müller (1884; the language of Ibn 'Abī 'Uṣaybiʿa's biographical lexicon of medical scholars). Of primary importance is the critical edition of the Arabian Nights by Mahdī (1984): most of the preceding editions consisted in an adaptation of the text to Classical norms and did not give an insight in the real language of the texts. On folktales, see Lebedev (1993); on colloquial poetry in al-'Andalus, see Corriente (1980) and Zwartjes (1995).

The best manual for Judaeo-Arabic is Blau (1965); it contains a large appendix about the Hebrew element in Judaeo-Arabic, as well as an appendix on the characteristics of Muslim Middle Arabic. An anthology of texts in Judaeo-Arabic was published by Blau in 1980. On the early orthography of Judaeo-Arabic, see Blau and Hopkins (1984).

For Christian Arabic, Blau (1966–7) is fundamental; an older publication on the language of Arabic texts written by Christians is Graf (1905); on the literature of the Arab Christians, see Graf (1944–66). The Arabic psalm translation in Greek letters was edited by Violet (1902); see also the remarks in the section on phonology in Hopkins (1984: 1–61). The text in Coptic letters was edited partially by Casanova (1902) and fully by Sobhy (1926); for an analysis, see Blau (1979). An edition of the *vita* of 'Abū Mīnā (Menas) and analysis of its language is in Jaritz (1993). The Arabic of the Bible translations is studied by Bengtsson (1995) on the basis of the translation of the Book of Ruth.

On the controversy about the use of dialect in literature, see Diem (1974: 96–125). Woidich and Landau (1993) produced 'Aḥmad il-Fār's farces in Egyptian dialect from the beginning of the twentieth century, with extensive notes on their language. Analysis of a work in contemporary colloquial Egyptian (Saʿd ad-Dīn Wahba's theatre play *Il-wazīr šāl it-tallāga*) in Malina (1987). A list of dialect words in Egyptian literature was compiled by Vial (1983).

9

The Study of the Arabic Dialects

9.1 THE STUDY OF THE ARABIC DIALECTS

In the preceding chapters, we have concentrated on the features which the Arabic vernaculars or dialects have in common as against the Classical Standard language. In that context, we have shown that they represent a different type of Arabic, rather than just a modified version of the Classical language. In this chapter and the next the focus will be on differences between the dialects, in particular the geographical variation and the separation into several dialect areas. The issue of the sociolinguistic variation between the dialects and the standard language will be reserved for Chapter 12.

The systematic study of dialect geography is a typical invention of Western European nineteenth-century linguistics. But it would be wrong to suppose that the Arabs themselves were not aware of the variation in speech in the Arabophone world. We have seen above that the grammarians accepted the variation in the pre-Islamic dialects and even collected the variants, because in their view these belonged to the corpus of pure Arabic speech (p. 39). They were not interested, however, in the urban dialects that arose all over the empire. In accordance with their views on the Arabic language, they regarded these as erroneous and refrained from mentioning them in their writings. But those outside the grammatical tradition did show an interest in the linguistic difference between the various parts of the empire and its causes. At an early date, al-Ǧāḥiẓ (d. 255/868) informs us that 'the people in the cities talk according to the language of the Bedouin immigrants that had settled there, which is why you find lexical differences between the people of Kūfa and Baṣra and Syria and Egypt' (*wa-'ahl al-'amṣār 'innamā yatakallamūna ʿalā luġat an-nāzila fīhim min al-ʿArab, wa-li-ḏālika taǧidu l-iḫtilāf fī 'alfāẓ min 'alfāẓ 'ahl al-Kūfa wa-l-Baṣra wa-š-Šām wa-Miṣr, Bayān* I, 38). In Kūfa, he adds, the immigration of Persians to the city brought in a number of Persian words: the inhabitants of this city say *ǧahār-sūǧ* (Persian *čahār* 'four' + *sū(ǧ)* 'road') where the Basrans say *marbaʿa* for a crossroads, and they use words such as *ḫiyār* instead of *qiṯṯā'* 'cucumber', and *wāzār* instead of *sūq* 'market' (Persian *ḫiyār, bāzār*). The topic of linguistic variation is restricted almost exclusively to writings such as these, as well as the books of the Arab historians, geographers and travellers. They sometimes inform us about different pronunciations in various areas and about the lexical variation in the areas which they visited. The most extensive description of the ways of talking in the Islamic empire and the differences between the various regions was given by al-Muqaddasī (d. 335/946) in his *Kitāb 'aḥsan at-taqāsīm fī maʿrifat al-'aqālīm* 'The best arrangement for the knowledge of the regions'. For all the provinces visited by him, he systematically discusses their linguistic peculiarities and supplies a list of lexical and phonetic regionalisms.

In other writers, the emphasis is on the social distribution of linguistic features. We find for instance in Ibn Ḫaldūn (*Muqaddima*, ed. Beirut, n.d., pp. 557–8) a chapter dedicated to the differences between sedentary and Bedouin speech, entitled 'The language of the sedentary population and the city-dwellers is an independent language, differing from the language of Muḍar' (*fī 'anna luġa 'ahl al-ḥaḍar wa-l-'amṣār luġa qā'ima bi-nafsihā li-luġa Muḍar*). In this chapter, he explains that the way in which city people talk differs essentially from the language of the *Ǧāhiliyya* (the language of Muḍar, the ancestor of the Qurayš through whom they traced their descendance from ʿAdnān, the ancestor of all Northern Arabs) and from the language of the contemporary Bedouin, for instance by their omitting the declensional endings, a phenomenon called by the grammarians *laḥn*. Each region has its own dialect, the eastern dialects differing from the western dialects, and the Andalusian dialect being different from both.

As we have seen above (p. 102), Ibn Ḫaldūn ascribes the changes in the Arabic language to the contact with the population of the conquered territories, and in this connection he again correlates the differences between the various dialects with the presence of other ethnic groups. Thus, the peculiarity of the dialect of the Maghreb is explained by him with a reference to the Berber presence: 'it has become a different language, a mixed one, and the foreign language has gained the upper hand in it' (*wa-ṣārat luġa 'uḫrā mumtaziǧa wa-l-ʿAǧamiyya fīhā 'aġlab*). Similarly, he says, the contact with speakers of Persian and Turkic in the East has brought changes to the dialects spoken in the Islamic East.

In one passage, the historian demonstrates that he is very much aware of the peculiarities of Bedouin speech:

> One of the phenomena that happen in the speech of these Arabs until this day … is their special way of pronouncing the *q*. They do not pronounce it at the place of articulation of the urban people, as it is mentioned in the books on Arabic, namely between the back of the tongue and the opposite point of the upper palate. They do not pronounce it at the place of articulation of the *k*, either, which is somewhat lower than the place of the *q* on the tongue and the upper palate, but they pronounce it at a place that is somewhere in the middle between the *q* and the *k*. (*wa-mimmā waqaʿa fī luġa hāḏā l-ġayl al-ʿarabī li-hāḏā l-ʿahd mā kānū min al-'aqṭār ša'nuhum fī n-nuṭq bi-l-qāf fa-'innahum lā yanṭuqūna min maḫraǧ al-qāf ʿinda 'ahl al-'amṣār kamā huwa maḏkūr fī kutub al-ʿarabiyya 'annahu min 'aqṣā l-lisān wa-mā fawqahu min al-ḥanak al-'aʿlā wa-mā yanṭuqūna bihā 'ayḍan min maḫraǧ al-kāf wa-'in kāna 'asfal min mawḍiʿ al-qāf wa-mā yalīhi min al-ḥanak al-'aʿlā kamā hiya bal yaǧī'ūna bihā mutawassiṭatan bayna l-kāf wa-l-qāf, Muqaddima*, p. 557)

This is an accurate description of one of the best-known differences between Bedouin and sedentary speech, the realisation of /q/. We have seen above (Chapter 6, p. 89) that in Sībawayhi's description of the *qāf*, it is classified as a voiced (*maǧhūr*) phoneme. Ibn Ḫaldūn does not mention that most sedentary dialects realised it as a voiceless phoneme, but emphasises the difference in place of articulation. In grammatical texts, one looks in vain for any reference to such variations in speech.

When in the nineteenth century European scholars started to become interested in the colloquial varieties of the Arabic language (cf. above, Chapter I, p. 6), this new trend did not always meet with approval in the Arab countries themselves. Since the dialects were a non-prestigious variety of the language, interest in their structure for its own sake was regarded as suspect. An exception is the situation in Egypt, where an interest in lexical regionalisms can be witnessed as early as the sixteenth century. In his dictionary entitled *Daf' al-'iṣr 'an kalām 'ahl Miṣr* ('The removal of the burden from the language of the people of Egypt'), Yūsuf al-Maġribī (d. 1019/1611) intends to record the way in which Arabic is spoken in Egypt. He criticises some of the 'errors' that Egyptians make, but in many cases he defends the Egyptian way of speaking by showing that it is related to Arabic. Even when he disapproves of 'errors' his examples are a precious source of information about early Egyptian Arabic:

> The people in Egypt, including some of the elite, say without thinking, for instance *fulān 'ad huwwa 'amal kaḏā* 'someone acted like this' or *'ad huwwa gā* 'look, he came'. There is no way of correcting such an expression; what they mean is *hā huwa* or *hāḏā huwa*. (*an-nās fī Miṣr yaqūlūna ḥattā ba'ḍ al-ḫawāṣṣ bi-ġayr fikr fulān 'ad huwwa 'amal kaḏā 'aw 'ad huwwa gā maṯalan hāḏihi l-lafẓa lā ḥīla fī taṣḥīfihā wa-murāduhum ma'nā hā huwa 'aw hāḏā*, Yūsuf al-Maġribī, *Ḍaf' al-'iṣr*, facsimile edn, Moscow, 1968, p. 3b)

In the nineteenth century, however, even in Egypt many people felt that the role of the Classical language as the uniting factor in the Arab world was threatened by too much attention to the dialects, symbols of the fragmentation of the Arab world. There was some truth in this suspicion, since in some cases the colonial authorities actively promoted the use of the dialect. In Algeria, for instance, the French for some time outlawed the teaching of Classical Arabic, which was replaced by the Algerian dialect, and in Egypt the British authorities actively supported experiments by Orientalists to replace the Arabic script with the Latin script as a medium for the Egyptian dialect. As a result, dialectology became associated with the divisive policy of the colonial authorities, and the dialectologist was regarded as a tool of imperialism. In addition, orthodox circles condemned any attempt to study the dialects as detrimental to the language of the *Qur'ān*.

In the modern period, it remains difficult in the Arab world to arouse interest in the dialects as a serious object of study. Many speakers of Arabic still feel that the dialect is a variety of language without a grammar, a variety used by children and women, and even in universities there is a certain reluctance to accept dialect studies as a dissertation subject. This is not to say that there are no Arab dialectologists. Many Arab linguists have applied their expertise to their native dialect, and some of the best dialect monographs have been written by Arab linguists. But on the whole, one may say that the study of dialectology still suffers from the drawbacks mentioned here.

Apart from the 'political' problem in Arabic dialectology, researchers are also confronted by a general problem of dialectological research, that of the observer's paradox. This is not a specific problem in the study of Arabic dialects, although the study of these dialects is particularly affected by it. Researchers are always faced by a paradox in that they wish the speakers of the dialect to speak as informally as possible, but it is precisely the attention to their speech which forces the speakers to upgrade their dialect and talk as 'correctly' as possible. In a situation of diglossia (see Chapter 12), this problem is even more intense than elsewhere, since there is a constant temptation for the speakers to move upwards on the speech continuum, even without the presence of a dialectologist. The result is manifest in a considerable number of dialect monographs and collections of dialect texts, which exhibit many traces of classicising. Dialect grammars often state, for instance, that the dialect has two ways of expressing possession, one with the Classical Arabic construct state and another with the analytical genitive. Such a statement is true as a synchronic observation, since many speakers indeed use the Classical construction because of the prestige of the standard language. But from a diachronic point of view, it would appear that the Classical construction is an intruder in the structure of the (sedentary) dialects, in which the analytical genitive replaced the Classical construction, at least in some contexts. The degree of emphasis which one places on the presence of both constructions in the dialect partly depends on the informants: when dialectologists choose to talk to the learned men of a village, they are bound to receive a highly upgraded kind of dialect in return. Besides, the grammatical descriptions often ignore the fact that in some cases the coexistence of the two constructions has brought about a new differentiation in function. In most dialects, the two possessive constructions have come to mark the opposition between alienable and inalienable possession (for instance, *laḥmi* 'my flesh'/*il-laḥm bitāʿi* 'my meat').

The upgrading of local dialect forms does not always have to take the form of classicisms. In cases of competing forms, informants will often choose the one that is identical to the prestige dialect, either a local one or, more often, the dialect of the capital. This applies even to those instances where the prestige form is not identical to the Classical form, whereas the local form is. In areas where an interdental and a dental realisation of /ṯ/ compete, the former is often avoided because it is associated with rural or Bedouin dialects, even though it is generally used in Qur'ānic recitation. Likewise, in some areas in the Egyptian Delta, the diphthongs /ay/ and /aw/ are avoided in conversations with outsiders and replaced with Cairene /ē/, /ō/.

In some speech communities, the presence of a low-prestige variant that is identical to the Classical form may lead to the avoidance of the latter in upgrading. One particularly striking example of this phenomenon is mentioned by Holes (1987: 74–6). Both in Kuwait and in Bahrain, the standard dialect realisation of Classical /ǧ/ is /y/. In Kuwait, upgrading leads to the replacement of /y/ with /ǧ/, which sounds more literate. In Bahrain, however, there is a Shiʿite minority that consistently uses /ǧ/. As a result, Sunnites in Bahrain never use /ǧ/ in upgrading, because this variant is associated with the non-prestige Shiʿite dialect.

9.2 THE CLASSIFICATION OF THE DIALECTS

Geographical linguistic variation is typically studied with the help of dialect maps that show the distribution of certain features over an area by means of imaginary lines drawn on the map (isoglosses). The isoglosses are imaginary lines, and their value depends to a great deal on the density of the points on which information is available. Typically, however, they occur in bundles, and when the bundle is strong enough it becomes possible to distinguish between dialect areas that differ markedly from other areas. This phenomenon is best seen in the case of geographical obstacles such as mountain ranges, which act as a boundary between areas. In other cases, the transition from one dialect to another tends to be gradual, with transitional zones in between. A dialect map is a synchronic representation of the dialects spoken in an area, but in many cases it is possible to infer from the data on the map something about the diachronic development of the area. Very often they tell us something about the relative chronology of the features, since as a rule the periphery of the area preserves the oldest features, that have not yet been reached by innovations from the prestige dialect of a cultural or political centre. The existence of transitional zones may be an indication of contacts between the speakers of different dialects.

Dialect atlases remain the most important tool for dialect geography and dialect classification. At the moment, atlases are available for only some of the areas of the Arabophone world. The oldest atlases were made of the Syro-Lebanese area by Bergsträßer (1915) and of the area around Ḥōrān and Palmyra by Cantineau (1940, 1946), a remarkable achievement for that time. In the modern period, the geographical distribution of the Egyptian dialects of the Šarqiyya was studied by Abul Fadl (1961), and a complete atlas of all Egyptian dialects (except Cairene) was produced by Behnstedt and Woidich (1985, 1987, 1988, 1994). Behnstedt also produced an atlas of the North Yemenite dialects (1985, 1992), while his atlas of the Syrian dialects is in course of publication. For the other areas, there are partial maps and dialect monographs, but on the whole the dialect map of the Arabophone world exhibits large blank spaces, especially so in the case of the Arabian peninsula. Even in the case of Egypt, our knowledge of other varieties than Cairene Arabic was sketchy until fairly recently.

The synchronic record of the dialect map represents innovations as clear-cut phenomena that are either present or absent. But on closer inspection, some dialect maps visualise the gradual introduction of an innovation in the form of an accumulation of phenomena (*terrace landscape*, or in German *Staffellandschaft*). One example is that of the *'aktib/niktibu* dialects in the Egyptian Delta. All dialects of the Maghreb are characterised by the prefix *n-* of the first person singular of the imperfect verb. This is one of the most frequently-cited isoglosses in Arabic dialectology, which divides the Western from the Eastern dialects. Moroccan Arabic has *nəktəb/nkətbu* 'I write/we write', whereas Eastern Arabic, for instance Syrian Arabic, has *'əktob/nəktob*. The *n-* prefix is also found in Maltese Arabic and in those sub-Saharan dialects that derived from a North African variety. The borderline between the Western and the Eastern dialects lies in the Egyptian Delta. There are two competing explanations for this development. The first explanation posits a change in the singular *nəktəb*

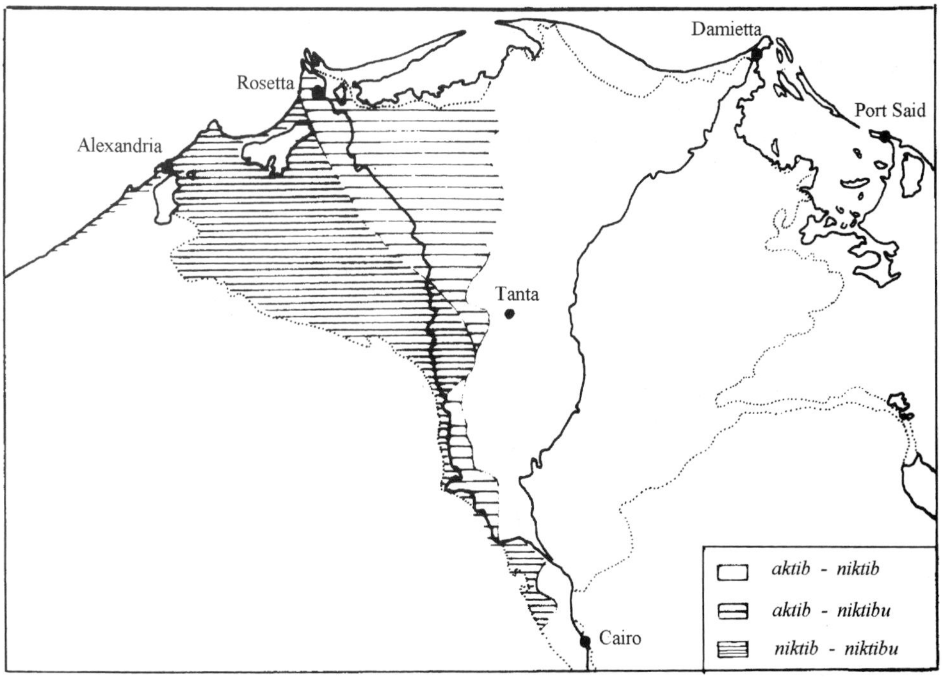

Map 9.1 Pronominal prefixes of the first person in the Egyptian Delta (after Behnstedt and Woidich 1985: map 211)

which is explained as contraction of the personal pronoun with the verb *'anā aktubu*; in this explanation, the plural is regarded as an analogous formation on the basis of the new singular. The second explanation starts from the plural form, which is explained as an analogous formation to the forms for the second and the third person plural *tkətbu, ikətbu*, the singular form being a secondary development. The dialect map of the Delta shows that between the two areas there is an area with *'aktib/niktibu*, which makes the latter explanation much more likely (see Map 9.1).

Another example is that of the pronoun of the first person singular in Yemenite dialects (Behnstedt 1985: 9, Map 38): in one area both the independent pronoun and the suffix are gender-neutral (*'ana/-ni*), more to the West there are a few areas where the independent pronoun has a masculine form *'ana* and a feminine one, *'ani*; finally, in the Tihāma both the independent pronoun and the object suffix have two forms (*'ana/'ani* and *-na/-ni*); in the latter area the suffix *-na* was no longer available for the first person plural, which therefore changed to *-iḥna*, as in the dialect of the Egyptian oasis of Farafra (cf. below, p. 137; see Map 9.2).

When a feature reaches a certain area, it will not affect mechanically every single item that it encounters. In many cases, for instance, an innovation spreading from an urban centre to the countryside will first affect the most frequent vocabulary items, thus creating a split in the vocabulary. The historical circumstances of the contact between both areas will determine the subsequent development. When contact becomes permanent, eventually the innovation

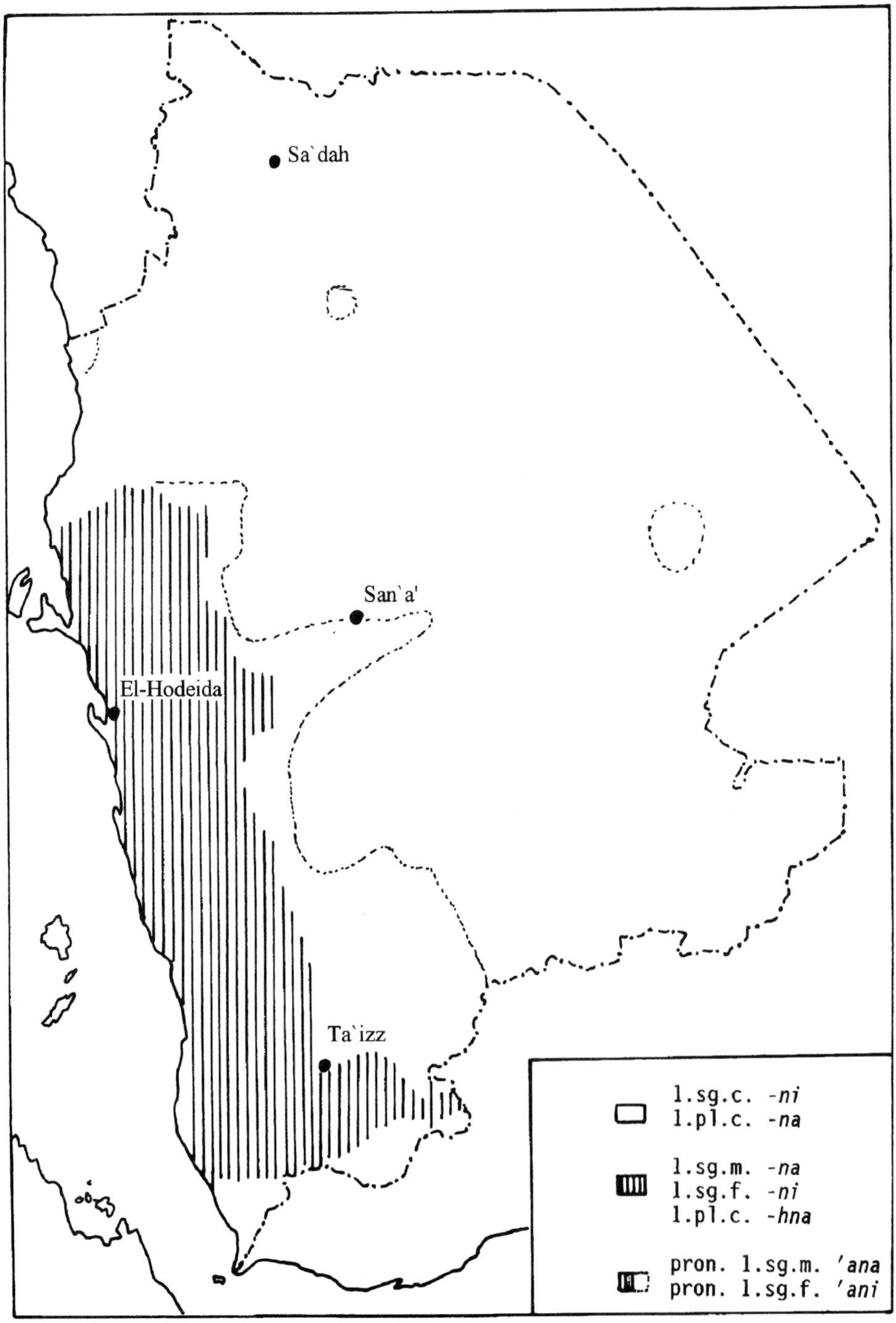

Map 9.2 Pronominal suffixes of the first person in the Yemenite dialects (after Behnstedt 1985: map 38)

will spread across the entire lexicon. But when the innovatory influence is withdrawn in mid-course or when loyalty towards the local dialect acts as a counterinfluence, the non-affected items are left in their original state, so that from a diachronic point of view the vocabulary gives the impression of a 'mixed' nature.

In most Arabic dialects, a certain amount of 'mixing' took place during the second stage of arabicisation when Bedouin tribes from the Arabian peninsula spread across the Islamic empire. The resulting contacts between sedentary and Bedouin speakers affected the lexicon in particular. In Uzbekistan Arabic, for instance, the usual realisation of Classical /q/ is voiceless /q/, but there are a few words containing a Bedouin voiced /g/, e.g. *gidir* 'pot', *giddām* 'before', *galab* 'to turn around'. This phenomenon is widespread over the Arabophone world. In Moroccan sedentary dialects, for instance that of Rabat, a few lexical items have Bedouin /g/, as in Uzbekistan Arabic, e.g. *gəmḥ* 'wheat' (Classical Arabic *qamḥ*), *gəmṛa* 'moon' (Classical Arabic *qamar*), *gədra* 'pot' (Classical Arabic *qidr*), *gəṛn* 'horn' (Classical Arabic *qarn*). It may be added that, inversely, in Bedouin dialects with the realisation /g/, there are usually some lexical items with /q/, for instance in the Moroccan dialect of Skūra *qbəṛ* 'grave', *qbīla* 'tribe', *qsəm* 'to divide'.

A well-documented case of dialect contact is that of the dialects in the Western oases in Egypt (Farafra, Da<u>h</u>la, <u>H</u>arga; cf. below, p. 161). According to Woidich's interpretation of the structure of these dialects (1993), some of the features which they exhibit, such as the prefix *n-* in the first person singular of the imperfect verb, may have been introduced in the course of contact with later invading Bedouin from the west, in particular the Banū Sulaym on their migrations back east. The dialect mixing in the oases demonstrates another result of dialect context, namely accommodation and overgeneralisation. As an example, we may mention the word-final stress in these dialects, which resembles that in Maghreb dialects. Contrary to what happens in the Maghreb dialects, however, the dialects of the oases also have word-final stress when the penultimate syllable is long, or when the final syllable ends in a vowel, e.g. in Farafra *minžál* 'sickle', *bayt^{s}iḥníy* 'our house'. This is probably to be interpreted as a generalisation of the rule in the Maghreb dialects. When the inhabitants of the oases came into contact with dialects in which many words were stressed on the final syllable, they overgeneralised in their attempt to accommodate to these dialects and extended the rule to all words.

The development of dialectal koines is a special case of dialect contact. Many of the Middle Eastern capitals, such as Amman and Baghdad, have gone through a period of rapid urbanisation, in which thousands of migrants flocked to the capital from the countryside, bringing with them their rural dialects. The ensuing mixture of dialects led to the emergence of more and less prestigious varieties, depending on the relative social and political power of the speakers involved (cf. below, Chapter 10, p. 160, on the emergence of Cairene Arabic). Within the confines of the national states, the new dialect of the capital started to exert an enormous influence on the neighbouring areas. In Iraq, for instance, the *gilit* dialect of the Muslims of Baghdad has become the prestige dialect, and speakers from the countryside tend to switch from their own local dialect to the dialect of the capital (even when features of their own dialect are closer to the Classical language, e.g. in the realisation of the Classical /q/!). A good example is the speech style of the Iraqi president Saddam Hussein, who in his public speeches has adapted to the Baghdad Muslim dialect – with *g* for Classical *q* – rather than the countryside dialect of his birthplace Tikrit, which belongs to the *qəltu* group of dialects and has a voiceless realisation of the *q*. The voiceless realisation is associated with both countryside and minority varieties. The latter association is also found in the case of Bahrain mentioned above (p. 133).

In Egypt, the dialect of Cairo has spread over a large area in the Delta. The map of the realisation of /q/ and /ğ/ in the central Delta shows an oblong area leading from Cairo to Damietta, in which the Cairene forms /g/ and /'/ are used, whereas the rest of the Delta has /ğ/ and /g/ (see Map 9.3, after Behnstedt and Woidich 1985: 31–2 and Map 15). After the decline of Alexandria as the main port of Cairo in the fourteenth century, the principal trade route ran from the capital along the eastern branch of the Nile to Damietta, as is shown by the concentration of trade centres along this route in the Middle Ages (see Map 9.4). Nowadays, the road from Cairo to Alexandria is the main artery in the Delta, and Cairene influence is indeed visible in Alexandria (/g/ and /'/), though not in the surrounding area. The configuration of the dialect map shows that Cairene Arabic influence corresponded to the frequency of trade contacts. Another conclusion that may be drawn from this configuration is that the realisation of /ğ/ as /g/ is not a recent development, but goes back at least to the flourishing period of the Damietta route.

The levelling influence of Cairene Arabic is also manifest in the speech patterns of recent migrants from the countryside to the capital. In a recent survey

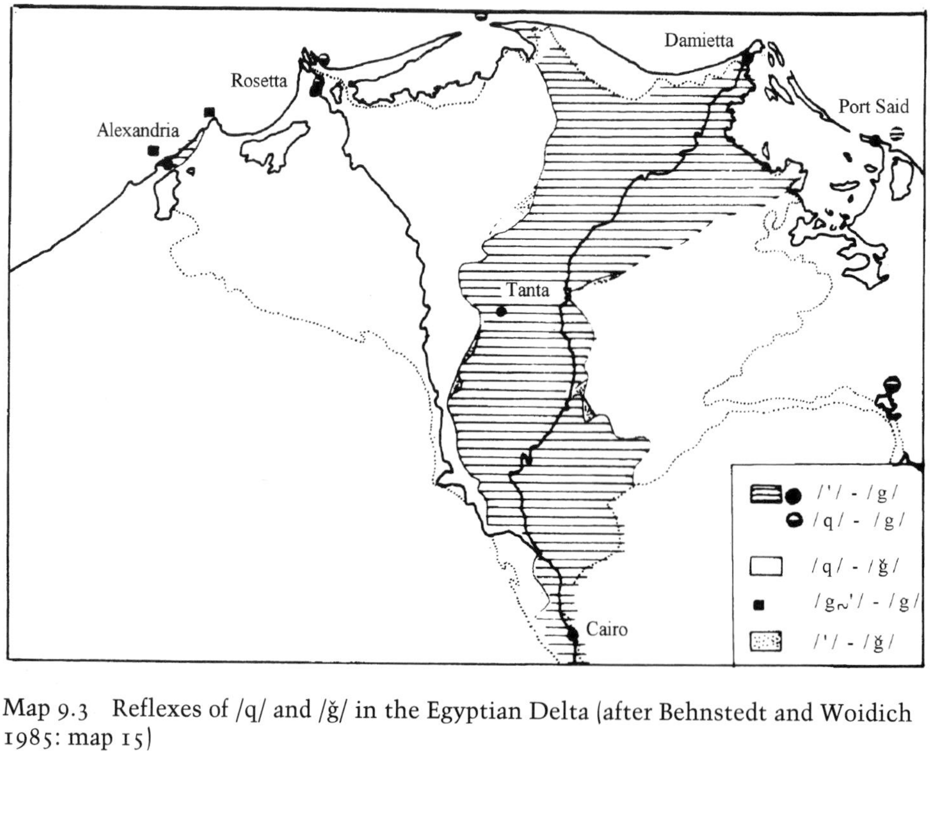

Map 9.3 Reflexes of /q/ and /ğ/ in the Egyptian Delta (after Behnstedt and Woidich 1985: map 15)

of these speech patterns, C. Miller (1996) has shown that the first generation of rural migrants has accommodated partially to Cairene Arabic: they replace their Saʿīdī genitive exponent with Cairene *bitāʿ*, for instance, but retain the Saʿīdī realisation of /q/ as /g/. The pattern of accommodation corresponds to those features of Cairene Arabic that had already been taken over in urban centres outside Cairo. The second generation of migrants adapts entirely to Cairene Arabic and loses all traces of Southern Egyptian speech.

The process of koineisation is a rapid process, which even spreads outside the borders of the national states. The Egyptian dialect in particular has become known all over the Arab world, partly as a result of the export of Egyptian movies and television soaps, which are broadcast almost everywhere, and partly as the result of the fact that in many countries Egyptian teachers were hired to help in setting up an education system. In most countries, almost everybody understands Egyptian Arabic, and sometimes the speakers are even able to adapt their speech to Egyptian if need be. In Yemen, for instance, foreigners who speak Arabic are automatically classified as Egyptians, and in communicating with them Yemenis will tend to use Egyptian words and even take over Egyptian morphology. The Yemenite continuous verbal particle *bayn-* (first person)/ *bi-* (second and third person) is sometimes used for habitual meaning as well under the influence of the Egyptian use of *bi-*. Often the Egyptian verbal particle *raḥ-/ḥa-* is used for the future instead of Yemeni *ša-*. Many typically Egyptian words have become *de rigueur* even in normal everyday conversation, e.g. *kwayyis* 'o.k.', *muš* 'not' and *kida* 'like this, so', sometimes Yemenised as *kiḏa*.

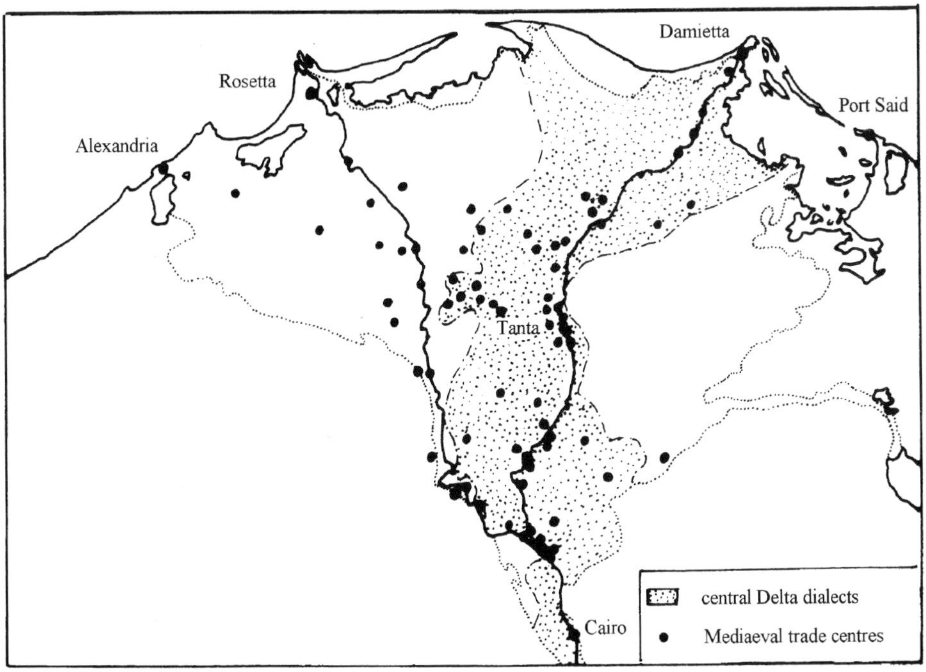

Map 9.4 Medieval trade centres in the Egyptian Delta (after Behnstedt and Woidich 1985: map 551)

Any attempt at a classification of dialects is, of course, arbitrary. The selection of different isoglosses as distinguishing marker leads to different divisions. The classification on the basis of phonetic features may lead, and often does lead, to results that differ from classifications on the basis of, for instance, lexical distribution. Besides, isoglosses almost never delimit two areas sharply: there are almost always transitional zones between them, in which the phenomenon in question applies partially or only in part of the lexicon. Still, the geographical distribution of the isoglosses often corresponds to the intuitive distinction between dialect groups by the speakers of the dialects themselves.

Other methods of classifying dialects are based on the historical chronology of settlement. In North Africa, for instance, one can distinguish different layers of settlement, in which different groups of speakers of Arabic participated. On the other hand, these layers are mostly not independent from each other, and, although different in origin, the resulting dialects have often been subject to profound mutual influence. In North Africa, the dialects of the urban areas were never completely isolated from the rural and nomadic dialects, and the settlement pattern was never permanently fixed for all time: nomadic groups entered the sedentary sphere of influence, and depending on their respective prestige and power either their dialect or the urban dialect was modified. The net result was that within each region a constant process of convergence took place.

Another method of classifying the dialects is along sociolinguistic lines. But this, too, runs counter to the development in most areas. The mutual influence between higher and lower registers of the language usually leads to a regional colouring of the local realisation of Standard Arabic, on the one hand, and homogenisation of the dialects through influence of the standard language, on the other.

The conclusion may be that a classification of dialects country by country, although not linguistic in nature, may not even be the worst alternative. Especially after the Arabic-speaking countries gained their independence, there was a certain amount of linguistic pull from one centre, mostly the capital, so that within each country there was a tendency towards homogenisation. In this sense, one may speak of the Algerian dialect, the Syrian dialect or the Yemeni dialect in the sense of the prestige dialect of the capital. Obviously, the influence of the dialect of the capital had its limits and in each country deviant regional dialects remained in use. Dialect enclaves within the boundaries of the national states are not necessarily doomed to disappear: factors of local pride may effectively promote the survival of the dialect, as for instance the dialect of Dēr iz-Zōr in Northern Syria, which is of a Mesopotamian type amid a Syro-Lebanese dialect area.

In some regions, dialect loyalty takes place along denominational lines. In North Africa, special varieties of Jewish Arabic have been recorded in some of the large cities such as Fes and Tunis, which go back to the earliest period of arabicisation and have not followed later innovations. In other countries, the dialects of heterodox minorities, such as the Christians and the Jews in Baghdad and the Shiʿites in Bahrain, were not affected by secondary bedouinisation but preserved their original sedentary features, whereas the language of the Muslim (Sunnite) majority developed a number of nomadic traits.

9.3 BEDOUIN AND SEDENTARY DIALECTS

Any classification of the Arabic dialects has to take into account a complicating factor: the coexistence of Bedouin and sedentary dialects in all areas. We have seen above that in the early centuries of the Islamic empire the Bedouin dialects were regarded as the only true representatives of the Classical language. The Bedouin were supposed to speak pure Arabic – i.e. with the declensional endings, *'i'rāb*, literally 'making it sound like true Bedouin Arabic' – but in the course of time the Arab grammarians conceded that not even the Bedouin could escape the effects of sedentary civilisation. As early as the time of Ibn Ǧinnī (d. 392/1002), grammarians could not help but notice the adverse effects of prolonged exposure to sedentary speech. Although some Bedouin tribes maintained a reputation of purity of speech, in reality they spoke a language that was no longer Classical Arabic – whether this happened before or after the advent of Islam remains disputed (cf. above, Chapter 3). In modern times, all dialects, regardless of whether they are spoken by the sedentary population or by nomads, are clearly of the New Arabic type, for instance in that they do not have any declensional endings. Yet, it can easily be shown that in some respects the Bedouin dialects are more conservative than the sedentary dialects.

This is more or less confirmed by the history of settlement. We have seen earlier that the process of arabicisation took place in two stages (Chapter 7). During the first stage, the sedentary dialects with their high rate of innovation came into being. The second wave of arabicisation generated the rural and nomadic dialects of Arabic all over the Arab world. According to some theories, the newly-arriving Arab tribes were responsible for a higher degree of homogeneity in the linguistic make-up of the Islamic empire, since unlike the urban dialects their dialects had not yet changed in the constant interaction between people of several languages.

As a general principle, isolation leads to linguistic conservatism, whereas areas of high rates of interaction exhibit many phenomena of reduction and simplification. As a result, it is impossible to distinguish between discrete dialect areas in the urban dialects, which form a continuum only broken by natural barriers. Within the sedentary areas, it is possible to distinguish core areas, however, around political and cultural centres, from which linguistic innovations fan out in a wave-like pattern. Between adjacent core areas, transitional areas come into being as competing innovations clash. The nomadic dialects on the other hand may be regarded as discrete dialects, which are maintained even when the members of the tribe disperse over a large area. They reflect in their linguistic features the history of their migratory pattern. From the Naǧd area in Saudi Arabia, for instance, tribes such as the ʿAniza, the Šammar, the Muṭayr and the Ḍafīr migrated to the north and the east over a large geographical area, but their dialects still reflect the original kinship, in a manner somewhat reminiscent of the relations between the Indo-European languages in the old family-tree model (cf. above, p. 10, and see Map 9.5). Outside the peninsula and in some regions within it, for instance the Ḥiǧāz, the difference between sedentary population and nomads takes on a social significance, the Bedouin/sedentary dichotomy usually correlating with linguistic, and sometimes occupational or religious, contrasts. In some parts of the Arabian

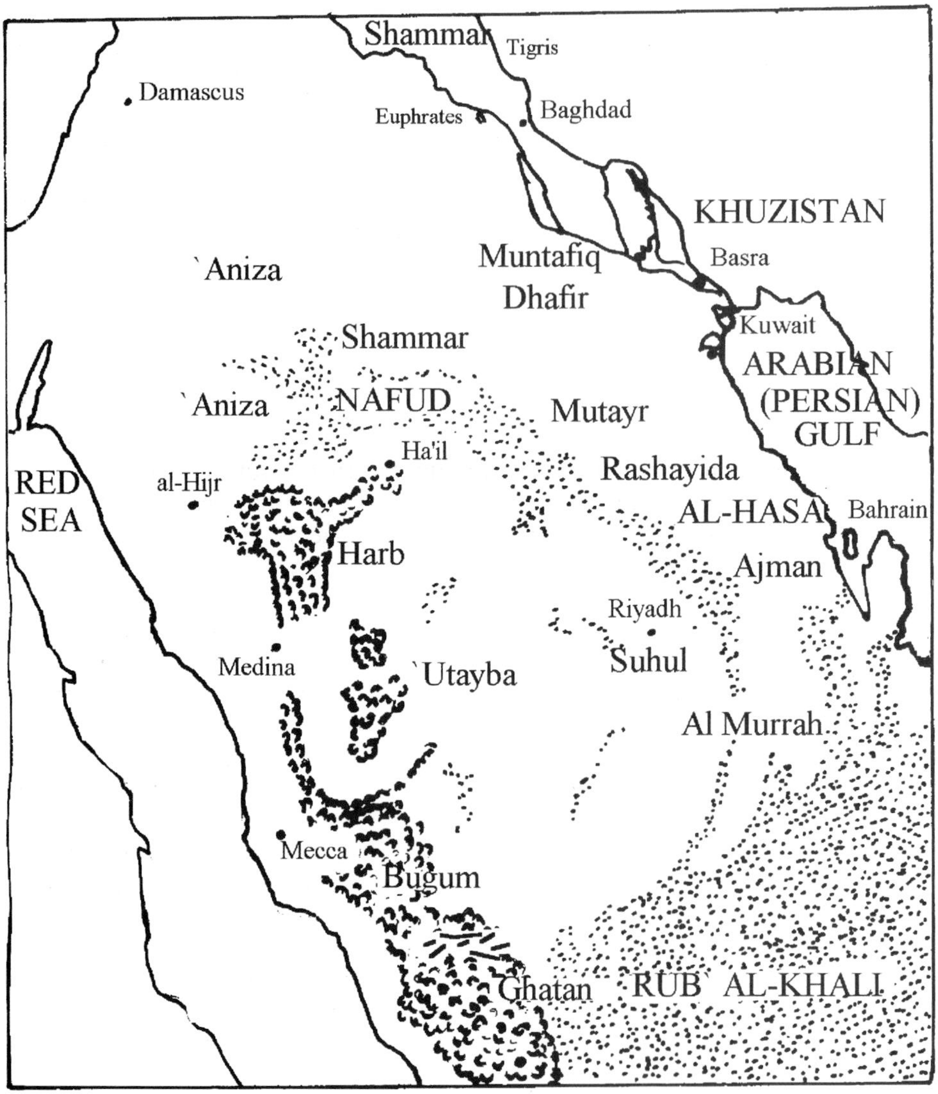

Map 9.5 Tribal areas in North Arabia (after Ingham 1994c: xvii)

peninsula, however, especially in the northern Nağd, the linguistic differences are between tribes, regardless of whether the members of the tribes lead a settled life or roam the desert. Some sections of the Šammar, for instance, are nomads, but regularly return to their sedentary kinsmen in the oases, with whom they form one tribe, both socially and linguistically.

From the beginning of the Islamic period, and of course even in pre-Islamic times, there have been constant migrations of Bedouin groups. The original conquests in the first centuries of the Hiğra were carried out largely by nomadic tribes, and they were followed by later Bedouin migrations from the peninsula. The eleventh-century invasion of the Banū Sulaym and the Banū Hilāl in North Africa shows that this process went on even at a later period. In all such cases, the Bedouin immigration set in motion a process of arabicisation in the countryside. Some of the Bedouin groups eventually settled down and adopted a sedentary kind of dialect. But in other cases, settled areas were bedouinised secondarily, for instance Marrakesh in Morocco, il-Biḥēra in the Western delta in Egypt, some of the Arabic dialects in Israel, the speech of the Muslims in Baghdad, or the dialect of the Sunnites in Bahrain. As a result, it is impossible to set up a list of canonical features distinguishing nomadic from sedentary dialects, although it is possible to speak of characteristic Bedouin features.

If one takes the dialects of Bedouin collectively, it turns out that in some respects they are more conservative than the sedentary dialects in the same area. The following features may be mentioned as generally typical of Bedouin dialects spoken by nomads. Because of the processes of secondary bedouinisation, it is clear that several of these features are also found in dialects that are spoken by a sedentary population.

- preservation of the interdentals: almost all Bedouin dialects preserve the Classical /ṯ/ and /ḏ/; the resulting phoneme from the merger of Classical /ḍ/ and /ḍ/ is always /ḏ̣/ in these dialects, e.g. in Naǧdī Arabic *ḏ̣arab* 'he hit'/*ḏ̣alāl* 'shadow' as against Classical Arabic *ḍaraba*/*ḏ̣alāl*.
- voiced realisation of the /q/ as /g/ (cf. above, Chapter 4, p. 42); already in the Classical period, the voiced realisation of the /q/ was regarded as a shibboleth for the Bedouin character of a dialect; it may have been the original pronunciation of this phoneme in Classical Arabic (cf. above, Chapter 2, p. 21).
- preservation of the gender distinction in the second and third person plural of pronouns and verbs; thus for instance the dialect of the Naǧd distinguishes between *ktibaw* 'they wrote [masculine]' and *ktiban* 'they wrote [feminine]', where related dialects in Iraq have only *ktibaw* without gender distinction, as in all sedentary dialects in the Arab world.
- the third person singular masculine of the pronominal suffix in the sedentary dialects is *-u*, *-o*; in the Bedouin dialects it is usually *-ah*, *-ih*.
- the use of the dual in the nouns is much more widespread in the Bedouin dialects than in the sedentary dialects.
- in most Arabic dialects, the prefix vowel of the verb is *-i-*, a phenomenon already found in some of the pre-Islamic dialects (*taltala*), but some of the Bedouin dialects of North and East Arabia have *-a-* as prefix vowel; in the Naǧdī Arabic paradigm the alternation (apophony) of the preformative vowel still reflects the situation in some of the pre-Islamic dialects (cf. above, Chapter 3): in this dialect, *a* appears before imperfect stem vowel *i*, and *i* before *a*, e.g. *yaktib* 'he writes', but *yismaʿ* 'he hears'.
- there is a tendency in the Bedouin dialects towards a more frequent use of the direct annexation in possessive construction; although all Bedouin dialects have a genitive exponent, they tend to restrict its use both semantically and syntactically to a larger extent than the sedentary dialects do; in North Africa, the Western Bedouin dialects distinguish themselves from the sedentary dialects in the same area by not using the genitive exponent *d-*, *dyal*.

- the agreement with inanimate plurals in the Bedouin dialects is with the feminine singular, as in the Classical language, rather than with the plural.

These features are characteristic of almost all Bedouin dialects. In addition, there are specific features characterising the Bedouin dialects of the Arabian peninsula, which will be dealt with below (Chapter 10). In general, the distinction between Bedouin and sedentary dialects is made on the basis of a few criteria, the most important ones being the voiced realisation of the Classical /q/ and the preservation of the Classical interdentals; in morphology, the gender distinction in the plural of the verb is often regarded as an important criterion.

The conservatism of the Bedouin dialects contrasts with the reduction or simplification of linguistic structure in those areas where there is intensive interaction between Bedouin and sedentary population, for instance in Southern Iraq, along the Gulf Coast and even in Mecca, which has a mixed population with many immigrants from outside the peninsula. In comparing the Bedouin dialects in the peninsula with the related dialects outside the peninsula, Ingham (1982) points out that many of the conservative traits of the Arabian dialects, such as the retention of the internal passive and causative, the gender distinction in the second/third person plural of the verb, the indefinite marker *-in* and the anaptyctic vowel in final clusters as in *šift/šifit* 'I saw', *galb/galub* 'heart', tend to disappear the farther away one gets from the Bedouin heartland, as happens in the Mesopotamian and Gulf varieties of the Central Arabian dialects.

Since all dialect areas in the Arabophone world have undergone the two stages of the arabicisation process, in each linguistic area a distinction has to be made between sedentary and Bedouin dialects. Bedouin dialects are found both in the eastern Arab world and in the west. The area in which Bedouin dialects are spoken in Syria, Mesopotamia and North Arabia is actually a kind of dialect continuum, in which it is difficult to distinguish discrete dialects. Two migratory movements, one from Central Arabia (Nağd) to the north, another from southern Mesopotamia to the Gulf, disrupt the geographical partition in this area. There is a large degree of interdependence between the settled areas and the nomadic tribes that are attached to them, even when they originally come from elsewhere. In Southern Mesopotamia, the nomads dominated the settled population and took over as rulers when they set up their summer camps in the settled areas instead of going back to the Nağd. In the oral literature of these tribes, or rather tribal units, composed of groups of different origin, there are often references to earlier dwellings. In Syria, there is a continuous process of migration between the peninsula and the Syrian *bādiya*. We have seen above (p. 12) that according to some theories the Semitic languages developed in just such a permanent process of interchange between desert and settled area.

Because of their constant migrations, it is difficult to set up geographically delimited dialect areas for Bedouin dialects; in fact in most cases it is impossible (cf. Ingham 1982). Sometimes an isogloss provides a clear demarcation line, but others that are potentially just as essential provide a completely different demarcation. Only in those cases where there are clear-cut geographical or political barriers is it possible to speak of a discrete dialect zone. The speakers themselves very often have a clear intuition of the differences between dialects, but the problem is that such judgments are usually based on idiosyncrasies. When there are no barriers, the dialect zones gradually merge, creating transitional zones for each individual feature between them. For the sedentary groups, ethnic origin is not a determining factor, and their acceptance or rejection of innovations is based on the relative force of attraction of different cultural/political centres. In the case of nomadic groups, the ethnic origin and the tribal relations are of the utmost importance in classifying the dialects, so that it is impossible to define them only geographically. An exception is formed by the area of the Ǧabal Šammar in Northern Saudi Arabia, which thanks to its location within easy reach of grazing grounds has maintained a stable population with both nomadic and sedentary sections of the tribe of the Šammar.

The Eastern Bedouin dialects are those spoken in the Arabian peninsula and the Gulf states, the Syro-Mesopotamian desert, and Southern Jordan, the Negev and the Sinai. The Western Bedouin dialects are spoken all over North Africa. Usually they are divided into two groups: the dialects of the area in which the Banū Sulaym settled (Tunisia, Libya and western Egypt); and those that belong to the territory of the Banū Hilāl (western Algeria and Morocco).

9.4 THE PRESENTATION OF THE DIALECTS

The usual classification of the Arabic dialects distinguishes the following groups:

1. dialects of the Arabian peninsula
2. Mesopotamian dialects
3. Syro-Lebanese dialects
4. Egyptian dialects
5. Maghreb dialects.

It is not always clear on what criteria this current classification is based. In some cases, purely geographical factors may have influenced the classification (e.g. the Arabian peninsula). We have seen above that each of these areas was arabicised in two separate processes, of which the first one resulted in innovatory sedentary dialects, whereas the second one brought into being local rural and nomadic dialects that in some respects retained some of the features of Old Arabic. The time-span between the two movements differs in each area. We have seen in Chapter 7 that in Syria and Mesopotamia sedentary and urban dialects already coexisted in the period before Islam. Most of the Bedouin dialects in this area belong to speakers who are still in contact with tribes in the interior of the peninsula. In Egypt and North Africa, on the other hand, there was a large chronological distance between the two movements, in North Africa more than four centuries. This chronological distance may explain the lesser degree of conservatism in the Bedouin dialects of North Africa: they stem from tribes that prior to their migration to North Africa had already been subjected for a long time to influence from sedentary speakers. The chronological distance may also explain why in spite of the different origin of the sedentary and the Bedouin dialects it is still possible to speak of a dialect area in North Africa and in Egypt. All dialects of North Africa, for instance, exhibit the central feature of the North African dialects, the prefix *n-* of the first person singular of the imperfect verb. These dialects arrived when there were already prestigious cultural and political centres; and although the Bedouin represented the new military power in the region, they could not avoid the centripetal influence of the sedentary dialects.

In Chapter 10, we shall therefore stick to the traditional distinction of five dialect areas. Each area will be presented briefly, with a survey of the most important representative dialects, the most characteristic features and a number of text samples that illustrate the idiosyncrasies of each dialect. Chapter 13 will be devoted to the dialects of the various language islands of Arabic, i.e. varieties of Arabic that are spoken outside the Arabophone world in linguistic enclaves in an environment in which other languages predominate. Examples of such language islands are Maltese Arabic, Cypriot Maronite Arabic, the Arabic of Uzbekistan and Afghanistan, the Arabic dialects of Central Anatolia, and the creolised Arabic of Uganda and Kenya (Ki-Nubi). The dialects spoken in the linguistic enclaves ultimately derive from dialect groups in the central areas, Cypriot Maronite Arabic being a Syro-Lebanese type of dialect, Maltese being a North African type of dialect, and so on. But their isolation from the Arabophone world and their lack of exposure to the Classical language have contributed to the preservation of features that were lost elsewhere. The contact with the dominant languages of the region has led to borrowings and innovations that are not present elsewhere either. For these reasons, it is preferable to treat the dialects of the linguistic enclaves separately.

The text samples illustrating the major dialect varieties illustrate a major problem of dialect recordings, that of the transcription. The usual transcription of Classical Arabic is phonemic; allophonic variants are not represented in Arabic script, nor in the transcription. Some texts of Arabic dialects are recorded in a phonemic transcription as well, whereas others aim at a complete phonetic transcription with all variants. In Syrian Arabic (below, p. 154), for instance, in most environments Classical Arabic /i/ and /u/ have merged in one phoneme, usually represented with /ə/, as in the Syrian text sample below. In this transcription, no allowance is made for the different phonetic realisations of /ə/. Depending on the environment, /ə/ may have the following allophones:

- fronted [ɪ] as in English *pit*, before plain dentals, without back vowels or emphatic consonants, e.g. /sətt/ [sɪtt];
- between [e] as in English *pet* and [ʌ] as in English *putt*, before pharyngals, e.g. /nəḥna/ [neḥna];
- backed [u] as in English *put*, in an emphatic environment, e.g. /ḍədd/ [ḍudd].

The choice of allophone is dictated by the environment and has nothing to do with the etymological origin of the vowel. Older transcriptions of Syrian Arabic wrote *sitt, ḍudd* in an effort to represent the pronunciation as accurately as possible. Such a phonetic transcription is also used, for instance, in Singer's (1958a) collection of texts from the dialect of Tetouan and in that of D. Cohen (1964) of the Jewish Arabic of Tunis. In both collections, a large number of symbols represent the various allophones of the vowels in different environments. Both systems have their advantages: the phonemic transcription shows the structural properties of the dialect, whereas the phonetic transcription makes it easier to pronounce the text samples. In the text samples, the transcription of the original source has been preserved as much as possible, so that some texts are written in a phonemic, others in a phonetic transcription.

FURTHER READING

There are no methodological introductions to Arabic dialectology, but the introduction to Behnstedt and Woidich's dialect atlas of the Egyptian dialects (1985: 11–42) offers a valuable substitute.

Dialect geography used to be one of the poor points in Arabic linguistics, although the situation is improving. The first surveys were made by Cantineau (dialect atlas of the Ḥōrān, 1940, 1946) and by Bergsträßer (dialect atlas of the Syro-Lebanese dialects, 1915). Dialect maps of the Lebanese dialects were produced by Fleisch (1974). More recently, an extensive dialect atlas of the Egyptian region was produced by Behnstedt and Woidich (1985, 1987, 1988, 1994, 1999); thus far, it consists of an atlas with commentary, two volumes of texts, and an Egyptian–German glossary. Behnstedt also produced a dialect atlas of the North Yemenite region (1985, 1992), and a Syrian dialect atlas by his hand is being published. But the fact remains that large parts of the Arabophone area are literally *terra incognita*, in particular the Arabian peninsula, North Africa and sub-Saharan Africa.

On the older sources for Egyptian Arabic, see Doss (1996). For the Egyptian influence in the Yemenite dialect, see Diem (1973b: 15–19). On the problem of the /q/–/g/ reflexes in Bedouin dialects, see Behnstedt and Woidich (1982). The transitional dialect between Western and Eastern dialects in the Egyptian delta is discussed by Behnstedt (1978); for the contact phenomena in the Western oases in Egypt, see Woidich (1993). The relationship between urbanisation and dialect change is discussed by Holes (1995b). For the accommodation to Cairene Arabic in Egypt, see C. Miller (1996). For speech variation in Baghdad, see Abu-Haidar (1988b, 1990).

The problem of the representation of Bedouin and sedentary layers is discussed by Ingham (1982), from whom most of the remarks about the distinction between Bedouin and sedentary dialects in Arabia and Syro-Mesopotamia above have been derived. On Ibn H̱aldūn's description of Bedouin speech, see Brett (1995). General data about the classification of Bedouin dialects and their features are given by Rosenhouse (1984). Cadora (1992) correlates the data of Arabic dialectology with the way of life of the speakers (his term for this approach being 'ecolinguistics').

10
The Dialects of Arabic

10.1 DIALECTS OF THE ARABIAN PENINSULA

The Arabian peninsula, the homeland of the Arab tribes, remains the least-known dialect area of the Arabophone world. In pre-Islamic times, there was probably a division into Eastern and Western dialects (cf. above, Chapter 3), but subsequent migrations have changed the geographical distribution of the dialects considerably. All Bedouin dialects in this area now belong to the new type of Arabic, although generally speaking they are more conservative than the dialects outside the peninsula. In the urban centres of the Gulf the majority speak typologically Bedouin dialects, whereas the Shiʿite minorities speak sedentary dialects.

Recent attempts at classification by Ingham (1982) and Palva (1991) distinguish four groups:

1. North-east Arabian dialects: these are the dialects of the Nağd, in particular those of the large tribes ʿAniza and Šammar. This group is divided into three subgroups: the ʿAnazī dialects (including the dialects of Kuwait, Bahrain (Sunnī) and the Gulf states); the Šammar dialects (including some of the Bedouin dialects in Iraq); and the Syro-Mesopotamian Bedouin dialects (including the Bedouin dialects of North Israel and Jordan).
2. South(-west) Arabian dialects (dialects of Yemen, Hadramaut and Aden, as well as the dialects of the Shiʿite Baḥārna in Bahrain).
3. Ḥiğāzī (West Arabian) dialects: to this group belong the Bedouin dialects of the Ḥiğāz and the Tihāma, which are not very well known; it is not yet clear what the relationship is between these dialects and those of the urban centres in this area, chiefly Mecca and Medina.
4. North-west Arabian dialects: the dialects of the Negev and the Sinai, as well as those of Southern Jordan, the eastern coast of the Gulf of ʿAqaba and some regions in north-western Saudi Arabia are sometimes thought to form a distinct group, which Palva (1991) calls the North-west Arabian dialects.

In Chapter 9 (p. 143) we have seen that outside the Arabian peninsula Bedouin dialects in general are characterised by a number of features that set them off clearly from the sedentary dialects in the same area (e.g. the voiced realisation of the /q/, the retention of the interdentals, and the gender distinction in the second and third person plural of the verbs and the pronouns). The Bedouin dialects in the Arabian peninsula are even more conservative than those outside it in the sense that they do not partake of many of the reducing and levelling innovations that are found outside the peninsula. The most conservative type is represented by Nağdī Arabic; those Bedouin dialects of South Iraq and the Gulf states that are related to them exhibit more innovations. In the peninsula, the nomadic/sedentary dichotomy does not function in the same way as outside, since many tribes also have settled members with whom there is frequent interaction both economically and socially. As a result, all dialects including the sedentary ones exhibit Bedouin features.

Among the conservative features of the Bedouin dialects in the Arabian peninsula, the following three may be mentioned. First, many Bedouin dialects have preserved the use of an indefinite marker *-an*, *-in*, *-en*, mostly as an optional feature, sometimes even as a mere metric device in oral poetry; this indefinite marker clearly derives from the Classical *tanwīn*, which has lost its function as a case marker of indefinite words and has become a marker for indefinite words when these are specified. In the dialects of the Nağd, the marker is used regularly before modifiers to a noun, whether adjectives, or relative clauses, or prepositional clauses, e.g. *bēt-in kibīr* 'a big house'; *kalmit-in gālōhālī* 'a word which they said to me', *ğiz'-in minh* 'a part of it', as well as in adverbial expressions that in Classical Arabic would have the ending *-an*, for instance *maṯal-in* 'for example', *mbaccir-in* 'early'. Second, some Bedouin dialects preserve the causative as a productive form, for instance in the dialect of the Rwala *'abʿad/yibʿid* 'to move away'; *'aẖbar/yiẖbir* 'to inform' (Prochazka 1988: 42, 47). Third, in some of the dialects, the internal passive is still productive, mainly in the North-east Arabian dialects, for instance in the dialect of the Ḥāyil *kitab/ktib* 'to write/to be written'; *ḍarab/ḍrib* 'to hit, to be hit' (Prochazka 1988: 28, 116). This is not a completely exclusive feature of the Arabian Bedouin dialects, since traces are also found in some of the Bedouin dialects of North Africa.

Apart from these conservative tendencies there are also innovations, especially in the North-east Arabian dialects. These have the so-called *gaháwa* syndrome, in which an *a* is inserted after a guttural + consonant, with subsequent stress shift. In Nağdī Arabic, for instance, the imperfect of *ḥafar* 'to dig' is **yáḥfir* > **yáḥafir* > *yḥáfir* (but *kitab* 'to write', imperfect *yaktib*). The *gaháwa* syndrome is also found in other regions, where Bedouin dialects were brought by migration, for instance, in the Egyptian dialects south of Asyūṭ.

Most North-east Arabian dialects are characterised by affrication of /g/ < /q/, and of /k/; this affrication is conditioned by the phonetic environment since it only takes place near front vowels (for a similar feature in the *gilit* dialects of Mesopotamia, possibly under Bedouin influence, see below, p. 157). In Syria and Mesopotamia, the Bedouin dialects have *ğ*, *č*, whereas the Bedouin dialects of Arabia usually have more fronted variants: g^y, d^z (*ǵ*) for *g*; t^s (*ć*) for *k*. As examples, we may quote from the dialect of the Rwala Bedouin *ṯiǵīl* 'heavy', *ǵilīl* 'few'; *ćam* 'how much?', *mićān* 'place' (Classical Arabic *ṯaqīl*, *qalīl*; *kam*, *makān*).

The West Arabian (Ḥiğāzī) dialects are not very well known. They include the dialects of those sedentary centres that already existed before the coming of Islam, for instance Mecca and Medina. In Islamic times, many tribes from this area migrated to the west, so that the Bedouin dialects in the Syrian desert, the

Negev and ultimately those in North Africa probably derive from dialects spoken in this area. The dialects of this group are distinguished from the East Arabian dialects by the absence of the affrication of /k/ and /q/. The dialect of Mecca, although related to the Bedouin dialects in the region, has some of the characteristics of sedentary dialects. It has lost the interdentals and the gender distinction in the plural of verbs and pronouns. Meccan Arabic has a genitive exponent (*ḥagg*), as well as verbal aspectual particles (*bi-* and *ʿammāl* for the continuous aspect and *rāyiḥ-* for the future), which are not normally used in the Bedouin dialects. The realisation of /q/ in Mecca is /g/ as in the Bedouin dialects. In some respects, the dialect of Mecca seems to be close to the varieties of Arabic found in Upper Egypt and the Sudan.

The dialect map of Yemen is complicated because the geographical fragmentation of the area has produced a great deal of dialect variation. Behnstedt (1985: 30–2) distinguishes the following main areas: the Tihāma dialects; the *k-* dialects; the South-east Yemenite dialects; the dialects of the central plateau (e.g. the dialect of Ṣanʿāʾ); the dialects of the southern plateau; the dialects of the northern plateau; and the North-east Yemenite dialects. But even this subdivision is not a complete representation of the entire area: there are many mixed zones, and some of the areas will probably have to be subdivided when more data become known.

The area of the *k-* dialects in the western mountain range (see Map 10.1) is characterised by the use of verbal forms in the perfect with *-k-* instead of *-t-*, e.g. for Classical Arabic *katabtu/katabta* 'I/ you have written' *katabku/katabka*, *katabk^{w}/katabk*, *katūbk/katabk*, or even *katubk/katabk*. There is reason to believe that this area has undergone extensive influence from South Arabian. Its settlement may even go back to the period before Islam, when Arab tribes invaded the South Arabian empires and settled there. After this region had come under Islamic sway, its dialect became known as Ḥimyaritic. In al-Hamdānī's description of the Ḥimyaritic language (cf. above, p. 38) this *k-* ending is displayed prominently in examples such as *kunku* 'I was', *bahalku* 'I said'.

The dialects of the Shiʿites in Bahrain, which belong to a sedentary type, are related to dialects in South-eastern Arabia, Oman and Yemen. The linguistic situation in Bahrain is not unlike that in Baghdad. In both areas, the heterodox minorities (in Baghdad Christians and Jews, in Bahrain Shiʿites) speak a sedentary type of Arabic, whereas orthodox Sunnite speech exhibits secondary bedouinisation. The picture is confused, however, since there are considerable differences between the Baḥārna dialect of the villages and that of the urban centres. In the villages, for instance, Classical Arabic /q/ is realised as a voiceless post-velar stop /ḳ/, whereas in the capital al-Manāma Baḥārna speakers have /g/, just like the Sunnites. This may be due to borrowing from the prestigious dialect or an old trait.

The Baḥārna dialects have in common the realisation of the Classical Arabic interdentals as /f/, /d/, /ḍ/, for instance in *falāfah* (< *ṯalāṯa*) 'three'. They also share the absence of the *gahāwa* syndrome of the Bedouin dialects (e.g. Baḥārna *ʾaḫḍar* as against Sunnite *ḫaḍar* 'green') and the formation of the feminine third person singular of the perfect verb (e.g. Baḥārna *šarabat* or *širbat* as against Sunnite *šrubat* 'she drank'). A characteristic trait of the Baḥārna dialects, linking them with the dialect of Oman and the Arabic of Uzbekistan (cf. below, p. 215),

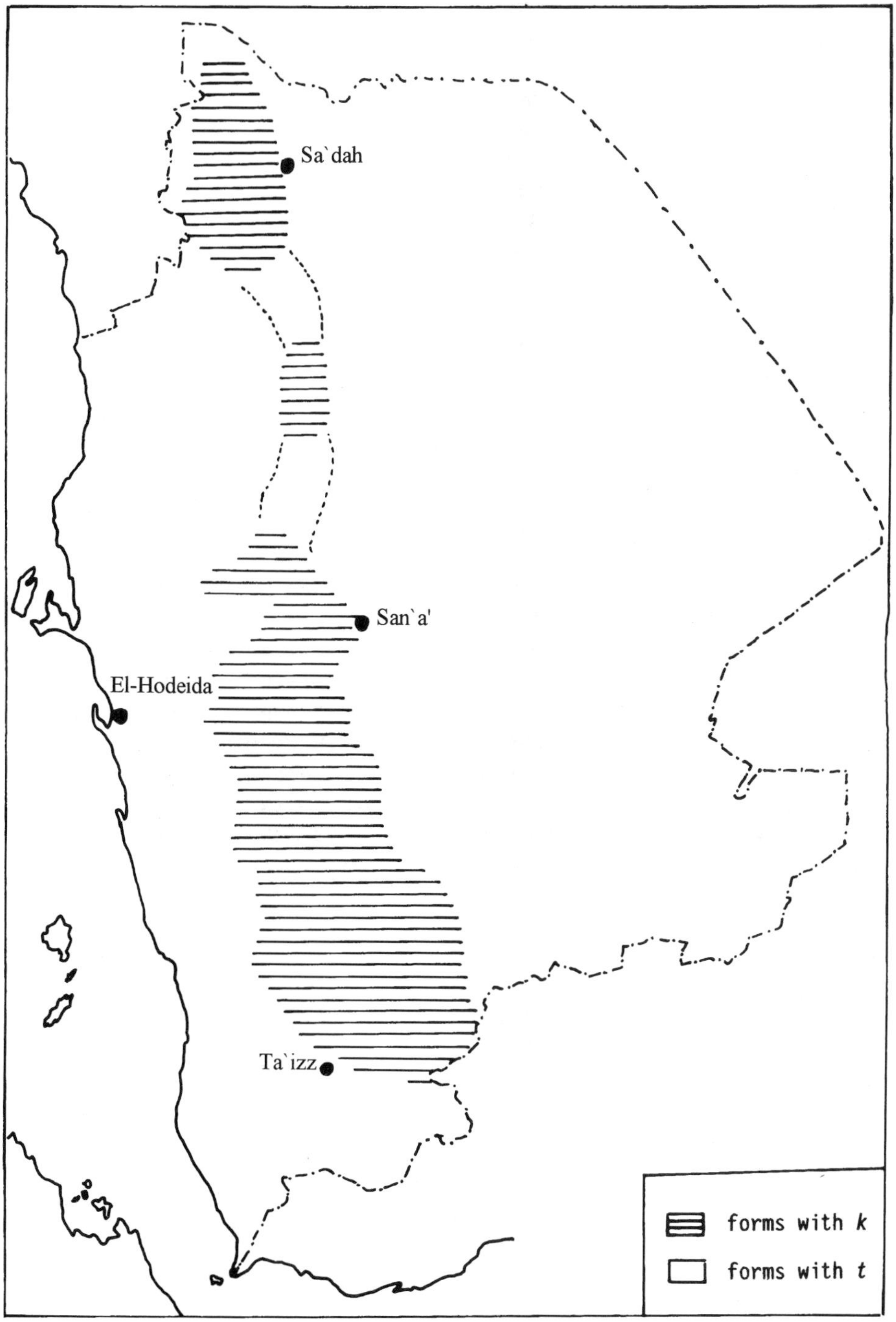

Map 10.1 The perfect verb in the Yemenite dialects (after Behnstedt 1985: map 68)

is the use of an infix *-inn-* in the participle with suffix, which is used for a perfective aspect, e.g. *šār-inn-eh* 'he has bought it', *msawwit-inn-eh* 'she has made it'.

Text 1: North-east Arabian, Šammar (after Ingham 1982: 130)

1. *had̲ōḷa iš-šilgān fa-d̲ōḷa ġazwīn ʿala ḥwēṭāy u baʿad ma h̲ad̲aw al-bil nhajaw il-ḥwēṭāt ʿala h̲eil u h̲ad̲ōham, h̲ad̲ōham yaʿni ʿugub maʿraktin ṭuwīlih*	1. These are the Šilgān and they were raiding the Ḥuwayṭāt and when they had taken the camels, the Ḥuwayṭāt took them on horses, I mean, they took them after a long fight.
2. *u yōm inn hum h̲ad̲ōhum u fassu–h̲aw ḥitta hdūmaham, mā h̲allaw ʿalēham hidūm*	2. And when they had taken them, they stripped them even of their clothes, they did not leave their clothes on them.
3. *hād̲a h̲awiyyam bin ah̲īham jīd ar-rubūʿ iksumōh il-ḥwēṭāy iksumōh miʿrijᵊlu miʿfah̲ᵊd̲u u gāl: yā h̲awāli rūḥu ana rajjālin abamūt wintam rūḥu lahalkam*	3. This was their companion, their cousin Ǧīd ar-Rubūʿ, the Ḥuwayṭāt maimed him in his foot, in his thigh and he said: 'O my uncles, go! I am a man who will die; go you to your families!'

Text 2: Meccan Arabic (after Schreiber 1970: 109)

1. *hāda kān wāḥid riǧǧāl wu-hāda r-riǧǧāl nassāy marra*	1. There once was a man and this man was very forgetful.
2. *wu-maratu tibġa mušš; gālatlu h̲ud hādi z-zubdīya w-hāda l-fulūs rūḥ ǧibli mušš*	2. His wife wanted *mušš* [cottage cheese]. She said to him: 'Take this bowl and this money and go buy me *mušš*'.
3. *gallaha 'iza nsīt; gālatlu lā 'inšaḷḷa mā tinsa 'inta ṭūl mā timši gūl mušš ʿašan lā tinsa*	3. He said to her: 'If I forget?' She said to him: 'No, by God, you won't forget; say all the way *mušš*, so that you don't forget'.
4. *gallaha ṭayyib; 'ah̲ad az-zubdīya w-al-fulūs wu-nadar yigūl mušš mušš mušš*	4. He said to her: 'Good!' He took the bowl and the money and kept saying *mušš mušš mušš*.
5. *laga 'itnēn biyiḍḍārabu; wigif yitfarriǧ ʿalēhum 'ilēn ġallagu l-miḍāraba; yifakkir 'ēš maratu gālatlu yištari*	5. He came across two men who were fighting. He stood there looking at them until they ended their fight; then he thought: 'What did my wife tell me to buy?'

10.2 SYRO-LEBANESE DIALECTS

The arabicisation of the Syro-Lebanese area began during the very first campaigns of the conquests and was no doubt facilitated by the presence of Arabic-speaking tribes in the Syrian desert and even in some of the sedentary areas. The Arab conquerors settled in the old Hellenistic cities in the area, such as Damascus and Aleppo, and it was there that the first varieties of New Arabic were spoken. These dialects were typical urban dialects with a fast rate of innovation.

There was no time-lag between a first and a second stage of arabicisation as in most other areas: the pre-Islamic pattern of Bedouin migration from the Syrian desert did not stop after the advent of Islam and remained a permanent fixture of the linguistic situation.

Because of the abundance of material, there is more or less a consensus about the classification of the dialects between the Mediterranean and the Syrian desert. Usually, all sedentary dialects in the area covering Lebanon, Syria, Jordan and Palestine are assigned to this group, the Bedouin dialects of the Syrian desert belonging to the dialects of the Arabian peninsula. In north-east Syria, dialects of the *qəltu* group of Mesopotamian dialects are spoken (e.g. the dialect of Dēr iz-Zōr). Across the border with Turkey, in the former district of Iskenderun (Alexandretta), the present-day province of Hatay, a dialect is spoken that is a continuation of the Syrian dialect area.

Most dialects in the Syro-Lebanese area exhibit the typically sedentary features of voiceless realisation of *q* as ', stops for interdentals, loss of gender distinction in the second and third person plural of pronouns and verbs. All dialects have preserved the three long vowels *ā*, *ī* and *ū*. But the fact that they are all sedentary does not mean that they never have Bedouin features. Most Jordanian dialects, for instance, have /g/ for /q/, reflecting contact with Bedouin tribes. In the entire area, the prestige dialects of the capitals (Damascus, Beirut) are rapidly replacing the countryside dialects. This is an ongoing process that will contribute to the regional uniformity of the dialects.

The usual classification distinguishes three groups:

- Lebanese/Central Syrian dialects, consisting of Lebanese (e.g. the dialect of Beirut) and Central Syrian (e.g. the dialect of Damascus); the latter group also includes the dialect of the Druzes; the Maronite Arabic of Cyprus (cf. below, Chapter 13, p. 212) is usually assigned to the Lebanese dialects.
- North Syrian dialects, e.g. the dialect of Aleppo.
- Palestinian/Jordanian dialects, consisting of the Palestinian town dialects, the Central Palestinian village dialects and the South Palestinian/Jordanian dialects (including the dialects of the Ḥōrān).

The first group is sometimes distinguished from the other two by the keyword *byiktub/biktub* (third person singular and first person singular of the imperfect of the verb *ktb* 'to write'); in the other two groups, these forms are *biktub/baktub*. Thus we have, for instance, in the Central Syrian dialect of Damascus *byəktob/bəktob* 'he writes/I write', but in the dialect of North Syrian Aleppo *bəktob/baktob*.

A second distinction between the North Syrian and the Lebanese/Central Syrian group concerns the working of the *'imāla*. In the North Syrian dialects, *'imāla* is a historical process that has led to the change *ā* > *ē* in the neighbourhood of an *i* vowel, e.g. in the dialect of Aleppo *lisān* > *lsēn* 'tongue', *ǧāmiʿ* > *ǧēmeʿ* 'mosque'. This change usually takes place even when the *ā* follows an emphatic or guttural consonant, e.g. *ṭāleb* > *ṭēleb* 'striving'. The historical development is to be distinguished from the synchronic rules governing the pronunciation of Classical Arabic /ā/, which ranges from [å] in the neighbourhood of emphatics or gutturals to [æ] elsewhere. We therefore find contrasting pairs such as *ṭēleb* 'striving' as the regular development of /ā/, and *ṭāleb* [ṭāleb] 'student', or *kēteb* 'writing' as against *kāteb* [kǣteb] 'writer', in which the second member is probably a loan from Classical Arabic, since it did not undergo the *'imāla*. In the pronunciation, there is a clear distinction between [ē] and [ǣ].

By contrast, in Lebanese Arabic, /ā/ is realised either as [ā̈] (*'imāla*) or [å̄] (*tafḫīm*), depending on the context, for instance in the dialect of Bišmizzīn: *mā̈t* 'to die' as against *ṣå̄r* 'to become'. But the distribution of these two variants is not always clear, since in some contexts both may occur, for instance *žå̄* 'to come' as against *žā̈b* 'to bring', which even leads to formal opposition pairs, such as *ktå̄b* 'write!' as against *ktā̈b* 'book'. In most Lebanese dialects, the diphthongs /ay/ and /aw/ have been preserved at least in open syllables. In closed syllables, they develop into /ē/ and /ō/ and become indistinguishable from the two allophones of /ā/, as in Tripoli. Since the context in which original /ay/ and /aw/ occur is not conditioned (for instance, /ē/ may occur after an emphatic consonant as in *ṣēf* 'summer'), the contrast between the two allophones of /ā/ has become phonemic.

The distinctions between the three groups are not clear-cut, however. The exact boundary between the Lebanese/Central Syrian and the North Syrian group cannot be determined with any degree of certainty. Likewise, there is an isogloss separating the Palestinian and the South Lebanese dialects from the rest, based on the behaviour of the short vowels. Palestinian Arabic and most Lebanese dialects have three short vowels, /a/, /i/ and /u/. The other dialects have preserved the opposition between /i/ and /u/ only in unstressed final syllables (often transliterated as *e* and *o*), whereas in all other environments they have merged into one vowel phoneme (transliterated as *ə*). The reduction of the opposition between /i/ and /u/ has been reinforced by their elision in all open, unstressed syllables. Thus, we find for instance in Damascene Arabic *kətob* < *kutub* 'books', with stress on the penultimate, but *ṭlūʿ*< *ṭulūʿ* 'ascent', with stress on the ultimate, and preservation of the long /ū/. Compare also *šəreb* < *šariba* 'to drink', with stress on the penultimate, and *t'īl* < *ṯaqīl* 'heavy', with stress on the ultimate, and elision of the short vowel. These two words exhibit yet another change: *a* > *i* because of the following *i* (otherwise the resulting form would have been **šareb*, **ta'īl*, since Damascene Arabic preserves the /a/ in unstressed syllables).

Within the group of the Lebanese dialects, a distinction used to be made between those which elide an unstressed /a/ in an open syllable, and those which do not. This distinction between 'parlers non-différentiels' vs. 'parlers différentiels', i.e. those which do not differentiate between the treatment of /a/, /u/ and /i/ and those which do, was taken by Cantineau to be one of the main isoglosses dividing the area. It runs through Beirut and constitutes a distinctive marker within the Lebanese dialects. South of Beirut we find, for instance *samaka* > *sámake* 'fish'; *ḍarabū* > *ḍárabu* 'they hit'; *qataltu* > *'atálᵉt* 'I hit', whereas north of Beirut we have *sámke, ḍárbu, 'tált*. Subsequent research has shown, however, that the details of the transition between the two areas are more complicated and that there is a large variation in the treatment of the /a/ that is not indicated by this isogloss alone.

Within the third group (the Palestinian/Jordanian dialects), the dialects of south Palestine and Jordan are sometimes distinguished from the others by the keyword *bəgūl* (first person singular of the imperfect of the verb *gāl* 'to say'). The voiced /g/ marks this group of dialects as former Bedouin dialects (or later bedouinised).

Synchronically, the treatment of consonant clusters in Syrian Arabic contrasts with that in Egyptian and other dialects, since an epenthetic vowel is inserted before the second rather than the third consonant in a cluster -CCC-, e.g. *yək*^{ə}*tbu* < *yəktbu* < *yəktubu*, *yəḥ*^{ə}*mlu* < *yəḥmlu* < *yəḥmilu* (these clusters originate as a result of the elision of *u* and *i* in an unstressed open syllable). The epenthetic vowel never receives stress.

In the entire area, the *b*-imperfect serves as a verbal marker. In Damascene Arabic, it indicates an intended future and is also used for assumptions, general facts and present actions. In combination with the *b*-prefix, the first person singular of the imperfect becomes *bəktob*, the first person plural *mnəktob*. We have seen above that in the North Syrian dialects the prefix of the first person singular has *-a-* instead of *-i-* > *-ə-*. The continuous aspect marker is *ʿam*, sometimes combined with *b-*; the expected future is expressed with the marker *laḥ(a)*, *raḥ(a)*. The verbal paradigm is as in Table 10.1.

katab	*katabu*	*yəktob*	*yəktbu*
katbet		*təktob*	
katabt	*katabtu*	*təktob*	*təktbu*
katabti		*təktbi*	
katabt	*katabna*	*'əktob*	*nəktob*

Table 10.1 The verbal paradigm in Damascene Arabic.

Text 3: Damascene Syrian Arabic (after Grotzfeld 1965: 130)

1. *la-nəḥkī-lak 'əṣṣət ḥayāti mən wa't li kənt bənt*	1. Let us tell you the story of my life from the time I was a girl.
2. *bəl-'awwal 'ana, wa't li kənt zġīre, kān žəsmi ḍʿīf ktīr, dāyman 'ana ḍʿīfe*	2. At first, at the time when I was young, my body was very weak, always I was weak.
3. *'ām waṣaf-li l-ḥakīm šamm əl-hawa, ma 'ə'der rūḥ ʿal-madrase ktīr*	3. Then, the doctor prescribed me fresh air, I couldn't go to school very much.
4. *baʿdēn fi 'əli ḫāl b-žabal Ləbnān, ḫūri, 'ām 'āl: lāzəm trūḥi la-hunīke, tġayyri hawa, tə'ʿdī-lek, la-'ənno l-ḥakīm manaʿ 'ənnek trūḥi ʿal-madrase*	4. Afterwards, I have an uncle in the Mount Lebanon, a priest, he said: 'You must go there, change the air, you'll stay, because the doctor has forbidden you to go to school.
5. *hunīk hənne fātḥīn madrase, w-ʿandon ṣəbyān w-banāt bəl-madrase*	5. There, they have opened a school, and they have boys and girls in the school'.

Text 4: Lebanese Arabic (Bišmizzīn) (after Jiha 1964: 90)

1. *kān fi marra biz-zamān ḥurmi ʿumra sabʿīn sini badda titžawwaz, ṭifråni*	1. Once upon a time there was a woman whose age was seventy years, who wanted to marry, [but she was] without a penny.

2. *šăfit šabb ʿa zwaʾa, ʾål: baddi ʾăh̲du, kif baddi ʾiʿmil ta ʾăh̲du?*	2. She saw a young man to her taste and said: 'I want to take him, what can I do in order to take him?'
3. *ṣår trūḥ tžīb ḥuwwåṛa ṭṭammil wi-tḥuṭṭ bi-has-sandūʾ, ʿašr ṭnaʿšar yawm tʿabbi bi-has-sandūʾ ta ṣår yiṭlaʿ ʾinṭårayn*	3. She went and brought white earth, which she kneaded, and put it in this trunk, ten, twelve days she filled the trunk, until it became two *inṭār*.
4. *h̲allit iš-šah̲ṣ il bitḥubbu ta yumruʾ, ʾålitlu: ʿmăl maʿrūf ḥdåf maʿi has-sandūʾ!*	4. She waited until the man whom she loved came by, and said to him: 'Do me a favour, move this trunk with me!'
5. *făt haš-šah̲əṣ yḥarrik bi-has-sandūʾ, ma fī yḥarrik is-sandūʾ*	5. This man began to move this trunk, he was unable to move the trunk.
6. *ʾalla: tʾīl aš fī? ʾålitlu: yi tuʾburni ya ḥabībi, fī sīġåti w-ḥåžăti*	6. He said to her: 'Heavy! What is in it?' She said to him: 'May you bury me, my dear! [i.e. May you live longer than me!] In it are my jewels and my things.'

10.3 MESOPOTAMIAN DIALECTS

Although many of the details about the arabicisation of this area are still obscure, we know that it took place in two stages. During the early decades of the Arab conquests, urban varieties of Arabic sprang up around the military centres founded by the invaders, such as Baṣra and Kūfa. Later, a second layer of Bedouin dialects of tribes that migrated from the peninsula was laid over this first layer of urban dialects. Since Blanc's (1964) study of the dialects of Baghdad, it has become customary to regard all dialects of Greater Mesopotamia as belonging to one dialect area. Blanc found that in Baghdad there were three communal dialects, i.e. dialects connected with religious communities: Muslim Baġdādī, Christian Baġdādī and Jewish Baġdādī. He concluded that Muslim Baġdādī belonged to one layer of the Mesopotamian dialect map, Christian and Jewish Baġdādī to another, and indicated them with the terms *qəltu* and *gilit*, respectively, after their reflex of the Classical Arabic *qultu* 'I have said'. These two varieties were found to be present all over Mesopotamia in a rather complicated pattern of distribution, illustrated in Table 10.2 (Blanc 1964: 6; Jastrow 1973: 1):

	Muslims		non-Muslims
	non-sedentary	sedentary	
Lower Iraq	*gilit*	*gilit*	*qəltu*
Upper Iraq	*gilit*	*qəltu*	*qəltu*
Anatolia	*gilit*	*qəltu*	*qəltu*

Table 10.2 The distribution of *gilit* and *qəltu* dialects.

According to Blanc, the *qəltu* dialects are a continuation of the medieval vernaculars that were spoken in the sedentary centres of ʿAbbāsid Iraq. The *gilit* dialect of the Muslims in Baghdad is probably the product of a later process of bedouinisation that did not affect the speech of the Christians and the Jews in the city. This has led to the present-day difference along religious lines. It may be added that the Jewish dialect of Baghdad is not spoken in Baghdad any more, since most Jews left Iraq in 1950–1 and are now settled in Israel.

The *qəltu* dialects are further classified by Jastrow (1978) into three groups: Tigris dialects, Euphrates dialects and the Anatolian group (the latter will be dealt with below, Chapter 13). They all exhibit the typical features of sedentary dialects, such as the voiceless realisation /q/ or /ʾ/ of Classical /q/; the reduction of the short vowels to two, /a/ and /ə/ < /i/ and /u/; the change of the interdentals into dentals (in the Christian dialect of Baghdad); the loss of the gender distinction in the second and third person plural of pronouns and verbs. All *qəltu* dialects are characterised by the ending of the first person singular of the perfect verb *-tu*, as in the word *qəltu*. The relationship with the *gilit* dialects is demonstrated by the fact that the Mesopotamian *qəltu* dialects have the endings *-īn*, *-ūn* in the imperfect verb, as do the *gilit* dialects, e.g. in the dialect of Arbīl *yəʿməlūn* 'they make'. They also share with these dialects the genitive exponent *māl* and a future marker derived from *rāyiḥ*, e.g. *raḥ-*. The most common continuous aspect marker in the Mesopotamian *qəltu* dialects is some form derived from *qāʿid* 'sitting' > *qa-*.

In the *gilit* dialects, there are three short vowels, /i/, /u/, /a/, but interestingly these do not continue directly the Classical vowels. The vowel /a/ has been preserved in closed syllables, but in open syllables it has changed into /i/ or /u/, depending on the environment, e.g. *simač* < *samak* 'fish' as against *buṣal* < *baṣal* 'onion'. The short /i/ and /u/ have been preserved only in some environments, whereas in others they are both represented by either /i/ or /u/, e.g. *ḥāmuḏ̣* < *ḥāmiḏ̣* 'sour', as against *gilit* < *qultu* 'I said'. In the *gilit* dialects, the interdentals have been preserved, and the reflex of both /ḍ/ and /ḏ̣/ is realised accordingly as /ḏ̣.

Characteristic of all ʿIrāqī dialects is the conditioned affrication of both /q/ > /g/ and /k/ near front vowels (possibly a Bedouin feature; cf. above, p. 149); in the Muslim dialect of Baghdad, however, only /k/ is affricated, e.g. *čān* < *kāna* as against *yikūn* < *yakūnu*. In the pronominal suffix of the second person singular, this leads to a distinction between masculine *-(a)k* and feminine *-(i)č*, e.g. *bētak* as against *bētič* 'your house'.

Where the *qəltu* dialects usually preserve consonant clusters -CC at the end of the word, the *gilit* dialects insert an epenthetic vowel, *i* or *u* depending on the environment, e.g. *čalib* < *kalb* 'dog', *gaḷub* < *qalb* 'heart', and in the keyword for these dialects *gilit* < *qultu*. In consonant clusters -CCC-, an epenthetic vowel is inserted after the first consonant, e.g. *yuḏ̣rubūn* > *yuḏ̣rbūn* > *yuḏ̣urbūn* 'they hit'. The verbal paradigm of the Muslim dialect of Baghdad illustrates this phenomenon, as shown in Table 10.3.

kitab	*kitbaw*	*yiktib*	*yikitbūn*
kitbat		*tiktib*	
kitábit	*kitabtu*	*tiktib*	*tikitbūn*
kitabti		*tikitbīn*	
kitabit	*kitabna*	*'aktib*	*niktib*

Table 10.3 The verbal paradigm of Muslim Baġdādī.

In the verbal inflection, the Classical Arabic type of perfect verb *faʿal* has developed in accordance with the vowel rule given above into *fiʿal* or *fuʿal* depending on the environment, e.g. *ḍurab* as against *simaʿ*. In the inflection of the verb, the endings of the weak and the strong verbs have been levelled to a large degree. In some cases, this has led to the introduction of weak endings in the strong verb, as in many Bedouin dialects, e.g. *ḍurbaw* 'they hit', *kitbaw* 'they wrote', in which the ending *-aw* is derived from the inflection of the weak verb, cf. *bičaw* 'they cried'. Some of the *qəltu* dialects go even further in this direction and eliminate completely the distinction between weak and strong verbs (cf. above, p. 100). In the Muslim dialect of Baghdad, the continuous aspect marker is *dā-*, the future marker *raḥ-*, as in most Mesopotamian dialects. The participle is used for the perfective aspect (as in Uzbekistan Arabic), for instance in the Muslim dialect of Baghdad *wēn ḍāmm* ^{i}*flūsak* 'where did you put your money?'

Of special interest are the dialects spoken in the Iranian province of Khuzestan (called in Arabic ʿArabistān). Although the political developments of the last few decades have turned this area into a linguistic enclave, relations between the Arabs living there and their co-tribesmen in Iraq have never been completely disrupted. The Bedouin dialects in this region continue the Arabian dialect area (p. 148), but the sedentary dialects closely resemble the *gilit* dialects of Mesopotamia, in particular the dialects around Baṣra. As may be expected, the Arabic dialects of Khuzestan use many Persian loans, many of them in the administrative domain (e.g. *dānīšgāh* < Persian *dānešgāh* 'university'; *’ɪdāra* < Persian *edāre* 'office'), but also frequent words, such as *hassɪt* < Persian *hast* 'there is, there are'; *hīč* < Persian *hīč* 'nothing'. In the morphology, the presence of a clitic interrogative *-man* 'what, who' may be noted, as in *šífɪt-man* 'who did you see?'; *trīd tíštɪrī-man* 'which do you want to buy?' In some verbal forms, especially before pronominal suffixes, a suffix *-an* occurs, e.g. *’ašūfan* 'I see'; *’āẖḏanha* 'I shall take her'.

Text 5: Jewish Arabic from ʿAqra (after Jastrow 1990: 166–7)

1. *əzzawāğ mālna, ida wēḥəd kār-rād fad bənt, nəḥne ʿəddna mā kān aku yəmši maʿa, yəği, yəmši, la’*	1. Our wedding, when somebody loved a girl, it was not the case with us that he could go out with her, come and go, no.
2. *bass kān aṛāha faz-zāye, zāytayn, kān tīqəlla, kūrrīd nəği nəṭləbki, mən əmmki w-abūki*	2. But when he had seen her once, twice, he told her: 'We want to come and ask for your hand, from your mother and father'.
3. *hīya təqəllu … ida hīya kān təskīm, hīya kānət rāḍye, kān yəmšawn ʿənd əmma w-abūwa, əmmu w-abūhu, w-əẖtu, w-ẖawātu flān yəmšawn, yəʿməlūn kāvōd, yəʿməlūn qadər wēḥəd šān ellāẖ*	3. She told him … if she agreed, they went to her mother and father, his mother and father and his sister or sisters went, they honoured them, they paid each other respect.
4. *yəmšawn ʿənd əmma w-abūwa, yəqəllūləm kūrrīd bəntkəm, təʿṭaw-na šān ə́bənna, ə́bənna kīrīda, w-bəntkəm-əš kūtrīdu*	4. They went to her mother and father, and told them: 'We want you to give your daughter to our son, our son loves her and your daughter loves him, too'.

Text 6: Khuzestan Arabic (Khorramshahr)(after Ingham 1973: 550)

1. *halmēlām šlōn ıysawwūna?*	1. This fishtrap, how do they make it?
2. *ʿala šāṭi maṯal šaṭṭ farıd makān ıdgūm dgıṣṣlak ıssaʿaf*	2. On the bank of for instance a river, a place, you stand and cut off for yourself the palm fronds.
3. *'ılḫ̣ūṣ māla dgıṣṣa 'awwal*	3. You cut off their leaves first.
4. *hannōba dnabbıč ılwıḥda yamm ıṯṯānya lamman ma ṣṣīr hēč mıṯl ılḫ̣ıṣṣ*	4. Then you fix one beside the other so that it becomes like this, like a woven garden fence.
5. *ılḫ̣ıṣṣ maṯal mnılmadda tıṣʿad ıssımač yıṣʿad u mın yınzıl hāḏa ssımač yqıḍḏ̣a bhāḏa bılmēlām*	5. Then for instance when the high tide comes, the fish come up, and when the fish go down it catches them with the fishtrap.

10.4 EGYPTIAN DIALECTS

The early stages of the arabicisation of Egypt took place right at the beginning of the conquests. After the military conquest of the country and the establishment of a military camp at Fusṭāṭ, the urban population in Lower Egypt soon abandoned Coptic and adopted the new language. In the countryside and in Upper Egypt, the linguistic situation did not change for quite some time, and the arabicisation of this area was much more gradual than that of Lower Egypt. This part of the country was arabicised in the course of three centuries by Bedouin tribes that continued to immigrate from the Arabian peninsula to the west.

From Egypt, the Arabic language was brought along the Nile to the south, into Sudan and Chad. In the middle of the third/ninth century, the Arab tribes of Rabīʿa and Ǧuhayna in Upper Egypt pressed on southwards and steadily invaded the lands of Beja and Nubia. The present-day Arabic-speaking nomads in Sudan claim descendance from the tribe of Ǧuhayna, whereas the sedentary population in the Sudan call themselves Ǧaʿaliyyūn, after an alleged ʿAbbāsid scion, Ǧaʿal. In all probability, they are Nubians who were arabicised at an early stage, right after the conquest of Egypt and before the Bedouin migration.

Some of the Arabic varieties in Central and West Africa must have arisen in the course of expansion westwards of the Arab tribes in Sudan. The Arabs called the transcontinental savannah belt lying between the Sahara desert and the forest of Central Africa *bilād as-Sūdān* 'lands of the Blacks'. Along this belt, which stretches from Sudan through the Central African Republic, Chad and Cameroon to Nigeria, Arabic and Islam were brought to West Africa, and during this expansion some of the Chadian Arabic dialects and the Arabic of Nigeria arose (see Map 10.2). The latter is spoken in the north-east of Nigeria in the province of Bornu by approximately 200,000 people, who are usually called Shuwa by their neighbours, but who call themselves Arabs. They probably arrived here from the east in the second half of the fourteenth century. All dialects in the savannah belt are Bedouin dialects and belong to what has been called the *baggara* culture, i.e. the culture of cow-raising nomads who headed the migratory movement from east to west. Although much is still unknown about the Central African varieties of Arabic, it is clear that there are many common features linking Nigerian Arabic, Chadian Arabic and Sudanic Arabic, as Owens (1993) has shown.

Within Egypt, the following dialect groups are usually distinguished:

- the dialects of the Delta; a further division is made between the Eastern dialects in the Šarqiyya and the Western Delta dialects; in some respects the latter constitute the link between Egyptian Arabic and the dialects of the Maghreb, for instance in the use of *ni-...-u* for the first person plural of the imperfect in some of these dialects (cf. above, p. 134).
- the dialect of Cairo.
- the Middle Egyptian dialects (from Gizeh to Asyūṭ).
- the Upper Egyptian dialects (from Asyūṭ to the south); these are subdivided into four groups: the dialects between Asyūṭ and Nag Hammadi; the dialects between Nag Hammadi and Qēna; the dialects between Qēna and Luxor; and the dialects between Luxor and Esna.

Until recently, only the Cairene dialect had been studied relatively well. Yet, in spite of the wealth of information about the dialect of the capital, its history and its formative period are still unclear. If one compares the present-day dialect of the capital with descriptions of 'Egyptian' (i.e. Cairene) from the nineteenth century and with dialect texts from that period, it turns out that there is a considerable difference. Cairene from that period exhibits a number of features that have disappeared from the modern dialect, e.g. the passive with the prefix *in-* instead of *it-*; the pausal *'imāla -e* instead of the modern ending *-a*; the form of the pronominal suffix of the third person singular masculine in forms such as *mā šafuhš* 'they did not see him' instead of modern *mā šafuhūš*, as well as a number of lexical items, most striking among which is *maṛa*, which used to mean 'woman' and did not have the modern connotation of 'woman of ill repute, slut'. Features such as these are still found in the rural dialects, although not all are connected to the same dialect region.

According to Woidich (1994), the Cairene dialect of today must be regarded as a mixed dialect whose formative period was the second half of the nineteenth century, when there was an enormous influx of people from the countryside. As a result of this immigration, a number of features that until then had been current in the capital came to be stigmatised because they were identified with the low-prestige rural dialects of the new inhabitants. This process of stigmatisation remained operative in the twentieth century. In the movies of the 1920s and 1930s, the elite frequently use forms that nowadays would be regarded as vulgar, for instance the plural ending of verbs in *-um*, which is now restricted in educated Cairene speech to the verb 'to come' (*gum* 'they came'), but in the poor quarters of Cairo can still be heard in other verbs. Another example is that of the interrogative adjective *anho* 'which?', which in educated speech has been replaced by *ayy* under the influence of the standard language. The process of mixing of dialects in the nineteenth century not only led to the disappearance and stigmatisation of rural forms but also to the emergence of completely new forms as a result of hyperurbanisation and overgeneralisation, for instance in the case of the loss of the pausal *'imāla*.

With the growing influence of the mass media, Cairene speech has spread all over the country. This prestige of the speech of the capital is not a recent phenomenon. We have seen in Chapter 9 (p. 138) that on dialect maps of the

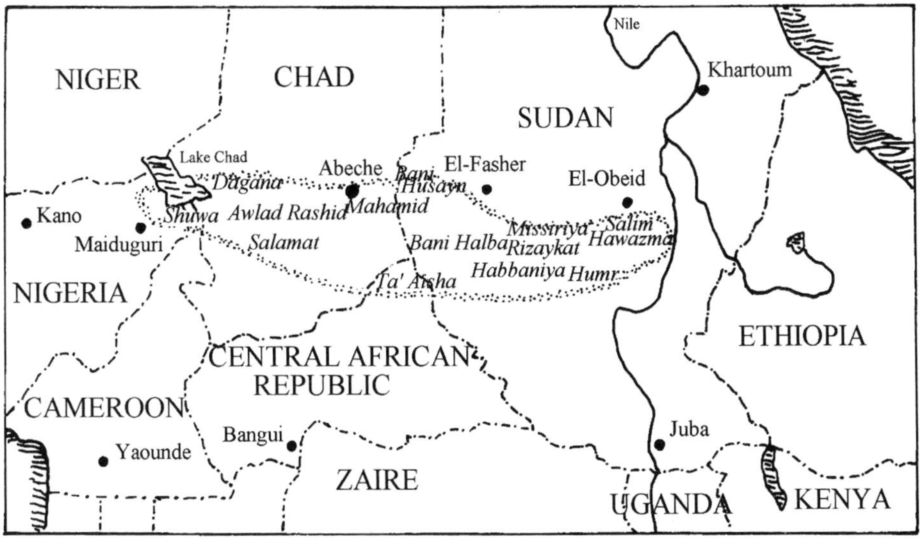

Map 10.2 Arab tribes in the Central African *baggara* belt (after Owens 1993: 17)

Delta the historical influence of Cairene Egyptian can still be traced following the ancient trade route that led from Cairo to the old port of Damietta (Dumyāṭ) in the Central Delta along the eastern branches of the Nile.

Egyptians themselves usually call all southern varieties of Egyptian Saʿīdī, in contrast with the prestige dialect of Cairo. One of the distinctive markers between the two groups is the realisation of Classical /q/ and /ǧ/: in Cairene Arabic these are realised as /ʾ/ and /g/, while in Upper Egypt they are pronounced as /g/ and /ǧ/ (or /g^y/ or even /d/). Another distinctive feature between the dialects of Cairo and some Delta dialects, on the one hand, and the Upper Egyptian dialects, on the other, is the system of stress assignment. In Cairene Arabic and in the Delta, the last heavy syllable (i.e. a syllable containing a long vowel and ending in a consonant or a syllable ending in two consonants) is stressed, e.g. *maʿzū́m* 'invited', *máṭʿam* 'restaurant', *bínti* 'my daughter'. When this syllable is followed by more than one vowel, the vowel immediately following it is stressed, e.g. *madrása* 'school', *bintáha* 'her daughter'. When there is no heavy syllable, the first vowel is stressed, e.g. *báraka* 'blessing'. This stress system is often called the *madrása* type, which contrasts with the *mádrasa* type of the Egyptian dialects south of Cairo. A long vowel before the stress is shortened, e.g. *ṭā́lib* 'student', but feminine *ṭalíba*; singular *maʿzū́m* 'invited', but plural *maʿzumī́n*. Unstressed *i*/*u* before or after stress are elided, unless they are word-final, thus: *ʿā́rif* 'knowing', but feminine *ʿárfa*, plural *ʿarfī́n*.

The dialects of the western parts of Egypt form the boundary with the dialects of the Maghreb, not only in the Delta, but also in the western oases. The dialects of the latter (Farafra, Baḥariyya, Daḫla and Ḫarga) are not very well known. Since they exhibit some West Arabic traits, it has been surmised that they are in some way related to the Arabic dialects of the Maghreb group. In Farafra, for instance, /t/ is pronounced affricated [t^s], as in many Maghreb dialects. Both in Farafra and in Baḥariyya, we find the typical pronominal suffixes for the first person of the imperfect verb (*niktib/niktibu*), that are usually regarded as the hallmark of Maghreb dialects. Besides, there are lexical similarities, e.g. the verb *dār/ydīr* 'to make, to do'. On the whole, however, the dialects of the oases seem to be much more related to the dialects of the Nile valley, especially the Middle Egyptian dialects. We have seen above (Chapter 9) that the structure of these dialects was the result of dialect contact. Originally, the inhabitants of the oases came from the Nile valley, and some of the features of their dialects may be regarded as archaic traits that were once present in the Middle Egyptian dialects but disappeared from them as a result of innovations. In the periphery, these traits remained and were not replaced by the later innovations. The features which these dialects have in common with the Maghreb dialects were probably introduced by later invading Bedouin from the west, in particular the Banū Sulaym on their migrations back east. During this process, too, the oasis of Siwa received its Berber dialect: it is the only place in Egypt where Berber is spoken.

In the Šarqiyya (Eastern Delta) and the Sinai, various Bedouin dialects are spoken. Recent research (de Jong 1996) has shown that some of the dialects in the Northern Sinai belong to the group of the Šarqiyya, whereas the dialects in the Eastern Sinai continue the Bedouin dialects of the Negev. Both groups are related to the dialects of North Arabia (cf. above, p. 148), most of them having arrived here in the first centuries of Islam, some perhaps even before the Islamic conquests.

In spite of the numerous differences, there are some common traits distinguishing the Egyptian Arabic dialects in Egypt from other dialect groups. All Egyptian dialects preserve the three short vowels of Classical Arabic, but /i/, /u/ are elided in open and unstressed syllables. There are five long vowels (/ā/, /ī/, /ū/, /ē/, /ō/), which are shortened in unstressed position, in Cairo even in stressed position before two consonants, as in the form *ʿarfa* mentioned above. Consonant clusters are treated differently in the various dialect groups; in Cairene Arabic in a cluster -CCC-, an epenthetic vowel is inserted before the third consonant, e.g. *iṣ-ṣabr^{i} ṭayyib* 'patience is good'. Historically, the epenthetic vowel sometimes received stress in accordance with the stress rules of Egyptian Arabic, as for instance in the verbal form *yiktíbu* < *yikt^{i}bu* < *yiktbu* < *yíktibu*.

The position of the demonstratives and the interrogatives in Egyptian Arabic is characteristic of this dialect, as well as of the related Sudanese Arabic dialects. The demonstratives for the near-deixis in the Egyptian dialects are variants of Cairene *da, di, dōl*, and always occur in postposition, e.g. (Cairene) *ir-rāgil da* 'this man', *il-fellaḥīn dōl* 'these peasants', sometimes even clitically as in *innaharda* 'today'. The position of the interrogatives is remarkable, too: whereas most Arabic dialects front the interrogatives, in Egyptian the interrogative retains its structural position in the sentence, e.g. *šuft^{i} mīn* 'whom did you see?'; *'alullak 'ē?* 'what did they tell you?' As an explanation for this phenomenon, Coptic substratal influence has been invoked (cf. above, p. 106).

In all Egyptian dialects, the imperfect has modal meaning; combined with an aspect marker *bi-* (Cairo, Delta) it expresses continuous or habitual aspect, combined with *ḥa-* it expresses future tense. The participle is an integral part of the verbal system. In a few verbs of perception or movement, it has present or future meaning, e.g. *ana šāyfo* 'I see him (now)' (contrasting with *ana bašūfo kull yōm* 'I see him every day'); in the other verbs it has resultative meaning, e.g. *ana wākil* 'I have eaten, I am satisfied'. The verbal paradigm of Cairene is as in Table 10.4.

katab	*katabu*	*yiktib*	*yiktibu*
katabit		*tiktib*	
katabt	*katabtu*	*tiktib*	*tiktibu*
katabti		*tiktibi*	
katabt	*katabna*	*'aktib*	*niktib*

Table 10.4 The verbal paradigm in Cairene Arabic.

Text 7: Cairene (after Woidich 1990: 337)

1. *iḥna fī l-ʿīd safirna yomēn wi-baʿdēn lamma rgiʿna kunna maʿzumīn ʿala l-ġada, ṛābiʿ yōm il-ʿīd, ʿand^{i} h̲alti*	1. During the feast we travelled two days and after that when we returned we were invited for dinner, the fourth day of the feast, at my aunt's.
2. *fa-ruḥna ʾana w-gōzi iḍ-ḍuhr^{i} taʾrīban is-sāʿa talāta, wi-staʾbilūna baʾa stiʾbāl gamīl giddan, bi-t-tirḥāb baʾa wi-ʾahlan wi-sahlan wi-ʾanistūna wi-šaṛṛaftūna wi-l-bēt nawwaṛ*	2. We went, my husband and I, in the afternoon around three o'clock, and they received us, a very beautiful reception, with welcome and 'hello' and 'you have made us happy' and 'you have honoured us' and 'may the house be illuminated'.
3. *huwwa kida dayman, il-ʿaʾilāt il-maṣriyya tḥibb^{i} tʾūl kalimāt kitīr ʾawi li-t-taḥiyya yaʿni*	3. It is always like that, Egyptian families love to say very many words, in greeting, that is.
4. *il-muhimm^{i} ʾaʿadna natabādal baʾa kalimāt it-tarḥīb diyyat li-ġāyit lamma h̲alti yaʿni ḥaḍḍaritlina l-ġada*	4. The important thing is, we exchanged those words of welcome until my aunt brought us dinner.

Text 8: Upper Egyptian (id-Dalawiyya) (after Behnstedt and Woidich 1988: 168)

1. *kān fī ṛādil ṣaʿīdi, w ḥabb izūr innabi*	1. There was a man from Upper Egypt and he wished to visit the prophet.
2. *fa lamma ṛāḥ izūr innabiy, taṛak filbēt ibnuw, wu lʿabde, w maṛatu*	2. And when he went to visit the prophet, he left at home his son, and his servant and his wife.
3. *w taṛak imʿāhum farrūde*	3. And he left with them a chicken.
4. *fa lamma taṛak ilfarrūde, fyōm ṭʾabb ṛādil takrūni, saḥaṛ ibmáṛatu, w ġaẉẉāha*	4. And when he left the chicken, one day a Sudanese sorcerer came, bewitched his wife and made her fall in love with him.
5. *ittakrūni da, ṣaʿīdi, ittakrūni miṣ-ṣaʿīd min gibli g̦awi*	5. This sorcerer was an Upper Egyptian, the sorcerer came from Upper Egypt, from the deep South.
6. *innáma ṛṛādil da grayyib šwayye, ġēr dukḥa*	6. But this man was somewhat from the North, not like that one.

7. *fa lamma saḥarlhe, ġíwitu, w ġiwīhe*

7. And when he bewitched her, she fell in love with him, and he fell in love with her.

8. *fa da fyōm w gallha: iḥna ʿayzīn nídbaḥu lfarrūde*

8. And he (came) one day and said to her: 'We want to slaughter the chicken'.

10.5 MAGHREB DIALECTS

In no other area of the Arabophone world has there been such a marked separation in time between the two stages of arabicisation. During the Arab conquests in the second half of the seventh century, the sedentary areas of North Africa were overrun by a relatively small group of invaders who settled mostly in existing urban centres, or in some cases in newly-established military camps, whence the new, urban varieties of Arabic were spread over the surrounding area. Some of the Jewish varieties of Arabic in North Africa go back to this early period, such as the Jewish Arabic of Tunis and Algiers. The greater part of the countryside remained entirely Berber-speaking. The second stage of arabicisation took place centuries later in the course of the invasion by the Banū Hilāl (tenth and eleventh centuries; cf. above, p. 96). During this stage, the Arabic language reached the countryside and the nomadic areas of North Africa, although it never managed to oust the Berber language completely (cf. above, p. 96, and see Map 10.3).

The group of the Maghreb dialects includes the dialects of Mauritania (*Ḥassāniyya*), Morocco, Algeria, Tunisia and Libya. In the literature, the dialects belonging to the two stages are often referred to as pre-Hilālī and Hilālī dialects, respectively. All pre-Hilālī dialects are sedentary dialects, spoken in cities and in those areas outside the cities that were arabicised early on, such as the Tunisian Sahel, and the regions north of some of the large urban centres, Constantine, Tlemcen and Fes. Usually two groups are distinguished:

- the Eastern pre-Hilālī dialects, spoken in Libya, Tunisia and eastern Algeria; these dialects are characterised by the preservation of the three short vowels.
- the Western dialects of the pre-Hilālī group, spoken in western Algeria and Morocco; these have only two short vowels and have developed an indefinite article from the Classical Arabic numeral *wāḥid*, e.g. in Moroccan Arabic *waḥd əl-mṛa* 'a woman', always used in combination with the definite article, possibly in analogy to the construction of the demonstrative with the article.

The Bedouin dialects of North Africa represent the Hilālī dialects; they are divided into the Sulaym in the East (Libya and southern Tunisia), the Eastern Hilāl (central Tunisia and eastern Algeria), the Central Hilāl (south and central Algeria, especially in the border areas of the Sahara) and the Maʿqil (western Algeria and Morocco). One group from the Maʿqil confederation, the Banū Ḥassān, settled in Mauritania, where the local dialect is still known under the name of Ḥassāniyya (see below, p. 167). Bedouin dialects are spoken not only in the rural areas, but also in some of the cities that were bedouinised at a later stage, for instance Tripoli.

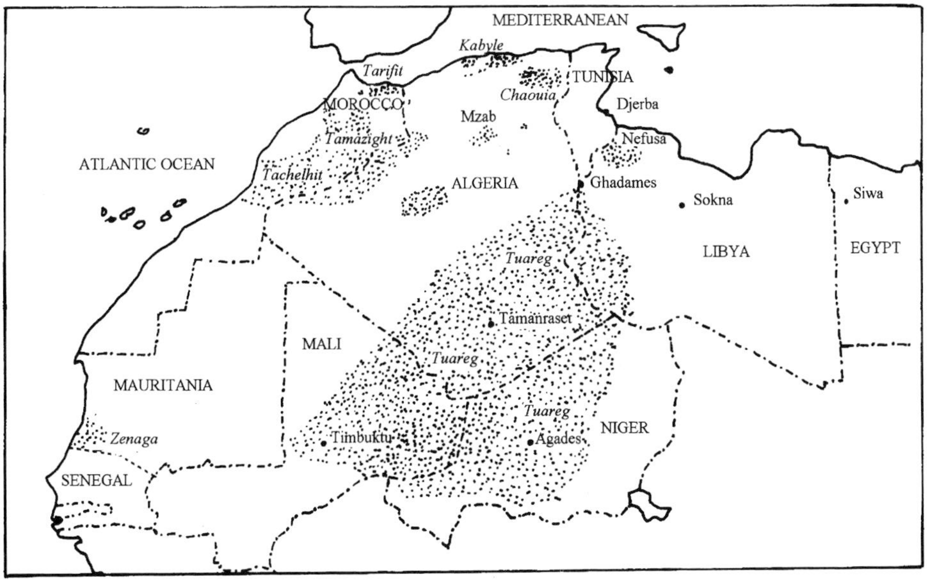

Map 10.3 Berber-speaking areas in North Africa

Libya is largely Bedouin-speaking; even the sedentary dialects of the urban centres such as Tripoli have been influenced by Bedouin speech. Tunisia is a transitional zone; its Bedouin dialects are related to those in Libya. Algeria is heterogeneous: in the Constantinois, both Bedouin and sedentary dialects are spoken, and this area is linked with Tunisia and with the Algérois; the Algérois is predominantly Bedouin; the Oranais has one important sedentary centre in Tlemcen, while the rest is Bedouin-speaking. In Morocco, Bedouin dialects are spoken in the plains and in recently-founded cities such as Casablanca; for the sedentary dialects, Rabat and Fes are the most important centres. In Mauritania, as we have seen, a Bedouin dialect is spoken. The dialect that was spoken in Spain (*al-'Andalus*) during the period of Islamic domination belonged to the Maghreb dialects, and so does the language of the linguistic enclave of Malta, which was conquered from Tunisia (cf. below, Chapter 13, p. 209).

The long coexistence between Arabic and Berber that is continued in the present countries of North Africa has marked these dialects (cf. p. 104). There has been a lot of discussion about the degree of interference in the Maghreb dialects, but the presence of loanwords from Berber is unmistakable, sometimes even in the use of certain nominal patterns. Of the latter, the pattern *tafəʿʿalət* is the most frequent; it serves to indicate professional activities, e.g. *taẖəbbazət* 'the profession of a baker'. The Ḥassāniyya dialect in particular has taken over a large number of Berber words, some of them together with their original plurals, e.g. *ärägäž/ärwägīž* 'man', *āḏrār/īḏrārən* 'mountain', *tāmūrt/tīmūrātən* 'acacia forest', with the typically Berber prefixes *ä-/ā-* (masculine) and *tā-/tī-* (feminine).

In spite of the linguistic diversity of North Africa, it may be regarded as one dialect area because of the common features shared by these dialects, which set them apart from the rest of the Arabophone world. There is one morphological feature in the verbal system that has served to classify the Maghreb dialects as one group: the prefix *n-* for the first person singular in the imperfect verb (cf. above, Chapter 9, p. 134), for instance Moroccan Arabic *nəktəb* 'I write'/*nkətbu* 'we write'. The boundary between the *n-* dialects and the Eastern dialects lies somewhere in western Egypt (cf. above, p. 137).

All Maghreb dialects (except the Eastern sedentary dialects) have a very simple vowel system, with only two short vowels, /ə/ (< /a/ and /i/) and /u/, and three long vowels, /ā/, /ī/, /ū/. In the dialect of Cherchell, this development has gone even further, with only one short vowel remaining.

Another striking feature in the phonology of all Maghreb dialects is the stress shift in words of the form *faʿal*, which among other things function as perfect verbs. Assuming that the original primary stress was on the penultimate, we may reconstruct the development as follows: *kátab* > *katáb* > *ktəb* 'to write', and likewise *žbəl* < *ğabal* 'mountain', *ʿrəb* < *ʿarab* 'Arabs', with elision of the short unstressed vowel. The only Maghreb dialect that has not undergone the stress shift is Maltese (cf. Maltese *kiteb*, *ġibel* 'stone, hill [in place names]', both with stress on the penultimate).

With regard to syllable structure, many Maghreb dialects have undergone a restructuring in sequences of the type CvCC, which was changed to CCvC, for instance in *qabr* > *qbəṛ* 'grave'; *saqf* > *sqəf* 'roof'. Since in many dialects there is a constraint against short vowels in open syllables, when such a sequence is followed by a vocalic ending the vowel 'jumps' back one position, e.g. **ktəbət* > *kətbət* 'she wrote'; **ḥməṛa* > *ḥəmṛa* 'red [feminine]. The constraint against short vowels in open syllables also operates in forms such as the second person plural of the imperfect verb, **təktəb-u* 'you [plural] write'; in Moroccan Arabic this becomes *tkətb-u*. In other Maghreb dialects, the outcome of this rule is different. Some of them, such as the dialect of the Muslims of Tunis, elide the vowel (*təktbu*), or reduplicate the first radical, such as the dialect of the Muslims of Algiers (*yəkkə́tbu*); other dialects have chosen still other solutions (*yə́kkətbu*, *tə́kətbu*, *yēkə́tbu*, *yḗkətbu*; cf. Fischer and Jastrow 1980: 254–6). The verbal paradigm of Moroccan Arabic demonstrates the effects of the phenomena mentioned above, as shown in Table 10.5.

ktəb	*kətbu*	*yəktəb*	*ykətbu*
kətbət		*təktəb*	
ktəbti	*ktəbtiw*	*təktəb*	*tkətbu*
		tkətbi	
ktəbt	*ktəbna*	*nəktəb*	*nkətbu*

Table 10.5 The verbal paradigm of Moroccan Arabic.

The system of derived measures has achieved a greater symmetry in the Maghreb than in the Eastern Arabic dialects. In Moroccan Arabic, for instance, the most frequent derived measures are the second measure (*ʿəlləm* 'to teach'), the third measure (*qatəl* 'to fight') and the eighth measure (*štġəl* or *štaġəl* 'to work'). From all measures, including the first (stem verb), a passive may be derived in *t-*, *tt-* or *n-*. Most Moroccan dialects have *tt-*, e.g. *ttəktəb* 'to be written', *ttšaf* 'to be seen', *ttəqra* 'to be recited', from the verbs *ktəb*, *šaf*, *qra*. Passives with *n-* occur mostly in the north and in Jewish varieties of Arabic. In some dialects, a wide variety of combinations occurs, for instance in the dialect of Skūra *tt-*, *n-*, *ttən-*, *ttnə-*, so that various forms have variants, e.g. *ttnəktəb/ttəktəb* 'to be written', *ttəssəḥsən/nəssəḥsən/ttnəssəḥsən* 'to be approved' (Classical *istaḥsana*).

The origin of these new passive formations is disputed. Since they occur in the stem verb as well, they must be new dialectal formations, possibly on the analogy of the Classical Arabic fifth measure *tafa*ʿʿ*ala* in the case of the *t-* forms, and from the Classical Arabic seventh measure *infaʿala* in the case of the *n-* forms. But it has also been proposed that these forms represent earlier Semitic categories, since a similar *t-* form occurs in Ethiopic and Aramaic. There may also be a connection with the Berber passive formation in *t-*, as Aguadé (1995: 66) suggests.

A special position is taken up by the Ḥassāniyya dialect of Mauritania. It has all the characteristic features of a Bedouin dialect, but apart from that we find here a series of unique innovations. In the phonological system, the dialect has a voiced /v/ that continues the Classical Arabic /f/, e.g. *vīl* < *fīl* 'elephant', *tọvla* 'girl'. The voiceless /f/ is restricted to certain environments: it occurs before a voiceless consonant, e.g. *fsəd* 'it was corrupted', in gemination, e.g. *wäffä* 'he terminated', and at the end of a word, e.g. *ʿṛaf* 'he knew'. Both consonants have an emphatic allophone in certain environments, just like most of the other consonants. As in all Arabic dialects, the two Classical phonemes /ḍ/ and /ḏ̣/ have merged, and since the dialect is a Bedouin dialect the resulting phoneme is interdental, /ḏ̣/. But in a number of words there is a phoneme /ḍ/ as the reflex of Classical /ḍ/, e.g. *qāḍi* 'judge', *ṛamaḍān* 'Ramadan'. These examples could be regarded as borrowings from the Classical language, but other words such as *vaḍl* < *faḍl* 'favour', *mṛọḍ* < *mariḍa* 'he became ill' seem to be original dialect words. In that case, Ḥassāniyya would be the only Western dialect to preserve traces of the original distinction. A third interesting feature is the presence of three palatalised phonemes, /t^y/, /d^y/, /ñ/ in a small number of words, most of them of Berber origin. Their phonemic status cannot be doubted, but their role in the language is minimal. Examples include *käwkt*^{y}*äm* 'to strike with the fist', *kand*^{y}*a* 'syphilis', *Bäññug* '[proper name]'.

In the verbal system of Ḥassāniyya, apart from the usual derived measures there is a special measure with the prefix *sa-*, e.g. *sagbäl* 'he went south', *saḥmaṛ* 'he made red', *säktäb* 'he made someone his secretary'. The most probable explanation for this verbal form is a back-formation from tenth-measure verbs, e.g. from *stäsläm* 'to become a Muslim' a new form was created *säsläm* 'to make a Muslim'. This new measure then spread to all verbs. Another innovation is a new passive form that has developed for the second and third measure of the derived verb, and for the *sa-* forms (see Table 10.6). An unusual feature is the presence of a diminutive pattern for verbs, e.g. *äkäytäb* from *ktäb* 'to write', *ämäyšä* from *mšä* 'to leave'. Such forms are mostly used in combination with a diminutive noun subject.

	active	passive
perfect	*bah̲h̲ar* 'to perfume'	*ubah̲h̲ar* 'to be perfumed'
imperfect	*ibah̲h̲ar*	*yubah̲h̲ar*
perfect	*găbel* 'to confront'	*ugăbel* 'to be confronted'
imperfect	*igăbel*	*yugăbel*
perfect	*sagbäl* 'to go south'	*usagbäl* 'to be directed south'
imperfect	*isagbäl*	*yusagbäl*

Table 10.6 The formation of the passive in Ḥassāniyya.

Text 9: Moroccan Arabic (after Caubet 1993)

1. *gāl-l-ha: hākda? ēwa gləs hna! žbəd əl-flūs u-ʿṭā-ha u-gāl-l-ha: hna tgəlsi! ma- təmšiw-šḥətta ngūl-l-kum āžīw ʿand-i*	1. He said to her: 'So? Then sit here!' He pulled out the money and gave it to her and said to her: 'You sit here! Don't go until I tell you: come to me!'
2. *mša där wāḥəd-əl-bṛa ʿand-əl-feṛṛān, gāl-l-u: dīr əl-feṛṛān yəsh̲on, yəsh̲on bezzäf, bəzzäf!, gāl-l-u: wah̲h̲a!*	2. He went to send a letter to the (attendant of the) oven, and told him: 'Heat it up, heat it up, very much!' He said to him: 'Alright!'
3. *ēwa ʿayyəṭ l-žūž-d-əl-būlīs, gāl-l-hum: rəfdu hād-əṣ-ṣəndūq!, rəfdu hād-əṣ-ṣəndūq u-ddāw-əh l-əl-fəṛṛān, ddāw-əh ṛmāw-əh f-bīt-nāṛ*	3. Then he called two policemen, and told them: 'Take this box!' They took this box and brought it to the oven, they brought it and threw it into the fire-place.
4. *ēwa, ya sīdi, bqa ka-yttəḥṛəq ḥətta māt dāk-əl-ʿabd*	4. Yes sir, it kept on burning until that slave died.

Text 10: Ḥassāniyya (after Cohen 1963: 252)

1. *ya qē^{y}r ṛkabnāhöm mʿa ṣṣbāḥ mən ʿand lh̲yām, madkurānna ḥayya v zərr Āfṭūṭ mən tall šaṛg; hāḏa nhāṛ, nhāṛ mtīn*	1. But we rode in the morning from the tents, a camp site had been mentioned to us near Āfṭūṭ ('the large plain') in the north-east; this is a day, a long day.
2. *ṛkabna mʿa ṣṣbāḥ u gəlna ʿanna lā bəddānna mən ngayyəlu ḏīk lḥayya vīh ārwāgīž gāʿ aṣḥāb ənna u vīh zād ṣadīqāt aṣḥabāt əṃṃ^{w}alli*	2. We rode in the morning and we said to ourselves: 'We have to take a rest in that camp site'. In it were men that were friends of ours and there were moreover female friends, too.

3. *ṛkabna mən vamm u gəmna mḥarrkīn; ḥma ənnhāṛ; hāḏa vaʿgāb əṣṣayf, ənnhāṛāt māhȫm ḥāmyīn ya qēʸr əššams ḥayya*

3. We rode from there and we got moving; the day became hot; it was the end of the summer, the days were not hot, but the sun was strong.

4. *mnēʸn ḥma əʿlīna ənnhāṛ, brək awṣayrīt, mnayn brək tbārəkna mʿāh u gām*

4. When the day became at its hottest, our young animal broke down; when it broke down, we took care of it, and it stood up.

FURTHER READING

The most complete handbook of Arabic dialects is that of Fischer and Jastrow (1980); the progress in our knowledge of the Arabic dialects is obvious when we compare this handbook with the sixteen-years-older survey by Brockelmann (1964) in the *Handbuch der Orientalistik*. Fischer and Jastrow give a general survey of the structure of Arabic dialects, followed by a discussion of each individual dialect group, with sample texts of the most important dialects. There is a rather short historical introduction. A recent survey is Kaye and Rosenhouse (1997). Short introductions to the Arabic dialects are available in Polish (Danecki 1989) and in Italian (Durand 1995). On dialect atlases, see above, Chapter 9.

A few monographs may be mentioned that concern themselves with general features across all dialects: Fischer (1959) on the deictic system; Janssens (1972) on the stress patterns; Eksell Harning (1980) on the genitive construction; Czapkiewicz (1975) on the aspectual system; Retsö (1983) on the passive voice.

For each of the dialect groups mentioned in this chapter, we shall indicate the most important grammars, dictionaries and monographs.

Dialects of the Arabian Peninsula

The classification and structure of the North-east Arabian dialects is relatively well known, the best survey being that of Ingham (1982); for the dialects of Eastern Arabia and the Gulf states, see Johnstone (1967). A reference grammar of Gulf Arabic is Holes (1990). For the Bedouin dialects outside the Arabian peninsula, see the older study of Cantineau (1936, 1937); more recent studies are by Rosenhouse (1984, general survey), Blanc (1970b, the dialects of the Negev) and de Jong (1996, the dialects of the Sinai). Palva (1991) proposes a new classification of what he calls the North-west Arabian dialects.

About the position of the Shiʿite dialects in Bahrain, see Prochazka (1981), Holes (1983, 1984, 1987) and Al-Tajir (1982). The dialect of Oman, which is important because of its expansion to Zanzibar and its contacts with the Swahili-speaking inhabitants of East Africa, is still known primarily through the old description by Reinhardt (1894); and see Brockett (1985).

The dialects of Central Arabia are dealt with by Prochazka (1988) and Ingham (1982); a reference grammar of Naǧdī Arabic was produced by Ingham (1994b), from whom the Naǧdī examples were taken. The dialects of the Ḥiǧāz are less well known; on the sedentary dialect of Mecca, see Schreiber (1970), Ingham (1971), Bakalla (1979) and Sieny (1978); on the Bedouin dialects, see Toll (1983).

The dialects of Yemen used to be one of the most neglected topics in Arabic dialect geography; apart from the older literature such as Rossi (1939), there was only a sketch of some of the dialect features by Diem (1973b). Recent publications by Behnstedt include a dialect atlas (1985) and a glossary (1992); there are some monographs on individual dialects (sketch of the dialect of Saʿdah by Behnstedt 1987; syntax of Ṣanʿāʾ Arabic by Watson 1993; dialects of the Central Tihāma by Greenman 1979). On the whole, the situation in North Yemen has been studied more extensively than that in South Yemen. A learning grammar of Ṣanʿānī Arabic was published by Watson (1996).

Syro-Lebanese Dialects

Syria and Lebanon are probably the best-researched dialect area in the Arab world. A classic article on the classification of Syrian, Lebanese and Palestinian dialects is Cantineau (1938).

There are two books on the Syrian dialect of Damascus in the Richard Slade Harrell Arabic Series: a reference grammar (Cowell 1964) and an English–Syrian Arabic dictionary (Stowasser and Ani 1964). A comprehensive dictionary of Levantine Arabic is that of Barthélemy (1935–69); a supplement was published by Denizeau (1960). The dialect of Damascus has been the subject of a detailed description by Grotzfeld (1964), who also wrote a number of texts together with Bloch (1964). A syntactic study of Damascene Arabic was published by Bloch (1965). The dialect of Aleppo is described by Sabuni (1980), from whom the examples were taken. On the dialect of the province of Hatay in Turkey, see Arnold (1996).

For the Lebanese dialects, see Fleisch (1974), a collection of dialect geographical studies. An older syntactic study of the Lebanese dialects is that of Feghali (1928). Individual dialects were described by El-Hajjé (1954, the dialect of Tripoli), Jiha (1964, the dialect of Bišmizzīn) and Abu-Haidar (1979, the dialect of Baskinta). The data about the isogloss of /a/ loss in unstressed syllables are to be found in Janssens (1972: 108–14).

For Palestine dialects, on the syntax of Palestinian Arabic see Bauer (1909), Blau (1960, the dialect of Bir Zēt) and Piamenta (1966).

For Jordanian Arabic, on the classification of the Jordanian dialects see Cleveland (1963) and a sociolinguistic study by Suleiman (1985).

Mesopotamian Dialects

For the dominant dialect of Baghdad, there is a complete set of materials in the Richard Slade Harrell Arabic Series: reference grammar (Erwin 1963), basic course (1969) and dictionaries (Clarity, Stowasser and Wolfe 1964; Woodhead and Beene 1967); grammatical sketch in Malaika (1963).

The classic work on the communal dialects of Baghdad is Blanc (1964). Our main source for the *qəltu* dialects is Jastrow's two-volume study on these dialects, their classification and their characteristics, accompanied by a large collection of texts (Jastrow 1978, 1981); for a survey, see Jastrow (1994). The same author has also published extensively on individual dialects of this group, for instance his study on the dialect of Mosul (1979) and on the Jewish Arabic of

ʿAqra and Arbīl (1990). A study on the verbal syntax of a Mesopotamian dialect, the dialect of Kwayriš, is by Denz (1971). For the *qəltu* dialects of Anatolia, see Chapter 13, p. 224.

On the Arabic of Khuzestan, there are three studies by Ingham (1973, 1976, 1994a).

Egyptian Arabic

One of the oldest dialect grammars is that of Spitta-Bey (1880) of Egyptian Arabic; it represents an effort to describe the Egyptian (Cairene) dialect as it was actually spoken at the time. Later grammars include Tomiche (1964), a reference grammar, and Mitchell (1962), Salib (1981) and Ahmed (1981), which are intended as learning grammars with conversations and exercises. A complete course developed in the Michigan series is Abdel-Masih, Abdel-Malek and Badawi (1978–9). Woidich (1990) is a manual for the Egyptian dialect; because of its empirical basis, it contains many aspects of Cairene grammar not included in the reference grammars. A transformational grammar of Egyptian Arabic was produced by Wise (1975). On the phonology of Cairene Arabic, see Broselow (1976, 1979).

Monographs on individual dialects are by Woidich (e.g. 1979, 1980, the dialect of il-ʿAwāmṛa; 1993, the dialects of the oases); Abulfadl (1961, the dialects of the Šarqiyya); de Jong (1999, the dialects of the Sinai that form a bridge between Egypt and the Eastern dialects). On the history of Cairene Arabic and the formative period of this dialect, see Birkeland (1952), Woidich (1994, 1995) and Woidich and Landau (1993: 49–75). A dictionary of the Cairene dialect was published by Badawi and Hinds (1986). The dialect atlas of Behnstedt and Woidich was mentioned above, p. 147.

Sudanese Arabic is much less well known than Egyptian Arabic; on the dialect of Khartoum, see Trimingham (1946); a dictionary of colloquial Sudanese is by Qāsim (1972); there is a monograph on the Bedouin dialect of the Šukriyya by Reichmuth (1983). On the Arabic of Chad, see Kaye (1976), Roth (1979), Owens (1985) and Tourneux and Zeltner (1986). A dictionary of Chadic Arabic is by Roth-Laly (1969).

An older study on the Arabic dialects of Central Africa is Kampffmeyer (1899). On the westward expansion of Arabic in the sub-Saharan region, see Braukämper (1994). On the Arabic dialect of Nigeria, see Owens (1993, 1994); a dictionary of Nigerian Arabic is by Kaye (1982).

Maghrebi Dialects

A general study of the Maghreb dialects is Ph. Marçais (1977). Most of the available didactic materials concern the Moroccan dialect. There is a complete set of manuals in the Richard Slade Harrell Arabic Series: reference grammar (Harrell 1962), basic course (Harrell 1965) and dictionaries (Harrell 1966; Harrell and Sobleman 1963). A complete handbook of Moroccan Arabic is Caubet (1993). The Dutch–Moroccan/Moroccan–Dutch dictionary of Otten (1983) deserves special mention because of its consistent orthography, which could be regarded as a step towards standardisation of the dialect. This orthography is also used in a recent course for Moroccan Arabic in Dutch (Hoogland 1996).

Other varieties of Moroccan Arabic are described by Singer (1958a, 1958b, the dialect of Tetouan) and Aguadé and Elyaacoubi (1995, the dialect of Skūra). For Algerian, see Ph. Marçais (n.d., the dialect of Djidjelli) and Grand'henry (1972, the dialect of Cherchell). For Tunisian, see the manual by Singer (1984) and Talmoudi (1980, 1981, 1984b, the dialect of Sousse). For Libyan, there is a reference grammar of Eastern Libyan by Owens (1984); on the dialect of Cyrenaica, see Laria (1996). For the early history of the dialects of the Maghreb, Corriente's (1977) study of the Arabic dialect of al-'Andalus is an important contribution.

Of special interest are the dialects of the Jewish communities in North Africa, e.g. the dialect of the Jews of Tunis (D. Cohen 1964, 1975); the dialect of the Jews of Algiers (M. Cohen 1912); the dialect of Tafilalt (Heath and Bar-Asher 1982). The Ḥassāniyya dialect is described by D. Cohen (1963) and Zavadovskij (1981); a study on this dialect was published by Taine-Cheikh (1994); there is an extensive dictionary in course of publication by Taine-Cheikh (1988–).

11
The Emergence of Modern Standard Arabic

11.1 INTRODUCTION

In 1798, Napoleon Bonaparte's brief expedition to Egypt brought this province of the Ottoman empire into direct contact with Western Europe. This marked the beginning of a period in which European culture, at first primarily from France, but later from England as well, began to infiltrate the Arab world. At first, the reception of new ideas was promoted by the government: Muḥammad ʿAlī, who governed Egypt from 1805 until 1848, stimulated the translation of books and articles from French, mostly on technical subjects, but political and cultural topics were also included. In this way, the concepts of the French Enlightenment became part of the intellectual atmosphere of the country. The introduction of new political ideas stimulated the rise of Arab nationalism, which in the second half of the nineteenth century centred around the position of Arabic as the language of the Arab world. At the same time, the confrontation with Western ideas led to a debate about the compatibility of these ideas with the tradition of Islam, and, on a linguistic level, about the capacity of the Arabic language to express the new notions. In this chapter, we shall deal with four topics: the position of Arabic in the nineteenth century; the adaptation of Arabic vocabulary to the modern period; the reform of grammar; and the changes in the structure and phraseology of the language.

11.2 THE REBIRTH OF ARABIC

When the French conquered Egypt, the Egyptian writer al-Ǧabartī (d. 1825), who witnessed the invasion, wrote an account in which he informed his compatriots about the political situation in Europe and the relations between the European nations. For the first time, political notions and institutions that were alien to the Islamic point of view had to be described in terms that were comprehensible to a Muslim audience. Throughout the nineteenth century, Arabic translators were active as intermediaries who attempted to express the notions of one culture in the language of the other (cf. Ayalon 1987). It was, for instance, hard to find an Arabic equivalent for the European notion of 'constitutional government'. In some translations, 'constitutional monarchy' became a *malakiyya muqayyada* (after the French *monarchie limitée*), i.e. a monarchy that was limited by laws, in the Middle Eastern context almost a contradiction in terms. The notion of man-made laws was equally difficult to grasp. The Middle East knew only a religious law (*šarīʿa*), sometimes complemented by temporary regulations by the ruler (*qawānīn*). For a long time, translators hesitated to use the verb *šarraʿa* for the Western concept of 'legislation', but at the end of the nineteenth century this became the current term for the activity of a legislative assembly. The term *dustūr* became the regular term for 'constitution'; originally this term had denoted a code, or a collection of laws. Once *dustūr* had been introduced as a term for the constitution, 'constitutional government' could be translated with *ḥukūma dustūriyya*.

It was equally hard to reproduce the idea of 'citizenship' in a society that consisted of a ruler and his subjects. Initially, the Arabic translators used the term *raʿiyya* 'flock, subjects' to indicate all people under a government, so that *ḥuqūq ar-raʿiyya* came to indicate the concept of 'civil rights'! Because of its connotations, this term was increasingly often avoided by the translators and replaced with the more neutral term *šaʿb* 'people', for instance in combinations such as *ḥukūmat aš-šaʿb bi-š-šaʿb* 'government of the people by the people' and *ṣawt aš-šaʿb* 'vox populi', and also in *mağlis aš-šaʿb* 'people's assembly, House of Commons'. Only in the twentieth century, when the concept of *waṭan* 'fatherland' had become familiar, could a term such as *muwāṭin* for 'citizen' gain currency (Ayalon 1987: 43–53).

The representative character of the government in many European countries constituted another problem for a translator wishing to explain the structure of European society. One of the first terms to indicate a representative was *wakīl*, originally a representative of the ruler or a mandatory. At first, this was the term used in combinations such as *wukalāʾ ar-raʿiyya* or *mağlis al-wukalāʾ*. At the end of the nineteenth century, it was replaced by *nuwwāb* from *nāʾib* 'replacing'. In some cases, the choice of terms represented a deliberate attempt on the part of the rulers to manipulate the ambiguity of the terminology. When the term *šūrā* was introduced to indicate the institution of a parliament, this term had overtones of a consultative body (cf. the Ottoman *meşveret*), and in choosing this term rulers could emphasise the limited powers of the body concerned. An alternative term *dīwān* had the same disadvantage – or advantage – of being closely connected to the sphere of influence of the ruler. In the end, the much vaguer term *mağlis* 'session' (or sometimes the European loan *barlamān*) seemed better suited to express the novel character of the new institution. This last example illustrates the process by which from a confusion of terms eventually the best term was selected, i.e. the term that was least contaminated with old concepts (cf. Rebhan 1986).

A complication in the study of the introduction of political terminology in Arabic in the nineteenth century is the fact that in many cases we have insufficient information about the exact path by which the terms were introduced. Neologisms invented by writers from the beginning of the nineteenth century such as al-Ǧabartī played an important part, but they were not the only source for the lexical innovations. In some cases, translators could go back to pre-Ottoman Arabo-Islamic sources, such as the terminology in Ibn H̱aldūn's (d. 757/1356) *Muqaddima*, from which they borrowed words like *istibdād* 'despotic rule' for 'absolutism', *šūrā* 'council to elect a caliph' for 'constitutional government', and *fitna* 'fight between Islamic factions' for 'revolution'. Most of these words were replaced later by more neutral, less Islamic terms (for instance, *fitna* by *ṯawra*, originally 'unrest, stirring').

Some of the terms that were introduced into Arabic went through an

Ottoman stage. When in the second half of the nineteenth century the Young Ottomans formulated their ideas about government and political structure, they often borrowed words from Arabic that had not been current or did not have a specifically political meaning in Arabic. At a later stage, some of these terms were reintroduced into Arabic together with their newly-acquired meaning, for instance the words for 'government' (*hükümet*, Arabic *ḥukūma*) and 'republic' (*cumhuriyet*, Arabic *ǧumhūriyya*). Other terms that Ottoman Turkish had borrowed from Arabic never became popular in the Arab world, for instance the term *mabʿūṯ* (from Arabic *baʿaṯa* 'to send') that was used for the representatives in the Ottoman *Hey'et-i Mebʿūsān* in 1876. Another example is the word *millet* (Arabic *milla* 'religious community') that was applied in the nineteenth century by the Ottoman administration to other nations, but was replaced in the Arab world by *'umma*.

Yet another category is constituted by those terms that were created independently in the Arab world to express Western political notions. At first, these notions had been borrowed together with the foreign word, for instance *kūmūnizm* or *kūmūniyya* for 'communism', or *sūsyāl* or *sūsyālist* for 'socialist', but most foreign words were soon replaced by Arabic equivalents. Many of them were derived from existing roots or words through analogy (*qiyās*), e.g. *ištirākī* 'socialist' (from *ištaraka* 'to share'), which came to be preferred to *iǧtimāʿī* (from *iǧtamaʿa* 'to gather') and *šuyūʿiyya*, which was coined in the twentieth century for 'communism' (from *šā'iʿ* 'common [property]'). In most cases, the original European (English or French) term shone through in the selected root, but inevitably the Arabic equivalents introduced new connotations as well. The term *ištirākī*, for instance, suggests 'sharing', which underscores one aspect of socialism, the sharing of the means of production.

The new role of Arabic as a medium for political ideas naturally affected its societal position as well. During the centuries of Ottoman rule, Turkish had become the language of power and government in the Arab world, and although Classical Arabic had always remained the language of religion and to a certain extent, of culture, it had lost its function as administrative language of the empire (cf. also above, Chapter 5). The official status of Turkish in the Ottoman empire did not mean, however, that it was universally understood. In the Arab provinces, less than 1 per cent of the population actually knew Turkish. In practice, therefore, the local authorities and the courts had to have recourse to translators in order to facilitate contacts with the local populace. Most of the locally-produced documents were either in Arabic or bilingual.

When at the end of the nineteenth century nationalism began to emerge in the Arab world, it was invariably linked with the Arabic language, whether this nationalism was pan-Arabic as in Syria, or regional as in Egypt. The linkage between Arab identity and the Arabic language did not call into question the framework of the Ottoman empire and usually went no further than a request for improvement in the status of Arabic in the provinces. On more than one occasion, complaints were made about the lack of understanding between the local populace and the government's representatives, and local authorities often stressed the need to send officials who were familiar with the local language. In Egypt, the use of Arabic for administrative purposes had increased steadily throughout the nineteenth century, and at the end of the century most of the official correspondence was carried out in Arabic. Nonetheless, any discussion in the Ottoman Parliament by Arab delegates about the position of Arabic immediately led to objections by those who felt that the position of Turkish as the official language of the Ottoman empire was threatened. In 1909, the use of any other language than Turkish in legal cases was explicitly forbidden, and in 1910 a request to the Ottoman Parliament to accept petitions written in Arabic was turned down.

The Arab Congress that convened in 1913 in Paris called for a measure of provincial autonomy within the Ottoman empire and at the same time claimed for Arabic the status of official language, both in the Ottoman Parliament and in local government. On the part of the central government, the loss of the Ottoman areas in the Balkans led to a renewed interest in the position of the Arab provinces. In 1913, petitions in Arabic in predominantly Arabic-speaking areas were allowed, and official decrees were published with an Arabic translation. Officially, Arabic was even accepted as the language of education and legal cases, but probably this new policy was implemented only in central areas such as Syria and Lebanon. None of these requests and measures should be construed as signs of disloyalty towards the central government; in most cases they were meant as support for the central government and as a means of strengthening the ties between the provinces and the capital.

The reaction to European ideas differed in the various Arab provinces. In Egypt, the period after the Napoleonic conquest was characterised by an emphasis on the special character of Egyptian society, history and culture. Some intellectuals even began to write about the Egyptian nation (*waṭan*) as something transcending the Muslim community (*'umma*). The keywords of this development were modernisation and reform, albeit without a concrete programme, and always within the framework of the Ottoman empire. At first, these writers did not respond negatively to European culture, but in the course of the nineteenth century the increasing political presence and influence of the European countries (Tunisia 1881, Egypt 1882) and their special ties with the Christian minorities altered the attitude towards Europe. Thinkers such as Ǧamāl ad-Dīn al-'Afġānī (1839–97) and Muḥammad ʿAbduh (1849–1905) opposed British imperialism, while at the same time emphasising the need to reform Islamic thinking and education. In their view, this reform should not consist in the wholesale borrowing of Western notions, but in a revival of the old Islamic virtues: Islam was a rational religion and perfectly capable of coping with the new problems. European ideas could be helpful in some respects, but because of its inherent virtues Islam had nothing to fear from them. The term *Nahḍa* 'awakening, revival' is sometimes used to indicate the spirit of this period, in which some reformers expected Islam to experience a renaissance, after the dark ages of uncritical repetition of established doctrine (*taqlīd*). In this view, an acquaintance with Western culture and ideas served as a catalyst for the revival of Islamic and/or Arabic culture.

In the Levant, the reaction to nationalism developed in a different way from Egypt. The Arab Christians in Greater Syria had never completely severed the ties with the Christians of Europe, and from the seventeenth century onwards there had been a constant interchange between the Maronites and the learned (often religious) institutions of Italy and France. For these Christians, the problem of a conciliation between Islam and Western ideas did not pose itself, and they could adopt these new ideas without any risk to their own identity. For them as non-Muslims, an Islamic empire held no appeal, and they were apt to stress the separation between Arabic and Islam. While in Egyptian nationalist circles the role of the Egyptian nation was emphasised, Syrian nationalism owed a great deal to Arab Christians, which partly explains its more markedly pan-Arab flavour. In accordance with their views on the unifying role of language rather than religion, Lebanese Christians played an important role in the revival of Arabic studies in the late eighteenth and early nineteenth centuries (for instance, Nāṣif al-Yāziǧī, 1800–71).

After the start of the First World War, the political conflicts between the provinces and the central government were phrased increasingly often in terms of the opposition Arabs/Turks. The Arab revolt of 1916 aimed at the establishment of an Arab kingdom to provide a home for all those of Arab descent who spoke Arabic. Although Arab thinkers often disagreed among themselves about the future form which their nation should take, they all agreed on its being an Arabic-speaking nation. It is true that in spite of efforts to realise a secular state in the Arab world, as Atatürk had done in Turkey, Islam remained the most important binding element. But, for most political thinkers, Islam was intrinsically and indissolubly connected with Arabic. Thus, for instance, Šakīb 'Arslān (1896–1946) held that the community was defined by its religion, and since Arabs formed the core of the Islamic *'umma*, Arabic was the true language of Islam, so that every Muslim had to learn Arabic. Arguing the other way round, Sāṭiʿ al-Ḥuṣrī (1880–1968) asserted that it was precisely language that defined a nation, and therefore, the Arab nation should include all those who speak Arabic. In this respect, he opposed both the Islamic nationalists, who wished to unite all Muslims, and the regional nationalists, such as the Egyptians, whose first priority was to obtain statehood for a geographically-defined nation.

11.3 THE REFORM OF THE LEXICON

The nineteenth century witnessed the development of a periodical press in Arabic, at first in Syria and later in Egypt as well. The first Arabic periodical was the Egyptian government newspaper *al-Waqā'iʿ al-Miṣriyya* (1828), established by Muḥammad ʿAlī. The involvement of Arab Christians in the publication of private newspapers ensured the emphasis on its Arabic character. The activities of language reformers in Syria, such as Fāris aš-Šidyāq (1804–87) and Buṭrus al-Bustānī (1819–83), gave an impetus to the much-needed modernisation of the lexicon. Al-Bustānī, for instance, published the first modern large-scale dictionary of Arabic, *al-Muḥīṭ*, which borrowed heavily from the Classical dictionaries, to be sure, but nevertheless aimed at the incorporation of all exciting new ideas and concepts in an Arabic garb.

This is not to say that there was a consensus among Arab linguists about the best way to deal with the influx of Western notions into the Arabic language. Just as political thinkers differed in their ideas about Islam and Islamic civilisation and its relationship to Western/Christian culture, the language-reformers ranged from those who believed that in itself the Arabic lexicon was sufficient to express anything needed in this modern age, to those who strongly advocated the wholesale adoption of Western words and a complete revision of the lexicon. The more careful approach of the moderates resembled the ideas of some of the political thinkers of this period. They maintained that in itself Arabic was the perfect language, but people had started to corrupt it. What was needed was a return to the purity of the Classical language.

In the process of modernisation of the language at the beginning of the twentieth century, the Arab Academies played a central part. Modelled after the great language academies of Europe – both the Academy of Damascus and the Academy of Cairo, for instance, were founded with explicit reference to the example of the Académie Française – their aim was to implement the ideas about the place of Arabic in the modern world that had become commonplace in the *Nahḍa*. During his short-lived reign in Syria, King Fayṣal expressed concern about the quality of the educational system and the preservation of the cultural heritage in the form of libraries, manuscript collections and museums. The *Dīwān al-maʿārif* that was installed for this purpose came under the presidency of Kurd ʿAlī, who had been the founder of the National Library (*Dār al-Kutub az-Ẓāhiriyya*). In 1919, the second task of the council, the cultivation of the Arabic language, was entrusted to what became the first language academy in the Arab world, *al-Mağmaʿ al-ʿIlmī al-ʿArabī*, nowadays called *Mağmaʿ al-Luġa al-ʿArabiyya bi-Dimašq* 'The Academy of the Arabic Language in Damascus'.

From the start, the goal of the Academy was twofold: to guard the integrity of the Arabic language and preserve it from dialectal and foreign influence, on the one hand, and to adapt the Arabic language to the needs of modern times, on the other. The same two functions appear in the charter of the Academy of Cairo (*Mağmaʿ al-Luġa al-ʿArabiyya al-Malikī*, since 1955 called the *Mağmaʿ al-Luġa al-ʿArabiyya*), founded in 1932 by Fu'ād I. In practice, the main function of the Cairene academy since 1960 has been the creation of new Arabic terminology, as well as the reform of both Arabic script and grammar. New terms are introduced through a complicated process of consultation and deliberation: they are proposed in the many subcommittees of the academy, each responsible for a specific field of knowledge, and after approval by the general assembly of the academy they are published in its journal. Usually the introduction of a new term leads to long and sometimes heated discussions in the proceedings of the Academy, and it may take years before a proposed term finally finds its way into the dictionaries and technical vocabularies of the Academy.

The academies of Iraq (*al-Mağmaʿ al-ʿIlmī al-ʿIrāqī*, established in 1947) and Jordan (*Mağmaʿ al-Luġa al-ʿArabiyya al-'Urdunnī*, established in 1976) are of more recent date and of secondary importance in the process of language modernisation. It appears that the Iraqi academy concentrates more on the edition of Classical texts in an effort to contribute to the *'iḥyā' at-turāṯ* 'resuscitation of the heritage', whereas the Jordanian academy serves as an instrument in the arabicisation of education in Jordan. There have been some attempts to create a pan-Arabic association of language academies, but the national academies guard their independence and autonomy jealously so that cooperation on a higher level is at most a cherished ideal and does not seem to have led to any concrete results.

The most urgent problem of language reform was that of the expansion of the lexicon. In addition to their confrontation with European political ideologies at the beginning of the nineteenth century, the Arab provinces were confronted by a host of new technical notions and objects, for which names had to be invented. The lexical expansion for political and technical terminology in this period parallels that in another period in which the Arabic language incorporated an entirely new vocabulary, that of the eighth/ninth centuries, when the translation of Greek logical, medical and philosophical writings required the invention of many new words (cf. above, Chapter 5).

A major difference between the Classical period of the translations and the modern period is the degree of uniformity. At first, the translators of the Classical period had been free to create their own terminology, but, with the establishment of the translators' academy by al-Ma'mūn, terminology in the 'Greek' disciplines such as medicine, philosophy and logic became increasingly uniform. In the twentieth century, even more so than in the nineteenth, the expansion of the lexicon was undertaken simultaneously in many different places. In the nineteenth century, one could say that the major centres, Egypt and Syria, were at least in touch with each other, and some of the people who worked on the modernisation of the language in Egypt had come from Syria. But in the twentieth century, every country undertook its own voyage on the way to the modernisation of the lexicon, and not even the Academies were able to unify the 'national' terminologies. In some fields, of course, the differences in terminology constituted an acute threat to the cooperation between scholars and scientists from the various Arab countries, for instance in the field of medicine and physical sciences, and for some of these technical disciplines pan-Arabic word lists were, indeed, compiled.

The following methods may be distinguished in the creation of new vocabulary:

1. borrowing of the foreign word
2. integration of the foreign word morphologically and/or phonologically
3. analogical extension of an existing root
4. translation of the foreign word
5. semantic extension of an existing word.

These methods do not represent successive stages in the creation of vocabulary: they are different ways of coping with the introduction of new notions in a civilisation. There is a certain tendency, however, to go through them successively, starting with the wholesale borrowing of foreign words, which are then gradually adapted to the structure of the language. The actual choice of a new word depends on many factors, such as the nature of the notion to be translated and the cultural and political circumstances. Often, a new notion is introduced in the form of a close approximation of the foreign word. Such foreign loans are usually printed in Latin letters between brackets or transliterated and written in quotation marks. Thus, one may find today in popular scientific texts word like 'laser' in Arabic transliteration, followed by the same word in Latin letters. A similar procedure is sometimes followed with proper names.

Although both in the Classical period and in modern times there were purists who strove for the complete elimination of all foreign loans from the Arabic language, most people were willing to admit them on the condition that they were adapted to the structure of Arabic, both in their phonetic shape (no foreign sounds and no combinations of consonants that are not allowed in Arabic) and in their morphological pattern. In the Classical period, this procedure of arabicisation (*taʿrīb*) was very successful, the number of unadapted words remaining minimal. In the modern period, the Academies adopted a restrictive policy, only allowing loans in scientific terminology. Many nineteenth-century political loans (such as the above-cited *kūmūnizm*) were replaced eventually by Arabic terms, while purely scientific and technical terms (such as *hīdrūkarbūn* 'hydrocarbon', *klūrūfūrm* 'chloroform') retained their foreign shape.

The real controversy arose around the question as to whether or not foreign words could be used as productive roots for new derivations. In Classical Arabic, once a foreign word had been admitted and adapted, it behaved like any other Arabic word, but in the modern period the Academies tried to restrict new derivations to scientific terminology. While some people deplored this invasion of the Arabic language, preferring to leave the foreign words in their original shape in order to set them apart from the Arabic stock, others saw in arabicisation the best solution to preserve the integrity of the language. Once a foreign word was introduced, scientists soon derived words like *tamağnuṭ* 'magnetisation' (from *mağnaṭīs*) and *mubastar* 'pasteurised' (from *bastara* 'to pasteurise'). But the powerful mechanism of root-abstraction did not stop at scientific terminology. Just as the dialects reanalysed foreign words and integrated them into their lexicon, writers did not hesitate to produce new derivations from accepted loans. Numerous examples for this procedure may be cited, e.g. the verbs *talfaza*, *talfana* from *tilifizyūn*, *tilifūn*; or the broken plurals *ʾaflām*, *bunūk* from the nouns *film*, *bank*. In spite of the resistance of the Academies, some of these derivations were commonly accepted.

Even those who admitted foreign loans usually conceded that at least in theory the most elegant solution was to replace foreign words with 'pure' Arabic words. In this context, the structure of the language was a relevant factor. In Germanic languages, the possibility of building compounds invites the speakers of the language to invent new combinations of existing words to express foreign notions and objects (neologisms). In Arabic, on the other hand, the possibility of using compounds was extremely limited, but the language had another device at its disposal for the formation of new words, the so-called *qiyās* 'analogy',

pattern	meaning	examples
mifʿal, mifʿāl, mifʿala	instrument	*miğhar* 'microscope' *minẓār* 'telescope' *mirwaḥa* 'fan'
-iyya	abstract noun	*iḥtirāqiyya* 'combustibility'
fiʿāla	profession	*qiyāda* 'leadership' *ṣiḥāfa* 'journalism'
faʿʿāl	professional	*sawwāq* 'driver' *ṭayyār* 'pilot'
fuʿāl	disease	*buwāl* 'diabetes' *buḥār* 'seasickness'

Table 11.1 Approved patterns of word-formation in Modern Standard Arabic.

which consisted in the application of morphological patterns to borrowed or existing sets of radicals. In internal *qiyās*, existing roots were used for this purpose. In its efforts to regulate the formation of new words, the Academy of Cairo declared certain morphological patterns to be productive, meaning that they might be used legitimately to create neologisms (see Table 11.1).

In the examples of *qiyās* given here, the construction of the new term is original, but in many cases the meaning of the foreign word determines the selection of the radicals. In such cases, we speak of a loan translation (calque, *Lehnübersetzung*). Combinations of words that serve as set expressions are usually modelled on a foreign example. The Arabic expression for 'satellite', for instance, *qamar ṣinā'ī* (literally 'artificial moon') is probably a translation from French (or Russian?). Even when the Arabic expression does not have a direct foreign equivalent, the English or French term shines through, for instance in the term for 'heading', *la'iba l-kura bi-r-ra's* (literally 'to play the ball with the head'), in football terminology. Loan translation also accounts for a large number of idiomatic expressions and metaphors, especially in the language of the media. In the course of time, such translations become part of the Arabic phraseology and are no longer regarded as foreign. The most frequently-quoted example of a loan expression is *la'iba dawran* 'to play a role'. Another example of loan translations is a variation in the use of prepositions under the influence of foreign idioms, e.g. *iltaqā/iltaqā ma'a* 'to meet/to meet with', and the development of syntactic calques, such as *mā 'iḏā* to translate English 'whether', e.g. *sa'ala mā 'iḏā*.

The most highly-regarded device for the expansion of the lexicon in Arabic, albeit not necessarily the most successful one, was the semantic extension of an existing word by giving it a modern meaning. Attempts to revive old Bedouin vocabulary in the search for new words were seldom successful, probably precisely because they had fallen into disuse and were therefore unfamiliar to the average speaker. One example of a term that did succeed is that of the word for 'train', *qiṭār*, originally meaning 'caravan'. But the associated word *hādiya* 'lead-camel' was never accepted for 'locomotive' (which became *qāṭira* instead). Revived words owed their success mostly to the efforts of one author, for instance *ǧarīda* 'newspaper' (originally 'strip of palm-leaf used for writing') and *maǧalla* 'journal' (originally 'codex, book'), introduced by aš-Šidyāq and al-Yāziǧī, respectively. Many of the proposals of the Academies, however, never gained general acceptance because they were regarded as too artificial, for instance, *ǧammāz* 'swift-footed [ass]' for 'tram' (remained *trām*), or *'irzīz* 'sound of thunder' for 'telephone' (remained *tilifūn*, although *hātif*, a Classical Arabic word meaning 'unseen man whose voice is heard', is becoming increasingly frequent).

In spite of the extreme productiveness of the nominal and verbal patterns of the Arabic language, the lexicon-builders kept looking for additional means of lexical expansion. In most Western languages, the use of Latin and Greek prefixes and suffixes provides a powerful means of expanding the scientific lexicon, which is absent in Arabic derivational morphology. At an early stage, combinations with the negations *lā-* and *ġayr-* were used to coin equivalents to Greek terms with the privative prefix *a-*. In modern times, these served as a model for the introduction of prefixes into the Arabic lexicon, at first only with the negations, e.g. *lā-* (*lā-nihā'ī* 'infinite', *lā-'adriyya* 'agnosticism'), *ġayr-* (*ġayr-šar'ī* 'illegitimate', *ġayr-mašrū'* 'illegal'). Later, several prepositions were used in this function, e.g. *šibh-* (*šibh-ǧazīra* 'peninsula', *šibh-rasmī* 'semi-official'), *qab-* (*qab-tārīḫ* 'prehistory'). Morphologically, these words behave as compounds: from *lā-nihā'ī* we may derive, for instance, the substantive *al-lā-nihā'iyya* 'the infinity', in which the article precedes the entire combination.

In Classical Arabic, there was a limited possibility of deriving new roots from combinations of words (called *naḥt*), usually delocutive verbs from nominal expressions, e.g. *basmala* 'to say "in the name of God" (*bi-smi llāhi*)', or *ḥamdala* 'to say "praise be to God!" (*al-ḥamdu lillāhi*)', or adjectives from compound names, e.g. *ḥanafī* 'belonging to 'Abū Ḥanīfa', or *ʿabqasī* 'belonging to ʿAbd al-Qays'. In modern times, initiatives to use this method of coining new words in the creation of scientific vocabulary became so popular that in 1953 the Academy of Cairo felt compelled to issue a ruling. According to the Academy, the method of *naḥt* was admissible only in scientific language, and the resulting terms had to be transparent. Words like *faḥmā'iyyāt* 'carbohydrates' (< *faḥm* 'carbon' + *mā'* 'water') and *ḥalma'a* 'to hydrolyse' (< *ḥallala* 'to dissolve' + *mā'* 'water') satisfied these conditions. Likewise, combinations with *kahra-* 'electro-', e.g. *kahra-maġnaṭīsī* or even *kahraṭīsī* 'electro-magnetic', *kahra-ri'awī* 'electro-pneumatic', *kahra-kīmiyā'ī* 'electro-chemical', and *šibh-* 'pseudo-' found favour with the Academy.

Generally speaking, however, the attitude of the Academy vis-à-vis compounds was conservative, and most proposals were deemed to be contrary to 'the spirit of the Arabic language'. Words like *'arbariǧl* 'quadruped' (< *'arbaʿ* 'four' + *riǧl* 'foot'), *qaṭǧara* 'laryngotomy' (< *qaṭʿ* 'cutting' + *ḥanǧara* 'throat'), or *sarmana* 'somnambulism' (< *sayr* 'going' + *manām* 'sleep') met with disapproval. Even more extreme proposals, such as *mutamāṯir* 'polymer' (< *mutamāṯil* 'homogeneous' + *mutakāṯir* 'multiple') or *musǧanāḥiyyāt* 'orthoptera' (< *mustaqīm* 'straight' + *ǧanāḥ* 'wing') were rejected outright, because of their lack of transparency. On the other hand, adjectival compounds have become relatively common, e.g. *šarq-'awsaṭī* 'Middle Eastern', *ra'smālī* 'capitalist', *barmā'ī* 'amphibian' (< *barr* + *mā'*), *'umamī* 'UN-' (< *al-'umam al-muttaḥida*), *mā fawqa l-banafsaǧī* 'ultra-violet', *taḥta l-'aḥmar* 'infra-red'.

Usually, within one semantic domain all methods to coin new words are used simultaneously, even though there is a tendency to go through certain stages. A few examples from modern vocabulary may illustrate the coexistence of different methods in the creation of a set of terms. In football terminology, all foreign terms have been replaced by Arabic words:

calque by extension	
ḍarba	'kick'
partial calque	
murāqib al-ḫuṭūṭ	'linesman'
compound calques	
ḍarba rukniyya, ḥurra, al-marmā, al-ǧazā'	'corner (kick)', 'free kick', goal kick' 'penalty (kick)'
ḥāris al-marmā	'goalkeeper'
neologisms	
marmā	'goal'
tamrīr	'pass'

paraphrases
laʿiba l-kura bi-r-raʾs 'to head'
semantic extension
tasallul 'offside' (lit. 'infiltration')
muḥāwara 'dribble' (lit. 'to trick someone in a debate')

This example also shows that it may be difficult to classify a new term. The word *marmā* 'goal', for instance, could be regarded as a neologism ('place where one throws'), or as the semantic extension of an existing term, meaning 'target'.

In computer terminology, the wish to go with the times and appear sophisticated competes with a tendency to purism that leads to the replacement of the English terms by neologisms. The omnipresent *kumbyūtur* (or similar transliterations) seems to be on the way out, and it is very possible that the actively-promoted *ḥāsūb* 'calculating machine' will, indeed, win eventually. Some Arabic computer terms have already become current, such as *munassiq al-kalima* 'word-processor', *šāša* 'computer screen' and *bank al-maʿlūmāt* 'databank'.

Finally, the example of modern linguistic terminology in Arabic demonstrates the opposition between the purism of the Academies and the attitude of modern linguists. There is no consensus on the name of 'linguistics' itself. In the Eastern Arab world, *ʿilm al-luġa* or *luġawiyyāt* is quite accepted, but linguists in the Maghreb object to the traditional term and replace it by *ʾalsuniyya* or *lisāniyyāt*. The official Arabic equivalent of two central notions in modern linguistics, 'morpheme' and 'phoneme', is in the form of a paraphrase, *ʿunṣur dāll* 'signifying element' and *waḥda ṣawtiyya* 'phonetic unit' (word list of ALECSO). But most linguists simply transliterate the English terms, *mūrfīm* and *fūnīm*. One linguist (Mseddi 1984) coined completely new terms, *ṣayġam* (containing the element *ṣīġa* 'form') and *ṣawtam* (containing the element *ṣawt* 'sound').

11.4 STANDARD ARABIC IN THE MODERN WORLD

Both vocabulary creation and regional variation are factors that have contributed to the gradual modification of the Classical language, so that it can no longer be regarded as identical with the modern variety of the language, usually called Modern Standard Arabic. Ideologically, of course, the modern language is still the same as the language of the *Qurʾān* and the Classical period, but in practice it is easy to see that there are differences, not all of them lexical. On the one hand, this is because many of the idiosyncrasies of the Classical language have become obsolete. Thus, for instance, one seldom finds in a modern text the constructions of a verbal noun with subject and object that are quite common in Classical texts. Similarly, some categories have become obsolete, e.g. the energetic *yaktubanna*. On the other hand, the modern language has developed new grammatical devices, in particular in the language of the media, which is heavily influenced by European languages. One of the most characteristic features of this language is the extensive use of verbal constructions with the dummy verb *qāma bi-* as a substitute for active verbs, e.g. *qāma bi-ziyāra* instead of *zāra* 'to visit'. In passive constructions, the verb *tamma* is used as a substitute, e.g. *tamma tawqīʿ al-ittifāqiyya* 'the agreement was signed', instead of a passive verb. Other characteristics of the language of the media include the limited use of the coordinative particle *fa-* and its replacement by *wa-*, and the extensive use of expressions like *wa-ḏālika, kull min* in enumerations.

In literary prose, the differences between Classical Arabic and Modern Standard Arabic are much less marked because authors tend to classicise their style, both in syntax and in the selection of the vocabulary. In some cases, however, the use of colloquial language, particularly in Egyptian literature, may create a new difference. The choice of informal registers is a further source of variation between the Arab countries as well. But lexical differences are responsible for most of the regional variation in Standard Arabic. In spite of the fact that the Standard Arabic language is regarded as the most powerful symbol of Arab unity, and in spite of the unifying work of the Academies, one immediately recognises a Moroccan text from an Egyptian text or a text from the Gulf states. Partly, this variation is caused by differing local traditions in the creation of new vocabulary. Partly, it is also a result of the different colonial history of the regions involved. In North Africa, for instance, there is a natural tendency to look at French examples and model the text, even on the level of syntax and stylistics, on a French example. One finds, for instance, *al-wazīr al-'awwal* (← French *premier ministre*) instead of the usual term *ra'īs al-wuzarā'*; *ḥuqūq* (← French *droits*) instead of *rusūm*. Stylistic expressions include *sāmī l-muwaẓẓafīn* (← French *hauts fonctionnaires*), *wuḍi'a fī l-isti'māl* (← French *mettre en usage*), *bi-'unwān* (← *à titre de*), and the use of prepositions with verbs like *taḥādaṯa ma'a* (← French *s'entretenir avec*). In some cases, North African phraseology was not directly inspired by French, yet differed from that in the Arab East, as in the choice of the dummy verb *waqa'a* in expressions like *waqa'a našr al-bayān* 'the publication of the declaration took place', where Eastern Arabic would use *tamma* or *ǧarā*. In Arab countries without a French colonial past, English usually replaced French as a model. In Egypt, for instance, France and French had been the model for most attempts at modernisation in the nineteenth century, but after the First World War, this role was taken over by Britain.

The reintroduction of Arabic as the official language of the Arab countries also raised the question of its role in education. The poor standards of language instruction were a constant source of concern, and since the nineteenth century there has been a call for simplification of the grammatical system. Some scholars claimed that Arabic in itself was perfectly well suited to accommodate contemporary needs, if only it was purified from the corruption that had crept in. They believed that the main obstacle to the general use of the standard language in society was the failure of the educational system to reach large parts of the population. There was, of course, a logistical problem because of the lack of schools and teachers, but most specialists agreed that this in itself did not explain the lack of success in teaching Standard Arabic to those children who did attend schools. Even today, hardly anybody after graduation is able to write flawless Arabic, let alone extemporise in speaking, and there is a general antipathy towards 'grammar', even among those who advocate the use of Standard Arabic.

The two keywords in the discussion were *tabsīṭ (taysīr) an-naḥw* 'simplification of grammar' and *tabsīṭ al-luġa* 'simplification of language', but the distinction between the two notions tended to become blurred. In the 1950s, a grammatical text was rediscovered, which sparked off a renewed interest in the matter of grammar teaching. Ibn Maḍā' was a grammarian from Cordova (d.

592/1196) who wrote about the refutation of the grammarians (*Kitāb ar-radd ʿalā n-nuḥāt*), proposing the abolition of the concepts of *ʿamal* 'governance' and *qiyās* 'analogy' from grammar. Among the scholars who occupied themselves with this text was the Egyptian linguist Šawqī Ḍayf, who maintained that this text was the solution to the problems of Arabic language teaching. With the abolition of *ʿamal* and *qiyās* from grammar, he asserted, it should be much easier to teach Arabic. Abstract discussions among the Arab grammarians, some of which had found their way into the current textbooks for schools, did nothing to enhance the understanding of the language and merely served the theoretical interests of the grammarians. His proposal to replace the Arabic notions of 'nominal sentence' and 'verbal sentence' (cf. above, p. 80) with the Western concepts of 'subject' and 'predicate' could, however, hardly be called a major improvement. Other proposals, too, were terminological in nature only. They involved the introduction of a new notion of 'complement' (*takmila*), and the replacement of the traditional terms *muḍāf* and *muḍāf 'ilayhi* for the constituents of the genitive construction by the term *mağrūr bi-l-'iḍāfa*. The success of these proposals has been limited.

Others concerned themselves with the simplification of the language itself, but in most cases this resulted in nothing more than a general plea for simplification without detailed proposals about the abolition of syntactic or morphological features from the language. Some scholars proposed to leave out the vowels of declension, which, however, leaves the declensional system intact, since in the sound masculine plural a choice must still be made between nominative *-ūn* and genitive/accusative *-īn*. Others called for the simplification of the syntactic rules for the numerals to be replaced by the rules of the dialect. More extreme proposals, such as those of 'Anīs Frayḥa and Georges al-H̱ūrī, involved the abolition of the feminine plural in the pronouns or the use of the masculine plural instead of the feminine plural in all parts of speech. Since none of these proposals was integrated into a comprehensive didactic concept, they have remained largely unproductive. Nowadays there are very few proponents of this road towards an 'easier language' (*luġa muyassara*).

The entire discussion about a simplified language has remained sterile, even when it was moved to a sociolinguistic level. In particular, in Egypt, it has become fashionable to hold that between the level of the standard language (*fuṣḥā*) and that of the dialect (*ʿāmmiyya*) there is an intermediate level, variably called *al-luġa al-mutawassiṭa* 'the intermediate language' or *luġat al-muṯaqqafīn* 'language of the intellectuals' (cf. Chapter 12). This variety, many people assert, would fill the gap between the artificial standard and the lower levels of the language continuum. The best that one could say about this sociolinguistic approach is that it legitimises the informal standard speech of many educated Egyptians. More than speakers from other Arab countries, they tend to leave out most of the declensional endings and freely use a number of dialect expressions.

On the whole, the trend in written Arabic has been towards a stricter regulation of the level of speech, rather than towards an increasing flexibility in the application of the rules. At this point, a distinction should be made between the practice in Egypt and the Levant, on the one hand, and North Africa, on the other. In North Africa, the most pressing problem after independence was how to replace the dominant French language with Arabic, preferably at all levels of society, but at the very least in education. As a consequence, simplification of the Classical language was not an issue. Since Arabic and French had to compete for the status of language of prestige, in the eyes of most language-reformers it would be wrong to devalue the Classical language by debasing it with dialect influence or with the abolition of grammatical rules. Discussions in North Africa on arabicisation (*taʿrīb*) concentrate on the introduction of Arabic in domains where formerly French had been the dominant language, whereas in other parts of the Arab world *taʿrīb* usually means the introduction of Arabic equivalents of foreign words, particularly in scientific language.

In recent times, various didactic projects have been set up for the compilation of a basic word list for use in primary schools and for the composition of a basic grammar that includes only the most frequent constructions of the standard language. The essential vocabularies from Tunisia and Lebanon do not seem to have had much impact on the various national educational systems. But there is one project that was based on an explicit didactic and linguistic concept, the Arabic version of the American children's programme Sesame Street (*Iftaḥ yā Simsim*). In the memorandum prepared by the makers of the programme, three categories of linguistic phenomena in Standard Arabic were distinguished: indispensable features of Standard Arabic that were to be used in spite of their absence in the dialect (e.g. the case endings); features that should be used sparingly (e.g. the passive form of the verbs); and features that should be avoided altogether (e.g. the superlative *al-ʾafʿalu*, the prepositions *ka-* 'like' and *siwā* 'except'). In the language of the programme, these principles have been followed rather closely. Moreover, the players, including the small children who play an essential part in the Sesame Street concept, make remarkably few performance errors in their use of Standard Arabic. On the whole, colloquialisms are used very infrequently, and yet there is a certain informal quality in the discourse, achieved mostly by the use of intonational patterns and interjections rather than the introduction of grammatical and/or lexical items from the colloquial language.

The *Iftaḥ yā Simsim* experiment proves that it is indeed possible to use an informal register of Modern Standard Arabic. It is true that in some Arab countries, in particular Egypt, the programme was criticised because it allegedly contained too many colloquial items. But on closer observation it turns out that this criticism was biased: the pronunciation of the *ǧīm* as [ǧ] rather than [g] can hardly be regarded as a regionalism, and the selection of lexical items in any pan-Arabic programme will probably never satisfy everybody. The future will have to decide whether or not the introduction of an informal register of Standard Arabic stands any chance.

FURTHER READING

The classic work on the period of the *Nahḍa* and the new ideas about the Arab nation that were developed in this period is Hourani (1970). Information about the linguistic question in the Ottoman empire is in Prätor (1993: 67f., 164–72, 217f.). For the development of modern Arabic lexicography and its historical roots, see Gätje (1985); in his history of Arabic lexicography, Haywood (1965) also deals with the activities of aš-Šidyāq and al-Bustānī; see also Sawaie (1987, 1990).

The role of the academies is discussed by Hamzaoui (1965, 1975) and Khafaifi (1985); Ali (1987) discusses the various methods of word-formation and contains (pp. 146–8) a list of approved patterns of lexical creation. A large amount of material on the methods and activities of the academies may be found in the journals which they publish regularly, *Maǧalla Maǧmaʿ al-Luġa al-ʿArabiyya bi-Dimašq* (Damascus, since 1921), *Maǧalla Maǧmaʿ al-Luġa al-ʿArabiyya* (Cairo, since 1935), *Maǧalla al-Maǧmaʿ al-ʿIlmī al-ʿIrāqī* (Baghdad, since 1950).

On the development of Arabic vocabulary, see the studies of Monteil (1960) and Stetkevych (1970); a comparison with the translations from Greek in the Classical period is in Bielawski (1956). The examples of the emerging political terminology in the nineteenth century in this chapter have been taken from Rebhan (1986), Ayalon (1987) and Lewis (1988). The examples of football terminology are derived from ʿAbd al-Ǧawād (1977); for linguistic terminology in Modern Arabic, see Shraybom-Shivtiel (1993) and Darir (1993), as well as the dictionaries of linguistic terms by Mseddi (1984) and R. Baalbaki (1990).

For the linguistic tendencies in the language of the media, Ashtiany's (1993) course of Media Arabic contains many interesting examples. The examples of French influence on Modern Standard Arabic in North Africa in this chapter were taken from Kropfitsch (1977, 1980) and Chaabani (1984).

Proposals for the simplification of grammar and/or language are discussed by Diem (1974: 129–36) and in Šawqī Ḍayf's introduction to his edition of Ibn Maḍā' (1982). The classic article on language choice in the teaching of Arabic as a second language is Ferguson (1962). A recent collection of articles on the problem of setting up a curriculum in Western departments of Arabic is Agiùs (1990). A report on an essential vocabulary selected by Moroccan, Algerian and Tunisian linguists is given by Mahmoud (1982). Specifically on the subject of the language of *Iftaḥ yā Simsim*, see Abu Absi (1990).

On the possibility of composing transfer grammars of Arabic, see Kouloughli (1979). Ryding (1990) may be cited as a practical attempt at a mixed grammar; her solutions include the introduction of frequent lexical items from the colloquial (*rāḥ*, *ǧāb*, *lāzim*), the elimination of case and mood inflection, and the use of function words from colloquial speech (*lissā*, *šū*, *miš*, and so on); cf. also Alosh (1994). Another approach is that of Woidich and Heinen-Nasr (1995), who aim at an integration of the two language varieties by starting with the colloquial language, but introducing from the beginning lexical items from the standard language, and gradually mixing the two varieties, so that at the end of the first year the student has spoken skills in colloquial Arabic and written skills in Standard Arabic.

Within the range of strictly standard grammars and manuals for Arabic, a number of courses may be mentioned: Ziadeh and Winder (1957); Krahl and Reuschel (1980, 1981), a comprehensive course, covering not only grammar but also stylistics, aiming at the training of interpreters of Arabic, Eastern European style, but available now in a revised non-socialist version; Fischer and Jastrow (1977), Fischer (1986) and Woidich (1985), intended for traditional departments of Arabic in Europe; Abboud and McCarus (1983; first published 1968), an audio-lingual approach with a large number of drills, intended for departments of Arabic in the USA.

Curiously enough, there are almost no reference grammars of Modern

Standard Arabic; the largest is Cantarino (1974–5), which is based on a predominantly literary corpus. Smaller surveys of the structure of the language are Beeston (1968), Pellat (1985) and Kouloughli (1994); a sketch of the modern language is given by Wild (1982). A comprehensive handbook on all aspects of Modern Standard Arabic is by Holes (1995a); although it is not a grammar in the strictest sense of the word, its systematic treatment of the structure of the language with extensive references to the existing literature makes this a very useful introduction to Modern Standard Arabic.

As regards dictionaries of Modern Standard Arabic: the Arabic–Arabic dictionaries, most of which were published in Lebanon, lean heavily on the Arabic lexicographical tradition. Buṭrus al-Bustānī's *Muḥīṭ al-muḥīṭ*, which was compiled in the nineteenth century, is still available in modern printings (e.g. Beirut, 1987); under the auspices of ALECSO, ʿAlī al-Qāsimī edited *al-Muʿǧam al-ʿarabī al-ʾasāsī* (Beirut: Larousse, 1989). Bilingual dictionaries were also published in Lebanon: English–Arabic (M. Baalbaki 1991); Arabic–English (Rohi Baalbaki 1988); French–Arabic (Hajjar 1983); Arabic–French (*Munǧid* 1990). The number of Western dictionaries of Arabic is considerable, the best-known being Wehr's (1952, 1959) Arabic–German dictionary, which was based on a corpus of literary and journalistic texts. Wehr's dictionary was translated into English and expanded by Cowan (1961; approximately 28,000 items; the fourth edition of 1979 contains more than 40,000 items). The fifth edition of the original Arabic–German dictionary appeared in 1985 in a thoroughly revised version, containing approximately 50,000 items. Dictionaries with Arabic as target language include: German–Arabic: Schregle (1974; 45,000 items; also Arabic–German 1981–); French–Arabic: Reig (1987; also Arabic–French); English–Arabic: Doniach (1972).

12
Diglossia and Bilingualism

12.1 THE NATURE OF DIGLOSSIA

In written Arabic, the choice between the standard norm and the colloquial language appears to be relatively uncomplicated: in writing, Standard Arabic is always used. But even here, problems of selection may arise. One complication derives from the fact that many people possess only a limited knowledge of the standard norm. For these people, Standard Arabic remains the target, but in writing it they make many mistakes. This results in the so-called Middle Arabic texts that have been discussed above (Chapter 8). A further complication may arise when for ideological or literary reasons writers decide to compose their literary writings in an approximate version of the colloquial language. Even these authors usually mix their colloquial language with elements from the standard language.

In spoken Arabic, the situation is even more complicated. Perhaps the best analogue to the situation in the Arabic-speaking countries would be that of a hypothetical modern France, where all newspapers and books are written in Latin, speeches in parliament are held in Latin, and in churches the only language used by the priests is Latin. On the other hand, people talking in a bar use French, people at home or among friends use French. In school, the official language of the classroom is Latin, but during the breaks between classes students use French among themselves, and so do the teachers. We know, of course, that the situation in France is not like this; but things could have been different, had the standard norm not switched from Latin to vernacular French in the fifteenth and sixteenth centuries.

In Arabic-speaking countries, the actual situation is very much like the hypothetical situation sketched here for France. At first sight, there appear to be two varieties of the language, the Classical standard, usually called *fuṣḥā*, and the colloquial language, usually called *ʿāmmiyya* or (in North Africa) *dāriǧa*, and in Western publications, 'dialect' or 'vernacular'. These two varieties divide among themselves the domains of speaking and writing: the standard language is used for written speech and for formal spoken speech, whereas the colloquial language is used for informal speech. The colloquial language is everybody's mother tongue; people only learn the standard when they go to school. In 1930, William Marçais called such a linguistic situation 'diglossia' (French *diglossie*), a term that he had borrowed from the literature on the linguistic situation in Greece and which gained general currency after the appearance in 1959 of an article by Charles Ferguson with the title 'Diglossia'. Ferguson compared the linguistic situation in the Arabic-speaking countries with that in Greece, in

German-speaking Switzerland and in Haiti. In all four areas, there seems to be a similar functional distribution between two varieties of the same language (*fuṣḥā*/*ʿāmmiyya*, *kathareúousa*/*dhimotikí*, *Hochdeutsch*/*Schwyzertüütsch*, *français*/*créole*). In Ferguson's terminology, these two varieties are called 'high variety' (H) and 'low variety' (L).

The terms 'high' and 'low' reflect the standing of the two varieties in the linguistic community. The low variety is held in very low esteem, and the name by which speakers refer to it normally implies a humble position: *ʿāmmiyya* literally means 'common' or 'vulgar', while other names are *sūqiyya* 'language of the market', *munḥarifa* 'deviant', and so on. The high variety, on the other hand, is prestigious: it is the language of a cultural, and often religious, heritage. In some cases, speakers even deny the existence of the low variety and claim that they only speak the high variety. In reality, the low variety is the mother tongue of all speakers, whereas the high variety is a second language that is almost never used in improvised speech.

The theoretical framework of Ferguson's model for the linguistic situation in the Arabic-speaking countries has been refined by subsequent studies in three important respects. In the first place, Ferguson's model restricted the notion of 'diglossia' to situations where the low variety was genetically related to the high variety, of which it was a simplified version. In later publications this restriction was lifted, and the notion of 'diglossia' was expanded to include any functional distribution of linguistic varieties, whether these were languages or dialects or registers. The functional distribution in the Arabic-speaking countries is nothing but a special case of a general phenomenon of sociolinguistic variation in all speech communities.

In the second place, the existence of a functional distribution between varieties does not imply that all speakers have an equal command of these varieties. In extreme cases, most speakers know only one variety, a non-prestigious colloquial kind of language, whereas a small elite uses a stilted variety of a cultural language, mostly an imported one. In the Arab world, an example of such a situation is Algeria just before independence: the majority of people in the speech community knew only Arabic and at the most a smattering of French, but a small group of intellectuals had been raised and educated in French and lost the ability to speak Arabic. Several linguists, among them Fishman (1967, 1972) and Gumperz (1962), therefore proposed to distinguish between a sociolinguistic and a psycholinguistic approach. In their terminology 'diglossia' is reserved for the sociolinguistic notion of a functional distribution of linguistic varieties. For the psycholinguistic notion of the speakers' command of these varieties, they adopted the term 'bilingualism'. In a speech community that is both diglossic and bilingual, there is a well-defined distribution of domains between more than one variety, and the members of the speech community actually know these varieties.

A third modification of Ferguson's model concerns the distinction of two discrete varieties. In his framework, the two varieties are mutually exclusive, and the speaker has to choose one or the other by a process of code-switching. In reality, the speaker never opts for one variety or the other, but moves along a continuum of speech, of which the two varieties are only the extremes. In such a situation, code-switching does not imply selecting a discrete variety, but positioning one's utterance along a scale of linguistic variation. Extralinguistic factors determine the position on this scale. Obviously, the span of the continuum that individuals control depends on their linguistic proficiency, which in its turn is determined to a large degree by their education and upbringing.

Much of the terminological confusion in the literature has been created by the use of the term 'diglossia' both in Ferguson's sense and in the modified sense. In Ferguson's model, 'diglossia' is only used for the relationship between *fuṣḥā* and *ʿāmmiyya*, whereas the functional division between French and Arabic in North Africa was termed by him 'bilingualism'. In what follows, the term 'diglossia' will be used in the modified sense of a linguistic situation in which several speech varieties divide among themselves the domains of verbal communication. The term 'bilingualism' will refer to the individual's proficiency in more than one speech variety. In a speech community that is both diglossic and bilingual, all speakers are able to vary their linguistic behaviour along a continuum according to extralinguistic factors that are connected both with the discourse context and the speaker's socioeconomic status.

Various efforts have been made to subdivide the continuum between the two extremes of Standard Arabic and dialect into intermediary varieties. Arab linguists often mention, for instance, a middle language (*al-luġa al-wusṭā*), also called 'the language of the intellectuals' (*luġat al-muṯaqqafīn*). This is supposed to be a form of standard Arabic that does not use case endings, follows the colloquial pronunciation and freely introduces colloquial words, while retaining the general structure of the standard language. An even finer distinction is found in Badawī's (1973) study of the sociolinguistic situation in Egypt. He rejects the strict dichotomy in Ferguson's model of two varieties, H and L, for the Egyptian situation (and possibly for other regions of the Arabic world as well) and sets up five different levels, which he regards as discrete, i.e. which have their own characteristic set of features setting them apart from the other sectors of the continuum (see Table 12.1).

There is not much empirical research on the actual distribution of speech levels in Egypt, or for that matter in any Arab country, but what studies there

I	*fuṣḥā at-turāṯ* 'Classical Arabic' only used in Qur'ānic recitation
II	*fuṣḥā al-ʿaṣr* 'Modern Standard Arabic' the standard form of the language used in writing and sometimes on formal occasions in speaking
III	*ʿāmmiyyat al-muṯaqqafīn* 'colloquial of the intellectuals' the formal spoken language of educated people
IV	*ʿāmmiyyat al-mutanawwirīn* 'colloquial of the literate' the informal spoken language of educated people
V	*ʿāmmiyyat al-'ummiyyīn* 'colloquial of the illiterate' the language in which the illiterate talk

Table 12.1 The five levels of Egyptian Arabic according to Badawī (1973).

are confirm that the strict dichotomy of Ferguson's model does not correspond to the actual situation. Elgibali (1985), for instance, shows that in accordance with Badawī's predictions there is a continuous flow in the distribution of sociolinguistic markers, such as the realisation of /q/ and /ṯ/, the use of aspectual markers in the verb, and word order and declensional endings. Yet, only the upper and lower level (Ferguson's H and L, Badawī's level V and I) could be called discrete levels with a characteristic set of features. The middle part of the continuum cannot be divided into separate levels. In his test results, the informal register of each level has the same distribution as the formal level of the second lowest level. For instance, the distribution of the /q/–/'/ variable among the five levels of spoken Egyptian turned out to be as in Table 12.2. The same distribution applied to the other sociolinguistic markers in his study.

While there are some studies relating the use of certain speech variables to speech situations, there is hardly any statistical material on the correlation between linguistic variables and socioeconomic factors. A classic work on the correlation between religious affiliation and dialect variety is Blanc's (1964) study of the communal dialects of Baghdad (cf. above, p. 156). A more recent study is Holes' (1987) extensive analysis of the communal varieties in Bahrain, where a Sunnite Bedouin dialect represents the standard variety, whereas the Shi'ite minority, the Baḥārna, speak a sedentary dialect. Holes emphasises the different social meanings which variants obtain in this community (cf. above, p. 133) and rightly assumes that an adequate account of the sociolinguistic situation should include the entire range of styles that people have at their disposal. In his survey he arrives at the relevant variables by setting up implicational scales, i.e. by observing the co-occurrence of certain variants in the speech of his respondents. The most important outcome of his analysis is the interdependence between linguistic form and social meaning. This is especially manifest in

oral level	source material	/q/ percentage
informal MSA	e.g. newscasting, university lectures (arts)	45
formal educated colloquial	e.g. university lectures (science)	44
informal educated colloquial	e.g. intra-group conversations among professors	35
formal literate colloquial	e.g. popular television programmes	34
informal literate colloquial	e.g. intra-group conversations among shopkeepers	22
formal illiterate colloquial	e.g. conversations between employers and employees	23
informal illiterate colloquial	e.g. intra-group conversations among workers	0

Table 12.2 Distribution of /q/ in spoken Egyptian (after Elgibali 1985).

those cases where Baḥārna forms agree or disagree with the Standard Arabic form. In the case of the word for 'fish' (Standard Arabic *samaka*), both Baḥārna and Sunnites have *smiča*; accordingly, when upgrading their speech they will turn both to the Standard Arabic form. In the case of the word for 'sunset' (Standard Arabic *maġrib*), the Baḥārna have *maġrib*, while the Sunnites say *mġarb*; in this case, Baḥārna literates tend to switch to the Sunnite form, whereas the Sunnites upgrade by turning to the Standard Arabic form (Holes 1987: 170ff.).

A related topic to that of the communal varieties is that of male/female speech, which has become relatively popular in Western sociolinguistics but remains a neglected field in Arabic sociolinguistics. There is a general dictum in Western sociolinguistics that on average women tend to conform to standard/prestige variants more than men and that they are more conservative with regard to linguistic change. This rule has been called into question for non-Western societies, where men tend to use the standard variants more than women. In Jordan, for instance, female students are reported by Suleiman (1985: 45) to switch from rural to urban dialect varieties to a much larger degree than male students. Yet, men tend to use more Standard Arabic, which is the variety for public appearances, in which women participate far less than men. The contrast between Western and non-Western speech patterns disappears when we realise that the standard variety should not be identified automatically with Modern Standard Arabic. In the case of the Jordanian students, it is the urban dialect that is regarded by most speakers as the prestige variety. Modern Standard Arabic, on the other hand, is seen as part of the male domain.

An important contribution to the study of intra-colloquial variables is Walters' (1991) extensive survey in the small town of Korba in Tunisia. One of the variables which he studied is that of final /-ā/, which in Tunisian Arabic becomes /ɛ:/ by *'imāla*. In the dialect of Korba, this variable is realised by three variants: the standard variant [ɛ:], and two raised variants, [ɪ:] and [ɨ:], which are regarded by the speakers as local and non-prestigious. Walters shows that the Tunisian standard variant is used most by young male speakers, followed by young females, then older males, and then older females. His results are important for several reasons. In the first place, they demonstrate that the use of the standard variant correlates with a combination of gender, age and education rather than gender alone: those female speakers who used the variant [ɛ:] had studied in Tunis. In the second place, most young speakers, both male and female, still use the raised variants with some speakers when they are back in the village, thus showing that these variants have become a marker of group identity.

12.2 LANGUAGE CHOICE AND LANGUAGE ATTITUDE IN DIGLOSSIA

Since we do not have enough data to set up full-scale correlations between socioeconomic class and the use of H/L variants, it would be premature to try to define sociolectal varieties with some measure of independent status. We are somewhat better informed about those extralinguistic factors determining language choice that are linked to the speech situation itself. The most relevant factors in the speech situation are the interlocutor, the topic and the setting. These factors can be ordered along a scale that goes from the private to the public domain. At the end of the scale, we might have an official spokesman, for instance a minister, talking on a public topic in a formal setting, for instance a radio interview: he will be forced to use a variety approaching Standard Arabic as much as possible. At the other end of the scale, friends talking in a pavement café about private affairs will use colloquial language, with a minimum of interference from the standard language.

The influence of these factors manifests itself when in a given situation one of them changes. When the minister in his radio interview is asked about his private life (rather unlikely in the Arab media!), his speech will change accordingly into the direction of the dialect. When the friends talking in the bar switch from private matters to a discussion about politics, their speech will immediately betray interference from the standard language. Since language choice takes place on a continuum, these changes do not take the form of code-switching from one variety to another, but manifest themselves in a larger percentage of features from the opposite variety.

One of the characteristics of the diglossia situation is the effect that speakers have on each other. Hardly any data are available on this topic, but in Diem's (1974) transcription of radio dialogues an impression can be formed of the way in which speakers accommodate to each other's level. In one conversation, for instance, a reporter is interviewing the secretary general of the Cairene Language Academy. At the beginning, he still uses phrases like *yaʿni, nifham min kida ʾinnu ʾabl ʾinʿiqād l-muʾtamar is-sanawi bitibʾa fīh ligān bitabḥaṯ qarārāt* 'that means, we understand from this that before the opening of the yearly conference there are committees that investigate proposals', in which colloquial /ʾ/ for /q/, continuous marker *bi-* and colloquial expressions like *min kida* are freely used. But when his interviewee keeps talking more or less Standard Arabic, within the space of one minute this same interviewer ends up saying things like *law ʾaradna ʾan naʾẖuḏ namūḏağan li-ẕālik* 'if we used an example for this' (Diem 1974: 76), which is almost absurdly Classical in its phonology and morphology.

A reverse example may be found in a Lebanese interview between a reporter and a literary critic, in which the reporter stubbornly uses colloquial Lebanese, whereas the critic says things like *bi-ṣūra ʿāmmah ʾal-mawsim kān ʾižābī – ižābī ʾawwalan min ḥays il-kammiyyi wa-sāniyan min ḥays ʾan-nawʿiyyi* 'generally speaking the season was positive, in the first place positive as to quantity, in the second place as to quality' with exaggerated Classical style (note the glottal stop in the article and the realisation of the Classical interdental /ṯ/ as /s/). But in the end he cannot resist the colloquial style of the reporter, and after a few minutes he talks like this: *fī taʾrīban ši miyyit maʿriḍ bi-s-sine* 'there are approximately 100 expositions each year', with /ʾ/ for /q/ and dialectal *ši* and *fī* (Diem 1974: 77).

These two examples show that the level of speech of each of the participants in a discourse event affects the speech of the others: speakers have a tendency to accommodate to the other's level and feel obliged to upgrade or downgrade their speech. This tendency is, however, not automatic: in conversations, people may talk to each other on a different level for an extended period of time, without bowing to the level of their interlocutor. In other words, the discourse factors that determine language choice do not operate mechanically. To a certain extent, they select the variety that one uses in a specific speech situation by correlating the formality of the situation with the choice of linguistic variants. But it is equally true to say that the speakers' linguistic choices also reflect their evaluation of the speech situation. With their choice of variants, they indicate to the other participants how they see their role, what they think about the topic, which kind of setting they wish to take part in.

This complicated interaction between extralinguistic factors and linguistic choice is controlled by the associations that the speakers connect with the varieties of speech current in their community. The low variety of the language is associated with low education, since the standard language is taught and learnt at school, and hence with illiteracy and poverty, since people with a poor education cannot make a career. The standard language, on the other hand, is associated with higher education, success in society and a high socioeconomic class, even though the colloquial language is also used by people from a higher socioeconomic class as an informal language. Looked at from a different perspective, the colloquial language as the language of family and home is associated with the in-group, with intimacy and friendship, whereas the high variety is associated with social distance and official relationships. The use of Standard Arabic may thus be a sign of respect, but also of creating a distance between speakers. The use of colloquial language may be derogatory, but also a sign of intimacy or modesty, somewhat in the way that the use of first names in English may signal either familiarity or social contempt.

The difference between most Western speech communities and the Arabic-speaking world is the much larger linguistic distance that exists between colloquial Arabic and the standard language, which forces the speakers to make decisions much more frequently than in Western speech communities. Since the colloquial and the standard language are not discrete varieties, but only abstract constructs at the extremes of a continuum, linguistic choice does not involve a two-way selection, but rather a mixture of variants. In many cases, the selection of a few markers suffices to convey the attitude of the speaker. In radio programmes, for instance, the speakers usually start from a written text in Standard Arabic, but in reading it they let themselves be influenced by the target group. In programmes for housewives or farmers, the structure of the Standard Arabic text remains unchanged, but at regular intervals colloquial markers are inserted, such as the realisation of the standard /q/ as /'/, the possessive particle *bitāʿ*, the undeclinable relative *illī*, the use of the continuous marker *bi-*, and so on. These markers signal to the audience the intention of the speaker, which is to create an atmosphere of intimacy and warmth (as in the text quoted above in Chapter 8 on Middle Arabic, p. 127). Likewise, the use of Standard Arabic markers, such as the use of the coordinative particle *fa-*, the use of passive forms, or in general the insertion of case endings, may be practised by speakers when they wish to impress upon their audience the importance of the occasion or the topic.

The choice of linguistic markers takes place partly on a conscious level and may be manipulated, for instance, for commercial reasons. In the language of the media and especially in advertisements in Egypt, the level chosen correlates with the nature of the product that is being sold and with the target group. Important public commodities such as loans and insurance policies are 'sold' to a predominantly male audience by the use of high varieties of the language, but producers of food and detergents mainly cater to housewives and accordingly advertise their products in colloquial language. The advertisers have to strike a fine balance between the intimacy and familiarity of the colloquial language and the prestige and intellectual level of the standard language.

On the political level, a rather spectacular case of this manipulation of linguistic variation is to be found in the political speeches of the late President Nasser. He used to begin his speeches at an elevated level, spoken slowly and rhythmically, because of the formality of the situation. But then his sentences would become gradually more and more colloquial, spoken in a faster tempo, until he reached a purely colloquial level. At the end of his speech, he would conclude with a few sentences in pure Standard Arabic. Such a mixture reflects the inherent problem for politicians in the Arab world: on the one hand, by identifying with colloquial speech they wish to involve their audience, who for the most part do not use or even understand the higher levels of Standard Arabic; on the other hand, they cannot simply switch to colloquial language, since this would be regarded as an insult to their audience.

This brings us to the political associations connected with the choice of varieties. Since the standard language is regarded by most Arabs as the most significant unifying factor of the Arab world, it also serves as a symbol of Arab unity. Most political parties in the Arab world at least officially propagate this unity, so that politicians are under severe pressure to use standard language, even though their constituents do not understand it. We have seen above (p. 175) that from the end of the nineteenth century the Arabic language played a central role in the emergent nationalist movement in the Arab provinces of the Ottoman empire. After independence, each country officially declared its adherence to pan-Arab nationalism (*qawmiyya*) with the Arabic language as the national language of all Arabs. From this point of view, the use of dialect stands for regionalism (*'iqlīmiyya*), which is regarded as detrimental to the unity of the Arab world. On the other hand, in some countries the vernacular came to be valued as an important ingredient of the national identity (*waṭaniyya*).

Not surprisingly, of all Arab countries, Egypt is the one with the most marked tendency towards the use of the dialect. Egypt has always been characterised by a large degree of regional nationalism aiming at the establishment of an Egyptian identity, and the Egyptian dialect is certainly an important component of this identity. Speeches in the Egyptian parliament are often given in something approaching the colloquial language, which would be unheard of in other Arab countries. An interesting example is the last speech given by the late President Sadat in parliament in 1981. The day after his assassination, it appeared in the newspapers in a colloquial version, with a note by the publisher that there had been no time to 'translate' it into standard language. Nasser's speeches have been mentioned above; it is remarkable that the pattern described there does not occur in any of the speeches which he gave abroad. The reason is obvious: any suggestion of Egyptian nationalism would have endangered the already tense relations with Syria in the United Arab Republic.

The relatively favourable attitude towards the dialect in Egypt is visible in all social contexts. In interviews on television, even in speeches in parliament, colloquial elements are freely used. There is a lot of public interest in the colloquial language, somewhat comparable to the way in which Schwyzertüütsch is cultivated in German-speaking Switzerland. Literary works regularly contain colloquial elements, especially in the dialogues; and theatre plays, even when they were written originally in Standard Arabic, are often staged in dialect. People proudly commented on the publication of Badawi and Hinds' (1986) dictionary of the Egyptian *ʿāmmiyya*. Many language schools offer courses in Egyptian dialect for foreigners. Debates about the language question did take place in Egypt (cf. above, Chapter 10), but the point is that in Egypt such debates did not create a scandal, whereas elsewhere in the Arab world experiments involving the use of dialect were regarded with much more suspicion.

The Egyptian attitude towards the use of dialect is also very much in evidence in international pan-Arabic conferences where Egyptian delegates unhesitatingly use colloquialisms in their speech while delegates from other Arab countries do their best to avoid such colloquialisms at all costs. Private interviews with Egyptian politicians and even with religious authorities, after a start in obligatory standard formulae, often switch to colloquial Egyptian. This is not to say that in Egypt the negative effects of the colonial heritage are not visible at all: here too, dialect research has been frustrated by university officials who still view the emphasis on dialect as a means to divide the Arab world.

We have seen earlier that the relationship between the regional dialects and the dialect of the capital is another factor that has to be taken into account in the explanation of linguistic behaviour. The tendency on the part of the regional dialect-speakers to level towards the dialect of the capital goes back a long time, as we have seen in the dialect map of the Delta. In its present form, Cairene Arabic originated probably at the end of the nineteenth century (cf. above, Chapter 10), when the influx of speakers from the countryside led to a stigmatisation of the rural dialects that has continued until today. As a result, new migrants to the capital tend to shift wherever possible to Cairene Arabic.

The attractive force of Cairene Arabic is also at work outside the Egyptian borders. One of the explanations for the use of colloquialisms by Egyptians in a pan-Arabic context may be that their dialect is universally known in the Arabophone world on account of the numerous Egyptian movies and soap-operas that are exported to all Arab countries. This has led to a situation where most people can understand the Egyptian dialect at least partly, but not the other way round. A second reason is the large number of Egyptian teachers working abroad: thousands of Egyptian teachers were invited to come to the North African countries after independence because of the shortage of people who could teach in Arabic. In recent times, many Egyptians have been working temporarily in the Gulf states and in Saudi Arabia. A large number of Egyptian teachers worked in Yemen during and after the Nasser period, so much so that nowadays any Arabic-speaking foreigner in Yemen is automatically regarded as an Egyptian teacher. In the Yemenite dialect, Egyptian colloquialisms are rapidly gaining a position as prestige variants (cf. above, p. 139).

12.3 THE LANGUAGE QUESTION IN NORTH AFRICA

The diglossic situation sketched above also obtains in North African countries, but there the situation is complicated by the presence of a second prestigious language, the language of the former colonial power, France. In the older literature on this topic, the situation is often described as one of 'bilingualism' in accordance with the original version of Ferguson's model, which used this term for a situation in which two unrelated languages were used within one speech community (cf. above, p. 189). Acording to the newer versions of the model, the sociolinguistic relationship between French and Arabic may be termed 'diglossia', whereas 'bilingualism' refers to the degree of command of both languages by the speakers. Unlike the situation in the former English colonies, the French authorities followed a colonial policy that aimed at the assimilation and integration of the indigenous population. The official point of view was that France did not colonise other countries in order to exploit them, but in order to bring them French civilisation. French officials regarded the colonial policy as France's *mission civilisatrice*, an attitude certainly not shared by all French colonists (*colons*), who opposed any effort to educate the indigenous population.

During the long years of French occupation (Morocco 1912–56; Algeria 1830–1962; Tunisia 1881–1956), the population of the 'colonies' was constantly exposed to French language and culture. Even though the official aim – to educate the indigenous population as inhabitants of the French empire with equal rights – was rarely, if ever, put into practice, it remained the framework in which relations between French and Arabs were defined. In practice, only a small elite of the Arab inhabitants of the colonies got a chance of learning French. These people became gallicised to such a degree that they adopted French language, literature and culture as their own; when it turned out that even with this education and attitude they would never be accepted as real French citizens, this small class of French Arabs became the core of the opposition movement to French domination. For the population at large, some knowledge of French was indispensable in their dealings with the French administration, but most people were denied any formal education in the language.

During the colonial period, some half-hearted efforts were made by the colonial administration to introduce bilingual education for Arabic-speaking children, but in the few schools that provided this system Arabic was relegated to the position of an extracurricular curiosity. In the first period after independence, this situation was more or less perpetuated. In bilingual schools, French remained the language of instruction for 'important' subjects, such as mathematics, physics and economics, whereas Arabic was used in classes in literature, history and religious education. Although for political reasons Arabic was declared the national language, French remained the main language of the schools and the administration. In all three Maghreb countries, campaigns for arabicisation were set up at an early stage to change this linguistic situation, both in education and in the administration. While the background to these campaigns was similar, there were noticeable differences in the course that they took in the three countries involved, analysed in detail by Grandguillaume (1983). These differences can be explained by several factors: the length of the French presence, the number of French colonists, and the presence of a Berber minority.

In Tunisia, the French left behind a sizeable bilingual elite; Berber did not play a role here, since it was only spoken in the south by no more than 5 per cent of the population. After independence, arabicisation became the official policy of the government, but at a slow pace. Although certainly dedicated to the introduction of Arabic himself, the first president of Tunisia, Bourguiba, was not in favour of a hasty transfer. In his own public speeches, he tended to use an intermediate register, and on several occasions he declared that Classical Arabic was not the language of the Tunisian people. This became one of the key notions of the language debate in Tunisia: arabicisation should not aim at the wholesale introduction of a standard form of the language, but allow for a considerable amount of bilingualism and, at least according to some people, proper attention to the Tunisian dialect.

Although in the public debates the importance of arabicisation was stressed, many intellectuals feared the reintroduction of orthodox Islam in the thoroughly secularised society of Tunisia as the result of exaggerated arabicisation. In the administration, arabicisation was not carried out systematically, even though some ministries were arabicised completely, for instance the Ministries of Justice and Interior Affairs in 1970. But at the same time, many people still professed their preference for a bilingual approach and did not want to lose what they regarded as an achievement of Tunisian society. Besides, many people agreed with Bourguiba that the proper Arabic language of Tunisia was the Tunisian dialect.

In the Tunisian schools, a revolutionary reform was started in 1958. It aimed at the arabicisation of the school system by setting up a two-track curriculum which gave the parents the option of sending their children either to a monolingual Arabic stream (*section A*) or to a bilingual French/Arabic stream (*section B*). The problems were predictable: lack of teaching materials, lack of teachers proficient in teaching in Arabic, and, most of all, lack of interest on the part of the parents, who wished to provide their children with the best chance of succeeding in society, which meant sending them to a bilingual school. After ten years, the project was officially abandoned and the *sections A* disappeared. Some measure of arabicisation was carried out, however, and the first three years in primary education remained completely Arabic, as did some of the disciplines in secondary education (philosophy, geography, history).

In more recent years, the situation in Tunisia has changed in favour of Arabic. Even at the university level, there is constant pressure on the teachers to adopt standard Arabic for their classes, and even those teachers who believed that it was impossible to teach their specialised subject in Arabic have by and large abandoned the exclusive use of French. In the 1990s, an additional factor became the emergence of Islamic fundamentalism as a powerful faction. On the whole, the fundamentalists are against any form of education in French and wish to give Arabic its rightful place in the curriculum. Where before this period arabicisation in Tunisia had never been a matter of principle, the language question now threatens to become linked with religious issues.

The linguistic situation in Morocco is determined by several factors. In the first place, the country has the largest Berber minority of all Maghreb countries, some estimates going as high as 50 per cent. In the second place, the French language played an important practical role because of the commercial relations between Morocco and Europe. In the third place, the language question was always closely connected with the political situation because of the connection with the throne: after King Mohammed V's return to an independent Morocco in 1956, the monarchy, Islam and the Arabic language became an unbreakable triad.

In the colonial period, the degree of schooling was very low. The overwhelming majority of the pupils in the French schools were French, and only a very small number of Moroccan children actually went to these schools. In 1945, for instance, the number of French pupils was 45,000, that of Moroccan pupils 1,150! Contrast this with the total amount of pupils in primary and secondary schools in 1957, just after independence: primary 530,000; secondary 31,000; and in 1965: primary 1,000,000, secondary 130,000 (Grandguillaume 1983). The only alternative for Moroccan pupils in the colonial period was that of the traditional schools, starting with the *kuttāb* and culminating in the traditional university of the Qarawiyine in Fes.

In the period after independence, several attempts were made to arabicise the schools. But plans for a complete arabicisation of primary schools and at a later point of secondary schools in 1959 were postponed because of the practical problem of actually introducing Arabic education in the sciences. At the present time, all government schools are completely arabicised for the first four years, while the next three are bilingual but with the emphasis on French in a ratio of 1:2. In secondary schools, the ratio Arabic:French varies between 1:2 and 1:1. Higher-level education is divided between the two languages according to subject matter. Apart from the government schools, there are quite a large number of private schools, Qur'ānic and foreign, which are free in their language choice.

The campaigns to arabicise the administration were mostly half-hearted. As a political issue, arabicisation was important, especially in the context of establishing Arabic as the only language of the country to counter the influence of Berber. In practice, even after thirty years, several departments retained the use of French as a working language. According to many reports, the employees in the *Bureaux d'arabisation*, whose express aim was to support and guard arabicisation, continued to use French among themselves when discussing the language problems of the country! It is small wonder, then, that the outward appearance of the larger cities, at least as far as the 'European parts' are concerned, remains French to a large degree. Bookshops still sell French newspapers and books, signs and advertisements are in French, and in the French-style cafés one orders one's coffee in French.

The third Maghreb country, Algeria, knew the longest period of French presence and harboured the largest number of French *colons*. The country was virtually a French province from 1830, and independence was fought for in a bitter war that ended in 1962. The situation of Arabic in French Algeria was precarious. There was constant pressure to prohibit instruction in Classical Arabic, culminating in the edict of 1936 that declared Arabic a foreign language. Whatever education existed in a language other than French was in dialectal Arabic or in Berber. When in 1961 de Gaulle made Arabic compulsory again in the *écoles du 1er degré*, this was much too late to change the situation. Like the other Maghreb countries, Algeria made Arabic the national language and Islam the national religion, but this did not change the fact that many Algerians were not proficient in Standard Arabic, and sometimes not even in dialectal Arabic. In 1963, for instance, there was a proposal in the National Assembly to translate the proceedings of the meetings into Arabic. Apparently, most of the debates were held in French, since many of the delegates would have been unable to talk in any kind of Arabic. The proposal met with general approval, but, as the prime minister pointed out, it would be impossible to find enough trained translators to do the job, so for the time being the proceedings had to remain in French!

Right from the start, it was recognised that arabicisation should begin in education; but the beginnings of the arabicisation programme were altogether modest (seven hours in Arabic in primary education). Because of the almost total absence of teachers, 1,000 Egyptian teachers were imported right away, later to be followed by another 1,000 from Syria. After the coup d'état of 1965, in which Boumediene became president, arabicisation became part of a centralised policy. In about ten years, most of primary education was arabicised, there was a lot of progress in secondary education, and even at the universities the pressure became more intense to switch to Arabic.

In the period just before independence, the French had created a corps of Algerian state employees to take over the administration when they had to leave. These 100,000 or so employees jealously guarded their privileged position and were loath to accept any change in the linguistic situation. In 1968, the government decreed that state employees had to take an exam within three years to prove their proficiency in Arabic, but this measure turned out to be futile. In 1980 the edict was repeated, however, and this time it was enforced, aiming at total arabicisation by 1985. The arabicisation of the Algerian administration has succeeded to a degree not attained in any other Maghreb country.

The introduction of Arabic in the Algerian mass media and in the public domain was very much connected with the dominant Islamic movement. In Morocco, Islamic feelings were usurped by the monarchy, and Tunisia chose a largely secularist way. In Algeria, however, Islam was not supported by the socialist government, but became a popular movement which actively supported the struggle for the replacement of French with Arabic. In 1976, within the course of one night, all French street names, billboards, advertisements, and so on disappeared from the streets of Algiers, and other towns followed suit. Probably these measures were not always taken by officials, and in some cases the popular movement acted autonomously. The success of arabicisation has been so complete that in the civil war that has torn the country apart in the 1990s the language question is no longer an issue.

Thus far, we have only spoken about the linguistic situation in North Africa. In the Eastern Arab world, Lebanon and Syria also belonged to the French sphere of influence. In Syria, most traces of French presence have been wiped out; Lebanon is a special case because of the presence of a large number of Arab Christians (Maronites). From a very early date onwards, the Lebanese Christians established contact with the Christian church in Europe: Maronites studied in the Vatican, and later in Paris, thereby strengthening the ties between Christians and Europe. After the troubles of 1860 between Maronites and Druze, the European powers intervened and signed with the Ottoman Porte an agreement on the status of Lebanon, which was to become an autonomous mutasarrifate rather than belong to the province of Syria. In this area the Maronites were in the majority, and Christian missionaries became highly active (in 1866 the Syrian Protestant College was founded, later to become the American University of Beirut, and in 1875 the Catholic Université Saint Joseph). The interference of the Western powers, especially France, led to the adoption of French as a cultural language by educated Christians before the turn of the nineteenth century.

In the turmoil of the Mandate period in which France dominated Lebanon (1918–43), the Maronites were constantly striving to establish a Greater Lebanon, independent of the Arab nation. When France finally conceded independence, Maronites continued to dominate in spite of the fact that they no longer constituted the majority due to the inclusion of large Muslim areas, such as the Biqāʿ and the south. Their only chance was, therefore, a special form of Lebanese nationalism, which emphasised the bicultural and bilingual character of the Lebanese nation.

In pre-civil war publications by Lebanese Maronites, the coexistence between French and Arabic in Lebanon used to be viewed in a favourable light. Abou (1961, 1962), for instance, published a survey of language use and a study in which he shows himself to be an enthusiastic proponent of the bicultural entity that Lebanon should remain. In such publications, the historical role of Lebanon as an intermediary between Europe and the Levant was emphasised and the advantages of bilingual education in general were extolled. At the same time, the statistics in Abou's book demonstrate the difference between the Muslim and the Christian population with regard to proficiency in French. It goes without saying that, since the civil war, much has changed, and it is safe to say that the linguistic landscape will never be the same again. Unfortunately, nothing much is known about the present situation, but so much is certain: French has lost its dominant position to a large degree. In Beirut itself, there is a growing contrast between East Beirut, where French is still used, and West Beirut, where it has been replaced to some extent by English in its role as channel to the international community.

12.4 LANGUAGE CHOICE AND LANGUAGE ATTITUDES IN NORTH AFRICA

During the French period, the French language had acquired such a symbolic value that even though it was the language of the former colonisers, and even though officially Arabic became the new national language, knowledge of French was still regarded as an essential key to success. In spite of the official policy of introducing the Arabic language (*taʿrīb*) into domains that had formerly belonged to French, it has taken people a long time to get used to the idea that Arabic can serve just as well as French as an official language. As a cultural language, French continues to play an important role, and one still overhears well-educated Moroccans and Tunisians switching in midstream from one language to the other.

As far as proficiency in French is concerned, the linguistic situation has changed, too. During the colonial period, only a very small proportion of the people received an education in a school system which was based entirely on French. As a result, this elite became bilingual in French and in the vernacular, and in some cases, depending on the situation at home and the degree of schooling, French even became their dominant language. In extreme cases, particularly in Algeria, this led to virtual monolingualism in French. Most members of the elite, whether they continued using the vernacular at home or switched to French completely, had virtually no knowledge of Standard Arabic and were unable to read or write in that language. After independence, this situation became unstable, and with the introduction of Standard Arabic in the school system it disappeared. A few older individuals in the Maghreb countries may still refuse stubbornly to learn Standard Arabic, but on the whole the pressure on them to use Standard Arabic in their professional life has become inescapable.

Apart from the elite who had most access to the French school system, anyone who came into contact with the French language during the colonial period acquired at the very least the minimal knowledge of (informal) French that was needed for dealings with the authorities or French colonists. These people developed a kind of bilingualism in which French was definitely subordinate, since for them the primary language was their vernacular. The degree of knowledge of French depended on the amount of exposure and the nature of the contacts with the French authorities and colonists. After independence, a similar type of bilingualism continued to exist, but nowadays its degree is a function of the amount of schooling. By contrast with the colonial period, in the post-colonial period anyone who goes to school has to learn Standard Arabic as well.

There are hardly any statistics on the knowledge of French and Standard Arabic in North Africa. In Table 12.3 an estimate is given for 1968 on the basis of numbers of graduates in various types of schools.

Although these figures have no doubt changed in the last few decades, they reflect a reality which still obtains in North Africa. There are two prestige languages that compete for the same domains: Standard Arabic and French. The colonial past has strongly influenced speakers' attitudes towards the two languages. Bentahila (1983) studied these attitudes with the help of a matched guise technique that has been designed to bring out people's reactions to the use of language varieties. The findings of these experiments were that Moroccans are indeed influenced by the language spoken: in general, French is regarded more favourably than Arabic, provided that the French is of high quality. Speakers of French are perceived as modern, sophisticated, educated and important, whereas the same speakers, when speaking in Arabic, are rated higher on features such as sociability and friendliness. Interestingly, most of the respondents regarded the use of mixed codes very negatively. Asked about the advantages of bilingualism, i.e. proficiency in both languages, two thirds of the respondents maintained that it is advantageous for both individuals and society, especially in education. Interestingly, at the same time most respondents favoured

	Tunisia	Morocco	Algeria
Arabic only	300,000	400,000	100,000
bilinguals	500,000	700,000	300,000
French only	100,000	100,000	900,000
total	900,000	1,200,000	1,300,000
	20 per cent	10 per cent	12 per cent

Table 12.3 Language proficiency of literates in North Africa (after Gallagher 1968: 148).

arabicisation, provided that it was carried out in Classical Arabic, while at the same time supporting the continuation of bilingualism. Likewise, almost all respondents asserted that Arabic was an appropriate language for the teaching of science, but at the same time they preferred the teaching of science in French. Such reactions illustrate the deep conflict between people's attitudes and their 'official' point of view in a post-colonial bilingual society.

Data on the actual language choice between Arabic and French in Moroccan society are available, but most studies on North Africa lump together Standard Arabic and dialect under one category 'Arabic' that is contrasted with French. In Bentahila's (1983) study of the choice between Arabic and French in Morocco, the respondents, all of whom were bilingual, stated that they spoke predominantly Arabic with elderly people, poor people and family, and predominantly French with doctors and employers. When ranking the domains of the language varieties, Bentahila found that Moroccan Arabic was used least in education and most at home, while French was used least among friends and most in education. Among friends, the preferred variety was a mixture of Arabic and French.

An interesting contrast is provided by the respondents' reactions to questions about their preferred variety in the written and the spoken media (see Table 12.4). The comments that accompanied these reactions show the kinds of associations that people have with the two varieties: French is preferred because of the content of messages in French, whereas Arabic is preferred out of a sense of duty towards the nation.

As for the relationship between standard and vernacular, there seems to be a tendency on the part of the speakers to use hypercorrect standard language. No doubt, this tendency is connected with the need to compete with the prestige of the French language, which forces speakers to speak as correctly as possible when they are using Standard Arabic. In the media, speakers using Standard Arabic pronounce the article in juncture as *'al-*, apparently in an effort to avoid the dialect form *l-*; they also tend to supply declensional endings even in pausal position, where no speaker in the Eastern Arabic-speaking world would ever use them. Consequently, switches in speech are characterised by sharp contrasts, as in the following utterance taken from a Moroccan radio programme:

s=87	French	mixed	Arabic	blanks
newspapers read	37	53	15	4
newspapers preferred	58	13	26	12
books read	45	54	7	3
books preferred	62	14	20	13
radio listened to	25	60	19	5
radio preferred	54	14	27	14
television preferred	55	26	20	8
films preferred	79	13	6	11

Table 12.4 Preferred language varieties in the media in Morocco (after Bentahila 1983: 68, 70).

> *wa-ḥaqīqa 'anna l-mutaffarižīn k-tašfu 'unṣur mən 'anāṣir l-masraḥ lli ġad-ikun ḥaqīqa fə-l-mustəqbal fī mīdān l-masraḥ nažāḥan bāhir* 'Really, the audience discover one of the elements of the theatre that in future will have a resounding success in the field of theatre' (Forkel 1980: 93)

or in the following utterance:

> *'aškuru l-'aḫ 'la had l-furṣa lli tutāḥ lī baš n'əbbər 'an ra'yī ḥawl dawr l-'iḏā'a* 'I thank my colleague for this opportunity granted to me to express my opinion about the role of the media' (Forkel 1980: 85)

The juxtaposition of high-standard expressions and dialect utterances (*ġad-ikun* with aspectual marker – *nažāḥan* with accusative ending; *lli* dialect relative – *tutāḥ* passive verb) is typical of media speech in North Africa.

In most studies of language choice, the position of Berber is hardly mentioned at all in spite of the fact that a large minority of the population are bilingual in Arabic/Berber. The marginal position of Berber has to do with the effects of the French colonial period. In 1930, the French issued an edict (*daher berbère*) about the position of Berber, in which they put an end to the teaching of Arabic in Berber-speaking areas. Education in both French and Berber was promoted, and several measures were taken to create a distance between speakers of Berber and speakers of Arabic. Although there was never any evidence of actual collaboration with the French authorities, the association of the Berber cause with French imperialism has remained strong in both Morocco and Algeria. In both countries, public support for Berber culture and language was strictly forbidden; in Algeria, all Berber publications were prohibited in 1976. The campaigns for arabicisation were no doubt also directed against the large number of Berber speakers, who had to send their children to Arabic schools. As a result, almost all Berber-speakers, except in remote regions of the Rif, are at least partly bilingual in Arabic and Berber.

In Morocco, an astonishing *volte-face* was introduced by the king himself in 1994, when he publicly announced that Berber language and culture were an important factor in Moroccan society. He therefore ordered the introduction of Berber as a language of instruction in primary schools. It is too early to say whether this new development will actually lead to changes in the position of the Berber language. In Algeria, the state has tried in recent years to incorporate Berber aspirations within its own policy; an official Centre d'Etudes Berbères was established in the south, but it is no exaggeration to say that all such aspirations continue to be viewed with suspicion by the central government. Attempts by the fundamentalist factions to ally themselves with the Berber cause have been scarce, and on the whole the fundamentalists view the Berbers as possible heterodox Muslims.

The lengthy period of coexistence of French and Arabic naturally left traces in the linguistic structure. We have seen above (p. 184) that in the form of Standard Arabic that is current in North Africa, French idiomatic patterns can be detected. In the vernacular, too, a host of French borrowings have been integrated. According to Heath (1989), the integration of loanwords from another language must necessarily be preceded by a period of intensive code-mixing. Judging from other situations of code-mixing, it appears more likely that the most integrated loans from French date back to a period in which most people had only a superficial knowledge of French. Only at a later stage, when there was a larger number of true bilinguals, did the number of *ad hoc* borrowings increase.

Heath pays special attention to the pattern of integration of French loans into Moroccan Arabic. At an earlier stage, Spanish loans had been integrated into the language on the basis of the Spanish infinitive (e.g. *fṛinaṛ-t* 'I braked', *n-fṛinaṛ* 'I brake' < Spanish *frenar*). But, for French loans, the basic form seems to have been a generalised stem ending in a vowel. In the *-er* conjugation in French, many forms end in a vowel sound (e.g. *déclarer* 'to declare', *déclaré, déclarez, déclarais*); according to Heath, these forms provided the canonical pattern for loanwords, imperfect *y-ḍiklaṛi*, perfect *ḍiklaṛa*, analogous to the Moroccan weak verbs in *-a/-i*. As we shall see below (Chapter 13, p. 211), in Maltese, too, the category of the weak verbs provided a suitable pattern for foreign loans. Other examples of French loans include *blisa/yblisi* 'to wound' (French *blesser*); *kuṇṭṛula/ykuṇṭṛuli* 'to supervise' (French *contrôler*); *ṣuṭṭa/yṣuṭi* 'to jump' (French *sauter*). From most of these verbs, a passive and a participle may be formed, e.g. *ttblisi* 'to be wounded', *mblisi* 'wounded'. With regard to nouns, it may be noted that their gender is determined by the presence or absence of an end-vowel; thus, for instance, *duš* 'shower' (French *la douche*) is masculine in Moroccan Arabic, whereas *aṇṭiṛṇa* 'campus' (French *l'internat*) is feminine. Many nouns borrowed from French have a plural in *-at* (e.g. *dušat, gaṛat*, plural from *gaṛ* 'station', French *gare*). But broken plurals for borrowed nouns are fairly common, e.g. *gid* 'tourist guide', plural *gyad* (French *guide*), *mašina* 'train', plural *mašinat* or *mwašn* (French *machine*), *tnbr* 'stamp', plural *tnabr* (French *timbre*).

A special case of code-mixing between French and vernacular Arabic is that of the so-called *Franco-Arabe*, a mixed code that is used predominantly by students and completely bicultural families in Morocco, Tunisia and Lebanon. As an illustration, we may quote a sentence quoted by Abou (1962: 67), in which French and (Lebanese) Arabic alternate even within conjunctions (*avant mā*):

> *yā laṭīf kīf ed-dine b-titġayyar, c'ētait en été avant mā ṣāret el-mašēkil, imagine-toi inno les X: kil ši ils ont fait, mā ḥadan qallon un seul mot* 'My dear, how the world is changing! It was in the summer before the problems began, imagine that the X family, whatever they did, nobody said a single word to them'

Most users of *Franco-Arabe* would not call this a language in its own right, and when students use it this is generally frowned upon. Nevertheless, speaking with a constant mixing of French and Arabic is highly popular in certain circles, especially with youngsters in peer-groups in certain intimate settings. Its maintenance is dependent on the status quo: as soon as the linguistic situation changes, as it did for instance in Lebanon after the civil war, the use of *Franco-Arabe* will stop. Because of its *ad hoc* character, it cannot be regarded as a new code, since the speakers seldom use it at home and they themselves do not feel that it is a separate language. The general attitude towards the mixing of codes is negative, most people viewing this mixed register as a sign of insufficient linguistic proficiency and detrimental to the social development of children.

The study of *Franco-Arabe* with its frequent use of code-mixing is of importance for our knowledge of the nature of bilingualism. In spite of its seemingly improvised and haphazard appearance, it seems that it obeys certain syntactic constraints: in other words, speakers avoid certain combinations and seem to favour others. Abbassi (1977: 162–3) notes, for instance, that it is perfectly acceptable to use combinations such as *mšina l-dak la salle de cinéma* 'we went to that movie-theatre'; *al-lawwal dyal le mois* 'the first of the month'; *saknin f-une grande maison* 'they live in a big house', *umm kaltum kanet une chanteuse mumtaza* ''Umm Kalṯūm was an excellent singer', in which Arabic demonstratives, genitive exponents, prepositions or nouns are combined with French nouns and adjectives. The reversed combinations (**cette qāʿat as-sinima*; **le début du šhar*, **dans waḥəd ḍ-ḍaṛ*, **une excellente muġanniya*) would, however, be less acceptable. Similar constraints are found in research in the Netherlands about the language of Moroccan youngsters who use a mixture of Moroccan Arabic and Dutch (cf. below, Chapter 13).

FURTHER READING

The term 'diglossia' became current in studies on Arabic after Marçais (1930); most of the sociolinguistic literature starts with Ferguson (1959), which provoked a large number of reactions: see for instance MacNamara (1967), McLoughlin (1972), Kaye (1972), El-Hassan (1977) and others. One of the first studies in which the notion of 'diglossia' was applied to the linguistic situation in an Arab country (Iraq) is Altoma (1969). A diachronic study of diglossia in the Classical Arab world is Corriente (1975). Theoretical discussion of the model is in Fishman (1967, 1972), Gumperz (1962) and Britto (1985). There is a comprehensive bibliography on diglossia, in which the number of items on Arabic diglossia is substantial: see Fernández (1993).

Theoretical aspects of the analysis of variation in contemporary Arabic speech communities are discussed by Holes (1987) in his study on the sectarian variation in the dialects of Bahrain; valuable methodological remarks also in Owens (1998; variation in Arabic in Nigeria) and Haeri (1997, Egyptian Arabic).

For the linguistic situation in Egypt, Badawī (1973) is a classic and also one of the very few publications in Arabic about a sociolinguistic topic; for an empirical evaluation of Badawī's model, see Elgibali (1985). Diem's (1974) study of radio Arabic has been mentioned in the text; the book contains transcribed texts that were taken from speeches, interviews and conversations. On the pattern of Nasser's speeches, see Holes (1993) and Mazraani (1996). Not much is known about the use of classicisms in colloquial speech, but the radio texts in Diem provide many examples of people trying to upgrade their speech. There is no analysis of the range of classical markers actually being used; on this topic, see also above, Chapter 8, and in a different region Palva's (1969a) study of the use of classicisms in Bedouin speech in Jordan.

Attitudinal research in the Arab world remains poorly represented; attitudes towards foreign languages have been studied by Bentahila (1983; French/Arabic in Morocco), Suleiman (1985; English/Arabic in Jordan), Zughoul (1984; English/Arabic in Jordan), Abu-Haidar (1988a; English/Arabic in Iraq) and Amara (1999; Hebrew/Arabic in the West Bank and Israel).

The difference between male and female speech in Tunisia and Egypt is discussed by Walters (1989, 1991) and Haeri (1992, 1997); they both emphasise the methodological need to distinguish between Western and non-Western speech communities. A survey of recent research in male/female differences in Arabic dialects is in Rosenhouse (1996).

On the linguistic situation in North Africa, there is quite a large literature. The French colonial policy that led to the present-day linguistic situation is discussed in Bidwell (1973) and Gallup (1973). On linguistic policies in Morocco, Algeria and Tunisia in the period after independence, see Grandguillaume (1983); a few case studies on the process of arabicisation are available, e.g. Hamzaoui (1970) on the arabicisation of the traffic police in Tunisia; Riguet (1984) on the arabicisation of the schools in Tunisia.

The older literature on Tunisia and Morocco provides an interesting point of comparison with the present-day situation; since these publications originated in the period just after independence, the writers were very much involved in what was happening; see e.g. Garmadi (1968), Maamouri (1973) and Gallagher (1968). A modern study on standard/vernacular diglossia in Moroccan radio Arabic is Forkel (1980), which has the same design as Diem's study on Egyptian (and Syro-Lebanese) radio Arabic. On diglossia in Tunisia, see Talmoudi (1984a).

On Lebanon, only older publications (such as Abou 1961, 1962) are available, which are interesting from the historical point of view.

Abbassi (1977) is a useful survey of the sociolinguistic situation in Morocco and includes a sketch of the syntactic constraints in *Franco-Arabe*; for an older study on the use of *Franco-Arabe* among students, see Ounali (1970). On French/Arabic code-switching, see Bentahila and Davies (1983); cf. below, Chapter 13, p. 222, on Dutch/Arabic code-switching. The most important study on French loanwords in Moroccan Arabic is Heath (1989), with extensive lists of borrowed words. On French loanwords in the Algerian vernacular, see Hadj-Sadok (1955). For a case study of English loanwords in an Arabic dialect, that of al-Ḥaṣā in Saudi Arabia, see Smeaton (1973).

13
Arabic as a Minority Language

13.1 INTRODUCTION

In the course of history, some speakers of Arabic have become isolated from the central area. Living among people who speak a different language and in order to function in society they have to use the dominant language of their neighbours, while continuing to speak Arabic among themselves as a home language. Usually, in such linguistic enclaves (called in German *Sprachinsel*) the home language has little prestige, and the speakers depend on the official language in their everyday dealings. Because of the frequent code-switching and the many integrated loans, their language is subject to all kinds of linguistic pressure from the dominant language (adstratal influence). The linguistic enclaves therefore present a general interest for the study of language contact.

The study of the Arabic linguistic enclaves also contributes to our knowledge of the history of Arabic. The classicising influence of the standard language was considerably weaker here than in the central empire. In some respects, therefore, the structure of these dialects reflects an earlier form of spoken Arabic in the areas to which they were exported, without the pressure from the Classical language, which in the core area acted as a target for most speakers (cf. above, p. 109). There is, however, no direct correlation between the date of cut-off and the present structure of these dialects. Hardly any linguistic enclave, with the possible exception of Maltese, was ever completely isolated from the central area, and in most cases the speakers maintained some form of contact with the prestigious centres of the Islamic empire, be it only because of their adherence to Islam.

In this chapter, we shall briefly discuss the linguistic situation of a number of linguistic enclaves in which Arabic is spoken, and we shall also deal with the linguistic situation of the many Arab immigrants in Western Europe and America.

13.2 MALTESE

When in 256/870 the Tunisian Aghlabids conquered the island of Malta, the inhabitants were Christians who probably spoke some kind of Romance dialect. During the period of Muslim domination, the entire population took over the Arabic language. If we believe the report by the geographer al-Ḥimyarī (cf. Brincat 1991), for some 180 years after the conquest there were no inhabitants at all and the island was repopulated with Arabic-speaking people afterwards. In any case, the language of the original inhabitants did not leave any traces in the Maltese language.

In 445/1054, the Normans conquered the island of Malta, but in the thirteenth century two thirds of the inhabitants were still Muslims according to a contemporary source. In the following centuries, these Muslims must have been either banished or converted to Christianity, and with their religion the Classical Arabic language disappeared as well. Their vernacular language remained in use, and, even though Latin and Italian were introduced as the languages of religion and culture, the Maltese vernacular was accepted as the language of contact between the priests and their flocks. The official language was Italian.

The earliest Maltese text that has been preserved dates from the second half of the fifteenth century (the *Cantilena* of Peter de Caxaro), but it was not until 1796 that Maltese was accepted as a language in its own right with Mikiel Vassalli's grammar, *Ktyb yl klym Malti* 'Book of the Maltese language'. After 1814, when Malta became a part of the British empire, English replaced Italian as the official language, but Maltese was introduced in the curriculum of the schools. In 1933, Maltese was recognised as the second national language, and after independence it became the official language of the Republic of Malta, written in a Latin orthography.

Despite efforts in the 1970s and 1980s by the Maltese government to emphasise the Arabic character of Maltese and introduce Arabic in the schools as a compulsory subject, most Maltese do not like to be reminded of the Arabic provenance of their language. They do not wish to be associated with the Arab world, and prefer to call their language a Semitic language. Older theories about the Punic origin of the language are no longer taken seriously, but at the University of Valletta the departments of Arabic and Maltese continue to be strictly separated.

A number of Arabic consonantal phonemes have merged in the language, but are still distinguished in the orthography: /q/ has become /'/, e.g. *qagħad* ['a:t] 'to sit' (Arabic *qaʿada*); /ʿ/ and /ġ/ have disappeared in most positions, but are still written as *għ*, e.g. *bogħod* [bo:t] 'distance' (Arabic *buʿd*); /ḥ/ and /h̠/ have merged in /ḥ/, written as *ħ*; /h/ has disappeared in most positions, e.g. *deher* [de:r] 'to appear' (Arabic *ẓahara*). All emphatic consonants have become non-emphatic. Yet, in spite of the fact that most Maltese regard their language as different from Arabic, almost all proposals for the orthography of the language were historicising: they attempted to restore the Arabic structure in writing in those cases where it had been destroyed by phonetic developments. Thus, the combinations *għa* and *agħ* are distinguished in the orthography, but pronounced similarly [a:] in words such as *għamlu* 'they did' (Arabic *ʿamilū*) and *jagħmlu* 'they do' (Arabic *yaʿmalū*).

The most striking feature of the language is the enormous amount of Italian and Sicilian loans, which have become completely integrated in the structure of the language. Although examples may be quoted from other dialects which accommodated foreign loans, Maltese Arabic is exceptional both in the amount of loans from Italian (and in recent times from English) and in the effect which the influx of loanwords had on the morphology of the language. The usual process of integration of loanwords in Arabic dialects is by root-abstraction (cf. above, p. 180), and this is the way in which older loans were incorporated in Maltese. In root-abstraction, the consonants of the foreign word constitute a new root in Arabic, to which Arabic morphological patterns may be applied. Italian *serpe* 'snake', for instance, was borrowed as *serp* and received a broken plural *srīp*; from Italian *pittore* 'painter' > Maltese *pittūr* a new verb *pitter* was coined.

As Mifsud (1995) demonstrates, the influx of foreign loans in Maltese was so massive that it led to a change in the morphological structure of the language, from a root-based to a stem-based morphology. The procedure of root-abstraction ceased to be productive, and foreign words were integrated in a different way. Most Italian verbs were borrowed on the basis of their imperative or the third person singular of the present; in Maltese, these verbs end in *-a*, e.g. Maltese *čēda* 'to give up' from the Italian verb *cedere*, or *falla* 'to fail' from the Italian verb *fallire*. This process was facilitated by the fact that the largest category of verbs in Maltese was that of the weak verbs, which also end in *-a*. Thus Italian loans such as *čēda* and *falla* became indistinguishable from Arabic Maltese verbs such as *meša* 'to walk', *mešša* 'to lead'. The same pattern also accommodated other verbs with more complicated stems, e.g. *splōda* 'to explode', *sōfra* 'to suffer'. The accumulation of Italian loans in this category led to a reinterpretation of the inflected forms: *meššeyna* 'we led', *falleyna* 'we failed' were interpreted not as the second measure of the radicals *m-š-y* with the ending *-na* (root + verbal pattern + suffix), but rather as a stem with a suffix, i.e. *mešš-eyna*. The Italian verbs received a Maltese imperfect, from one of the two categories of Maltese Arabic, in *-a* or *-i*, e.g. *salva/ysalva* 'to save' (Italian *salvare*); *solva/ysolvi* 'to solve' (Italian *solvere*), probably on the basis of their conjugation in Italian: verbs in *-are* received a Maltese imperfect in *-a*, those in *-ere*, *-ire* an imperfect in *-i*.

A similar development took place in the nominal system. Since Arabic nouns are usually triradical and most plurals are formed with discontinuous morphemes (broken plurals), foreign words are not easily integrated. In Maltese, the integration of Italian loans was accomplished by a reinterpretation of their form, by taking into account only the last two syllables of the word. Thus, Italian loans such as *umbrella* 'umbrella', *gverra* 'war' received the broken plurals *umbrelel* and *gverer*. In this way, the difference between Italian morphology operating with suffixes and Maltese Arabic morphology operating with discontinuous patterns was eliminated, and the way was opened for the introduction of any foreign loan. In recent times, however, there has arisen a tendency not to provide English words with broken plurals, but to borrow them together with their English plural morpheme *-s*, e.g. *telefon/telefons*.

Text 1: Maltese (from *L'Orizzont*, 9 May 1990)

1. *Is-sitwazzjoni tan-nuqqas ta' ilma qegħda dejjem tiggrava.*	1. The situation of the deficit of water is becoming graver all the time.
2. *Issa qegħdin jintlaqtu wkoll postijiet li rari kienu jkunu ffaċċjati bi problema ta' nuqqas ta' ilma.*	2. Now they are confronted with it in all places that were rarely faced with the problem of a deficit of water.
3. *Qed tikber ukoll il-pressjoni fuq it-Taqsima tal-Bowsers tad-Dipartiment ta' l-Ilma.*	3. The pressure is becoming greater on the Bowsers Section of the Department of Water.
4. *Minkejja li għandhom erba' linji tat-telefon, tlieta minnhom diretti, aktar iva milli le ssibhom 'engaged' – iċċempel meta ċċempel.*	4. Although they have four telephone lines, three of them direct, more often than not you find them engaged – it rings when you ring.

13.3 CYPRIOT MARONITE ARABIC

Cypriot Maronite Arabic is the home language of a small community of the village of Kormakiti in north-west Cyprus. The presence of this Maronite community on the island dates back to the period between the ninth and twelfth centuries. After the Turkish invasion of Cyprus in 1974, most of the inhabitants of this community spread over the island, leaving behind in Kormakiti only about 500 people (1979). Of the 5,000 Maronites in Cyprus, these are the only ones bilingual in Greek and Arabic. Because of its peculiarities and in spite of the small size of the community, Cypriot Maronite Arabic is of great importance for the historical study of the Syrian and Mesopotamian dialects. Most of its traits are shared with the sedentary dialects of Greater Syria, for instance the verbal marker for the non-past *p(i)*, which goes back to the common Syro-Lebanese *bi-*. Borg (1985) also mentions a large number of common features between Cypriot Arabic and the so-called *qəltu* dialects of the Mesopotamian group, for instance the future marker *tta-* (< Classical Arabic) *ḥattā*, which is also used as a future marker in the Anatolian *qəltu* dialects, and the past marker *kan-*. According to him, these common features go back to a period in which there was a dialect continuum between the Mesopotamian dialects and the Syrian dialect area.

Three features lend the Cypriot Arabic dialect its 'exotic' character: the development of the Arabic stops; the reduction in morphological patterns; and the presence of numerous Greek loans. Probably under the influence of Greek phonology, the opposition voiced/voiceless has disappeared in the stops in this dialect. The realisation of these merged phonemes depends on the environment: they are realised as voiced stops between vowels, but as voiceless stops at the end of a word, e.g. [kidep], phonologically /kitep/, from Classical *kataba*. Before another stop, stops become spirants, e.g. *ẖtuft* < *ktupt* 'I have written', *paẖtop* from *p-aktop* 'I am writing'. In a cluster of three stops, the middle one is deleted, e.g. *pkyaẖpu* < *p-yaktpu* < *bi-yaktubu* 'they are writing'. This form also illustrates another instance of Greek influence, the insertion of *k* before *y*, as in *pkyut* < *buyūt* 'houses'. Cypriot Arabic has lost the emphatic consonants, but two of the interdentals have been preserved: *ṯ* as in *ṯawp* < *ṯawb* 'cloth', and *ḏ* going back to Classical *ḍ* and *ḏ̣* as in *ḏahr* < *ḏ̣ahr* 'back'. But the original voiced interdental *ḏ* has become *d/t*, as in *tapaẖ* < *ḏabaḥ* 'to slaughter'.

The number of plural nominal patterns has been reduced drastically; there are only five patterns corresponding to the broken patterns of the regular Arabic dialects. The ending *-at* has to a large degree replaced the various patterns, e.g. *patn*, plural *patnat* 'belly', *moẖẖ*, plural *moẖẖat* 'head'. It even appears as an ending for historical plurals, e.g. *ẖumat* < **luḥūmāt* 'kinds of meat' (Classical *luḥūm*) and *ẖpurat* 'graves' (Classical *qubūr*, with spirantisation of the *q* before a second stop). The genitive exponent is *tel* (masculine), *šayt* (feminine), *šat* (plural).

Greek loans cover a large part of the official but also of the everyday vocabulary, e.g. *kiryakí* 'Sunday', *tiléfono* 'telephone', *pólemo* 'war', *ayróplana* 'aeroplane', *ḏískolo* 'difficult', *záẖari* 'sugar', *maṯités* 'pupil', *ístera* 'later', and so on. As in similar linguistic situations it is often difficult to determine whether we are dealing with code-switching or with real loans. This is not the case with some of the functional words that have been borrowed, such as *kaṯe* 'each', as in *kaṯe-veẖen* 'everyone' (< Greek *kathe* + Arabic *wāḥid*), and suffixes such as the diminutive in *paytui* 'little house' (< Arabic *bayt* + Greek suffix *-oudhi*).

Text 2: Cypriot Arabic (after Borg 1985: 165)

1. *eẖen šípp ámma piẖúpp il-éẖte pínt, piváddi l-éẖlu u t-tatátu žump il-éẖla u kyitilpúa*	1. A youth when he falls in love with a girl, sends his parents and his godfather to her parents and they ask for her hand.
2. *an p-pínt u l-éẖl piritúẖ, tóte š-šípp kyítlop príka miẖ páyt ẖkáli u flús*	2. If the girl and the parents want him, then the youth requests a dowry, such as a house, land and money.
3. *an má-liẖon aš ma kyítlop, tóte l-iproksenyá kyintẖírpu*	3. If they do not have what he requests, then they break off the engagement.
4. *an piẖúppa ma kálpu, pkyaẖúta ma áš ma kyatúa éẖla*	4. If he loves her with his heart, he takes her whatever her parents give.
5. *piẖóttu aška zmán kyaʿatézzu pšan tentžáwzu, u ẖost áḏa l-izmán, pitáylpu l-páyt u š-šáya tel-ʿarús, w-ístera pitáylpu l-iẖár tel-ʿórs*	5. They determine how much time they need to get married and during this time they prepare the house and the things of the bride and then they prepare the date of the wedding.

13.4 ANATOLIAN ARABIC

After the Seljuk conquest of Anatolia, not all traces of Arabic dialects disappeared. When in the course of the next centuries Turkish became the official language of the Seljuks and later of the Ottoman empire, Classical Arabic remained the language of religion and, to a certain degree, that of culture; the status of colloquial Arabic, however, changed drastically. Most speakers eventually switched to Turkish or Kurdish, but in a few areas in Central Anatolia some communities retained the use of Arabic as their home language, most speakers being bilingual or trilingual.

In Jastrow's classification (1978) of the Mesopotamian *qəltu* dialects, the Anatolian Arabic dialects constitute one of the three subgroups. The total number of speakers lies around 140,000, most of whom are bi- or trilingual in Arabic, Kurdish and Turkish. The dialects are subdivided into five groups: Diyarbakır dialects (spoken by a Jewish and Christian minority, now almost extinct); Mardin dialects; Siirt dialects; Kozluk dialects; and Sason dialects. There are two larger cities where Arabic is spoken, Mardin and Siirt, although in the latter Arabic is being replaced gradually by Turkish.

Compared to the other dialects of the *qəltu* group, the Anatolian dialects have deviated much more from the Classical type of Arabic. There are various distinctive markers that immediately classify a dialect as Anatolian, such as the suffix *-n* instead of *-m* in the second and third person plural (e.g. in Mardin Arabic *baytkən* 'your house', *baytən* 'their house') and the negation *mō* instead of *mā* with the imperfect. But these traits are minor details compared to some other features that contribute to the exotic character of Anatolian Arabic.

There is a great deal of variation between the dialects, both in phonology and in morphology. The Arabic interdentals, for instance, have developed in each dialect differently: in Mardin /ṯ/, /ḏ/, /ḏ̣/; in Diyarbakır /t/, /d/, /ḍ/; in Siirt /f/, /v/, /ṿ/; in Kozluk/Sason /s/, /z/, /ẓ/ (for instance *ḏ̣ahər, ḍahər, ṿahr, ẓahər*, all from Arabic *ḏ̣ahr* 'back'). This demonstrates the fact that they have gone through separate developments.

In morphology, too, there is a great deal of variation between the dialects. The genitive exponent, for instance, differs: some dialects use a reflex of **ḏī-la* (relative pronoun + preposition *li-* 'for'), e.g. *dīla, ḏīl, ḏēl*; others use a combination of *lē* + *l-*, e.g. *lē* in Daragözü. The Anatolian dialects are particularly rich in verbal particles. They not only have an aspectual prefix for the actual present (*kū-*), but also a prefix for the future (*ta-, tə-* < *ḥattā* 'until'; sometimes *də-*), the continuous past (*kān, kən, kā*), the perfective (*kəl, kūt, kū*) and the anterior past (*kə, kan, kāt* with the perfect verb).

A major innovation is the development of a copula from the personal pronoun, usually placed after the predicate. In the dialect of Qarṭmīn, for instance, we find sentences such as *ṯəmm əğğəbb ḏayyəq-we* (< *huwa*) 'the opening of the well is narrow', *əlmērge mfállate-ye* (< *hiya*) 'the meadow is without an owner', *ənti mán-ənti?* 'who are you?', *žib-u* '(it) is the wolf'. A further development is the demonstrative copula with the demonstrative elements *k-* and *hā-*, e.g. in the same dialect *əbnu kū qəddām əmmu* 'his son is before his mother', *kw* (< *k-* + *hā*) *zlām mayyət* 'there is a dead man', *kēh* (< *k-* + *hā* + *hā*) *maṛa* 'over there is a woman' (examples from Jastrow 1978: 131–42). The simple copula is also found in the Christian Arabic of Baghdad, but the proliferation of forms and new functions is only found in Anatolia.

The lexicon of the Anatolian dialects is marked by a large number of loanwords from Turkish and Kurdish. Most of the Turkish loans are in the domains of administration and the army, e.g. (Daragözü) *damanča* 'pistol' (Turkish *tabanca*), *čəfta* 'gun' (Turkish *çifte*). Some of the Turkish loans are themselves of Arabic origin, e.g. (Mḥallami) *ḥaqsəz* 'unjust' (Turkish *haksız* < Arabic *ḥaqq* + Turkish *sız*). The Kurdish loans often concern agricultural and household items, such as (Daragözü) *qāzə́ke* 'jar', *tōv* 'sowing-seed', *ğōt* 'plough', but also current words such as *dōst* 'friend'. The first example contains the Kurdish diminutive *-ik*.

The older loans have been integrated into the language, both phonologically and morphologically, for instance by acquiring their own broken plurals, e.g. (Mḥallami) *panṭūr/panēṭīr* 'trousers' (< Turkish *potur*). In this case, there can be no doubt that we are dealing with a real loan. But very often the speakers use foreign words without modifying their phonetic shape, even when there is a perfectly good synonym available in their own dialect. In such cases, the use of the foreign word is the effect of the bilingual situation, which leads the speakers to code-switch from their own language to the prestige language. This explains the large number of *ad hoc* loans occurring only once in the corpus that was used for a recent count (Vocke and Waldner 1982). According to this count, 24 per cent of the lexicon of the Anatolian dialects consists of foreign loans. The dialects differ with respect to the language from which they borrow most: in Daragözü 32 per cent of the lexicon is foreign, of which 5 per cent is Turkish, 12 per cent is Kurdish and the rest of unknown etymology, whereas in Mardin, of

15 per cent foreign loans 12 per cent is Turkish, 0.5 per cent is Kurdish and the rest of unknown origin. Most of the foreign loans do not belong to the most frequent vocabulary, since in running speech only about 5 per cent of the words are of non-Arabic origin.

An interesting phenomenon is the use of verbo-nominal expressions with the verb *sawa* 'to do, make' of the type that is usually found in loans from Arabic in other languages, rather than the other way round (cf. below, Chapter 14). In Anatolian dialects, many expressions of this kind are found, not only with Turkish words, but also with Arabic words: *sawa talafōn* 'to call by telephone', *sawa īšāra* 'to give a sign', *sawa mḥāfaza* 'to protect'. In all likelihood, these constructions are a calque of Turkish expressions with *etmek* (cf. below, Chapter 14, p. 235).

Text 3: Daragözü Arabic (after Jastrow 1973: 118)

1. *lōm mēḥəd malǧaləm kəntu qfā lxašne, ġalámi k^{ə}ẓarbo fāk əlpāl, w nā lē ʿīyantu šīwaʿd m^{ə}havṛās-va īǧi*	1. One day I was with the goats, behind the hill, my goats were climbing the slope, and suddenly I saw something coming from the top of the hill.
2. *qəltu wəḷḷā ukkā īžba zzīb, īyantu zīb-u*	2. I said: 'O, my God, that looks like the wolf!' I looked, it was a wolf.
3. *hama ǧā ma ǧā, rakəb əlġalme, r^{ə}kába, w gəndāra mfō lḥaǧəṛ*	3. Right when he came, he jumped upon a goat, he jumped upon her, and rolled her from the stone.
4. *nā lē ʿīyantu qōqə́ta sāġē fṣəmmu*	4. Suddenly I saw how he took her head in his mouth.
5. *saytu ʿlayu rətto hárətto, kalb^{ə}na waʿd k^{ə}fī čāḷo, zīyaqtūllu čāḷo, čāḷo-ǧi mbaržēr-va ǧā saynu šəbər waʿd ṭalaḥ, w-ǧā ʿlayu*	5. I shouted at him *rətto hárətto*. We had a dog, Čāḷo, I called to him: 'Čāḷo!' Čāḷo came from downhill, his tongue hanging out of his mouth, and he came upon him.

13.5 UZBEKISTAN AND AFGHANISTAN ARABIC

During the 1960s, information became available on an Arabic dialect spoken in the (then) Soviet Republic of Uzbekistan. Since Western Arabists did not have access to this region, the only fieldwork was done by the Soviet Arabists Vinnikov and Tsereteli. Through their publications, scholars learned that an Arabic dialect was spoken in the Qašqa Darya (1,000 speakers in 1938) and Bukhara (400 speakers in 1938) regions of Uzbekistan. Most of them were bi- or trilingual, Tajik and Uzbek being the current languages in the community. Their dialect turned out to be related to the Mesopotamian and Anatolian *qəltu* dialects, but it had developed in a special way. According to fieldwork carried out in 1996 by Dereli (1997), the inhabitants of the villages of Ǧogari and Arabkhane still use Arabic in their daily contacts, although they code-switch constantly to Uzbek and Tajik.

The origins of the Uzbekistan community of speakers of Arabic are controversial. According to some traditions, the Arab presence in Transoxania and the islamisation of this area date back to the time of Qutayba ibn Muslim, governor of Khurāsān, who conquered Bukhara and Samarqand in 87/709–10. Others link the Arab presence with Timur Lenk's conquests in the fourteenth century, or with Bedouin migrations from Afghanistan in the sixteenth century. In all likelihood, there were different stages of arabicisation in this area, which would explain the mixed character of the lexicon.

Our lack of knowledge is even greater in the case of the Arabic spoken in Afghanistan. The first publication in a Western language concerning remnants of Arabic in Afghanistan appeared in 1973. At that time, there were approximately 4,000 speakers of an Arabic dialect in Northern Afghanistan in the provinces of Balkh and Ǧawzǧān. Most speakers were bilingual in Arabic and Persian (Tajik). They belonged to a closely-knit community that observed a strict endogamy, and felt proud of their Arabic descent. According to the local tradition, they descended from the tribe of Qurayš and had been brought to this region by Timur Lenk in the fourteenth century. On the whole, their dialect seems to be closely related to the dialect spoken in Uzbekistan. They exhibit the same double reflex of the Classical *q*, disappearance of the emphatic consonants and sibilant realisation of the interdentals. Unlike Uzbekistan Arabic, Afghanistan Arabic seems to have preserved, however, the two phonemes /ḥ/ and /ʿ/.

Belonging as it does to the *qəltu* group, Uzbekistan Arabic exhibits many of the typical features of a sedentary dialect. There are, however, traces of Bedouin influence, since not all words show the voiceless reflex of Classical Arabic *q*: side by side, we find here *gidir* 'pot' and *qalb* 'heart' (cf. above, p. 137). Sometimes, but not always, the variants belong to different dialect regions, e.g. the word for 'heart' in the Ǧeinau dialect is given as *galib*. In the group of interdentals, the situation is similar: the usual reflex of the Classical interdentals must have been *ṯ, ḏ, ḏ̣*, which probably under Tajik influence developed into *s, z, ẓ*, e.g. *sūb* 'cloth' < *ṯawb*, *orẓ* 'earth' < *'arḍ*. It appears that in most cases emphatic consonants were de-velarised, so that *ḏ̣* becomes simple *z*. But in some words the Classical interdentals are represented by dentals, e.g. in the demonstratives *hād, hādi* 'this', and *dūk, dīki* 'that'.

The definite article of Classical Arabic has disappeared in Uzbekistan Arabic, but there is a new indefinite article, *fat* (< *fard*), as in Mesopotamian Arabic. In the nouns, broken plurals are restricted to a few words; most masculine animate nouns have a plural in *-īn*, e.g. *wazīrīn* 'ministers', *uḫwīn* 'brothers'; feminine animate and inanimate nouns have the ending *-āt*, e.g. *ummāt* 'mothers', *šiyāt* 'things', *rāsāt* 'heads', *balbetāt* 'doors' (< *bāb il-bēt* 'door of the house'). In nominal phrases, the attribute (adjective or relative clause, sometimes a second noun) may be linked to the head noun with the help of the suffix *-in* or *-hin*, e.g. *mu-hin aḥmar* 'the golden water', *šiyāt-in ġāli ġāli* 'very expensive goods', *fat ḥağart-in kabīra* 'a large stone'; with a relative clause: *fat bint-in tibki* 'a girl who is crying', *ādami-n min alla il miḫōf* 'a man who fears God' (with relative *il*, and imperfect with the non-past particle *mi-*); with another noun: *nuṣṣ-in lēl* 'the middle of the night'. The origin of this suffix is not quite clear; it may be connected with the Persian *izafet* construction, or etymologically related to the Arabic relative *'ayna* 'where'.

In the verbal system, the participle has become the current form for completed actions, and it has lost its nominal functions. In combination with pronominal suffixes, the participial forms have undergone a reanalysis in the following way. From *zōrib* 'he has hit' (< *ḍārib* 'hitting') with the pronominal object suffix, *zorb-in-nī* 'he has hit me', a new form with pronominal subject suffix was developed, *zorbin-ī*, meaning 'I have hit'; in the same way *zorbin-ak* 'you have hit'. In their turn, these forms may be connected with objective suffixes, e.g. *zorbinīk* 'I have hit you', *zorbināh* 'I have hit him', *zorbinīhim* 'I have hit them'; *zorbinakāni* 'you have hit me', *zorbinakāh* 'you have hit him', *zorbinakāhum* 'you have hit them'.

Uzbekistan Arabic is unique among Arabic dialects in having a word order subject–object–verb, as against subject–verb–object in all other dialects. This word order may have originated as a stylistic alternative to the normal word order, in which the object was fronted. In an environment in which Uzbek (a verb-final Turkic language) was spoken, the alternative word order was reinforced and became the canonical one. When the object is definite, there is a resumptive suffix in the verb. As a result, we now have in Uzbekistan Arabic sentences such as

> *fat ādami baqarīn kom-misūq-nāyim*
> a man cows [past]-he tends-[continuous]
> 'a man was tending cows'

> *zaġīr ḥağara fīdu ḫadāha*
> young the-stone hand-his he-took-it
> 'the young man took the stone in his hand'

A similar order applies to other sentence constituents such as the predicate in:

> *ʿō sámaka anā maṣōr-mi*
> still a-fish I I-remain-[interrogative particle]
> 'shall I then remain a fish?'

If the explanation given above is correct, this would be a good example of a change that started as a stylistic discourse alternative that was reinforced by the influence of Uzbek, the dominant adstratal language.

Text 4: Uzbekistan Arabic (after Vinnikov 1956: 192)

1. *fat šī il mebīʿ kon, fat walád kun ʿéndu, fat bint kun ʿéndu, bíntu i-ḫaṭīb sabára*	1. There was a trader, he had a son, he had a daughter, he promised his daughter to the preacher.
2. *šī šarā, wey wáladu i-fat madínt-in wáḥad ġadāk šī taybīʿ*	2. He bought something, with his son he went to a city in order to sell something.
3. *ḫaṭīb i-máratu qōl: hamat bínt šī il mebīʿ iláy wurīya; bint kun tístaḥi mínnu*	3. The preacher said to his wife: 'Show me this daughter of the trader'. The girl was ashamed before him.
4. *mart ḫaṭīb qōlet: mawūra iléyk! ana móġdi fi béyta, rāsi fi giddāma maḥeṭṭā^h tatfillā^h; hint min waro ḥāyṭ ʿáyyin, miššūfa*	4. The wife of the preacher said: 'I'll show her to you! I'll go to her house, put my head before her, in order for her to clean it; you look from behind the wall, you'll see her!'

13.6 ARABIC CREOLES IN AFRICA: THE CASE OF KI-NUBI

A special case of linguistic enclave is the one documented example that we have of an Arabic dialect which developed in a process of pidginisation/creolisation. Pidginisation is a process in which a reduced variety of a language develops as a means of communication between speakers of different languages. They acquire a second language as their common means of communication in a short period of time without any formal teaching. Such a reduced language or pidgin may remain in use for a long time as an auxiliary language. When speakers of different languages start intermarrying, they communicate in the reduced variety and transmit it to their children. These acquire the pidgin language as their first language and through expansion and grammaticalisation creolise it, i.e. transform it into a new natural language or creole. Most known cases of pidginisation/creolisation involve Indo-European languages (English, French, Dutch, Portuguese, Spanish) that were turned into creoles by the slaves exported to the New World from Africa.

In the nineteenth century, when the Egyptian, later the Anglo-Egyptian, army attempted to 'pacify' the Sudan, they recruited in Upper Egypt and in the Sudan many soldiers from the indigenous peoples. In the garrison camps around Edfu, the only means of communication was a pidginised form of (Egyptian/Sudanese) Arabic used by the subalterns in their contacts with the recruits, most of whom belonged to the Nubian tribe. Since the arabicisation of the Egyptian army was not carried out before 1860, this pidginised form of the language probably goes back to an Arabic pidgin that had been current in the area for centuries in commercial contacts, in particular the slave trade, between Egypt and the Sudan. After the Mahdist revolt in 1882, the German commander of the army, Emin Pasha, became isolated in the south and joined the English army in Kenya and Uganda; many of the Nubian soldiers followed him and eventually settled down in these British colonies. Some of them took indigenous wives, and in these mixed marriages the language of communication was the Arabic pidgin which they had learned in the army camps in the Sudan. The children of these marriages started to creolise the language, and the result is the creolised variety of Arabic that continues to be spoken in both countries by fewer than 50,000 people; it is usually known as Nubi (or Ki-Nubi with the Bantu prefix for the names of languages).

An interesting aspect of the history of this dialect is the development in the Southern Sudan. After the Mahdist revolt, the pidgin variety of Arabic remained in use as the *lingua franca* of the area. It became known locally as Juba Arabic, after the capital of the Southern Sudan, where it was particularly common. In the last few decades, the increase in bilingual marriages in the capital has led to the emergence of a group of native speakers of Juba Arabic who speak a creole that in many respects resembles the Ki-Nubi of Uganda and Kenya. We have seen above (p. 110) that the increasing influence of Standard Arabic and Khartoum Arabic might eventually lead to a restructuring of Juba Arabic in the direction of a 'normal' Arabic dialect.

Nubi exhibits many of the features of 'classic' creolised languages, such as Jamaican English or Haitian Créole. Its phonemic system has undergone a drastic restructuring compared to the source language from which it derives, probably a form of Upper Egyptian. The emphatic consonants have merged with their non-emphatic counterparts; /ḥ/ and /ʿ/ have disappeared; /ẖ/ and /ġ/ have merged and become /k/. The reflexes of Classical Arabic /q/ and /ğ/ in Nubi correspond to the Upper Egyptian origin of the language: /g/ and /ğ/. Word-final consonants have in many cases been dropped. A few examples may demonstrate to what extent Nubi words differ from their Arabic source: *rági* 'man' (Arabic *rağul*; Egyptian Arabic *rāgil*), *sondú* 'box' (Arabic *ṣandūq*), *sokolá* 'things' (plural **šuġūlāt* from Arabic singular *šuġl*). Many words were taken over by Nubi together with the Arabic article, e.g. *láádum* 'bone' (Arabic *al-ʿaẓm*), *lasía* 'evening' (Arabic *al-ʿašiyya*), *lifíli* 'elephant' (Arabic *al-fīl*).

Like most other creoles, Nubi has only one verbal form, probably derived from the Arabic imperative, e.g. *ábinu* 'to build' (Arabic *banā*), *álabu* 'to play' (Arabic *laʿiba*), *áángulu* 'to remove' (Arabic *naqala*), *ááriğa* 'to return' (Arabic *rağaʿa*). The verbal form is used for all persons and may be expanded with a large number of aspectual particles:

rúa 'to go' (< Arabic *rāḥ*; imperative *ruḥ*)
áána rúa 'I went' (punctual past)
áána bì-rúa 'I shall go' (future)
áána gí-rúa 'I am going' (continuous)
áána bì-gí-rúa 'I shall be going' (future continuous)
áána káàn-rúa 'I had gone' (pluperfect)
áána káàn-gí-rúa 'I was going' (past continuous)
áána káàn-bì-rúa 'I would go' (hypothetical)

Many verbs end in a suffix *-u*, which may either be a remnant of the object pronoun *-hu*, functioning as a transitiviser, or originally a marker of the plural.

The nominal forms usually do not distinguish between singular and plural, although there seems to be a marker for plurality *-ā*, as in *laáğer*/plural *laağerá* (Arabic *al-ḥağar*) 'stone'. Sometimes groups of human beings may be indicated with a collective prefix *nas-*, derived from the Arabic word *nās* 'people', as in *nas-babá* 'fathers [collective]'; *nas-yalá* 'children [collective]'. Adjectives sometimes have a form in *-in* to denote the plural. The genitive exponent *ta* clearly derives from Egyptian Arabic *bitāʿ*; it is used both with nouns and with pronominal suffixes (e.g. *taí* 'my', *táki*, *to*, *tína*, *tákum*, *toúmon*).

The lexicon is built on an Arabic basis, but contains a large number of Swahili and recently-acquired English loans. In some cases, pairs of synonyms exist that are indicative of the close relationship between the Nubis and the Bantu-speaking environment, e.g. *áseti* (Arabic *ʾasad*)/*síímba* (Swahili *simba*) 'lion'; *bééda* (Arabic *bīḍ*)/*mayáái* (Swahili *mayai*) 'egg'; *gemís* (Arabic *qamīṣ*)/*šáti* (Swahili *shati* < English *shirt*). There is one frequent verb that has been taken over from Swahili, *wéza* 'to be able', although there is an Arabic equivalent *ágder* (Arabic *qadira*).

Text 5: Ki-Nubi Arabic (after Heine 1982: 50)

1. *núbi kúlu má aanás ta béle alí úmon fógo dé íla wazée yaá ğá wéledú*	1. All the Nubis are not people of the country in which they are, except the elders, they came and got children.

2. *yalá kamán wéledú, úmon alí kubar-ín dé mútu, yalá al fádul dé kúlu aanási ğedid-ín*	2. The children, too, got children; those who were old, died; the children who were left behind, they were all new people.
3. *gén ta núbi, úmon gí gén bakán wái, gén fu kámbi*	3. The stay of the Nubis, they are staying in one place, they stay in a village.
4. *úmon áágu bádu, úmon gí lébisí gumási, káánzu, bóuzá tróúz, šátí, kóti ma tóróbús, dé sáfa fi sáfa ta rugal-á*	4. They like each other; they wear clothes, gowns, knickerbockers, shirts, jackets and hats. This concerning the men.
5. *nuswán gí lébis kurbába, gemís, tóob, fi kurá úmon gí lébis borotús ma ndála*	5. The women wear a *gurbaba*, shirts, upper cloth; on their legs they wear clogs and sandals.
6. *úmon gí másatú rásu, úmon gí gídu adán ma nyangáratu ta kipín ma kisááfu*	6. They plait their hair, they pierce their ear and nose with ear-rings and nose-rings.

13.7 ARABIC IN MIGRATION

No survey of the role of Arabic in the world would be complete without at least a brief reference to the large numbers of speakers of Arabic who emigrated to other parts of the world. From the earliest times, speakers of Arabic left their home countries and migrated to other countries, where they settled down and found a new livelihood in an environment where a different language was spoken. In the case of the historical Islamic conquest, they imposed their language on the population of their new countries, and these countries became part of the Arabic-speaking world. But in some cases Arabic became a minority language. A few instances of such a situation have already been mentioned above, namely the linguistic enclaves in Cyprus, Uzbekistan and Anatolia. But on a massive scale, this phenomenon occurred in modern times in those Western countries to which a considerable number of speakers of Arabic have migrated in the recent past, for instance, the migration of Lebanese to the USA and to Latin America, and the migration of Moroccans and Algerians to the countries of Western Europe (France, Britain, Belgium, the Netherlands and Germany).

Obviously, the migration as such had a tremendous psychological and sociological effect on the people involved. Here, we shall confine ourselves to the linguistic effects on the language of the migrants, which may be divided into two categories. On the one hand, the migrants found themselves in a situation in which they had to learn the dominant language of their new country, which threatened the survival of their own home language. On the other hand, even if they continued to speak their language of origin, their speech habits could not escape the influence of the surrounding language.

The two groups mentioned above, the migrants from Lebanon and those from the Maghreb countries, went through a different development, because of the difference in environment and even more because of the difference in make-up of the groups involved: the Lebanese mostly belonged to a relatively well-educated layer of society and found new jobs in trading and middle-class occupations, whereas most migrants from the Maghreb countries were employed in menial jobs or in industry. Moreover, the two waves of migration belong to different periods. The high tide of Lebanese migration to America took place in the nineteenth century and the first half of the twentieth century, whereas the migration from the Maghreb countries to Western Europe is a phenomenon of the 1960s and 1970s.

The situation of the Arab migrants in Latin America is relatively prosperous. Most of them work in the commercial sector, and all are fluent in Brazilian Portuguese or Spanish. Because they worked mostly in trading, they had to integrate quickly into the society and worked in close contact with Brazilians and Argentinians. Most members of the immigrant community have retained the use of Arabic dialect, and there is even a small amount of literary activity in Standard Arabic. Newcomers from Lebanon are incorporated into the community. The close trade relations between the Lebanese and the local population may be the explanation of the fact that their language contains a large number of loanwords from Brazilian Portuguese or Spanish, mostly in the domains of work and occupation, but also in the domain of family relationships (cf. Nabhan 1994):

> *sàbàt*, pl. *sàbàbīt* 'shoes' (Port. *sapato*)
> *ībrigadu* 'employee' (Port. *empregado*)
> *vẽdedor* 'salesman' (Port. *vendedor*)
> *fàbraka* 'factory' (Port. *fábrica*)
> *bi-l-atakado* 'wholesale' (Port. *no atacado*)
> *brimu*, *brima* 'cousin' (Port. *primo, prima*)

and even a few verbs, such as

> *nawmar*, *bi-nawmir* 'to go on a date' (Port. *namorar*)
> *kawbar*, *bi-kawbir* 'to charge' (Port. *cobrar*)
> *vayaž*, *bi-vayež* 'to travel' (Port. *viajar*)

Since almost all migrants in Latin America are literate and belong to the educated part of the population, their situation is radically different from that of the migrants in Western Europe, who usually derived from rural regions, had no education and worked as unskilled manual labourers. Earlier research on the linguistic situation of Arab migrants in Western Europe concentrated almost exclusively on their acquisition of the new language. Applied linguists tried to find out which problems the migrants faced in the acquisition of their second language in order to help improve the teaching methods for this special group of learners. This type of research is less relevant for the history of the Arabic language.

In more recent studies, the migrant languages themselves are the focus of interest. Two basic fields of study may be distinguished, that of language loss and that of language mixing or code-switching. Language loss or language attrition refers to a general reduction in the proficiency of the speakers of the language. Immigrants often complain about the quality of the language of their children who were raised in the new country and speak their new language more fluently than the language of their parents. Second-generation children tend to code-switch a lot in their daily conversation, so that it is quite unnatural for them to engage in pure Arabic speech. It is questionable whether they ever possessed the features that they are supposed to have lost. Because of the relatively limited amount of exposure to the language of their parents, it is more likely that they never acquired these features completely. One might say therefore that their language is undergoing a process of shift, because it has lost the traditional domains in which it used to be spoken. For most immigrants in the Netherlands, Moroccan Arabic has been reduced to the status of a home language, and for the children of the third generation Dutch is encroaching even there upon the domain of Moroccan. At the receptive level, immigrant children continue to be able to communicate with their family in Moroccan Arabic. But at the productive level there is a marked inability to produce the correct forms. In a recent study of language loss among Moroccan adolescents in the Netherlands, El Aissati (1996) reports that their phonology is affected to such a degree that informants say things like *kbət* instead of *qbəṭ* 'he caught', *ḍaġṣa* instead of *ḍaṛṣa* 'tooth', or *msa, saf* instead of *mša* 'he went', *šaf* 'he saw', showing substitution of marked phonemes /q/, /ṛ/, /ṭ/, /š/ by unmarked /k/, /ġ/, /t/, /s/. They also fail to produce the correct plural patterns for such common words as *təʿləb*/*tʿaləb* 'fox', *qəṭṭ*/*qṭuṭ* 'cat', *ḥmar*/*ḥmir* 'donkey', resorting instead to general strategies of plural formation, e.g. *qiṭin*, *ḥmarin*, or completely garbled forms such as *təʿblitat*. One informant consistently used Dutch plural endings, producing forms such as *təʿləbs*, *qəṭṭs*, and *ḥmars*. When forced to speak Moroccan Arabic without code-switching, these adolescents frequently have to pause, searching for words, and their speech is marked by a simplified lexicon and sentence structure.

The process of language shift may partially be countered by the fact that the governments of the Western European countries developed a new policy towards the linguistic minorities in their countries, which involved the right of these minorities to be taught and educated in their 'own' language. In countries such as Sweden and the Netherlands, this right was realised by the large-scale establishment of a curriculum for Arabic in primary and secondary schools. A specific problem in the case of Moroccan immigrants is the fact that a large majority of them are Berber-speaking, so that it is not immediately obvious which language they should be instructed in. Besides, the issue of whether the high variety of the language (Modern Standard Arabic) or the vernacular should be the focus of instruction has not yet been solved.

For many of the immigrants' children, code-switching has become a normal mode of speech, somewhat like the *Franco-Arabe* that was mentioned above (Chapter 12); in some countries, one might even say that it constitutes a more or less institutionalised variety in the speech community of the immigrants, as in the case of the Beur-Arabic in France. In general, whenever languages of different status meet within one speech community, such patterns are bound to arise. Within this mode of speaking, switching between the two languages takes place not only between sentences (intersentential code-switching), but also within sentences (intrasentential code-switching). Such switches can occur at many syntactic positions, for instance between verb and object, as in *žib-liya / een glas water* 'bring me / a glass of water', or between verb and subject, as in *hna ka-ysəknu / zowel marokkanen als nederlanders* 'there are living here / both Moroccans and Dutchmen'. Switches can also occur before prepositional phrases, as in *u-təẖruž mʿa-hŭm / naar de stad* 'and you go with them / to the city', or even within a noun phrase, as in *bezzaf / moeilijkheden* 'many / difficulties', *f-/ zelfde tijd* 'at / the same time', *ši / informatie* 'some / information' (examples of Dutch/Moroccan code-switching from Nortier 1989: 124–40).

In recent models of code-switching, such as the one proposed by Myers-Scotton (1993), a distinction is made between the matrix language, which provides the function words of the message, and the embedded language, which provides the content words. The structure of the languages involved plays an important role in the solutions that speakers invent for the conflict between the two different grammars involved in the code-switching. French/Moroccan code-switching, for instance, differs in some respects from Dutch/Moroccan code-switching. When French items are used in a Moroccan matrix, either the French article is retained or an Arabic article is used, as in the examples noted by Nortier (1994) *dak la chemise* 'that shirt', *waḥəd l-paysage* 'a landscape', in which the rules of Arabic grammar require the use of an article after the demonstrative *dak* or the indefinite article *waḥəd* (cf. above, Chapter 12, p. 207). Likewise, Arabic articles are often retained when Arabic is used in another matrix (cf. the case of the Arabic loanwords in European languages: cf. below, Chapter 14). When Dutch and Moroccan are mixed in code-switching, however, the article is omitted, and one frequently hears combinations such as *dak opleiding* 'that education' or *waḥəd bedreiging* 'one threat'. The difference between French and Dutch in this respect suggests that the French article functions in a different way from the Dutch article, possibly because of its clitic nature.

Because of the complicated morphology of Moroccan Arabic verbal structure, not all foreign loans can be accommodated easily. We have seen above that Italian verbs were integrated completely into the structure of Maltese Arabic (cf. above, p. 210), and a similar ease of integration is reported about French loans in Moroccan and Algerian Arabic (cf. above, p. 206). Dutch verbs, on the other hand, are almost never integrated in this manner, most speakers preferring to use verbal compounds of the kind found in many languages to accommodate foreign loans. In most languages, such compounds combine a dummy verb from one language with a noun from another, in order to avoid the complicated problem of providing foreign verbs with inflection (cf. below, Chapter 14, pp. 233, 235, 237). In Dutch/Moroccan code-switching, the verb *dar/ydir* 'to do' is combined with the Dutch infinitive, for instance in *ka-tdir mʿahum voetballen* 'do you play soccer with them?', or with collocations of verb + noun, for instance *ḫəṣṣək tdirhum kans geven* 'you must give them a chance' (Boumans 1996). With such a strategy, the code-switching process is facilitated considerably.

As in most language contact situations, it is impossible to foretell what the future of Arabic in the migration will be. It is certainly not a purely linguistic matter, since political, ideological, cultural and perhaps even religious factors will determine the outcome. In the case of Latin America, a cultural community has been established that is proud of its Arabic heritage and cultivates Arabic language and literature. In such a situation, one may expect the presence of a lot of loanwords in the home language of the community, and at the same time a conscious effort to keep the two languages apart and prevent language loss of the home language. Most of the members of the community go to school and have a perfect command of the language of the host country.

In most European countries, on the other hand, it would seem that the process of language shift cannot be stopped, and, although there will always be individuals striving to preserve as much as possible the language of the old country, eventually most immigrant children will probably shift to the dominating language of the new country, even when the pressure is countered by explicit government policies. Phenomena like the frequent use of code-switching are highly unstable and likely to disappear within one generation.

In the case of the linguistic enclaves of Uzbekistan, Afghanistan, Anatolia and Cyprus mentioned at the beginning of this chapter, no policies of language preservation are available, and the minority language has no prestige whatsoever, so that it will probably die out in the near future. A possible exception is the Nubi community of Uganda, which is taking steps towards the preservation of its own language; they are aided by the relative social and political prestige of their community. In the case of Malta, the situation is, of course, completely different, since there the language has become the symbol of a recognisable national entity. Italian and more recently English have made some inroads into the domain of Maltese, but it seems that national pride is a sufficiently strong factor to counter this influence.

FURTHER READING

For Maltese, there is an extensive literature, ranging from grammars (Sutcliffe 1936) to basic courses (Aquilina 1956) and dictionaries (large dictionary by Aquilina 1987; smaller dictionaries by Busuttil 1976, 1977). In 1981, the first volume of a dialect atlas was produced by Aquilina and Isserlin (1981); there are many smaller studies on the history of the language and dialect geography by Aquilina (1970, 1976). Mifsud's (1995) study of loanwords in Maltese has already been referred to in the text. A handbook of Maltese was published by Vanhove (1993), which presents the most up-to-date description of the language. The dialect grammar of Schabert (1976) concentrates on the countryside dialects that have not gone through the development of the standardised language of Valletta. On the present sociolinguistic situation, see Mifsud and Borg (1994).

On Cypriot Maronite Arabic, almost the only source is Borg (1985). On Anatolian Arabic, see Jastrow's study of the *qəltu* dialects (Jastrow 1978, 1981); there are monographs on individual dialects, that of Daragözü by Jastrow (1973), and that of Mḥallamīye (Mardin) by Sasse (1971). A dictionary of the Anatolian Arabic dialects was produced by Vocke and Waldner (1982).

Recent fieldwork data on Uzbekistan Arabic were treated by Dereli (1997). The older literature is summarised in Fischer (1961); since then, a few articles have dealt with these dialects: Tsereteli (1970a, b); Versteegh (1984–6). Vinnikov (1962) has produced a dictionary of Uzbekistan Arabic, as well as a description of the language and the folklore of the Arabs of Bukhara (1956, 1969). Afghanistan Arabic was described summarily by Sirat (1973) and Kieffer (1980), and in somewhat more detail by Ingham (1994b). On the history of islamisation in Central Asia, see Akiner (1983).

About the varieties of Arabic in sub-Saharan Africa, see in the first place Owens (1985) and Prokosch (1986); on the variety called Turku, see Tosco and Owens (1993). A description of Nubi Arabic has been available since the unpublished dissertation of Owens (1977), but general interest in Nubi started after the first publication of a grammatical description by Heine (1982). Some publications concentrate on the history and development of Nubi and its relationship to the substratal languages (e.g. Owens 1990); others deal with the language from the point of view of general creole studies (cf. Miller 1994). On the variety of Nubi spoken in Bombo (Uganda), see Musa-Wellens (1994). Not much is known about the development of the language in the Southern Sudan (the so-called Juba Arabic), but see Mahmud (1979) and Miller (1985–6, 1987).

Although there is a large literature on both the psychological and the sociological effects of migration, there are surprisingly few linguistic studies of Arabic-speaking minorities. The linguistic situation in Brazil is treated by Nabhan (1994). For the situation in individual countries in Western Europe: France (Abu-Haidar 1994b); England (Abu-Haidar 1994a); Germany (Mehlem 1994). Compared to the literature about other countries, the literature about migrants' languages in the Netherlands is extensive: for a summary of this literature, see Extra and de Ruiter (1994). Problems of language attrition and language loss are dealt with by El Aissati and de Bot (1994) and El Aissati (1996). Dutch/Moroccan code-switching is discussed by Nortier (1989, 1994); the examples of the use of dummy verbs were taken from Boumans (1996). Early bilingualism in Moroccan children is treated by Bos and Verhoeven (1994). On the distinction between code-switching and borrowing, see, for instance, Heath (1989); many examples are in Myers-Scotton (1993).

14
Arabic as a World Language

14.1 INTRODUCTION

At a rough guess, approximately 150 million people use a variety of Arabic as their mother tongue. But the domain of Arabic does not stop at the boundaries of the Arabophone area. Throughout history, speakers of Arabic have frequently come into contact with speakers of other languages and affected their language, in its vocabulary or even in its morphosyntactic structure. In situations of contact between speakers of two languages the direction of the influence and its nature are determined by the relative prestige of both languages and by the history of their cohabitation. Wherever Arabic is spoken as a minority language in a region where another language is the prestige language, it is affected by the language of the host country, both in the so-called language islands and in the emigration (cf. above, Chapter 13). But as an international language it has affected in its turn other languages within its sphere of influence. There are two aspects to this role: Arabic as the language of trading, in particular in Africa; and Arabic as a religious language, in large parts of Africa, in Turkey, in Iran, in Pakistan, and in Malaysia and Indonesia.

In these regions, Islam was introduced as the new religion, but the language of the Arabs did not supplant the indigenous language as it had done in the central areas. Farsī (New Persian), for instance, was originally the language of one of the peripheral areas of the Sasanian empire, whose official language was Middle Persian (Pahlavi). Subordinate to Arabic during the first centuries of the Islamic conquest, Pahlavi continued to be used until the ninth century, but was supplanted by Farsī as the national language of Iran under the dynasty of the Samanids (cf. above, p. 71). In this position, it became the carrier of the religious message to the east. In Asia, the role of Arabic was restricted to that of the language of the *Qur'ān*; many Arabic loanwords in the indigenous languages, as in Urdu and Indonesian, were introduced mainly through the medium of Persian.

In all Islamic countries, the influence of Arabic is pervasive because of the highly language-specific nature of Islam. Since the Revealed book was inimitable, it could not be translated, and those who converted to Islam had to learn its language. Even when they did not learn to speak Arabic properly, they held the Arabic text of the *Qur'ān* in great awe. In all countries where Islam is a majority religion, religious instruction always involves a certain amount of instruction in Arabic. In some countries, children only learn to pronounce or write the text more or less correctly, without really understanding it. In other countries, there is a whole network of Qur'ānic schools offering instruction in Arabic. Linguistically, the presence of Arabic as a religious language is seen above all in the vocabulary, in which Arabic words abound. In many of the languages involved, two layers may be distinguished in the Arabic-based vocabulary. The first layer represents the original borrowings from the period of the Islamic expansion; these have usually been integrated completely into the lexicon of the language. The second layer consists of recent learned loanwords, which have been introduced through the scholarly elite, who aim to preserve to some degree the original Arabic pronunciation.

After the conquest of large parts of the Iberian peninsula in 711, the Arabs came into direct contact with a Romance-speaking population in Arab Spain (*al-'Andalus*), a contact which was to last until the end of the reconquest of the peninsula by the Christian kingdoms to the north in 1492. According to some scholars, during this prolonged contact the Arabic language all but replaced the native Romance of the population under their sway. A contemporary witness, the ninth-century Paulus Alvarus from Cordova, complains that the Christian youths of his time were more interested in Arabic poetry than in knowledge of Romance. According to others, Arabic never ousted Romance as a colloquial language, and even Latin may have remained in use as a cultural language. Certainly, there are traces of Romance throughout the period of Arab domination in the peninsula, but after the conquest of Toledo in 1085 by the Castilians its importance declined in those areas that remained in Arab hands, especially after the invasions of the Almoravids and the Almohads in the twelfth century. Yet, throughout the period of Islamic domination, there must have subsisted a considerable degree of bilingualism. The poets of *zağal*, such as Ibn Quzmān (d. 1160) used dialect and in the *muwaššaḥa*s we even find Romance in the refrains (*jarchas*; Arabic *ḫarğa*) in the same way that poets of this genre in the east used the vernacular to close their poems. In the following instance of such a *jarcha*, colloquial Arabic and Romance are mixed for stylistic reasons (Zwartjes 1995: 224):

> *álba díya esta díya / díya d-al-ʿanṣara ḥáqqa*
> *bestiréy mew al-mudabbáğ / wa-nišúqq ar-rumḥa šáqqa*
> 'A white day is this day / the day of Saint John, indeed'
> 'I shall put on my brocade dress / and break the lance'

The local dialect of the petty kingdom of Granada, which survived until the end of the *Reconquista* in 1492, contained a large number of Romance loans, as we know from the description of Pedro de Alcalá, who lists in his vocabulary of 1505 words like *xintilla* 'spark' (Spanish *centella*), *banq*, plural *bunúq* 'couch' (Spanish *banco*), *cornéja* 'crow' (Spanish *corneja*), with Arabic plural *caránic̦* and diminutive *coráyneja*.

The Arabs called the Romance dialect *lisān al-ʿAğam* or *ʿAğamiyya* 'language of the foreigners, non-Arabs' and the assimilated bilingual speakers *mustaʿribūn* 'those who have become like Arabs' (hence their name in Spanish, *Mozárabes*). When these people wrote down their own Romance language, they used the Arabic script; the literature in which their dialect has been preserved is often called *aljamiado* (< *al-ʿağamiyya*). There is another corpus of texts in Romance in Arabic script, the literature of the *Moriscos*, the Muslims who stayed behind after the *Reconquista* and compulsorily converted to Christianity in 1525 until their expulsion from the peninsula. Their use of the Arabic script does not mean that they knew Arabic: almost certainly some of them were monolingual in Romance.

The centuries of Arabic linguistic domination did not fail to affect the Romance language. The total number of Arabic loanwords in Spanish has been estimated at around 4,000; they cover almost the entire lexicon but are particularly numerous in the domains of warfare (*alcázar* 'fortress' < Arabic *qaṣr*, *almirante* 'admiral' < Arabic *'amīr*), agriculture (*albaricoque* 'apricot' < Arabic *barqūqa*, itself from Greek *praikokkia* < Latin *praecoquum*), commerce (*aduana* 'customs' < Arabic *dīwān*, *almacén* 'warehouse' < Arabic *maẖzan*) and building (*albañil* 'mason' < Arabic *bannā'*). The majority of the loans are nouns, most of them borrowed together with the Arabic article *al-*, but there are some adjectives of Arabic origin (e.g. *mezquino* < Arabic *miskīn* 'poor', *gandul* 'lazy' < Arabic *ġandūr* 'dandy', *azul* 'blue' < Arabic *lāzūrd* 'lapis lazuli'). There are even a few verbs that were borrowed from Arabic such as *halagar* 'to caress' (< Arabic *ḥalaqa* 'to shave'). The two Spanish words for 'so-and-so' are of Arabic origin, *fulano* (< Arabic *fulān*) and *mengano* (< Arabic *man kāna* 'who was it?'), and the Spanish interjection *ojalá* 'may God will' derives from the Arabic *wašallāh*. There is one example of a suffix, *-í*, that became moderately productive in Spanish; it occurs in the loanwords *baladí* 'insignificant' (< Arabic *baladī* 'rural'), but is also used in Spanish words such as *alfonsí* 'belonging to king Alfonso'. There is, however, little evidence of syntactic influence of Arabic in Spanish. Perhaps the conjunction *hasta* 'even, until' was taken from Arabic *ḥattā*. Semantically, Arabic influence may be seen in the large number of Spanish expressions containing God's name.

From Spain, a large amount of Arabic words were transmitted to other countries in Western Europe. We have seen above (Chapter 1, p. 2) that during the Middle Ages Arabic was regarded as the language of scholarship, not only in *al-'Andalus*, but also in the universities of Western Europe. After the fall of Toledo, many Arabic texts on mathematics, medicine, alchemy and astronomy were translated into Latin, and in the process a host of Arabic technical terms were borrowed in their original form. In mathematics, for instance, most European languages took over the word *algorithm*, derived from the name of al-H̱wārizmī, whose book *al-Ğabr wa-l-muqābala* 'Restoration and comparison' lived on in the term *algebra*. In astronomy, terms such as *almanac* (< *al-manāẖ* 'station of the Zodiac'), *azimuth* (< *as-samt* 'course, direction'), *zenith* (< *samt ar-ra's* 'vertical point in heaven'), *nadir* (< *naḏ̣īr* 'opposite'), and the names of many stars, such as *Betelgeuse* and *Aldebaran*, derive from Arabic. In medicine, many of the Latin terms that are still current are calques of Arabic terms that ultimately go back to Greek sources; thus, for instance, *retina* and *cornea* are translations of the Arabic words *šabakiyya* and *qarniyya*, rather than direct translations of the Greek terms.

Spain, however, was not the only source of Arabic loans in the European languages. There were other routes through which they could reach Europe, primarily through Italy, either via Arab Sicily, or via Venetian and Genoan traders. In some cases, the phonetic form of the word betrays its Spanish or Italian provenance. The italianised loans were usually taken over without the article, whereas Arabic loans in Spanish were often borrowed together with the Arabic article. Compare, for instance, the pairs Italian *carciofo* (North Italian *articiocco*)/Spanish *alcachofa* 'artichoke' (< Arabic *ẖaršūf*); *cotone*/*algodón* 'cotton' (< Arabic *quṭn*); *zucchero*/*azúcar* 'sugar' (< Arabic *sukkar*). In these three examples, the other European languages took the word from Italian.

14.2 ARABIC IN AFRICA

Arabic as a mother tongue is widespread in Africa, not only in the Maghreb and Egypt but also in the sub-Saharan areas and in East Africa. Leaving aside the special case of the Nubi in Uganda and Kenya (cf. p. 218), Arabic is the native language of many people in Sudan and Chad and of sizeable minorities in Nigeria and Niger. Even in those areas where Arabic never replaced the indigenous languages, it left behind a substantial heritage through the trading networks which the Arabs established all over the continent. The expansion of Islam brought many of the cultures in the northern half of the continent under the Islamic sphere of influence, which resulted in hundreds of loanwords in the domains of religion, culture and science.

The main expansion of Islam and Arabic in Africa took place along two routes of exploration and exploitation. One route followed the Nile to the Sudan, and from there went westwards along the savannah belt between the Sahara desert and the forest, through the region called by the Arabs the *bilād as-Sūdān* 'land of the Blacks'. The other route followed the Saharan trails to the south. The expansion of the Arabs along the savannah belt brought them in touch with Hausa-speaking people. Hausa, commonly regarded as a subgroup of the Afro-Asiatic languages, had spread from its main centres in Niger and Nigeria as a *lingua franca* over large parts of Central Africa. The history of the relations between the Arabs and the Hausa is reflected in the structure of the Arabic loanwords in their language. The oldest groups of loans is integrated completely into the structure of the language, with extensive adaptation to the phonology. Arabic /b/ is represented by /f/ (e.g. *littaafìi*, plural *lìttàtàafay* 'book' < Arabic *kitāb*), most of the gutturals have disappeared (e.g. *làabaarìi*, plural *làabàaruu* 'news' < Arabic plural *'aẖbār*; *maalàmii*, plural *maalàmaa* 'learned man' < Arabic *mu'allim*). The examples given here also demonstrate that the early loans from Arabic almost always contain the Arabic article and have been provided with a Hausa plural. The recent loans from Arabic are all in the domain of religion or Islamic sciences and represent a much closer approximation of the original form, for instance *nahawù* 'grammar' (< Arabic *naḥw*). If they contain an Arabic article, it has the form *'al* instead of colloquial *il-*, *l-*, *li-*, e.g. *àḷaadàa* 'custom' (< Arabic *'āda*), *àlhajìi* 'pilgrim' (< Arabic *ḥāǧǧī*), *àlbarkàa* 'blessing' (< Arabic *baraka*). There is a tendency among the religious learned men to pronounce even the older loans in an arabicised way, for instance by replacing /d/ deriving from Arabic /d̲/ with /z/.

Most of the Arabic loans in Hausa are substantives, but there are also a few Arabic conjunctions, such as *in*, *ìdan* 'if' (< Arabic *'in*, *'id̲an*), *sabòo dà* 'because' (< Arabic *sabab* 'reason' + Hausa *dà*) and *lookàcii dà* 'when' (< Arabic *al-waqt* 'time' + Hausa *dà*). In spite of the large difference between the two morphological systems, some Arabic verbs have been borrowed and integrated completely, e.g. *halàkaa* 'to destroy' (< Arabic *halaka*), *sàllamàa* 'to greet' (< Arabic *sallama*). Another way of integrating verbal notions in Hausa is by means of verbo-nominal compounds with the help of the verb *yi* 'to do', e.g. *yi kàráatuu* 'to read' (< Arabic *qirā'a* 'reading').

On the east coast of Africa, traders from South Arabia and Oman established contact with Swahili-speaking coast-dwellers. The name 'Swahili' derives from the Arabic word *sawāḥil* 'coasts' and was applied by the traders to those speakers of Bantu languages who came from the west to the east coast of Africa, settling there around the year 1000 CE between Somalia and Mozambique, in approximately the same period when the expanding Islamic traders arrived. Along the coast, a series of settlements and city states were established in which commercial transactions between the traders and the Bantus took place. The ʿUmānī dynasty of Zanzibar, who came to control the area from the seventeenth century onwards, stimulated the Swahili traders to go looking for ivory and slaves in the interior, and this resulted in a wave of expansion of Swahili in the nineteenth century to as far west as Zaïre.

The intensive contacts between Arabo-Islamic culture and Swahili culture led to the development of a literary tradition in Swahili, whose earliest documents go back to the twelfth century. The language was written in Arabic characters and served as the medium for a large religious and secular literature, especially in Zanzibar. During the colonial period, English influence partially replaced that of Arabic. There used to be a certain tension between the original native speakers of Swahili on the coast, who were Muslims and favoured Arabic as a source language for cultural and linguistic borrowings, and the inhabitants of the interior, for whom Swahili was only a vehicular language and who usually were not Muslims. The latter resented the ʿUmānī domination of the recent past and resisted Arabic influence, turning instead to English. After the Heligoland Treaty of 1890 when the sultanate of Zanzibar became a British protectorate, Arabic was replaced here and in the rest of East Africa in many domains by English and Swahili. In Zanzibar itself, Arabic remained the first official language up to the republican revolution of 1964, and even after that it continued to play a considerable role in education. In the rest of East Africa (Kenya, Tanzania, Uganda), in spite of the fact that on average half of the population is Muslim, knowledge of Arabic remains usually restricted to Qur'ānic teaching in the so-called *chuo* (plural *vyuo*) schools, and hardly anybody has any active knowledge of the language.

With the disappearance of the old-fashioned religious and cultural aristocracy, the influx of Arabic words more or less ceased. In recent times, however, there has been a renewed tendency in Tanzania and Kenya, where Swahili has become the national language, to replace English loans with words of Arabic origin; in most cases, these words already existed as alternatives and were regarded by the speakers as Swahili, e.g. *ripoti* is replaced with *taarifu* 'report', *korti* with *mahakama* 'court', *jaji* with *hakimu* 'judge', especially in scientific terminology (e.g. *elimunafsi* has become more current than the English *saikolojia*, *elimujamii* more current than the English *sosholojia*). The use of the Arabic script for Swahili has been abandoned, however, and only elderly people use it infrequently in private correspondence and religious instruction. The only country where Arabic has remained a national language is the tiny Islamic Federal Republic of Comoro, that recognises both Arabic and the local language

Shingazija (written in Arabic script) as national languages.

According to the dictionaries, approximately 50 per cent of the vocabulary of Swahili derives etymologically from Arabic. In modern journalistic Swahili, this drops to 30 per cent and in the colloquial language it is even less. The influence of Arabic has spread to many domains of the lexicon, foremost among them, of course, religion, but also law, politics, economy and trade, education and sciences. One example may suffice to show the dependence of the language on Arabic in the choice of abstract words: to express the notion of 'estimating, calculating, thinking', Swahili uses no fewer than four Arabic words, *kisi* 'to estimate, calculate' (Arabic *qāsa*), *fikiri* 'to think, reflect' (Arabic *fakara*), *kadiri* 'reckon, judge' (Arabic *qaddara*) and *hesabu* 'count, calculate' (Arabic *ḥasiba*), alongside a word derived from Persian, *bahatisha* 'to guess, speculate', and a Bantu word *pima* 'to measure'.

The degree of integration of Arabic loans in the structure of Swahili is high. Thus, we find for instance from the Arabic words *ʿilm* 'science, knowledge' and *muʿallim* 'teacher' the following Swahili derivatives"

> *elimu* 'science, education'
> *mwalimu*/plural *walimu* 'professor'
> *mtaalamu*/plural *wataalamu* 'scholar'
> *utaalamu* 'culture, erudition'
> *-taalamu* 'learned'
> *kutaalamu* 'to be specialised in'
> *kuelimisha* 'to teach, instruct'.

These derivatives show that the derivation goes across categories, and one Arabic noun may be used as point of departure for other nouns, adjectives and derived verbs. The example of *mwalimu/walimu* shows that Arabic words are integrated in the morphological pattern of Swahili plurals. In this case, the Arabic *mu-* in *muʿallim* is treated as the Swahili prefix of the first class of nouns, hence the plural with *wa-*; similarly *kitabu*/plural *vitabu*, on the pattern of the Swahili third nominal class (cf. *kitu*/plural *vitu* 'thing'). Arabic is also the source for many of the conjunctions and prepositions of Swahili, e.g. *kama* 'as', *kabla* 'before', *baada* 'after', *baina* 'between', *lakini* 'but', *wala* 'nor', *au* 'or', *zaidi* 'plus', *karibu* 'almost', and so on.

As in most African languages that came into contact with Arab traders, some of the numerals in Swahili were borrowed from Arabic: *situ* 'six' (< *sitta*), *saba* 'seven' (< *sabʿa*), *tisa* 'nine' (< *tisʿa*), and all decimals (e.g. *ishirini* 'twenty' < *ʿišrīna*, *arobaini* 'forty' < *'arbaʿīna*). But note that for 'eight' a Bantu word is used, *nane*, as for the numerals one to five (*moja*, *mbili*, *tatu*, *nne*, *tano*) and the word for 'ten' (*kumi*).

Even when contact with the Arabs was less intensive, linguistic borrowing took place on a large scale, as for instance in the Ful languages, spoken in a large area from Guinea to Chad. The approximately 550 vocabulary items derived from Arabic are almost all connected with Islam and trade and have been integrated to a large degree. One finds, for instance, for 'onion' *albasal* (< Arabic *baṣal* with the article). The final syllable of the word *-al* was interpreted as a Ful classifier as in the Ful word *lisal* 'branch', on whose plural *licce* the plural of *albasal* is built, *albacce*. Other loanwords were provided with a Ful classifier, e.g. *ḥarf* 'letter' > *harfeere*/plural *karfeeje*, or *dunyā* > *dunyaaru*/plural *duuniyaaru*. In some cases this led to virtual unrecognisability, for instance in *ḫinzīr* 'swine' > *hinjiiru*/plural *kinjiiji*. As in other African cultures, the contact with Islam led to the emergence of an intellectual and religious elite of scholars, who became well versed in Classical Arabic and wrote commentaries in Ful on Arabic religious texts. Their familiarity with Arabic manifests itself in a tendency to arabicise the pronunciation of Arabic loans, e.g. *ḏikru* instead of the popular *jikru*, or *zamaan* instead of the usual *jamanu*, *jamaanu*, *jamanuuru*.

A special case is that of Arabic influence in the Austronesian language Malagassy, the official language of Madagascar. Trading contacts with Arab traders go back several centuries, but it seems that the loanwords from Arabic in general use are restricted to the domain of astrology (called *alikilili* < Arabic *al-'iklīl* 'the head of Scorpio'). Still, there must have existed a literate tradition connected with Arabic, since in the south-west of Madagascar several clans still use a secret vocabulary of Arabic words (e.g. *maratsi* 'woman', Arabic *mar'a*, instead of usual Malagassy *vehivàvi*, or *dzoma* 'day', Arabic *yawm*, instead of usual *andru*). These clans still write Malagassy texts in a modified form of the Arabic script.

14.3 ARABIC IN IRAN

In the early centuries of Arab domination after the fall of the Sasanian empire, Arabic became both the dominant and the prestigious language of the Persian provinces. This situation changed with political developments (see Chapter 5): New Persian (Farsī) became the national language of the 'Abbāsid successor states in eastern Iran and Central Asia, but Classical Arabic retained its position as the language of the *Qur'ān*. At the present time, there is one province of Iran, Khuzestan, where Arabic is still spoken by an Arab minority (cf. above, Chapter 10, p. 158). Strangely enough, the Iranian authorities do not seem to find any contradiction between their treatment of the Arabic-speaking minority, who are not encouraged to cultivate their ethnic and linguistic background, on the one hand, and their reverence for Arabic as the language of the Holy Book, on the other.

From the beginning, contacts between Arabic and Persian were intensive. The amount of Persian loanwords in Arabic is considerable (cf. above, p. 62). Conversely, of all the languages with which Arabic came into contact, Persian is the one that was most influenced by this process. The number of Arabic loanwords is enormous, not only in the literary language, but even in everyday speech. From time to time there have been trends to de-arabicise Persian vocabulary, sometimes for political reasons; but the Arabic component of the language is so deeply rooted that it would be impossible to eradicate it completely.

Persian is written with the Arabic alphabet, with the addition of four letters (*p*, *č*, *ž*, *g*). Since a number of Arabic phonemes merged in the process of borrowing, the script has become ambiguous: Arabic /ṯ/, /s/, /ṣ/ are pronounced as /s/; Arabic /t/ and /ṭ/ as /t/; Arabic /ḏ/, /z/, /ḍ/ and /ḏ̣/ as /z/; Arabic /ġ/ and /q/ as /ġ/; Arabic /'/ and /'/ as /'/; and Arabic /ḥ/ and /h/ as /h/. All Arabic loans are written, however, according to Arabic orthography, which places an extra burden on Persian children learning to write.

Most of the Arabic loans are abstract words, in particular in the domains of religion, science, scholarship and literature. The full impact of Arabic can be seen especially in the morphology of these words: in many cases, Arabic words retain their original plural endings, e.g.

> *mo'allem/mo'allemin* 'teacher' (Arabic *muʿallim*)
> *mosāfer/mosāferin* 'passenger, traveller' (Arabic *musāfir*)
> *eǧtemā'i/eǧtema'iyūn* 'socialist' (Arabic *iǧtimāʿī*)
> *daraǧe/daraǧāt* 'degree' (Arabic *daraǧa*)
> *maġāle/maġālāt* 'article' (Arabic *maqāla*)
> *hejvān/hejvānāt* 'animal' (Arabic *ḥayawān*)

The plural ending *-āt* was applied even to words that were not of Arabic origin, e.g. *deh/dehāt* 'village' (the plural means 'country'), *mive/miveǧāt* 'fruit'. Broken plurals were often taken over together with their singular, e.g.

> *vaġt/'ouġāt* 'time' (Arabic *waqt*)
> *hāl/'ahwāl* 'situation' (Arabic *ḥāl*)
> *ġazā/'aġziye* 'food' (Arabic *ġaḏā'*)

In Modern Persian, it is quite common, however, to abandon the broken plural and supply the word with a Persian plural ending, e.g. *ẖabar-hā* 'news' alongside *'aẖbār* (Arabic *ẖabar/'aẖbār*), or *ketāb-hā* 'books' alongside *kotob* (Arabic *kitāb/kutub*). In some words, the broken plural is treated as a singular, e.g. *'arbāb* 'master' (Arabic *'arbāb*, plural of *rabb*), which may obtain a Persian plural ending, *'arbāb-hā* 'masters'.

The verbal morphology of Arabic is even less suited than its nominal morphology to integrate into the structure of Persian. Therefore, verbo-nominal compounds are used as a periphrastic device to avoid the need to inflect the Arabic loans. Most compounds contain the dummy verbs *kardan* 'to do' and *šodan* 'to become' in combination with Arabic verbal nouns, participles or adjectives. Examples abound:

> *mokātabe kardan* 'to correspond', lit. 'to make correspondence' (Arabic *mukātaba*)
> *ta'lim kardan* 'to teach', lit. 'to make instruction' (Arabic *taʿlīm*)
> *fekr kardan* 'to think', lit. 'to make thought' (Arabic *fikr*)
> *harakat kardan* 'to set out', lit. 'to make movement' (Arabic *ḥaraka*)
> *sabr kardan* 'to wait', lit. 'to make patience' (Arabic *ṣabr*)
> *maġlūb kardan* 'to defeat', lit. 'to make defeated' (Arabic *maġlūb*)

There is a regular correspondence between active compounds with *kardan* and passive with *šodan*:

> *'e'lam kardan* 'to announce'/*'e'lam šodan* 'to be announced' (Arabic *'iʿlām*)
> *razi kardan* 'to satisfy'/*razi šodan* 'to be satisfied' (Arabic *rāḍī*)
> *'asir kardan* 'to take prisoner'/*'asir šodan* 'to be taken prisoner' (Arabic *'asīr*)

When these compounds are connected with pronominal objects, the suffix is added to the nominal part of the compound, e.g. *ẖabar-ešan kard* 'he informed them', lit. 'he made their news'.

There is extensive borrowing even in the case of prepositions, often compounded with a Persian preposition, for instance *ba'd 'az* 'after' (Arabic *ba'da* + Persian *'az*), *bar lahe* 'for' (Persian *bar* + Arabic *lahu* 'for him') and *bar 'aleh* 'against' (Persian *bar* + Arabic *'alayhi* 'against him'), e.g. *qazi bar lahe u hokm dad* 'the judge made a judgment in his favour'. Many conjunctions in Persian are formed with Arabic words, e.g. *vaġtike* 'when' (Arabic *waqt* 'time'), *mādāmike* 'as long as' (Arabic *mā dāma*), *qabl 'az 'ānke* 'before' (Arabic *qabla*). As in other languages that have borrowed extensively from Arabic, certain indeclinable particles have been taken over as well, e.g. *hattā* 'even', *faġat* 'only', *dā'iman* 'continually', *bal* (usually with Persian suffix *keh*) 'but', *va* 'and', *'ammā* 'as for, but', *lākin* 'but'.

14.4 ARABIC IN THE OTTOMAN EMPIRE AND TURKEY

With the ascendance of the Seljuks in Anatolia, the position of Arabic as the language *par excellence* of the Islamic empire was eroded considerably. The Turkic dynasties adopted Persian as their literary language and retained Arabic only as the language of religion. In the Ottoman empire, Turkish became the official language of the state, but at the same time Persian and Arabic were maintained as the languages of culture. Collectively, the three languages were called the *elsine-i selāse* (with two Arabic words, *'alsina* and *ṯalāṯa*, and a Persian connective particle!); they constituted the cultural baggage of the intellectual elite. In the period between the fifteenth and the seventeenth centuries, the influence of the two cultural languages, Persian and Arabic, increased to such a degree that in some literary styles only the morphology and the structure of the text remained Turkish, whereas the lexical material was almost completely taken from the two other languages.

At the end of the Ottoman empire, there was an increasing tendency on the part of the Arab provinces to stress their right to linguistic autonomy, i.e. their right to use Arabic as an official language (cf. above, Chapter 11). This feeling was reinforced by the developments in the Turkish revolution. First the Young Turks and then Atatürk dissociated the notion of Islam from that of the Arabic language. In line with the secularisation of the new Turkish republic, there was to be no special place for the Arabic language, and this was formally symbolised by the abolition in 1928 of the Arabic script that had hitherto been used for the writing of Ottoman Turkish. The new emphasis on the Turkish identity brought with it a campaign to preserve or restore the purity of the Turkish language. Since the reformers regarded Turkish as the most perfect language on earth, it was inconceivable to them that its lexicon should include large quantities of Persian and Arabic words.

As a result of the language reform, many of the loanwords and constructions that were common in the Ottoman period have become obsolete, but even in modern Turkish a large number of loans from Persian and Arabic (or from Arabic through Persian) are still present. These loanwords can often be recognised because they are not subject to the strict rules of vowel harmony in Turkish, which forbid the combination of back vowels and front vowels within a word. A word such as *kitap* 'book' (< Arabic *kitāb*) with front vowel followed by back vowel does not obey the rules of vowel harmony, and a word such as *saat* 'hour' (< Arabic *sā'a*), if it were Turkish, would receive the possessive suffix *-ı*, but since it is an Arabic word it becomes *saat-i*. Certain phonetic changes take place in the process of borrowing: in the Ottoman spelling which used the Arabic script, the emphatic and pharyngal consonants of Arabic were distinguished but not pronounced. Since the spelling reform, the orthography no longer distinguishes these sounds, but follows the pronunciation (*a* often spelled as *e*; *w* as *v*; *ḥ*, *ẖ* as *h*, etc.).

Many Arabic nouns were borrowed together with their plural, so that in Ottoman Turkish it was customary to have, for instance, *hādise*, plural *havadis* (< Arabic *ḥādiṯa*/*ḥawādiṯ*) 'event', whereas in modern Turkish the plural is *hâdiseler*; likewise *akide*, plural *akait* (Arabic *'aqīda*/*'aqā'id*) 'dogma', nowadays *akideler*. Common words such as *kitap* 'book' always had a Turkish plural *kitaplar*. Some abstract nouns were borrowed in the feminine plural form, such as *edebiyat* 'literature', *tafsilât* 'details'; syntactically, these words are still treated as plurals.

Characteristic of Ottoman prose was the use of long compounds of Arabic origin, which, if they have not been abolished, remain in use as idiomatic single-word expressions, e.g. *kuvveianelmerkeziye* 'centrifugal force' (Arabic *quwwa* + *'an* + *al-markaz* + *iyya*) or *mukabeleibilmisil* 'retribution' (Arabic *muqābala* + *bi* + *al-miṯl*). In both examples, the connection between the main components of the compound word is made with the Persian suffix *-i-*, which in Persian (and in Persian loans in Turkish) indicates the genitive construction (*izāfet*). In Ottoman Turkish, these constructions were still productive, whereas in modern Turkish they have become fixed expressions. In constructions of Arabic nouns with Arabic adjectives, on the other hand, the agreement rules of Arabic are still followed, e.g. *aklı selim* (Arabic *'aql salīm*) 'common sense', but *esbabı mucibe* (Arabic *'asbāb mūğiba*) 'compelling circumstances'.

Just like Persian, Turkish has borrowed a large number of nouns that are used as postpositions. A few examples may suffice: *nisbetle* 'compared to' (Arabic *nisbatan li-*), *rağmen* 'in spite of' (Arabic *raġman*), *itibaren* 'from ... onwards' (Arabic *i'tibāran*), and even the pronominal expressions *leh* and *aleyh* (Arabic *lahu* and *'alayhi*) in the sense of 'for' and 'against', e.g. with Turkish pronominal suffixes *lehimizde* 'for us', *aleyhinde* 'against him'. Originally, Turkish did not have conjunctions, but it has borrowed the Arabic *wa-* (Turkish *ve*), presumably through Persian.

In Ottoman Turkish, the *nisba* adjective was still used in its function as an adjective; in adverbial expressions, a noun in the accusative (*ḥāl* construction) was preferred, so that *resmî* meant 'official', but *resmen* 'officially' (Arabic *rasmī*/*rasm*); likewise *zarurî* 'necessary', *zarureten* 'necessarily' (Arabic *ḍarūrī*/*ḍarūratan*). In Modern Turkish, the constructions with a *ḥāl* accusative are often replaced by the adjective with Turkish *olarak*, e.g. *resmî olarak* instead of *resmen*.

An interesting parallel between the pattern of borrowing in Persian and that in Turkish is the use of verbo-nominal compounds with the verbs *olmak* 'to be, become' and *etmek* (and synonyms) 'to do, make', e.g.:

> *sebep olmak* 'to cause' (Arabic *sabab*)
> *memnun olmak* 'to be pleased' (Arabic *mamnūn*)

refakat etmek 'to accompany' (Arabic *rafaqa*)
ziyaret etmek 'to visit' (Arabic *ziyāra*)
rica etmek 'to request' (Arabic *rağā'*)
tebdîl etmek 'to change' (Arabic *tabdīl*)

In Ottoman Turkish, such expressions were still understood as Arabic structures, so that for instance 'to change clothes' was expressed as *tebdîl-i qïyâfet etmek*, lit. 'to make a-change-of-clothes' with Persian connective *-i-*. In Modern Turkish, this would be expressed as *qïyâfeti tebdîl etmek*, lit. 'to-make-a-change clothes' (with accusative suffix *-i*), so that the syntactic tie between verb and noun has become much tighter. The passive of such constructions is made with *olunmak*, but in combinations with an Arabic infinitive of the seventh verbal measure, which has a passive meaning of itself, *etmek* is used, e.g. *intişar etmek* 'to be published' (Arabic *intišār*); the active voice is expressed by the Turkish causative: *intişar ettirmek* 'to publish'.

14.5 ARABIC IN THE INDIAN SUBCONTINENT

Contacts between the Islamic world and India go back as far as the ninth century, when Muslim traders ventured east, to India and China. The islamisation of the Indus valley took place much later, when it was conquered by the dynasty of the Ghaznavids in the eleventh century. The Ghaznavids, whose centre was Ghazna in Afghanistan, spoke Persian and, just like most dynasties in this area, used Persian as their literary language. The founder of the Mughal empire in 1526, Bābur, himself wrote in Chagatay Turkic, but at the Mughal court the literary language remained Persian, while the colloquial language was Urdu (also called Hindawī or Hindī), a Prākrit dialect from North India. Urdu had been used as the language of communication between Hindus and Muslims from the time of the Ghaznavids, and under the Mughal emperors it even became the medium of a vernacular literature. Because of the prestige of Persian, a large number of loans from that language entered Urdu during this period.

With the advent of the English, the harmonious relation between the languages, the vernacular and Persian, was disturbed, and the language question became a controversial issue. While in the western provinces the use of Urdu in Arabic/Persian characters was accepted even by Muslims, in the eastern provinces Hindus propagated the use of the same language, but under the name of Hindi, written in Devanagari characters. The matter of the script became the focus of the discussions. Eventually, Devanagari was adopted in India, and the Arabic script remained in use in Pakistan. For the representation of Urdu phonemes, a number of characters were added to the alphabet: retroflex consonants are indicated with a superscript letter *ṭ*, aspirated consonants with a following letter *h*.

With the separation between Pakistan and India, the two varieties of the language were separated, too. Urdu became the official language of Pakistan and of some Muslims in north-west India and retained its Arabic/Persian vocabulary, while Hindi became one of the two official languages of India (together with English). Hindus started a campaign to purify Hindi and replace the Arabic/Persian loans with words derived from Sanskrit. Modern literary Hindi has ousted a large part of the Persian vocabulary, but in the more colloquial registers of the language some of these words are still used.

Since the grammatical structure of Urdu and Hindi is practically identical, the difference between them is almost entirely lexical. There is a large number of synonym pairs, of which the Sanskrit word is used in literary Hindi and the Persian/Arabic word in colloquial Hindi and in Urdu, e.g. *uttar* (S.)/*javāb* (P./A.) 'answer'; *ṛtu* (S.)/*mausim* (P./A.) 'season, weather'; *ghar* (S.)/*makān* (P./A.) 'house' (Arabic 'place'); *pustak* (S.)/*kitāb* (P./A.) 'book'. It appears that all Arabic words passed through Persian before being introduced to Urdu, together with a large number of originally Persian words. This even applies to those Arabic words which were borrowed both in the singular and the plural form, e.g. *akhbār* 'newspaper' (< *'a*<u>*h*</u>*bār*, plural of Arabic <u>*h*</u>*abar* 'news'); *asbāb* 'tools, luggage' (< *'asbāb*, plural of Arabic *sabab* 'reason'). In Urdu, such plurals are usually treated as singular words. Arabic plurals in -*īn* (e.g. *hāzirīn* 'audience' < Persian < Arabic *ḥāḍirīn*) and -*āt* (e.g. *dehāt* 'villages, the countryside' < Persian *dehāt*) are distinguished from originally Urdu words in that they do not take the oblique marker -*õ*.

Just like Persian, Urdu contains a considerable number of prepositions, adverbial expressions and conjunctions taken from Arabic. It appears that in these categories, too, there was no independent borrowing from Arabic, but Persian always acted as the channel through which these words passed, e.g. *lekin* 'but', *va* 'and', *balki* 'but on the contrary' (< Arabic *bal* + Persian *keh*); *taqriban* 'approximately' (< Arabic *taqrīban*), *fauran* 'at once' (< Arabic *fawran*); *bilkul* 'entirely' (Arabic *bi-l-kull*); *barkhilāf* 'contrary to' (< Arabic <u>*h*</u>*ilāf* 'difference'), *bāvajūd* 'in spite of' (Arabic *wuǧūd* 'existence'), and so on.

In Urdu, as in Persian and Turkish, no Arabic verbs appear to have been borrowed, probably because of the morphological complexity of the Arabic verb, which prohibited morphological integration. Instead, verbo-nominal compounds are made with the help of the dummy verb *karnā* 'to do', possibly under the influence of the Persian verb *kardan* (cf. above), although similar compounds are made with Sanskrit words, e.g. *kā intazar karnā*/*kī pratīkṣā karnā* 'to wait for someone' (< Arabic *intiẓār*, verbal noun of *intaẓara* 'to wait, to expect'), *se inkār karnā* 'to refuse' (< Arabic *'inkār* 'refusal'). Passives are made with the verb *honā* 'to be, to become', e.g. *khātam honā*/*samāpt honā* 'to be finished' (< Arabic <u>*h*</u>*ātam*). Other verbs are also occasionally used, such as *denā* 'to give' (e.g. *kā javāb denā* 'to give an answer' < Arabic *ǧawāb* 'answer'), or *lenā* 'to take' (e.g. *kā badlā lenā* 'to take vengeance' < Arabic *badla* 'replacement, compensation').

The impact of Arabic and Persian on other modern Indian languages strongly correlates with the degree of islamisation which their speakers underwent. The two varieties of Bengali, spoken both in the Indian province of Bengal and in Bangladesh, formerly East Pakistan, differ considerably in their lexicon. In Bangladesh, which is predominantly Muslim, there is a growing tendency to replace older Sanskrit words with Arabic/Persian loans, especially in the domain of religion. In West Bengali, the literary language (*sādhu-bhāšā*) contains few loanwords, but in the colloquial language (*čalit-bhāšā*) some Sanskrit words have an Arabic/Persian synonym (e.g. *šǫbad* vs *khǫbor* (Arabic <u>*h*</u>*abar*) 'news', or *prakar* vs *buruǧ* (Arabic *burǧ*) 'fortress').

14.6 ARABIC IN EAST ASIA: THE INFLUENCE OF ARABIC ON MALAY AND INDONESIAN

The earliest contacts between the Islamic world and East Asia go back to the thirteenth and fourteenth centuries. The first signs of Arab presence date from this period in the form of tombstones in the Indonesian archipelago. Since the Malay language was firmly established in the Malayan peninsula and as a *lingua franca* in the Indonesian islands, Arabic was unable to gain the same position that it had obtained in the lands of the Middle East and North Africa, but there can be no doubt that as the language of the *Qur'ān* and Islam it exercised an enormous influence. This influence manifests itself in the use of Arabic loanwords in Malay and its modern offshoot Bahasa Indonesia, the national language of Indonesia; furthermore, in the use of Arabic script for the Malay language; and finally, in the use of Arabic as the religious language of most people.

The first preserved inscription in Arabic script dates from the fourteenth century, a legal edict that was found in Trengganu in the Malay peninsula, written in the variety of Arabic script that became known as Jawi. It is an adaptation of the Arabic alphabet with special additional signs for *c, g, ng, ny, p* and *v*, that was used in manuscripts from the sixteenth century onwards. In Indonesia, this script remained in use until the twentieth century, when it was replaced by a Latin orthography during the period of the Dutch administration in Indonesia.

The Indonesian Muslim community is the largest community of Muslims outside the Arab world. The vast majority of the population of about 160 million people are Muslims and regard Arabic as the holy language of their religion. It is therefore not surprising that the position of Arabic as a religious language is unshaken. Most Indonesians have a rudimentary knowledge of Arabic because of their Qur'ānic training. The secular curriculum, however, does not do very much to improve this knowledge, and, in spite of periodic attempts by the authorities to improve the level of Arabic, it is largely left to the so-called *pesantren* schools to train those who wish to learn in Arabic. The *pesantren* system has been very successful in setting up a religious curriculum on the pattern of the so-called 'Meccan' model, i.e. traditional transmission of texts with *'iǧāza* 'licence to transmit' and on the whole passive knowledge of the written language.

The number of words from Arabic in modern Indonesian is considerable; according to some estimates, at least 3,000 words may be traced back to an Arabic original. Naturally, many of these words are connected to religion, but there are Arabic loans all over the lexicon in such domains as politics, philosophy, zoology and botany, medicine, education and science. Many or most of the loans have probably come through the medium of Persian, as in the case of Urdu. In some cases, the exact provenance is still visible in the form of the word. Thus the word *hajam* 'indigestion' cannot have come directly from Arabic *haḍm* (since that would have resulted in **hadam*), but must have been taken from the Persian form of the word, *haẓm*. Just like in Persian, many Arabic feminine words were taken over with the ending *-at*, for instance *nasihat* (Arabic *naṣīḥa* 'advice', Persian *nasihat*).

The Indonesian words going back to Arabic range from complete expressions (e.g. *silaturahmi* 'friendship') to borrowed suffixes (e.g. the suffix *-i*/*-iah* which occurs in words of Arabic origin such as *abadi* 'eternal', *alami* 'natural', *ilmiah* 'scientific', but also in neologisms such as *gerejawi* 'church-' from Portuguese *gereja* 'church'). Some of the complete expressions that were borrowed may have belonged to a written tradition, since they retain the article in its unassimilated form, as in writing, e.g. *ahlulnujum* 'astrologers' (< Arabic *'ahl an-nuǧūm*) or *aldubul akbar* 'Great Bear' (< Arabic *ad-dubb al-'akbar*). Those expressions in which the article is assimilated probably belong to the spoken language, e.g. *ahlussunnah* 'people of the Sunna'.

Phonetically, the following developments may be noted. Arabic /ʿ/ and /'/ have merged in Indonesian borrowings, as in Persian, through which most of the Arabic words reached Indonesian. Both phonemes are pronounced with a glottal stop, represented in modern orthography by either ', or at the end of the syllable by *k* (pronounced '), as in *maklum* (Arabic *maʿlūm* 'known'), *iklan* (Arabic *'iʿlān* 'announcement'). Arabic /f/ is usually represented by *p*, e.g. *palak* 'celestial sphere' < Arabic *falak*; for such words, there is usually a learned variant with the 'correct' *f*. In a number of loans, Arabic /ḍ/ is represented by *l* or *dl*. Thus, for instance, the Arabic word *ʿaraḍ* 'obstacle' has become *aral* in Indonesian, *ḥāḍir* 'present' is *hadlir*, and *qāḍī* 'judge' is variably spelled as *kadi* or *kadli*. It is not certain whether this spelling renders an originally lateral pronunciation of the *ḍād*; we have seen (cf. above, p. 89) that in other languages, too, the *ḍād* is sometimes represented by a lateral phoneme.

Most of the loanwords are nouns, but just like Swahili the Indonesian language exhibits a remarkable ability to assimilate Arabic loanwords morphologically with the help of its many prefixes and suffixes. Thus we have from Arabic *'inkār* 'denial' the noun *ingkar*, but also the verb *mengingkari* 'to deny the truth', and from Arabic *ḥukm* 'judgment' the noun *hukum*, but also the verb *menghukumkan* 'to pronounce judgment'. Nominal compounds are also used, as for instance from *perlu* 'necessary' (< Arabic *farḍ*) *keperluan* 'need'. Abstract nouns are formed with the prefix *tata-*, e.g. *tata-hukum* 'legal order', *tata-kalimat* 'syntax' (< Arabic *kalima* 'word'). A few Arabic words may be regarded as roots themselves, for instance *fikir/pikir* 'to think'.

An interesting phenomenon in modern Indonesian is the coexistence of two variants of the same original, e.g. *fikir/pikir*, both derived from Arabic *fikra* 'opinion, thought', or *kadi/kadli*, both from Arabic *qāḍī* 'judge'. In the case of the Arabic word *farḍ* there are two common derivates, *perlu* meaning 'necessary', and the more official word *fard* 'obligatory [often in a religious sense]'. The semantic development of Arabic loans in Indonesian often shows the prestige of Western (especially Dutch) terms: compare for instance *tabib* (< Arabic *ṭabīb* 'physician'), which has become the current term for a traditional healer, against the modern *dokter*, derived from Dutch. In other cases, just as in Swahili (cf. above, p. 231), an Arabic equivalent is preferred over the Western word that is associated with the colonial period.

FURTHER READING

On the linguistic situation in al-'Andalus, see Zwartjes (1997: 5–22) and R. Wright (1982: 151–61). On the language of the Mozarabs and the relations between Romance and Arabic, see Galmés de Fuentes (1983; Romance loans in

Pedro de Alcalá pp. 213–44; cf. also Corriente 1988). Arabic in Sicily: Agiùs (1996). Dozy and Engelmann (1869) produced a list of Arabic words in Spanish and Portuguese; for Arabic words in French, see Devic (1876); for Arabic words in English, see Cannon (1994).

A question not touched upon here is the use of the Arabic script for other languages (Persian, Kurdish, Pashto, Kashmiri, Urdu, Sindhi, Ottoman Turkish, Uyghur, Malay, Berber) and the adaptations which it underwent in the process; for these alphabets, see Kaye (1995).

On Arabic in Africa, for general information on the spread of Islam in the continent, see Fisher (1970); on influence in Swahili and the development of Arabo-Swahili culture, see Haddad (1983) and Lodhi (1986). The examples from Ful and Malagassy have been taken from a collection of articles in *Langue arabe et langues africaines* (1983); on Malagassy, see also Faublée (1974), Beaujard (1998); on Arabic in Hausa, see Greenberg (1947).

The Arabic element in Persian is traditionally treated as a separate component in the standard grammars, for instance in Lambton (1961: 181–250) and Alavi and Lorenz (1972: 167–70, 174–8, 181–3), from which the examples have been taken. On the semantics of Arabic loans in Persian, see Asbaghi (1987) and Perry (1991).

Arabic words in Ottoman Turkish are dealt with in all standard grammars of Ottoman Turkish, e.g. Kissling (1960, especially pp. 45, 67, 152f., 243f.), from whom the examples quoted here are taken; on Arabic and Persian loans in Ottoman Turkish, see Battersby (1966); on the Turkish campaign for purity of the language, see Zürcher (1985).

On the language question in the Indian subcontinent, see Kanungo (1962). The examples of loan pairs in Hindi have been taken from Pořízka (1972). On the two varieties of Bengali, see Dil (1972).

On the role of Arabic in the first Malay grammars, see Ogloblin (1981); on Arabic loans in Indonesian, see Jones (1978), from whom most of the examples were taken. A general survey on the role of Arabic in Indonesia is given by Meuleman (1994). On Arabic loanwords in Acehnese, see Al-Harbi (1991).

Not all contact situations with Arabic could be dealt with here. For the linguistic situation in Israel, see Kinberg and Talmon (1994); on the Arabic component in Hebrew slang, see Kornblueth and Aynor (1974); on language attitudes and variation in Palestinian communities see Amara (1999). On linguistic contact between Egyptian Arabic and Nubian, see Rouchdy (1991). On linguistic contacts between Arabic and Berber, see Chaker (1984). An important collection on Arabic in al-Andalus, Daghestan, Bactria, Israel, Nigeria, Turkey is Owens (2000).

BIBLIOGRAPHY

Aartun, Kjell (1963), *Zur Frage altarabischer Tempora*. Oslo: Universitetsforlaget.

Abbassi, Abdelaziz (1977), *A Sociolinguistic Analysis of Multilingualism in Morocco*. Ph.D. thesis, University of Texas.

Abbott, Nabia (1939), *The Rise of the North Arabic Script and its Kur'anic Development*. Chicago: Chicago University Press.

— (1941), 'The development of early Islamic scripts'. *AI* 8, 65–104.

— (1972), *Studies in Arabic Literary Papyri*. III. *Language and Literature*. Chicago and London: University of Chicago Press.

Abboud, Peter and Ernest McCarus (1983), *Elementary Modern Standard Arabic*, I, II. Cambridge: Cambridge University Press [orig. pub. University of Michigan, 1968].

ʿAbd al-Ǧawād, Ḥasan (1977), *Kurat al-qadam: al-Mabādiʾ al-ʾasāsiyya, al-ʾalʿāb al-ʾiʿdādiyya, al-qānūn ad-dawlī*. Beirut: Dār al-ʿIlm li-l-Malāyīn.

Abdel-Masih, Ernest, Zaki N. Abdel-Malek and El-Said M. Badawi (1978–9), *A Comprehensive Study of Egyptian Arabic*, 3 vols. Ann Arbor: University of Michigan.

Abou, Selim (1961), *Enquête sur les langues en usage au Liban*. Beirut: Imprimerie Catholique.

— (1962), *Le bilinguïsme arabe–français au Liban: essai d'anthropologie culturelle*. Paris: Presses Universitaires de France.

Abu Absi, S. (1990), 'A characterization of the language of *Iftaḥ yā Simsim*: sociolinguistic and educational implications for Arabic'. *LPLP* 14, 33–46.

Abu-Haidar, Farida (1979), *A Study of the Spoken Arabic of Baskinta*. Leiden and London: E. J. Brill.

— (1988a), 'Arabic with English: borrowing and code-switching in Iraqi Arabic'. *Abhath al-Yarmouk*, Literature and Linguistics Series 6:1, 45–58.

— (1988b), 'Speech variation in the Muslim dialect of Baghdad: urban vs. rural'. *ZAL* 19, 74–80.

— (1990), 'Maintenance and shift in the Christian Arabic of Baghdad'. *ZAL* 21, 47–62.

— (1994a), 'Cross-dialectal interaction: examples from three Arabic speech communities in the UK'. *IJoAL* 20, 215–28.

— (1994b), 'Beur Arabic: continuity in the speech of second generation Algerian immigrants in France', in Aguadé et al. (1994), pp. 7–14.

Abul Fadl, Fahmi (1961), *Volkstümliche Texte in arabischen Bauerndialekten der ägyptischen Provinz Šarqiyya mit dialektgeographischen Untersuchungen zur Lautlehre*. Ph.D. thesis, University of Münster.

Agiùs, Dionisius A. (1990), *Diglossic Tension: Teaching Arabic for Communication*. Leeds: Folia Scholastica.

— (1996), *Siculo Arabic*. London & New York: Kegan Paul International.

Aguadé, Jordi, Federico Corriente and Marina Marugán (eds) (1994), *Actas del Congreso Internacional sobre Interferencias Lingüísticas Arabo–Romances y Parallelos Extra-Ibéricos*. Zaragoza: Navarro & Navarro.

Aguadé, Jordi and Mohammad Elyaacoubi (1995), *El dialecto árabe de Skūra (Marruecos)*. Madrid: Consejo Superior de Investigaciones Científicas.

Ahmed, Mokhtar (1981), *Lehrbuch des Ägyptisch-Arabischen*. Wiesbaden: O. Harrassowitz.

Akiner, Shirin (1983), *Islamic Peoples of the Soviet Union*. London: Kegan Paul International.

Alavi, Bozorg and Manfred Lorenz (1972), *Lehrbuch der persischen Sprache*. Leipzig: VEB Verlag Enzyklopädie.

Al-Harbi, Awwad Ahmad Al-Ahmadi (1991), 'Arabic loanwords in Acehnese'. *PAL* III, 93–117.

Ali, Abdul Sahib Mehdi (1987), *A Linguistic Study of the Development of Scientific Vocabulary in Standard Arabic*. London and New York: Kegan Paul International.

Al-Nassir, ʿAbd al-Munʿim ʿAbd al-ʿAmīr (1993), *Sibawayh the Phonologist: A Critical Study of the Phonetic and Phonological Theory of Sibawayh as Presented in his Treatise* Al-Kitab. London and New York: Kegan Paul International.

Alosh, M. Mahdi (1994), 'Arabic in the United States: the educated native speaker construct and its implications for curriculum design'. *IJoAL* 20, 55–86.

Al-Tajir, Mahdi Abdalla [= Mahdī ʿAbdallāh at-Tāǧir] (1982), *Language and Linguistic Origins in Baḥrain: The Baḥārnah Dialect of Arabic*. London: Kegan Paul International.

Altheim, Franz and Ruth Stiehl (1964–9), *Die Araber in der alten Welt*, 5 vols in 6 tomes. Berlin: W. de Gruyter.

Altoma, Salih J. (1969), *The Problem of Diglossia in Arabic: A Comparative Study of Classical and Iraqi Arabic*. Cambridge MA: Harvard University Press.

Amara, Muhammad Hasan (1999), *Politics and Sociolinguistic Reflexes: Palestinian Border Villages*. Amsterdam & Philadelphia: J. Benjamins.

Ambros, Arne (1994), 'Zur Inschrift von ʿĒn ʿAvdat: Eine Mahnung zur Vorsicht'. *ZAL* 27, 90–2.

Anawati, Georges C. (1975), 'Factors and effects of arabization and islamization in Medieval Egypt and Syria', in *Islam and Cultural Change in the Middle Ages*, ed. Speros Vryonis Jr, pp. 17–41 (= *Fourth Giorgio Levi della Vida Biennial Conference*). Wiesbaden: O. Harrassowitz.

Anghelescu, Nadia (1984), *Problemele limbii în cultura arabă*. Bucharest: University of Bucharest.

— (1986), *Limbaj şi cultură în civilizaţia arabă*. Bucharest: Editura Stiinţifică şi Enciclopedică. [French transl. by Viorel Visan, *Language et culture dans la civilisation arabe*. Paris: L'Harmattan, 1995.]

'Anīs, 'Ibrāhīm (1952), *al-Lahǧāt al-ʿarabiyya*. Cairo: Maṭbaʿa Lahǧāt al-Bayān al-ʿArabī.

Aquilina, Joseph (1956), *Teach Yourself Maltese*. London: English Universities Press.

— (1970), *Papers in Maltese Linguistics*. Valletta: Royal University of Malta.

— (1976), *Maltese Linguistic Surveys*. Msida: University of Malta.

— (1987), *Maltese–English Dictionary*, 2 vols. Malta: Midsea Books.

Aquilina, Joseph and B. S. J. Isserlin (1981), *A Survey of Contemporary Dialectal Maltese*, vol. I, *Gozo*. Leiden: E. J. Brill.

Arnold, Werner (1996), 'Arabian dialects in the Turkish province of Hatay'. *AIDA* II, 1–10.

Arnold, Werner and Peter Behnstedt (1993), *Arabisch–Aramäische Sprachbeziehungen im Qalamūn (Syrien)*. Wiesbaden: O. Harrassowitz.

Asbaghi, Asya (1987), *Die semantische Entwicklung arabischer Wörter im Persischen*. Stuttgart: F. Steiner.

— (1988), *Persische Lehnwörter im Arabischen*. Wiesbaden: O. Harrassowitz.

Ashtiany, Julia (1993), *Media Arabic*. Edinburgh: Edinburgh University Press.

Ayalon, Ami (1987), *Language and Change in the Arab Middle East: The Evolution of Modern Political Discourse*. New York and Oxford: Oxford University Press.

Ayoub, Georgine and Georges Bohas (1983), 'Les grammairiens arabes, la phrase nominale et le bon sens', in *The History of Linguistics in the Near East*, ed. Kees Versteegh, Konrad Koerner and Hans-Josef Niederehe, pp. 31–48. Amsterdam: J. Benjamins.

Baalbaki, Munir (1991), *al-Mawrid qāmūs 'inglīzī–ʿarabī*, 25th edn. Beirut: Dār al-ʿIlm li-l-Malāyīn.

Baalbaki, Ramzi Munir (1990), *Dictionary of Linguistic Terms: English–Arabic*. Beirut: Dār al-ʿIlm li-l-Malāyīn.

Baalbaki, Rohi (1988), *al-Mawrid qāmūs ʿarabī–ʾinglīzī*. Beirut: Dār al-ʿIlm li-l-Malāyīn.

Badawī, as-Saʿīd Muḥammad (1973), *Mustawayāt al-ʿarabiyya al-muʿāṣira fī Miṣr*. Cairo: Dār al-Maʿārif.

Badawī, as-Saʿīd Muḥammad and Martin Hinds (1986), *A Dictionary of Egyptian Arabic. Arabic–English*. Beirut: Librairie du Liban.

Bakalla, Muhammad Hasan (1979), *The Morphological and Phonological Components of the Arabic Verb (Meccan Arabic)*. London: Longman; Beirut: Librairie du Liban.

— (1982), *Ibn Jinnī, an Early Arab Muslim Phonetician: An Interpretative Study of his Life and Contribution to Linguistics (A Chapter from the History of Arabic Linguistics)*. London and Taipei.

— (1983), *Arabic Linguistics: An Introduction and Bibliography*. London: Mansell.

— (1984), *Arabic Culture Through its Language and Literature*. London: Kegan Paul International.

Barthélemy, A. (1935–69), *Dictionnaire arabe–français, dialectes de Syrie: Alep, Damas, Liban, Jérusalem*. Paris: Institut de France.

Bateson, Mary Catherine (1967), *Arabic Language Handbook*. Washington DC: Center for Applied Linguistics.

Battersby, H. R. (1966), 'Arabic and Persian elements in Ottoman Turkish (Osmanlıca)', in *Reşit Rahmeti Arat için*, pp. 93–141. Ankara: Türk Kültürünü Araştırma Enstitüsü.

Bauer, Leonhard (1909), *Das palästinische Arabisch, die Dialekte des Städters und des Fellachen: Grammatik, Übungen und Chrestomathie*. Leipzig: Hinrichs (repr. Leipzig, 1970).

Beaujard, Philippe (1998), *Le parler secret arabico-malgache du sud-est de Madagascar*. Paris: L'Harmattan.

Beck, Edmund (1946), 'ʿArabiyya, Sunna und ʿĀmma in der Koranlesung des zweiten Jahrhunderts'. *Orientalia*, new series, 15, 180–224.

Beeston, Alfred F. L. (1968), *Written Arabic: An Approach to the Basic Structures*. London: Cambridge University Press.

— (1981), 'Languages of pre-Islamic Arabia'. *Ar* 28, 178–86.

Behnstedt, Peter (1978), 'Zur Dialektgeographie des Nildeltas'. *ZAL* 1, 64–92.

— (1985), *Die nordjemenitischen Dialekte*, vol. I, *Atlas*. Wiesbaden: L. Reichert.

— (1987), 'Anmerkungen zu den Dialekten der Gegend von Ṣaʿdah (Nord-Jemen)'. *ZAL* 16, 93–107.

— (1992), *Die nordjemenitischen Dialekte*, vol. II, *Glossar (Buchstaben Alif-Dal)*. Wiesbaden: L. Reichert.

Behnstedt, Peter and Manfred Woidich (1982), 'Die ägyptišchen Oasen: ein dialektologischer Vorbericht'. *ZAL* 8, 39–71.

— (1985), *Die ägyptisch-arabischen Dialekte*, vol. I, *Einleitung und Anmerkungen zu den Texten*; vol. II, *Sprachatlas von Ägypten*. Wiesbaden: L. Reichert.

— (1987), *Die ägyptisch-arabischen Dialekte*, vol. III, *Texte. I. Delta-Dialekte*. Wiesbaden: L. Reichert.

— (1988), *Die ägyptisch-arabischen Dialekte*, vol. III, *Texte II. Niltaldialekte. III. Oasendialekte*. Wiesbaden: L. Reichert.

— (1994), *Die ägyptisch-arabischen Dialekte*, vol. IV, *Glossar Arabisch–Deutsch*. Wiesbaden: L. Reichert.

— (1999), *Die ägyptisch-arabischen Dialekte*, vol. V, *Glossar Deutsch-Arabisch*. Wiesbaden: L. Reichert.

Bekkum, W. Jacques van (1983), 'The "*Risāla*" of Yĕhuda Ibn Quraysh and its place in Hebrew linguistics', in *The History of Linguistics in the Near East*, ed. Kees Versteegh, Konrad Koerner and Hans-Josef Niederehe, pp. 71–91. Amsterdam: J. Benjamins.

Bellamy, James A. (1985), 'A new reading of the Namārah inscription'. *JAOS* 105, 31–51.
— (1988), 'Two pre-Islamic Arabic inscriptions revised: Jabal Ramm and Umm al-Jimāl'. *JAOS* 110, 369–85.
— (1990), 'Arabic verses from the First/Second century: the inscription of 'En 'Avdat'. *JSS* 25, 73–9.
Bengtsson, Per A. (1995), *Two Arabic Versions of the Book of* Ruth*: Text Edition and Language Studies*. Lund: Lund University Press.
Bentahila, Abdelâli (1983), *Language Attitudes among Arabic–French Bilinguals in Morocco*. Clevedon: Multilingual Matters.
Bentahila, Abdelâli and Eirlys E. Davies (1983), 'The syntax of Arabic–French code-switching'. *Lingua* 59, 301–30.
Bergsträßer, Gotthelf (1915), 'Sprachatlas von Syrien und Palästina'. *ZDPV* 38, 169–222 (+ maps XX–LXII).
— (1928), *Einführung in die semitischen Sprachen*. Munich (repr. Darmstadt: Wissenschaftliche Buchgesellschaft, 1963).
Bernards, Monique (1997), *Changing Traditions: al-Mubarrad's Refutation of Sībawayh and the Subsequent Reception of the* Kitāb. Leiden: E. J. Brill.
Bidwell, Robin (1973), *Morocco under Colonial Rule*. London: Cass.
Bielawski, Józef (1956), 'Deux périodes dans la formation de la terminologie scientifique arabe'. *RO* 20, 263–320.
Birkeland, Harris (1940), *Altarabische Pausalformen*. Oslo: Norske Videnskabs-Akademi.
— (1952), *Growth and Structure of the Egyptian Arabic Dialect*. Oslo: Dybwad.
— (1954), *Stress Patterns in Arabic*. Oslo: Norske Videnskabs-Akademi.
Bishai, Wilson B. (1960), 'Notes on the Coptic substratum in Egyptian Arabic'. *JAOS* 80, 225–9.
— (1961), 'Nature and extent of Coptic phonological influence on Egyptian Arabic'. *JSS* 6, 175–82.
— (1962), 'Coptic grammatical influence on Egyptian Arabic'. *JAOS* 82, 285–9.
Blachère, Régis (1961), *Eléments de l'arabe classique*. Paris: Maisonneuve & Larose (4th edn 1985).
Blachère, Régis, M. Chouémi and Claude Denizeau (1964–), *Dictionnaire Arabe–Français–Anglais*. Paris.
Blachère, Régis and Maurice Gaudefroy-Demombynes (1952), *Grammaire de l'arabe classique (Morphologie et syntaxe)*, 3rd edn. Paris: G.-P. Maisonneuve.
Blanc, Haim (1964), *Communal Dialects in Baghdad*. Cambridge MA: Harvard University Press.
— (1967), 'The "sonorous" vs. "muffled" distinctions in Old Arabic phonology', in *To Honor Roman Jakobson*, I, pp. 295–390. The Hague: Mouton.
— (1969), 'The fronting of Semitic g and the *qāl–gāl* dialect split in Arabic'. *Proceedings of the International Conference on Semitic Studies (Jerusalem 1965)*, 7–37. Jerusalem.
— (1970a), 'Dual and pseudo-dual in the Arabic dialects'. *Lg* 46, 42–57.
— (1970b), 'The Arabic dialect of the Negev Bedouins'. *The Israel Academy of Sciences and Humanities Proceedings* 4:7, 112–50.
Blau, Joshua (1960), *Syntax des palästinensischen Bauerndialektes von Bir-Zēt*. Walldorf-Hessen: Verlag für Orientkunde.
— (1965), *The Emergence and Linguistic Background of Judeo-Arabic: A Study of the Origins of Middle Arabic*. London: Oxford University Press (2nd edn Jerusalem: Ben Zwi, 1981).
— (1966–7), *A Grammar of Christian Arabic, Based Mainly on South-Palestinian Texts from the First Millennium*, 3 vols. Louvain: Imprimerie Orientaliste.
— (1969), 'Some problems of the formation of the Old Semitic languages in the light of

Arabic dialects'. *Proceedings of the International Conference on Semitic Studies held in Jerusalem, 19–23 July 1965*, pp. 38–44. Jerusalem: Israel Academy of Sciences and Humanities.

— (1970), *On Pseudo-corrections in some Semitic Languages*. Jerusalem: Israel Academy of Sciences and Humanities.

— (1972–3), 'On the problem of the synthetic character of Classical Arabic as against Judeo-Arabic (Middle Arabic)'. *JQR* 63, 29–38.

— (1977), *The Beginnings of the Arabic Diglossia: A Study of the Origins of Neo-Arabic*. Malibu: Undena.

— (1979), 'Some observations on a Middle Arabic Egyptian text in Coptic characters'. *JSAI* 1, 215–62.

— (1980), *Has-Sifrot ha-'aravit ha-yĕhudit: Pĕraqim nibḥarim* [*Judaeo-Arabic Literature: Selected Texts*]. Jerusalem: The Magnes Press.

— (1981), 'The state of research in the field of the linguistic study of Middle Arabic'. *Ar* 28, 187–203.

— (1982), 'Das frühe Neuarabisch in mittelarabischen Texten'. *GAP* I, 83–95.

— (1988), *Studies in Middle Arabic and its Judaeo-Arabic Variety*. Jerusalem: The Magnes Press.

Blau, Joshua and Simon Hopkins (1984), 'On early Judaeo-Arabic orthography'. *ZAL* 12, 9–27.

Bloch, Ariel A. (1965), *Die Hypotaxe im Damaszenisch-Arabischen, mit Vergleichen zur Hypotaxe im Klassisch-Arabischen*. Wiesbaden: F. Steiner.

Bloch, Ariel A. and Heinz Grotzfeld (1964), *Damaszenisch-Arabisch: Texte mit Übersetzung, Anmerkungen und Glossar*. Wiesbaden: F. Steiner.

Bobzin, Hartmut (1992), 'Geschichte der arabischen Philologie in Europa bis zum Ausgang des achtzehnten Jahrhunderts'. *GAP* III, 155–87.

Bohas, Georges (1981), 'Quelques aspects de l'argumentation et de l'explication chez les grammairiens arabes'. *Ar* 28, 204–21.

— (1985), 'L'explication en phonologie arabe'. *SHAG* I, 45–52.

— (1993), 'Le PCO et la structure des racines', in *Développements récents en linguistique arabe et sémitique*, ed. Georges Bohas, pp. 9–44. Damascus: Institut Français de Damas.

— (1995), 'Au-delà de la racine', in *Proceedings of the Colloquium on Arabic Linguistics Bucharest August 29–September 2, 1994*, ed. Nadia Anghelescu and Andrei A. Avram, I, pp. 29–45. Bucharest: University of Bucharest.

— (1997), *Matrices, étymons, racines: Eléments d'une théorie lexicologique du vocabulaire arabe*. Louvain: Peeters.

Bohas, Georges and Jean-Patrick Guillaume (1984), *Etude des théories des grammairiens arabes*. I. *Morphologie et phonologie*. Damascus: Institut Français de Damas.

Bohas, Georges, Jean-Patrick Guillaume and Djamel Eddine Kouloughli (1990), *The Arabic Linguistic Tradition*. New York and London: Routledge.

Bomhard, Allan R. (1984), *Toward Proto-Nostratic: A New Approach*. Amsterdam and Philadelphia: J. Benjamins.

Borg, Alexander (1985), *Cypriot Arabic: A Historical and Comparative Investigation into the Phonology and Morphology of the Arabic Vernacular spoken by the Maronites of Kormakiti Village in the Kyrenia District of North-Western Cyprus*. Stuttgart: Deutsche Morgenländische Gesellschaft.

Bos, Petra and Ludo Verhoeven (1994), 'Moroccan-Arabic Dutch bilingual development'. *IJoAL* 20, 119–50.

Boumans, Louis (1996), 'Embedding verbs and collocations in Moroccan Arabic/Dutch code-switching', in *Perspectives in Arabic Linguistics* 9, ed. Mushira Eid and Dilworth Parkinson, pp. 45–76. Amsterdam and Philadelphia: J. Benjamins.

Brame, Michael (1970), *Arabic Phonology: Implications for Phonological Theory and Historical Semitic*. Ph.D. thesis, MIT, Cambridge MA.

Branden, Albert van den (1950), *Les inscriptions thamoudéennes*. Louvain: Bureaux du Muséon.
Braukämper, Ulrich (1994), 'Notes on the origin of Baggara Arab culture with special reference to the Shuwa'. *SGA* 14, 13–46.
Bravmann, Max (1934), *Materialien und Untersuchungen zu den phonetischen Lehren der Araber*. Göttingen: W. F. Kaestner.
Brett, Michael (1995), 'The way of the nomad'. *BSOAS* 58, 251–69.
Brincat, Joseph M. (1991), *Malta 870–1054: Al-Himyarī's Account*. Valletta: Said International.
Britto, Francis (1985), *Diglossia: A Study of the Theory with Application to Tamil*. Washington DC: Georgetown University Press.
Brockelmann, Carl (1908–13), *Grundriß der vergleichenden Grammatik der semitischen Sprachen*, 2 vols. Berlin (repr. Hildesheim: G. Olms, 1966).
— (1964), 'Das Arabische und seine Mundarten'. *HdO* I:3, 207–45.
— (1965), *Arabische Grammatik. Paradigmen, Literatur, Übungsstücke und Glossar*, 16th edn, ed. Manfred Fleischhammer. Leipzig: VEB Verlag Enzyklopädie.
Brockett, Adrian A. (1985), *The Spoken Arabic of Khābūra on the Bāṭina of Oman*. Manchester: Journal of Semitic Studies.
Broselow, Ellen (1976), *The Phonology of Egyptian Arabic*. Ph.D. thesis, University of Massachusetts, Amherst.
— (1979), 'Cairene Arabic syllable structure'. *LA* 5, 345–82.
Bulliet, Richard W. (1990), *The Camel and the Wheel*, 2nd edn. New York: Columbia University Press (1st edn Cambridge MA: Harvard University Press, 1975).
Busuttil, E. D. (1976), *Kalepin: Dizzjunarju Ingliz–Malti*. Valletta: Muscat.
— (1977), *Kalepin (Dizzjunarju) Malti–Ingliz*. is-Sitt Harġa: A. C. Aquilina.
Cadora, Frederic J. (1992), *Bedouin, Village, and Urban Arabic: An Ecolinguistic Study*. Leiden: E. J. Brill.
Cannon, Garland (1994), *The Arabic Contribution to the English Language: An Historical Dictionary*. Wiesbaden: O. Harrassowitz.
Cantarino, Vicente (1974–5), *Syntax of Modern Arabic Prose*, 3 vols. Bloomington: Indiana University Press.
Cantineau, Jean (1930–2), *Le nabatéen*, 2 vols. Paris.
— (1932), 'Accadien et sudarabique'. *BSLP* 33, 175–204.
— (1935), *Grammaire du palmyrénien épigraphique* (= *Publications de l'Institut d'Etudes Orientales de la Faculté des Lettres d'Alger*, 4). Cairo.
— (1936, 1937), 'Etudes sur quelques parlers de nomades arabes d'Orient'. *AIEO* 2, 1–118; 3, 119–237.
— (1938), 'Remarques sur les parlers syro-libano-palestiniens'. *BSLP* 40, 80–89.
— (1940, 1946), *Les parlers arabes de Ḥōrān*. I. *Notions générales, grammaire*. II. *Atlas*. Paris: Klincksieck.
— (1960), *Etudes de linguistique arabe (Mémorial Jean Cantineau)*. Paris: C. Klincksieck.
Carter, Michael G. (1981), *Arab Linguistics: An Introductory Classical Text with Translation and Notes*. Amsterdam: J. Benjamins.
— (1990), 'Arabic grammar', in *Cambridge History of Arabic Literature. Religion, Learning and Science in the ʿAbbāsid Period*, ed. M. J. L. Young, J. D. Latham and R. B. Serjeant, pp. 118–38. Cambridge: Cambridge University Press.
Casanova, M. P. (1902), 'Un texte arabe transcrit en caractères coptes'. *BIFAO* 1, 1–20.
Caspari, C. P. (1887), *Arabische Grammatik*, 5th edn, ed. August Müller. Halle.
Caubet, Dominique (1993), *L'arabe marocain*. I. *Phonologie et morphosyntaxe*. II. *Syntaxe et catégories grammaticales, textes*. Paris and Louvain: Peeters.
Chaabani, Zinelabidine (1984), *Der Einfluß des Französischen auf das Arabische in Tunesien: Zur Beschreibung morphosyntaktischer Phänomene des Neuhocharabischen*. Frankfurt am Main: P. Lang.

Chaker, Salem (1984), *Textes en linguistique berbère: introduction au domaine berbère.* Paris: Centre National de la Recherche Scientifique.

Chejne, Anwar G. (1969), *The Arabic Language: Its Role in History.* Minneapolis: University of Minnesota Press.

Clarity, Beverly E., Karl Stowasser and Ronald Wolfe (1964), *A Dictionary of Iraqi Arabic: English–Arabic.* Washington, DC: Georgetown University Press.

Cleveland, R. L. (1963), 'A classification for the Arabic dialects of Jordan'. *BASOR* 167, 56–63.

Cohen, David (1963), *Le dialecte arabe ḥassānīya de Mauritanie (parler de la Gəbla).* Paris: Klincksieck.

— (1964), *Le parler arabe des juifs de Tunis*, vol. I, *Textes et documents linguistiques et ethnographiques.* The Hague and Paris: Mouton.

— (1970), 'Koinè, langues communes et dialectes arabes', in David Cohen, *Etudes de linguistique sémitique et arabe*, pp. 105–25. The Hague and Paris: Mouton.

— (1975), *Le parler arabe des juifs de Tunis*, vol. II, *Etude linguistique.* The Hague and Paris: Mouton.

Cohen, Marcel (1912), *Le parler arabe des juifs d'Alger.* Paris: Champion.

Comrie, Bernard (1991), 'On the importance of Arabic to general linguistic theory'. *PAL* III, 3–30.

Corriente, Federico (1971a), *Problemática de la pluralidad en semítico: el plural fracto.* Madrid: Consejo Superior de Investigaciones Científicas.

— (1971b), 'On the functional yield of some synthetic devices in Arabic and Semitic morphology'. *JQR* 62, 20–50.

— (1975), 'Marginalia on Arabic diglossia and evidence thereof in the *Kitab al-Agani*'. *JSS* 20, 38–61.

— (1977), *A Grammatical Sketch of the Spanish Arabic Dialect Bundle.* Madrid: Instituto Hispano-Árabe de Cultura.

— (1980), *Gramática, métrica y texto del Cancionero hispano-árabe de Abán Quzmán.* Madrid: Instituto Hispano-Árabe de Cultura.

— (1988), *El léxico árabe andalusí según P. de Alcalá (ordenado por raíces, anotado y fonémicamente interpretado).* Madrid: Universidad Complutense.

Cowell, Mark W. (1964), *A Reference Grammar of Syrian Arabic (Based on the Dialect of Damascus).* Washington DC: Georgetown University Press.

Cuvalay, Martine (1996), *The Arabic Verb: A Functional Grammar Approach to Verbal Expression in Arabic.* Ph.D. thesis, University of Amsterdam.

Czapkiewicz, Andrzej (1975), *The Verb in Modern Arabic Dialects as an Exponent of the Development Processes Occurring in them.* Wroclaw: Wydawnictwo Polskiej Akademii Nauk.

Dagorn, René (1981), *La geste d'Ismaël d'après l'onomastique et la tradition arabes.* Geneva: Droz.

Danecki, Janusz (1989), *Wstep do dialektologii jfzyka arabskiego.* Warsaw: Wydawnictwa Uniwersytetu Warszawskiego.

Darir, Hassane (1993), 'The unification of Arabic scientific terms: linguistic terms as an example'. *PCALL* I, 155–79.

Ḍayf, Šawqī (1968), *al-Madāris an-naḥwiyya.* Cairo: Dār al-Maʿārif.

— (1982), *Kitāb ar-radd ʿalā n-nuḥāt li-bn Maḍāʾ al-Qurṭubī.* 2nd edn. Cairo: Dār al-Maʿārif.

Denizeau, Claude (1960), *Dictionnaire des parlers arabes de Syrie, Liban et Palestine.* Paris: Maisonneuve.

Denz, Adolf (1971), *Die Verbalsyntax des neuarabischen Dialektes von Kwayriš (Irak) mit einer einleitenden allgemeinen Tempus- und Aspektlehre.* Wiesbaden: F. Steiner.

— (1982), 'Die Struktur des klassischen Arabisch'. *GAP* I, 58–82.

Dereli, Belgin (1997), *Het Uzbekistaans Arabisch in Djogari*. MA dissertation, University of Nijmegen.

Devic, L. Marcel (1876), *Dictionnaire étymologique des mots français d'origine orientale (arabe, persan, turc, hébreu, malais)*. Paris (repr. Amsterdam: Oriental Press, 1965).

Diakonoff, I. M. [Djakonov, Igor Mixailovič] (1965), *Semito-Hamitic Languages*. Moscow: Nauka.

Diem, Werner (1971), 'Zum Problem der Personalpronomina *hənne* (3. Pl.), *-kon* (2. Pl.) und *-hon* (3. Pl.) in den syrisch-libanesischen Dialekten'. *ZDMG* 121, 223–30.

— (1973a), 'Die nabatäischen Inschriften und die Frage der Kasusflexion im Altarabischen'. *ZDMG* 123, 227–37.

— (1973b), *Skizzen jemenitischer Dialekte*. Beirut and Wiesbaden: F. Steiner.

— (1974), *Hochsprache und Dialekt im Arabischen: Untersuchungen zur heutigen arabischen Zweisprachigkeit*. Wiesbaden: F. Steiner.

— (1976), 'Some glimpses at the rise and early development of the Arabic orthography'. *Orientalia*, new series, 45, 251–61.

— (1978), 'Divergenz und Konvergenz im Arabischen'. *Ar* 25, 128–47.

— (1979a), 'Studien zur Frage des Substrats im Arabischen'. *Der Islam* 56, 12–80.

— (1979b), 'Untersuchungen zur frühen Geschichte der arabischen Orthographie. I. Die Schreibung der Vokale'. *Orientalia*, new series, 48, 207–57.

— (1980a), 'Untersuchungen zur frühen Geschichte der arabischen Orthographie. II. Die Schreibung der Konsonanten'. *Orientalia*, new series, 49, 67–106.

— (1980b), 'Die genealogische Stellung des Arabischen in den semitischen Sprachen: ein ungelöstes Problem der Semitistik', in *Studien aus Arabistik und Semitistik Anton Spitaler zum siebzigsten Geburtstag von seinen Schülern überreicht*, ed. Werner Diem and Stefan Wild, pp. 65–85. Wiesbaden: O. Harrassowitz.

— (1981), 'Untersuchungen zur frühen Geschichte der arabischen Orthographie. III. Endungen und Endschreibungen'. *Orientalia*, new series, 50, 332–83.

— (1984), 'Philologisches zu den arabischen Aphrodito-Papyri'. *Der Islam* 61, 251–75.

— (1991), 'Vom Altarabischen zum Neuarabischen: Ein neuer Ansatz', in *Semitic Studies in Honor of Wolf Leslau*, ed. Alan S. Kaye, I, pp. 297–308. Wiesbaden: O. Harrassowitz.

Dil, Afia (1972), *The Hindu and Muslim Dialects of Bengali*. Ph.D. thesis, Stanford University.

Ditters, Everhard (1992), *A Formal Approach to Arabic Syntax: The Noun Phrase and the Verb Phrase*. Ph.D. thesis, University of Nijmegen.

Doniach, N. S. (1972), *The Oxford English–Arabic Dictionary of Current Usage*. Oxford: Clarendon Press.

Donner, Fred McGraw (1981), *The Early Islamic Conquests*. Princeton: Princeton University Press.

Doss, Madiha (1996), 'Comparative sources for the study of 17th century Egyptian Arabic'. *AIDA* II, 31–40.

Dossin, Georges (1959), 'Les bédouins dans les textes de Mari', in *L'antica società beduina*, ed. Francesco Gabrieli, pp. 35–51. Rome: Centro di Studi Semitici.

Dostal, Walter (1959), 'The evolution of Bedouin life', in *L'antica società beduina*, ed. Francesco Gabrieli, pp. 11–34. Rome: Centro di Studi Semitici.

Dozy, Reinhart (1881), *Supplément aux dictionnaires arabes*, 2 vols. Leiden: E. J. Brill (repr. Beirut: Librairie du Liban, 1968).

Dozy, Reinhart and W. H. Engelmann (1869), *Glossaire des mots espagnols et portugais dérivés de l'arabe*, 2nd edn. Leiden: E. J. Brill (repr. Amsterdam: Oriental Press, 1965).

Durand, Olivier (1995), *Introduzione ai dialetti arabi*. Milan: Centro Studi Camito-Semitici.

Eche, Youssef (1967), *Les bibliothèques arabes publiques et sémi-publiques, en Mésopotamie, en Syrie et en Egypte au Moyen Age*. Damascus: Institut Français de Damas.

Eid, Mushira (1990), 'Arabic linguistics: the current scene'. *PAL* I, 3–37.
Eksell Harning, Kerstin (1980), *The Analytical Genitive in the Modern Arabic Dialects.* (= *Orientalia Gothoburgensia*, 5.) Gothenburg: Acta Universitatis Gothoburgensis.
El Aissati, Abderrahman (1996), *Language Loss among Native Speakers of Moroccan Arabic in the Netherlands.* Ph.D. thesis, University of Nijmegen.
El Aissati, Abderrahman and Kees de Bot (1994), 'Moroccan Arabic in the Netherlands: acquisition and loss'. *IJoAL* 20, 177–92.
Elgibali, Alaa (1985), *Towards a Sociolinguistic Analysis of Language Variation in Arabic: Cairene and Kuwaiti dialects.* Ph.D. thesis, University of Pittsburgh.
El-Hajjé, H. (1954), *Le parler arabe de Tripoli.* Paris.
El-Hassan, S. A. (1977), 'Educated Spoken Arabic in Egypt and the Levant: a critical review of diglossia and related concepts'. *ArchLing*, new series, 8, 112–32.
Endreß, Gerhard (1982), 'Die arabische Schrift'. *GAP* I, 165–97.
Endreß, Gerhard and Dimitri Gutas (1992–), *A Greek and Arabic Lexicon: Materials for a Dictionary of the Mediaeval Translations from Greek into Arabic.* Leiden: E. J. Brill.
Ermers, Rob (1995), *Turkic Forms in Arabic Structures: The Description of Turkic by Arabic Grammarians.* Ph.D. thesis, University of Nijmegen.
Erwin, Wallace M. (1963), *A Short Reference Grammar of Iraqi Arabic.* Washington DC: Georgetown University Press.
— (1969), *A Basic Course in Iraqi Arabic.* Washington DC: Georgetown University Press.
Extra, Guus and Jan Jaap de Ruiter (1994), 'The sociolinguistic status of the Moroccan community in the Netherlands'. *IJoAL* 20, 151–76.
Fassi Fehri, Abdelkader (1982), *Linguistique arabe: forme et interprétation.* Rabat: Faculté des Lettres et Sciences Humaines.
Faublée, Jacques (1974), 'L'influence arabe dans le sud-est de Madagascar', in *Actes du Premier Congrès International de Linguistique Sémitique et Chamito-Sémitique Paris 16–19 juillet 1969*, ed. André Caquot and David Cohen, pp. 399–411. The Hague and Paris: Mouton.
Feghali, Michel (1928), *Syntaxe des parlers arabes actuels du Liban.* Paris: Geuthner.
Ferguson, Charles A. (1959a), 'The Arabic koine'. *Lg* 25, 616–30.
— (1959b), 'Diglossia'. *Word* 15, 325–40.
— (1962), 'Problem of teaching languages with diglossia'. *Georgetown University Monograph Series* 15, 165–77.
— (1989), 'Grammatical agreement in Classical Arabic and the modern dialects: a response to Versteegh's pidginization hypothesis'. *al-ʿArabiyya* 22, 5–17.
Fernández, Mauro (1993), *Diglossia: A Comprehensive Bibliography 1960–1990 and Supplements.* Amsterdam and Philadelphia: J. Benjamins.
Fischer, Wolfdietrich (1959), *Die demonstrativen Bildungen der neuarabischen Dialekte: ein Beitrag zur historischen Grammatik des Arabischen.* The Hague: Mouton.
— (1961), 'Die Sprache der arabischen Sprachinsel in Uzbekistan'. *Der Islam* 36, 232–63.
— (1972), *Grammatik des klassischen Arabisch.* Wiesbaden: O. Harrassowitz.
— (1982), 'Frühe Zeugnisse des Neuarabischen'. *GAP* I, 83–95.
— (1986), *Lehrgang für die arabische Schriftsprache der Gegenwart*, II. Wiesbaden: L. Reichert.
— (1995), 'Zum Verhältnis der neuarabischen Dialekte zum Klassisch-Arabischen'. *Dialectologia Arabica: A Collection of Articles in Honour of the Sixtieth Birthday of Professor Heikki Palva*, pp. 75–86. Helsinki: Finnish Oriental Society.
Fischer, Wolfdietrich and Otto Jastrow (1977), *Lehrgang für die arabische Schriftsprache der Gegenwart*, I. Wiesbaden: L. Reichert.
— (1980), *Handbuch der arabischen Dialekte.* Wiesbaden: O. Harrassowitz.
Fisher, Humphrey (1970), 'The Western and Central Sudan', in *The Cambridge History of Islam*, II, ed. P. M. Holt, Ann K. S. Lambton and Bernard Lewis, pp. 345–405. Cambridge: Cambridge University Press.

Fishman, Joshua A. (1967), 'Bilingualism with and without diglossia; diglossia with and without bilingualism'. *JSI* 23, 29–38.
— (1972), 'Societal bilingualism: stable and transitional', in *Language in Sociocultural Change*, ed. Joshua A. Fishman, pp. 135–52. Stanford: Stanford University Press.
Fleisch, Henri (1958), '*Mağhūra, mahmūsa*, examen critique'. *MUSJ* 35, 193–210.
— (1961), *Traité de philologie arabe*, vol. I, *Préliminaires, phonétique, morphologie nominale*. Beirut: Imprimerie Catholique.
— (1964), 'Arabe Classique et arabe dialectal'. *TJ* 12, 23–64 (repr. in Henri Fleisch, *Etudes d'arabe dialectal*, Beirut: Imprimerie Catholique, 1974, pp. 3–43).
— (1968), *L'arabe classique: esquisse d'une structure linguistique*, 2nd edn. Beirut: Dar el-Machreq.
— (1974), *Etudes d'arabe dialectal*. Beirut: Imprimerie Catholique.
— (1979), *Traité de philologie arabe*, vol. II, *Pronoms, morphologie verbale, particules*. Beirut: Dar el-Machreq.
Forkel, Fritz (1980), *Die sprachliche Situation im heutigen Marokko: eine soziolinguistische Untersuchung*. Dissertation, University of Hamburg.
Fraenkel, Siegmund (1886), *Die aramäischen Fremdwörter im Arabischen*. Leiden: E. J. Brill (repr. Hildesheim: G. Olms, 1962).
Fück, Johann (1950), *Arabiya: Untersuchungen zur arabischen Sprach- und Stilgeschichte*. Berlin: Akademie-Verlag [French transl. by Claude Denizeau, '*Arabīya: Recherches sur l'histoire de la langue et du style arabe*. Paris: M. Didier, 1955].
— (1955), *Die arabischen Studien in Europa bis in den Anfang des 20. Jahrhunderts*. Leipzig: O. Harrassowitz.
— (1964), 'Geschichte der semitischen Sprachwissenschaft'. *HdO* I:3, 31–9.
Gallagher, Charles F. (1968), 'North African problems and prospects: language and identity', in *Language Problems of Developing Nations*, ed. Joshua A. Fishman et al., pp. 129–50. New York: Wiley & Sons.
Gallup, Dorothea M. (1973), *The French Image of Algeria: Its Origin, its Place in Colonial Ideology, its Effect on Algerian Acculturation*. Ph.D. thesis, University of California, Los Angeles.
Galmés de Fuentes, Álvaro (1983), *Dialectología mozárabe*. Madrid: Gredos.
Garbell, Irene (1958), 'Remarks on the historical phonology of an East Mediterranean Arabic dialect'. *Word* 14, 303–37.
Garbini, Giovanni (1974), 'La position du sémitique dans le chamito-sémitique', in *Actes du Premier Congrès International de Linguistique Sémitique et Chamito-Sémitique Paris 16–19 juillet 1969*, ed. André Caquot and David Cohen, pp. 21–6. The Hague and Paris: Mouton.
— (1984), *Le lingue semitiche: studi di storia linguistica*, 2nd edn. Naples: Istituto Universitario Orientale (1st edn 1972).
Garmadi, Salah (1968), 'La situation actuelle en Tunisie: problèmes et perspectives'. *Revue Tunisienne des Sciences Sociales* 13, 13–24.
Gätje, Helmut (1985), 'Arabische Lexikographie: ein historischer Übersicht'. *HL* 12, 105–47.
Ǧindī, 'Aḥmad 'Alam ad-Dīn al- (1983), *al-Lahǧāt al-'arabiyya fī t-turāṯ*. I. *Fī n-niẓāmayn aṣ-ṣawtī wa-ṣ-ṣarfī*. II. *an-Niẓām an-naḥwī*. 2nd edn. Tripoli: ad-Dār al-'Arabiyya lil-Kitāb.
Graf, Georg (1905), *Der Sprachgebrauch der ältesten christlich-arabischen Literatur, ein Beitrag zur Geschichte des Vulgär-Arabisch*. Leipzig.
— (1944–66), *Geschichte der christlichen arabischen Literatur*, 5 vols. Città del Vaticano.
Grandguillaume, Gilbert (1983), *Arabisation et politique linguistique au Maghreb*. Paris: Maisonneuve & Larose.
Grand'Henry, Jacques (1972), *Le parler arabe de Cherchell (Algérie)*. Louvain-la-Neuve: Université Catholique de Louvain.

Greenberg, Joseph H. (1947), 'Arabic loan-words in Hausa'. *Word* 3, 85–97.
— (1950), 'The patterning of root morphemes in Semitic'. *Word* 6, 162–81.
Greenman, Joseph (1979), 'A sketch of the Arabic dialect of the central Yamani Tihāmah'. *ZAL* 3, 47–61.
Grohmann, Adolf (1958), 'The problem of dating early Qur'āns'. *Der Islam* 33, 213–31.
— (1966), 'Arabische Papyruskunde'. *HdO* I: 2, 1, 49–118.
— (1967), *Arabische Paläographie*. I. *Einleitung, die Beschreibstoffe, die Schreibgeräte, die Tinte*. Vienna: Österreichische Akademie der Wissenschaften.
— (1971), *Arabische Paläographie*. II. *Das Schriftwesen: Die Lapidarschrift*. Vienna: Österreichische Akademie der Wissenschaften.
Grotzfeld, Heinz (1965), *Syrisch-arabische Grammatik (Dialekt von Damaskus)*. Wiesbaden: O. Harrassowitz.
Gruendler, Beatrice (1993), *The Development of the Arabic Scripts: From the Nabataean Era to the First Islamic Century According to Dated Texts*. Atlanta: Scholars Press.
Gumperz, J. (1962), 'Types of linguistic communities'. *AL* 4, 28–40.
Haarmann, Ulrich (1988), 'Arabic in speech, Turkish in lineage: Mamluks and their sons in the intellectual life of fourteenth-century Egypt and Syria'. *JSS* 33, 81–114.
Haddad, Adnan (1983), *L'arabe et le swahili dans la République du Zaïre: etudes islamiques, histoire et linguistique*. Paris: SEDES.
Hadj-Sadok, Mahammed (1955), 'Dialectes arabes et francisation linguistique de l'Algérie'. *AIEO* 13, 61–97.
Haeri, Niloofar (1992), 'How different are men and women: palatalization in Cairo'. *PAL* IV, 169–80.
— (1997), *The Sociolinguistic Market of Cairo: Gender, Class and Education*. London & New York: Kegan Paul International.
Hajjar, Joseph (1983), *Mounged classique français–arabe dictionnaire moderne*, 5th edn. Beirut: Dar el-Machreq.
Hamzaoui, Rached (1965), *L'académie arabe de Damas et le problème de la modernisation de la langue arabe*. Leiden: E. J. Brill.
— (1970), 'L'arabisation au ministère de l'Intérieur: la brigade de la circulation de la garde Nationale'. *CERES* 3, 10–73.
— (1975), *L'académie de langue arabe du Caire: histoire et oeuvre*. Tunis: Université de Tunis.
Harrell, Richard Slade (1962), *A Short Reference Grammar of Moroccan Arabic*. Washington DC: Georgetown University Press.
— (1965), *A Basic Course in Moroccan Arabic*. Washington DC: Georgetown University Press.
— (1966), *A Dictionary of Moroccan Arabic: Moroccan–English*. Washington DC: Georgetown University Press.
Harrell, Richard Slade and Harvey Sobleman (1963), *A Dictionary of Moroccan Arabic: English–Moroccan*. Washington DC: Georgetown University Press.
Hartmann, Regina (1974), *Untersuchungen zur Syntax der arabischen Schriftsprache: eine generativ-transformationelle Darstellung*. Wiesbaden: O. Harrassowitz.
Hava, J. G. (1964), *Al-Faraid Arabic–English Dictionary*. Beirut: Catholic Press.
Haywood, John A. (1965), *Arabic Lexicography: Its History and Place in the General History of Lexicography*, 2nd edn. Leiden: E. J. Brill.
Heath, Jeffrey (1989), *From Code-Switching to Borrowing: A Case Study of Moroccan Arabic*. London and New York: Kegan Paul International.
Heath, Jeffrey and Moshe Bar-Asher (1982), 'A Judeo-Arabic dialect of Tafilalt (Southeastern Morocco)'. *ZAL* 9, 32–78.
Hebbo, Ahmed Irhayem (1970), *Die Fremdwörter in der arabischen Prophetenbiographie des Ibn Hischam (gest. 218/834)*. Dissertation, University of Heidelberg.

Hecker, Karl (1982), 'Das Arabische im Rahmen der semitischen Sprachen'. *GAP* I, 6–16.
Heine, Bernd (1982), *The Nubi Language of Kibera: An Arabic Creole*. Berlin: D. Reimer.
Henninger, Joseph (1959), 'La société bédouine ancienne', in *L'antica società beduina*, ed. Francesco Gabrieli, pp. 69–93. Rome: Centro di Studi Semitici.
Hetzron, Robert (1974), 'La division des langues sémitiques', in *Actes du Premier Congrès International de Linguistique Sémitique et Chamito-Sémitique Paris 16–19 juillet 1969*, ed. André Caquot and David Cohen, pp. 181–94. The Hague and Paris: Mouton.
— (1976), 'Two principles of genetic classification'. *Lingua* 38, 89–108.
— ed. (1997), *The Semitic Languages*. London: Routledge.
Höfner, Maria (1959), 'Die Beduinen in den vorislamischen arabischen Inschriften', in *L'antica società beduina*, ed. Francesco Gabrieli, pp. 53–68. Rome: Centro di Studi Semitici.
Holes, Clive (1983), 'Bahraini dialects: sectarian differences and the sedentary/nomadic split'. *ZAL* 10, 7–38.
— (1984), 'Bahraini dialects: sectarian differences exemplified through texts'. *ZAL* 13, 27–67.
— (1987), *Language Variation and Change in a Modernising Arab State*. London and New York: Kegan Paul International.
— (1990), *Gulf Arabic*. London and New York: Routledge.
— (1993), 'The use of variation: a study of the political speeches of Gamal Abd EnNasir'. *PAL* V, 13–45.
— (1995a), *Modern Arabic: Structures, Functions and Varieties*. London and New York: Longman.
— (1995b), 'Community, dialect and urbanization in the Arabic-speaking Middle East'. *BSOAS* 58, 270–87.
Hoogland, Jan (1996), *Marokkaans Arabisch: een cursus voor zelfstudie en klassikaal gebruik*. Amsterdam: Bulaaq.
Hopkins, Simon (1984), *Studies in the Grammar of Early Arabic Based upon Papyri Datable to Before A.H. 300/A.D. 912*. London: Oxford University Press.
Hospers, Johannes H. (1974), *A Basic Bibliography for the Study of the Semitic Languages*, II. Leiden: E. J. Brill.
Hourani, Albert (1970), *Arabic Thought in the Liberal Age (1798–1939)*. London: Oxford University Press.
Howell, Mortimer Sloper (1883–1911), *A Grammar of the Classical Arabic Language Translated and Compiled from the Most Approved Native or Naturalized Authors* (repr. Delhi: Gian Publishing House, 1986).
Huehnergard, J. (1991), 'Remarks on the classification of the Northwest Semitic languages', in *The Balaam Text from Deir 'Alla Re-evaluated. Proceedings of the International Symposium Held at Leiden, 21–24 August 1989*, ed. J. Hoftijzer and G. van der Kooij, pp. 282–93. Leiden: E. J. Brill.
Humbert, Geneviève (1995), *Les voies de la transmission du* Kitāb *de Sībawayhi*. Leiden: E. J. Brill.
Ingham, Bruce (1971), 'Some characteristics of Meccan Arabic'. *BSOAS* 34, 273–97.
— (1973), 'Urban and rural Arabic in Khuzistan'. *BSOAS* 36, 533–53.
— (1976), 'Regional and social factors in the dialect geography of Southern Iraq and Khuzistan'. *BSOAS* 39, 62–82.
— (1982), *North-east Arabian Dialects*. London and Boston: Kegan Paul International.
— (1994a), 'The Arabic language in Iran'. *IJoAL* 20, 103–16.
— (1994b), 'The effect of language contact on the Arabic dialect of Afghanistan', in Aguadé et al. (1994), pp. 105–117.
— (1994c), *Najdi Arabic: Central Arabian*. Amsterdam and Philadelphia: J. Benjamins.
Jamme, Albert (1967), 'New Hasean and Sabaean inscriptions from Saudi Arabia'. *OA* 6, 181–7.

Janssens, Gerard (1972), *Stress in Arabic and Word Structure in the Modern Arabic Dialects*. Leuven: Peeters.
Jaritz, Felicitas (1993), *Die arabischen Quellen zum heiligen Menas*. Heidelberg: Heidelberger Orientverlag.
Jastrow, Otto (1973), *Daragözü, eine arabische Mundart der Kozluk-Sason-Gruppe (Südostanatolien): Grammatik und Texte*. Nuremberg: H. Carl.
— (1978), *Die mesopotamisch-arabischen* Qəltu-*Dialekte*, vol. I, *Phonologie und Morphologie*. Wiesbaden: F. Steiner.
— (1979), 'Der arabische Mundart von Mossul'. *ZAL* 2, 36–75.
— (1981), *Die mesopotamisch-arabischen* Qəltu-*Dialekte*, vol. II, *Texte*. Wiesbaden: F. Steiner.
— (1982), 'Die Struktur des Neuarabischen'. *GAP* I, 128–41.
— (1990), *Der arabische Dialekt der Juden von ʿAqra und Arbīl*. Wiesbaden: O. Harrassowitz.
— (1994), 'The *qəltu* Arabic dialects of Mesopotamian Arabic', in Aguadé et al. (1994), pp. 119–23.
Jaussen, A. and R. Savignac (1909, 1914), *Mission archéologique en Arabie*. Paris.
Jeffery, Arthur (1938), *The Foreign Vocabulary of the Qur'ān*. Baroda: Oriental Institute.
Jiha, Michel (1964), *Der arabische Dialekt von Bišmizzīn: Volkstümliche Texte aus einem libanesischen Dorf mit Grundzügen der Laut- und Formenlehre*. Beirut: Orient-Institut.
Johnstone, Thomas M. (1967), *Eastern Arabian Dialect Studies*. London: Oxford University Press.
Jones, Russell (1978), *Indonesian Etymological Project*. III. *Arabic Loan-words in Indonesian*. London: School of Oriental and African Studies.
Jong, Rudolf de (1996), 'Aspects of phonology and morphology of dialects of the Northern Sinai littoral'. *AIDA* II, 105–13.
— (1999), *The Bedouin Dialects of the Northern Sinai Littoral: Bridging the Linguistic Gap between the Eastern and Western Arab World*. Ph.D. University of Amsterdam.
Kampffmeyer, Georg (1899), 'Materialien zum Studium der arabischen Beduinendialekte Innerafrikas'. *MSOS* 2, 143–221.
Kanungo, Gostha Behari (1968), *The Language Controversy in Indian Education: Historical Study*. Chicago: University of Chicago.
Kaye, Alan S. (1972), 'Remarks on diglossia in Arabic: well-defined versus ill-defined'. *Linguistics* 81, 32–48.
— (1976), *Chadian and Sudanese Arabic in the Light of Comparative Arabic Dialectology*. The Hague: Mouton.
— (1982), *A Dictionary of Nigerian Arabic*. Malibu: Undena.
— (1995), 'Adaptations of Arabic script', in *The World's Writing Systems*, ed. Peter T. Daniels and William Bright, pp. 743–62. London: Oxford University Press.
— and Judith Rosenhouse (1997), 'The Arabic dialects and Maltese', in Hetzron (1997: 263–311).
Khafaifi, Hussein Mabrok el- (1985), *The Role of the Cairo Academy in Coining Arabic Scientific Terminology: An Historical and Linguistic Evaluation*. Ph.D. thesis, University of Utah.
Khuli, Mohamed al- (1979), *A Contrastive Transformational Grammar: Arabic and English*. Leiden: E. J. Brill.
Kieffer, Charles M. (1980), 'L'arabe et les arabophones de Bactriane (Afghanistan). I. Situation ethnique et linguistique'. *WdI* 20, 178–96 [all published].
Kinberg, Naphtali and Rafael Talmon (1994), 'Learning of Arabic by Jews and the use of Hebrew among Arabs in Israel'. *IJoAL* 20, 37–54.
Kissling, Hans Joachim (1960), *Osmanisch-türkische Grammatik*. Wiesbaden: O. Harrassowitz.

Klein-Franke, Felix (1980), *Die klassische Antike in der Tradition des Islam*. Darmstadt: Wissenschaftliche Buchgesellschaft.

Klengel, Horst (1972), *Zwischen Zelt und Palast: Die Begegnung von Nomaden und Seßhaften im alten Vorderasien*. Vienna: A. Schroll.

Knauf, Ernst Axel (1988), *Midian: Untersuchungen zur Geschichte Palästinas und Nordarabiens am Ende des 2. Jahrtausends vor Christ*. Wiesbaden: O. Harrassowitz.

Kofler, Hans (1940–2), 'Reste altarabischer Dialekte'. *WZKM* 47, 60–130, 233–62; 48, 52–88, 247–74; 49, 15–30, 234–56.

Koningsveld, Pieter Sjoerd van (1976), *The Latin–Arabic Glossary of the Leiden University Library: A Contribution to the Study of Mozarabic Manuscripts and Literature*. Ph.D. thesis, University of Leiden.

Kopf, Lothar (1956), 'Religious influences on Medieval Arabic philology'. *SI* 5, 33–59.

Kornblueth, Ilana and Sarah Aynor (1974), 'A study of the longevity of Hebrew slang'. *IJSL* 1, 15–37.

Kouloughli, Djamel Eddine (1979), 'Pour une grammaire de transfert dialectes/arabe standard'. *Théorie Analyses* 2/3, 125–34.

— (1994), *Grammaire de l'arabe d'aujourd'hui*. Pocket-Langues pour Tous.

Krahl, Günther and Wolfgang Reuschel (1980, 1981), *Lehrgang des modernen Arabisch*. I, II/1–2. 4th edn. Leipzig: VEB Enzyklopädie.

Kropfitsch, Lorenz (1977), 'Der französische Einfluß auf die arabische Schriftsprache im Maghrib'. *ZDMG* 128, 39–64.

— (1980), 'Semantische Tendenzen im Neuhocharabischen'. *ZAL* 5, 118–36.

Lambton, Ann K. S. (1961), *Persian Grammar*. Cambridge: Cambridge University Press.

Landberg, Carlo de (1888), *Bāsim le Forgeron et Harun er-Rachid: Texte arabe en dialecte d'Egypte et de Syrie, publié d'après les manuscrits de Leyde, de Gotha, et du Caire*. Leiden: E. J. Brill.

Lane, Edward William (1863–93), *An Arabic–English Lexicon, Derived from the Best and the Most Copious Eastern Sources ...*, Book I, in eight parts [all published]. London and Edinburgh: Williams and Norgate (repr. Beirut: Librairie du Liban).

Langue arabe et langues africaines: Mémoire spécial du Centre d'Etudes sur le monde arabe et l'Afrique et du Centre d'Etudes sur l'Océan Indien occidental (1983), Paris: Conseil International de la langue française.

Laria, Massimo (1996), 'Some characteristic features of Cyrenaican Arabic'. *AIDA* II, 123–32.

Latham, Derek (1983), 'The beginnings of Arabic prose literature: the epistolary genre'. *CHAL* I, 154–79.

Lazard, G. (1975), 'The rise of the new Persian language'. *CHI* IV, 566–94.

Lebedev, Viktor Vladimirovič (1977), *Pozdnij srednearabskij jazyk (XIII–XVIII vv.)*. Moscow: Nauka.

— (1993), ''Anāṣir fūlklūriyya fī l-'adab al-'arabī fī l-qurūn al-wusṭā'. *al-Karmil* 14, 131–46.

Leder, Stefan and Hilary Kilpatrick (1992), 'Classical Arabic prose literature: a researchers' sketch map'. *JAL* 23, 2–26.

Leemhuis, Fred (1977), *The* D *and* H *Stems in Koranic Arabic: A Comparative Study of the Function and Meaning of the* fa''ala *and* 'af'ala *Forms in Koranic usage*. Leiden: E. J. Brill.

Levin, Aryeh (1994), 'Sībawayhi's attitude to the spoken language'. *JSAI* 17, 204–43.

Levy, Kurt (1936), *Zur masoretischen Grammatik: Texte und Untersuchungen*. Stuttgart: W. Kohlhammer.

Lewis, Bernard (1988), *The Political Language of Islam*. Chicago and London: Chicago University Press.

Lipiński, Edward (1997), *Semitic Languages: Outline of a Comparative Grammar*. Louvain: Peeters.

Littmann, Enno (1943), *Safaitic Inscriptions*. Leiden: E. J. Brill.

Lodhi, Abdulaziz Y. (1986), 'The status of Arabic in East Africa', in *On the Dignity of Man:*

Oriental and Classical Studies in Honour of Frithiof Rundgren, ed. Tryggve Kronholm and Eva Riad, pp. 257–62. Stockholm: Almqvist & Wiksell.
Maamouri, Mohamed (1973), 'The linguistic situation in independent Tunisia'. *AJAS* 1, 50–65.
McCarthy, John and Alan Prince (1990), 'Prosodic morphology and templatic morphology'. *PAL* II, 1–54.
McLoughlin, Leslie (1972), 'Towards a definition of Modern Standard Arabic'. *ArchLing*, new series, 3, 57–73.
MacNamara, J. (1967), 'Bilingualism in the modern world'. *JSI* 23:2, 1–7.
Mahdī, Muḥsin (1984), *Kitāb 'Alf layla wa-layla min 'uṣūlihi l-ʿarabiyya al-'ūlā*. Leiden: E. J. Brill.
Mahmoud, Y. (1982), 'Towards a functional Arabic'. *al-ʿArabiyya* 15, 82–9.
Mahmud, Ushari Ahmad [= ʿUsārī 'Aḥmad Maḥmūd] (1979), *Variation and Change in the Aspectual System of Juba Arabic*. Ph.D. thesis, Georgetown University, Washington DC.
Malaika, Nisar (1963), *Grundzüge der Grammatik des arabischen Dialektes von Bagdad*. Wiesbaden: O. Harrassowitz.
Malina, Renate (1987), *Zum schriftlichen Gebrauchs des Kairinischen Dialekts anhand ausgewählter Texte von Saʿdaddīn Wahba*. Berlin: K. Schwarz.
Marbach, Amikam (1992), 'Maʿnā l-muṣṭalaḥ "ʿArab" ḥasaba l-maʿāǧim wa-l-Qur'ān wa-l-Kitāb li-Sībawayh wa-Muqaddimat Ibn H̱aldūn'. *al-Karmil* 13, 145–78.
Marçais, Philippe (n.d.[1956]), *Le parler arabe de Djidjelli (Nord constantinois, Algérie)* (= *Publications de l'Institut d'Etudes Orientales d'Alger*, 16). Paris: Librairie d'Amérique et d'Orient Adrien-Maisonneuve.
— (1977), *Esquisse grammaticale de l'arabe maghrébin*. Paris: Maisonneuve.
Marçais, William (1930), 'La diglossie arabe'. *EP* 104:12, 401–9.
— (1961), 'Comment l'Afrique du Nord a été arabisée', in William Marçais, *Articles et Conférences*, pp. 171–92. Paris: Adrien-Maisonneuve.
Mazraani, Nathalie (1996), 'Style variation and persuasion in the speeches of Gamal Abdel Nasser'. *AIDA* II, 41–9.
Mehlem, Ulrich (1994), 'Linguistic situation and mother tongue teaching for migrants from Arab countries in the Federal Republic of Germany'. *IJoAL* 20, 249–69.
Meuleman, John H. (1994), 'Arabic in Indonesia'. *IJoAL* 20, 11–34.
Mifsud, Manwel (1995), *Loan Verbs in Maltese: A Descriptive and Comparative Study*. Leiden: E. J. Brill.
Mifsud, Manwel and Albert Borg (1994), 'Arabic in Malta'. *IJoAL* 20, 89–102.
Miller, Ann M. (1986), 'The origin of the modern Arabic sedentary dialects: an evaluation of several theories'. *al-ʿArabiyya* 19, 47–74.
Miller, Catherine (1985–6), 'Un exemple d'évolution linguistique: le cas de la particle "Ge" en "Juba Arabic"'. *MAS*, 155–66.
— (1987), 'De la campagne à la ville: évolution fonctionnelle de l'arabe véhiculaire en Equatoria (Sud-Soudan)'. *BCEPSP* 9, 1–23.
— (1994), 'Créolisation et acquisition: quelques phénomènes observés à propos de l'arabe du Soudan', in *Créolisation et acquisition des langues*, ed. Daniel Véronique, pp. 225–46. Aix-en-Provence: Publications Université de Provence.
Mitchell, T. F. (1962), *Colloquial Arabic: The Living Language of Egypt*. London: The English Universities Press.
Molan, Peter D. (1978), *Medieval Western Arabic: Reconstructing Elements of the Dialects of al-Andalus, Sicily, and North Africa from the* laḥn al-ʿāmma *Literature*. Ph.D. thesis, University of California, Berkeley.
Monteil, Vincent (1960), *L'arabe moderne*. Paris: Klincksieck.
Moscati, Sabatino (ed.) (1964), *An Introduction to the Comparative Grammar of the Semitic Languages: Phonology and Morphology*. Wiesbaden: O. Harrassowitz.

Mosel, Ulrike (1975), *Die syntaktische Terminologie bei Sībawaih*. Dissertation, University of Munich.
Motzki, Harald (1991), 'Der Fiqh des -Zuhrī: Die Quellenproblematik'. *Der Islam* 68, 1–44.
Moutaouakil, Ahmad (1989), *Pragmatic Functions in a Functional Grammar of Arabic*. Dordrecht: Foris.
Mseddi, Abdessalam [= ʿAbd as-Salām Musaddī] (1984), *Qāmūs al-lisāniyyāt, ʿarabī–firansī, firansī–ʿarabī*. Tunis: ad-Dār al-ʿArabiyya li-l-Kitāb.
Müller, August (1884), 'Über Text und Sprachgebrauch von Ibn Abī Uṣeibiʿa's Geschichte der Aerzte'. *SbBAW* V, 853–977.
Müller, Walter M. (1982), 'Das Altarabische der Inschriften aus vorislamischer Zeit'. *GAP* I, 30–6.
Munǧid (1990), *al-Munǧid al-ʿarabī al-firansī li-ṭ-ṭullāb*. Beirut: Dar el-Machreq.
Musa-Wellens, Ineke (1994), *A Descriptive Sketch of the Verbal System of the Nubi-Language Spoken in Bombo, Uganda*. MA dissertation, University of Nijmegen.
Myers-Scotton, Carol (1993), *Duelling Languages: Grammatical Structure in Code-switching*. Oxford: Clarendon Press.
Nabhan, Neuza Naif (1994), 'The speech of the Arabic-Lebanese in Brazil: a lexical study'. *IJoAL* 20, 229–47.
Nagel, Tilman (1983), 'Vom "*Qur'ān*" zur "Schrift": Bells Hypothese aus religionsgeschichtlicher Sicht'. *Der Islam* 60, 143–65.
Nebes, Norbert (1982), *Funktionsanalyse von* kāna yafʿalu*: Ein Beitrag zur Verbalsyntax des Althocharabischen mit besonderer Berücksichtigung der Tempus- und Aspektproblematik* (= *Studien zur Sprachwissenschaft*, 1). Hildesheim: G. Olms.
Negev, A. (1986), 'Obodas the God'. *IEJ* 36, 56–60.
Nishio, Tetsuo (1996), 'Word order and word order change of wh-questions in Egyptian Arabic: the Coptic substratum reconsidered'. *AIDA* II, 171–9.
Noja, Sergio (1989), 'Über die älteste arabische Inschrift, die vor kurzem entdeckt wurde', in *Studia semitica necnon iranica Rodolpho Macuch septuagenario ab amicis et discipulis dedicata*, pp. 187–94. Wiesbaden.
— (1993), 'A further discussion of the Arabic sentence of the 1st century A.D. and its poetical form', in *Semitica. Serta Philologica Constantino Tsereteli Dicata*, ed. R. Contini, F. A. Pennachietti and M. Tosco, pp. 183–88. Turin: S. Zamorani.
Nöldeke, Theodor (1891), 'Das arabische Märchen vom Doctor und Garkoch'. *AKAWB* 14, 1–54.
— (1897), *Zur Grammatik des klassischen Arabisch*. Wien (repr., ed. by Anton Spitaler, Darmstadt: Wissenschaftliche Buchgesellschaft, 1963 [with an appendix containing the handwritten notes of Nöldeke's private copy]).
— (1904), 'Das klassische Arabisch und die arabischen Dialekte', in Theodor Nöldeke, *Beiträge zur semitischen Sprachwissenschaft*, pp. 1–14. Strasburg: K. J. Trübner.
Nöldeke, Theodor and Friedrich Schwally (1961), *Geschichte des Qorans*, 2nd edn, ed. Gotthelf Bergsträßer and Otto Pretzl. Hildesheim: G. Olms.
Nortier, Jacomien (1989), *Dutch and Moroccan Arabic in Contact: Code-switching Among Moroccans in the Netherlands*. Ph.D. thesis, University of Amsterdam.
— (1994), 'Dutch–Moroccan code-switching in the Netherlands'. *IJoAL* 20, 193–214.
Noth, Albrecht (1973), *Quellenkritische Studien zu Themen, Formen und Tendenzen früh-islamischer Geschichtsüberlieferung*. I. *Themen und Formen*. Bonn: Selbstverlag des orientalischen Seminars der Universität Bonn.
Ogloblin, A. K. (1981), 'Tradicionnoe jazykoznanie v Indonezii i Malajzii', in *Istorija lingvističeskix učenij: Srednevekovyj vostok*, ed. Agnija Vasil'evna Desnickaja and Solomon Davidovič Kacnel'son, pp. 210–23. Leningrad: Nauka.
Orel, Vladimir E. and Olga V. Stolbova (1994), *Hamito–Semitic Etymological Dictionary: Materials for a Reconstruction*. Leiden: E. J. Brill.

Otten, Roel (1983), *Basiswoordenboek van het Marokkaans Arabisch: Marokkaans/ Nederlands, Nederlands/Marokkaans*. Muiderberg: Coutinho.
Ounali, Mohamed (1970), 'La langue des étudiants'. *CERES* 3, 167–213.
Owens, Jonathan (1977), *Aspects of Nubi Grammar*. Ph.D. thesis, University of London, School of Oriental and African Studies.
— (1984), *A Short Reference Grammar of Eastern Libyan Arabic*. Wiesbaden: O. Harrassowitz.
— (1985), 'Arabic dialects of Chad and Nigeria'. *ZAL* 14, 45–61.
— (1988), *The Foundations of Grammar: An Introduction to Medieval Arabic Grammatical Theory*. Amsterdam and Philadelphia: J. Benjamins.
— (1990), 'East African Nubi: bioprogram vs. inheritance'. *Diachronica* 7, 217–50.
— (1993), *A Grammar of Nigerian Arabic*. Wiesbaden: O. Harrassowitz.
— (1994), 'Nigerian Arabic in comparative perspective'. *SGA* 14, 85–175.
— (1998), *Neighborhood and Ancestry: Variation in the Spoken Arabic of Maiduguri, Nigeria*. Amsterdam & Philadelphia: J. Benjamins.
—, ed. (2000), *Arabic as a Minority Language*. Berlin & New York: Mouton de Gruyter.
Palva, Heikki (1969a), 'Notes on classicization in modern colloquial Arabic' (= *Studia Orientalia* 40:1–2). Helsinki: Snellmanink.
— (1969b), 'Notes on the alleged Coptic morphological influence on Egyptian Arabic'. *OS* 18, 128–36.
— (1991), 'Is there a North West Arabian dialect group?', in *Festgabe für Hans-Rudolf Singer*, ed. Martin Forstner, pp. 151–66. Frankfurt am Main: P. Lang.
Pellat, Charles (1985), *Introduction à l'arabe moderne*, new edn. Paris.
Penrice, John (1873), *A Dictionary and Glossary of the Kor-ān with Copious Grammatical References and Explanations of the Text* (repr. New York: Praeger, 1971).
Pérez Lázaro, José (1990), *Ibn Hišām al-Lajmī (m. 577/1181–1182)*, al-Madjal ilà taqwīm al-lisān wa-ta'līm al-bayān *(Introducción a la corrección del lenguaje y la enseñanza de la elocuencia): Edición crítica, estudio e índices*, 2 vols. Madrid: Instituto de Cooperación con el Mundo Árabe.
Perry, John R. (1991), *Form and Meaning in Persian Vocabulary: The Arabic Feminine Ending*. Costa Mesa, Cal. & New York: Mazda Publishers.
Petráček, Karel (1981), 'Le système de l'arabe dans une perspective diachronique'. *Ar* 28, 162–77.
— (1982), 'La racine en indoeuropéen et en chamitosémitique et leurs perspectives comparatives'. *AION* 42, 381–402.
— (1984), 'La méthodologie du chamitosémitique comparé: état, problèmes, perspectives', in *Current Progress in Afro-Asiatic Linguistics*, ed. James Bynon, pp. 423–62. Amsterdam and Philadelphia: J. Benjamins.
Piamenta, M. (1966), *Studies in the Syntax of Palestinian Arabic*. Jerusalem.
Poliak, A. N. (1938), 'L'arabisation de l'Orient sémitique'. *REI* 12, 35–63.
Pořízka, Vincenc (1972), *Hindština, Hindī Language Course*. Prague: Státní Pedagogické Nakladatelství.
Prätor, Sabine (1993), *Der arabische Faktor in der jungtürkischen Politik: eine Studie zum osmanischen Parlament der II. Konstitution (1908–1918)*. Berlin: Klaus Schwarz.
Prochazka, Theodore (1981), 'The Shī'ī dialects of Bahrain and their relationship to the Eastern Arabian dialect of Muḥarraq and the Omani dialect of al-Ristāq'. *ZAL* 6, 16–55.
— (1988), *Saudi Arabian Dialects*. London and New York: Kegan Paul International.
Prokosch, Erich (1986), *Arabische Kontaktsprachen (Pidgin- und Kreolsprachen) in Afrika*. Graz: Institut für Sprachwissenschaft, University of Graz.
Qāsim, 'Awn aš-Šarīf (1972), *Qāmūs al-lahğa al-'āmmiyya fī s-Sūdān*. Khartoum.
Rabin, Chaim (1951), *Ancient West-Arabian*. London: Taylor's Foreign Press.
— (1955), 'The beginnings of Classical Arabic'. *SI* 4, 19–37.

— (1960), ''Arabiyya'. *EI(2)* I, 564–6.
— (1969), 'The structure of the Semitic system of case endings', in *Proceedings of the International Conference on Semitic Studies held in Jerusalem, 19–23 July 1965*, pp. 190–204. Jerusalem: Israel Academy of Sciences and Humanities.
Ratcliffe, Robert R. (1998), *The 'Broken' Plural Problem in Arabic and Comparative Semitic*. Amsterdam & Philadelphia: J. Benjamins.
Rebhan, Helga (1986), *Geschichte und Funktion einiger politischen Termini im Arabischen des 19. Jahrhunderts (1798–1882)*. Wiesbaden: O. Harrassowitz.
Reckendorff, Hermann (1895–8), *Die syntaktischen Verhältnisse des Arabischen*, 2 vols. Leiden: E. J. Brill (repr. 1967).
— (1921), *Arabische Syntax*. Heidelberg: C. Winter.
Reichmuth, Stefan (1983), *Der arabische Dialekt der Šukriyya im Ostsudan*. Hildesheim: G. Olms.
Reig, Daniel (1987), *Dictionnaire arabe–français, français–arabe: as-Sabīl al-wāsiṭ*. Paris: Larousse.
Reinhardt, Carl (1894), *Ein arabischer Dialekt gesprochen in 'Oman und Zanzibar*. Stuttgart (repr. Amsterdam: Philo Press, 1972).
Retsö, Jan (1983), *The Finite Passive Voice in Modern Arabic Dialects*. Göteborg: University of Göteborg.
Revell, E. J. (1975), 'The diacritical dots and the development of the Arabic alphabet'. *JSS* 20, 178–90.
Riguet, Maurice (1984), *Attitudes et représentations liées à l'emploi du bilinguisme: analyse du cas tunisien*. Paris: Publications de la Sorbonne.
Robin, Christian (1992), *L'Arabie antique de Karib'īl à Mahomet: nouvelles données sur l'histoire des Arabes grâce aux inscriptions*. Aix-en-Provence: Editions Edisud.
Roman, André (1983), *Etude de la phonologie et de la morphologie de la koine arabe*, 2 vols. Aix-en-Provence: University of Provence.
Rosenhouse, Judith (1984), *The Bedouin Arabic Dialects: General Problems and a Close Analysis of North Israel Bedouin Dialects*. Wiesbaden: O. Harrassowitz.
— (1996), 'Features of women's speech in Arabic dialects: an interim survey'. *AIDA* II, 207–16.
Rosenthal, Franz (1968), *A History of Muslim Historiography*, 2nd edn. Leiden: E. J. Brill.
Rossi, E. (1939), *L'arabo parlato a Ṣan'ā': Grammatica, testi, lessico*. Rome.
Roth-Laly, Arlette (1969–), *Lexique des parlers arabes tchado-soudanais*. 1–. Paris: Editions du CNRS.
— (1979), *Esquisse grammaticale du parler arabe d'Abbéché (Tchad)*. Paris: Geuthner.
Rouchdy, Aleya (1991), *Nubians and the Nubian Language in Contemporary Egypt: A Case of Cultural and Linguistic Contact*. Leiden: E. J. Brill.
Ryding, Karin C. (1990), *Formal Spoken Arabic: Basic Course*. Washington DC: Georgetown University Press.
Saad, George Nehmeh (1982), *Transitivity, Causation and Passivization: A Semantico-syntactic Study of the Verb in Classical Arabic*. London and New York: Kegan Paul International.
Sabuni, Abdulghafur (1980), *Laut- und Formenlehre des arabischen Dialekts von Aleppo*. Frankfurt am Main: P. Lang.
Sáenz-Badillos, Angel (1993), *A History of the Hebrew Language*, trans. John Elwolde. Cambridge: Cambridge University Press [English translation of *Historia de la lengua hebrea*, Sabadell: Editorial AUSA, 1988].
Salib, Maurice (1981), *Spoken Arabic of Cairo*. Cairo: American University of Cairo Press.
Sasse, Hans-Jürgen (1971), *Linguistische Analyse des arabischen Dialekts der Mḥallamīye in der Provinz Mardin (Südosttürkei)*. Dissertation, University of Munich.
Sawaie, Mohammed (1987), 'Jurjī Zaydān (1861–1914): a modernist in Arabic linguistics'. *HL* 14, 283–304.

— (1990), 'An aspect of 19th-century Arabic lexicography: the modernizing role and contribution of Faris al-Shidyak (1804?–1887)', in *History and Historiography of Linguistics*, ed. Hans-Josef Niederehe and Konrad Koerner, I, pp. 157–71. Amsterdam and Philadelphia: J. Benjamins.

Schabert, Peter (1976), *Laut- und Formenlehre des Maltesischen anhand zweier Mundarten* (= *Erlanger Studien*, 16). Erlangen: Palm & Enke.

Schall, Anton (1982), 'Geschichte des arabischen Wortschatzes: Lehn- und Fremdwörter im klassischen Arabisch'. *GAP* I, 142–53.

Schen, I. (1972–3), 'Usāma ibn Munqidh's memoirs: some further light on Muslim Middle Arabic'. *JSS* 17, 218–36; 18, 64–97.

Schimmel, Annemarie (1982), 'Die Schriftarten und ihr kalligraphischer Gebrauch'. *GAP* I, 198–209.

Schippers, Arie and Kees Versteegh (1987), *Het Arabisch: norm en realiteit*. Muiderberg: Coutinho.

Schoeler, Gregor (1985), 'Die Frage der schriftlichen oder mündlichen Überlieferung der Wissenschaften im frühen Islam'. *Der Islam* 62, 201–30.

— (1989a), 'Weiteres zur Frage der schriftlichen oder mündlichen Überlieferung der Wissenschaften im Islam'. *Der Islam* 66, 38–67.

— (1989b), 'Mündliche Thora und Ḥadīth: Überlieferung, Schreibverbot, Redaktion'. *Der Islam* 66, 213–51.

— (1992), 'Schreiben und Veröffentlichen: zu Verwendung und Funktion der Schrift in den ersten islamischen Jahrhunderten'. *Der Islam* 69, 1–43.

Schregle, Goetz (1974), *Deutsch–arabisches Wörterbuch*, 2nd edn. Wiesbaden: O. Harrassowitz.

— (1981–), *Arabisch–deutsches Wörterbuch*. Wiesbaden: F. Steiner.

Schreiber, Giselher (1970), *Der arabische Dialekt von Mekka: Abriß der Grammatik mit Texten und Glossar*. Dissertation, University of Münster.

Semaan, Khalil I. (1968), *Linguistics in the Middle Ages: Phonetic Studies in Early Islam*. Leiden: E. J. Brill.

Serjeant, R. B. (1983), 'Early Arabic prose'. *CHAL* I, 114–53.

Sezgin, Fuat (1982), *Lexikographie bis ca. 430 H* (= *GAS* VIII). Leiden: E. J. Brill.

— (1984), *Grammatik bis ca. 430 H* (= *GAS* IX). Leiden: E. J. Brill.

Shahid, Irfan (1984), *Byzantium and the Arabs in the Fourth Century*. Washington DC: Dumbarton Oaks.

Shraybom-Shivtiel, Shlomit (1993), 'Methods of terminological innovation used by the Cairo Language Academy'. *PCALL* I, 195–202.

Sieny, Mahmoud Esma'il [= Maḥmūd 'Ismā'īl Ṣīnī] (1978), *The Syntax of Urban Hijazi Arabic (Sa'udi Arabia)*. London: Longman.

Singer, Hans-Rudolf (1958a), 'Neuarabische Texte im Dialekt der Stadt Tetuan'. *ZDMG* 108, 106–25.

— (1958b), 'Grundzüge der Morphologie des arabischen Dialektes von Tetuan'. *ZDMG* 108, 229–65.

— (1982), 'Der neuarabische Sprachraum'. *GAP* I, 96–109.

— (1984), *Grammatik der arabischen Mundart der Medina von Tunis*. Berlin and New York: De Gruyter.

— (1994), 'Die Beduinen als Träger der Arabisierung im islamischen Machtbereich', in *Gedenkschrift Wolfgang Reuschel. Akten des III. Arabistischen Kolloquiums, Leipzig, 21.–22. November 1991*, ed. Dieter Bellmann, pp. 263–74. Stuttgart: F. Steiner.

Sirat, Abdul-Sattār (1973), 'Notes on the Arabic dialect spoken in the Balkh Region of Afghanistan (annotated by Ebbe Egede Knudsen)'. *AO* 35, 89–101.

Smeaton, B. Hunter (1973), *Lexical Expansion due to Technical Change as Illustrated by the Arabic of Al Hasa, Saudi Arabia*. Bloomington: Indiana University Press.

Sobhy, Gregory P. G. (1926), 'Fragments of an Arabic manuscript in Coptic script in the Metropolitan Museum of Art', in *Egyptian Expedition, The Monasteries of the Wadi 'n Natrūn. I. New Coptic Texts from the Monastery of St. Marcus*, ed. H. G. Evelyn White. New York.

— (1950), *Common Words in the Spoken Arabic of Egypt, of Greek or Coptic Origin.* Cairo: Société d'Archéologie Copte.

Soden, Wolfram von (1960), 'Zur Einteilung der semitischen Sprachen'. *WZKM* 56, 177–91.

Sourdel-Thomine, Janine (1966), 'Les origines de l'écriture arabe: à propos d'une hypothèse récente'. *REI* 34, 151–7.

Spitaler, Anton (1953), Review of Fück (1950). *BiOr* 10, 144–40.

Spitta-Bey, Wilhelm (1880), *Grammatik des arabischen vulgärdialektes von Aegypten.* Leipzig.

Spuler, Bertold (1964a), 'Die Ausbreitung der arabischen Sprache'. *HdO* I:3, 245–52.

— (1964b), 'Der semitische Sprachtypus'. *HdO* I:3, 3–25.

— (1964c), 'Ausbreitung der semitischen Sprachen'. *HdO* I:3, 25–31.

Starcky, Jean (1966), 'Petra et la Nabatène'. *Dictionnaire de la Bible*, Supplément, VII, 886–1,017. Paris.

Stetkevych, Jaroslav (1970), *The Modern Arabic Literary Language: Lexical and Stylistic developments.* Chicago and London: University of Chicago Press.

Stiehl, Ruth (1971–3), 'Neue Liḥyanische Inschriften aus al-ʿU̱dayb', in Franz Altheim and Ruth Stiehl (eds), *Christentum am Roten Meer*, 2 vols, I, 3–40. Berlin: de Gruyter.

Stowasser, Karl and Moukhtar Ani (1964), *A Dictionary of Syrian Arabic: English–Arabic.* Washington DC: Georgetown University Press.

Suleiman, Saleh M. (1985), *Jordanian Arabic between Diglossia and Bilingualism.* Amsterdam and Philadelphia: J. Benjamins.

Suleiman, Yasir (1999), *The Arabic Grammatical Tradition: A Study in* taʿlīl. Edinburgh: Edinburgh University Press.

Sutcliffe, Edmund F. (1936), *A Grammar of the Maltese Language, with Chrestomathy and Vocabulary.* London: Oxford University Press.

Taine-Cheikh, Catherine (1988–), *Dictionnaire ḥassāniyya–français.* 1–. Paris: Geuthner.

— (1994), 'Le *ḥassānīya* de Mauritanie: un dialecte non-marginal de la périphérie', in Aguadé et al. (1994), pp. 173–99.

Talmon, Rafael (1985), 'Who was the first Arab grammarian? A new approach to an old problem'. *SHAG* I, 128–45.

Talmoudi, Fathi (1980), *The Arabic Dialect of Sūsa (Tunisia).* Gothenburg: Acta Universitatis Gothoburgensis.

—(1981), *Texts in the Arabic Dialect of Sūsa (Tunisia): Transcription, Translation, Notes and Glossary.* Gothenburg: Acta Universitatis Gothoburgensis.

—(1984a), *The Diglossic Situation in North Africa: A Study of Classical Arabic/Dialectal Arabic Diglossia with Sample Text in 'Mixed Arabic'.* Gothenburg: Acta Universitatis Gothoburgensis.

— (1984b), 'Notes on the syntax of the Arabic dialect of Sūsa'. *ZAL* 12, 48–85.

Téné, David (1980), 'The earliest comparisons of Hebrew with Aramaic and Arabic', in *Progress in Linguistic Historiography*, ed. Konrad Koerner, pp. 355–77. Amsterdam: J. Benjamins.

Toll, Christopher (1983), *Notes on Ḥiǧāzī Dialects: Ġāmidī.* Copenhagen: C. A. Reitzel.

Tomiche, Nada (1964), *Le parler arabe du Caire.* The Hague and Paris: Mouton.

Tosco, Mauro and Jonathan Owens (1993), 'Turku: a descriptive and comparative study'. *SGA* 14, 177–267.

Tourneux, Henry and Jean-Claude Zeltner (1986), *L'arabe dans le bassin du Tchad: le parler des Ulād Eli.* Paris: Karthala.

Trimingham, J. S. (1946), *Sudan Colloquial Arabic*, 2nd edn. London: Oxford University Press.

Troupeau, Gérard (1976), *Lexique-index du* Kitāb *de Sībawayhi*. Paris: Klincksieck.
Tsereteli, George V. (1970a), 'The verbal particle *m/mi* in Bukhara Arabic'. *FO* 12, 291–5.
— (1970b), 'The influence of the Tajik language on the vocalism of Central Asian Arabic dialects'. *BSOAS* 33, 167–70.
Ullendorff, Edward (1958), 'What is a Semitic language?' *Orientalia*, new series, 27, 66–75.
Ullmann, Manfred (1966), *Untersuchungen zur Rağazpoesie: ein Beitrag zur arabischen Sprach- und Literaturwissenschaft*. Wiesbaden: O. Harrassowitz.
'Umar, 'Aḥmad Muḫtār (1992), *Ta'rīḫ al-luğa al-'arabiyya fī Miṣr wa-l-Mağrib al-'Adnā*. Cairo: 'Ālam al-Kutub.
Vanhove, Martine (1993), *La langue maltaise*. Wiesbaden: O. Harrassowitz.
Versteegh, Kees (1984), *Pidginization and Creolization: The Case of Arabic* (= *Current Issues in Linguistic Theory*, 33). Amsterdam: J. Benjamins.
— (1984–6), 'Word order in Uzbekistan Arabic and universal grammar'. *OS* 33–5, 443–53.
— (1985), 'The development of argumentation in Arabic grammar: the declension of the dual and the plural'. *SHAG* I, 152–73.
— (1987), 'Arabische Sprachwissenschaft (Grammatik)'. *GAP* II, 148–76.
— (1990), 'Grammar and exegesis: the origin of Kufan grammar and the *Tafsīr Muqātil*'. *Der Islam* 67, 206–42.
— (1993a), *Arabic Grammar and Qur'ānic Exegesis in Early Islam*. Leiden: E. J. Brill.
— (1993b), 'Leveling in the Sudan: from Arabic creole to Arabic dialect'. *IJSL* 99, 65–79.
— (1994), 'The notion of "underlying levels" in the Arabic linguistic tradition'. *HL* 21, 271–96.
— (1995), *The Explanation of Linguistic Causes: Az-Zağğāğī's Theory of Grammar, Introduction, Translation and Commentary*. Amsterdam and Philadelphia: J. Benjamins.
— (1999), 'Loanwords from Arabic and the merger of *ḍ/ḏ'*/. *IOS* 19, 273–86.
Vial, Charles (1983), *L'égyptien tel qu'on l'écrit d'après un choix d'œuvres littéraires égyptiennes contemporaines*. Cairo: Institut Français d'Archéologie Orientale du Caire.
Vinnikov, Isaak Natanovič (1956), 'Fol'klor Buxarskix Arabov'. *AOASH* 6, 181–206.
— (1962), *Slovar' dialekta buxarskix Arabov* (= *PS* 10 [73]). Moscow and Leningrad: Izd. Nauka.
— (1969), *Jazyk i fol'klor buxarskix Arabov*. Moscow: Izd. Nauka.
Violet, E. (1902), *Ein zweisprachiges Psalmfragment aus Damaskus*. Berlin.
Vocke, Sibylle and Wolfram Waldner (1982), *Der Wortschatz des anatolischen Arabisch*. Dissertation, University of Erlangen.
Voigt, Rainer M. (1987), 'The classification of Central Semitic'. *JSS* 32, 1–21.
— (1988), *Die infirmen Verbaltypen des Arabischen und das Biradikalismusproblem*. Stuttgart: F. Steiner.
Vollers, Karl (1906), *Volkssprache und Schriftsprache im alten Arabien*. Strasburg: K. J. Trübner (repr. 1981).
Walters, Keith (1989), *Social Change and Linguistic Variation in Korba, a Small Tunisian Town*. Ph.D. thesis, University of Texas, Austin.
— (1991), 'Women, men, and linguistic variation in the Arab world'. *PAL* III, 199–229.
Watson, Janet C. E. (1993), *A Syntax of Ṣan'ānī Arabic*. Wiesbaden: O. Harrassowitz.
— (1996), *Sbaḥtū: A Course in Ṣan'ānī Arabic*. Wiesbaden: O. Harrassowitz.
Wehr, Hans (1952), Review of Fück (1950). *ZDMG* 102, 179–86.
— (1956), *Das Buch der wunderbaren Erzählungen und seltsamen Geschichten*. Wiesbaden: F. Steiner.
— (1979), *A Dictionary of Modern Written Arabic (Arabic–English)*, ed. J Milton Cowan. Wiesbaden: O. Harrassowitz.
— (1985), *Arabisches Wörterbuch für die Schriftsprache der Gegenwart: Arabisch–*

Deutsch, 5th edn. Wiesbaden: O. Harrassowitz (1st edn 1952).
Wild, Stefan (1965), *Das* Kitāb al-ʿain *und die arabische Lexikographie*. Wiesbaden: O. Harrassowitz.
— (1982), 'Die arabische Schriftsprache der Gegenwart'. *GAP* I, 51–7.
Wise, Hilary (1975), *A Transformational Grammar of Spoken Egyptian Arabic*. Oxford: B. Blackwell.
Woidich, Manfred (1979), 'Zum Dialekt von il-ʿAwāmṛa in der östlichen Šarqiyya (Ägypten). I. Einleitung, grammatische Skizzen und volkskundliches'. *ZAL* 2, 76–99.
— (1980), 'Zum Dialekt von il-ʿAwāmṛa in der östlichen Šarqiyya (Ägypten). II. Texte und Glossar'. *ZAL* 4, 31–60.
— (1985), *Übungsbuch zur arabischen Schriftsprache der Gegenwart*. Wiesbaden: L. Reichert.
— (1990), *Ahlan wa sahlan: Eine Einführung in die Kairoer Umgangssprache*. Wiesbaden: L. Reichert.
— (1993), 'Die Dialekte der ägyptischen Oasen: westliches oder östliches Arabisch?' *ZAL* 25, 340–59.
— (1994), 'Cairo Arabic and the Egyptian dialects'. *AIDA* I, 493–507.
— (1995), 'Das Kairenische im 19. Jh.: Gedanken zu Ṭanṭāwī's "*Traité de la langue arabe vulgaire*"', in *Dialectologia arabica. A Collection of Articles in Honour of the Sixtieth Birthday of Professor Heikki Palva*, pp. 271–87. Helsinki: Finnish Oriental Society.
Woidich, Manfred and Rabha Heinen-Nasr (1995), Kullu tamām: *Inleiding tot de Egyptische omgangstaal*. Amsterdam: Bulaaq.
Woidich, Manfred and Jacob M. Landau (1993), *Arabisches Volkstheater in Kairo im Jahre 1909: Aḥmad ilFār und seine Schwänke*. Stuttgart: F. Steiner.
Woodhead, Daniel and Wayne Beene (1967), *A Dictionary of Iraqi Arabic: Arabic–English*. Washington DC: Georgetown University Press.
Wright, Roger (1982), *Late Latin and Early Romance in Spain and Carolingian France*. Liverpool: F. Cairns.
Wright, William (1859–62), *A Grammar of the Arabic Language*, 2 vols. London (3rd revised edn by W. Robertson Smith and M. J. de Goeje, Cambridge: Cambridge University Press, 1896–8).
Zaborski, Andrzej (1991), 'The position of Arabic within the Semitic language continuum'. *BSA* 3–4, 365–75.
Zarrinkūb, ʿAbd al-Ḥusain (1975), 'The Arab conquest of Iran and its aftermath'. *CHI* IV, 1–56.
Zavadovskij, Ju. N. (1981), *Mavritanskij dialekt Arabskogo jazyka (Chassanija)*. Moscow: Nauka.
Ziadeh, Farhat J. and R. Bayly Winder (1957), *An Introduction to Modern Arabic*. Princeton: Princeton University Press.
Zimmermann, F. W. (1972), 'Some observations on al-Fārābī and logical tradition', in *Islamic Philosophy and the Classical Tradition: Essays Presented by his Friends and Pupils to Richard Walzer on his Seventieth Birthday*, ed. Samuel M. Stern, Albert Hourani and Vivian Brown, pp. 517–46. Oxford: Cassirer.
Zughoul, Muhammad Raji and Lucine Taminian (1984), 'The linguistic attitude of Arab university students: factorial structure and intervening variables'. *IJSL* 50, 155–79.
Zürcher, Erik-Jan (1985), 'La théorie du "langage-soleil" et sa place dans la réforme de la langue turque', in *La linguistique fantastique*, ed. Sylvain Auroux et al., pp. 83–91. Paris: J. Clims.
Zwartjes, Otto (1997), *Love Songs from al-Andalus: History, Structure and Meaning of the Kharja*. Leiden: E. J. Brill.
Zwettler, Michael (1978), *The Oral Tradition of Classical Arabic Poetry: Its Character and Implications*. Columbus: Ohio State University Press.

LIST OF ABBREVIATIONS

AI	*Ars Islamica*. Ann Arbor.
AIDA I	*Actes des premières journées internationales de dialectologie arabe de Paris*, ed. Dominique Caubet and Martine Vanhove. Paris: INALCO.
AIDA II	*Proceedings of the 2nd International Conference of L'Association Internationale pour la Dialectologie Arabe, Held at Trinity Hall in the University of Cambridge, 10–14 September 1995*. Cambridge: University of Cambridge, 1996.
AIEO	*Annales de l'Institut d'Etudes Orientales*. Algiers.
AION	*Annali del Istituto Orientale di Napoli*. Naples.
AJAS	*American Journal of Arabic Studies*. Leiden.
AKAWB	*Philosophische und historische Abhandlungen der königlichen Akademie der Wissenschaften zu Berlin*. Berlin.
AL	*Anthropological Linguistics*. Bloomington IN.
AO	*Acta Orientalia*. Copenhagen.
AOASH	*Acta Orientalia Academiae Scientiarum Hungaricae*. Budapest.
Ar	*Arabica. Revue d'Etudes Arabes*. Leiden.
al-ʿArabiyya	*al-ʿArabiyya. Journal of the American Association of Teachers of Arabic*. Columbus OH.
ArchLing	*Archivum Linguisticum: A Review of Comparative Philosophy and General Linguistics*. Leeds.
BASOR	*Bulletin of the American Schools of Oriental Research*. Jerusalem.
BCEPSP	*Bulletin du Centre d'Etude des Plurilinguismes et des Situations Pluriculturelles*. Nice.
BIFAO	*Bulletin de l'Institut Français d'Archéologie Orientale*. Cairo.
BiOr	*Bibliotheca Orientalis*. Leiden.
BSA	*Budapest Studies in Arabic*. Budapest.
BSLP	*Bulletin de la Société de Linguistique de Paris*. Paris.
BSOAS	*Bulletin of the School of Oriental and African Studies*. London.
CERES	*Cahiers du Centre d'Etudes et de Recherches Economiques de l'Université de Tunis*, série linguistique. Tunis.
CHAL	*The Cambridge History of Arabic Literature*. I. *Arabic Literature to the End of the Umayyad Period*, ed. A. F. L. Beeston, T. M. Johnstone, R. B. Serjeant and G. R. Smith. Cambridge: Cambridge University Press, 1983.
CHI	*The Cambridge History of Iran*. IV. *The Period from the Arab Invasion to the Saljuqs*, ed. R. N. Frye. Cambridge: Cambridge University Press, 1975.
Concordances	*Concordances et Indices de la Tradition Musulmane*, ed. A. J. Wensinck et al., 7 vols. Leiden: E. J. Brill, 1936–69.
Diachronica	*Diachronica. International Journal for Historical Linguistics*. Amsterdam.
EI(2)	*The Encyclopaedia of Islam*. Leiden: E. J. Brill, 1908–34. New edition prepared by a number of leading Orientalists. Leiden: E. J. Brill, 1960–.

EP	*L'Enseignement Public*. Paris.
FO	*Folia Orientalia. Revue des Etudes Orientales*. Cracow.
GAP	*Grundriß der arabischen Philologie*. I. *Sprachwissenschaft*, ed. Wolfdietrich Fischer. II. *Literaturwissenschaft*, ed. Helmut Gätje. III. *Supplement*, ed. Wolfdietrich Fischer. Wiesbaden: L. Reichert, 1983, 1987, 1992.
GAS	Fuat Sezgin, *Geschichte des arabischen Schrifttums*. Leiden: E. J. Brill, 1967–.
HdO	*Handbuch der Orientalistik*. Leiden: E. J. Brill.
HL	*Historiographia Linguistica*. Amsterdam.
IEJ	*International Education Journal*. Scarsdale NY.
IJoAL	*Indian Journal of Applied Linguistics*. Delhi.
IJSL	*International Journal of the Sociology of Language*. Berlin.
IOS	*Israel Oriental Studies*. Tel Aviv.
Der Islam	*Der Islam. Zeitschrift für Geschichte und Kultur des islamischen Orients*. Berlin.
JAL	*Journal of Arabic Literature*. Leiden.
JAOS	*Journal of the American Oriental Society*. New Haven CT.
JQR	*Jewish Quarterly Review*. Leiden.
JSAI	*Jerusalem Studies in Arabic and Islam*. Jerusalem.
JSI	*Journal of Social Issues*. New York.
JSS	*Journal of Semitic Studies*. Manchester.
al-Karmil	*al-Karmil. Studies in Arabic Language and Literature*. Haifa.
LA	*Linguistic Analysis*. New York.
Lg	*Language. Journal of the Linguistic Society of America*. Baltimore.
Lingua	*Lingua. International Review of General Linguistics*. Amsterdam.
Linguistics	*Linguistics: An Inter-disciplinary Journal of the Language Sciences*. London.
LPLP	*Language Problems and Language Planning*. Amsterdam.
MAS	*Matériaux Arabes et Sudarabiques*. Paris.
MSOS	*Mitteilungen des Seminars für Orientalische Sprachen, westasiatische Studien*. Berlin.
MUSJ	*Mélanges de l'Université Saint Joseph*. Beirut.
OA	*Oriens Antiquus. Rivista del Centro per le Antichità e la Storia dell' Arte del Vicino Oriente*. Rome.
Orientalia	*Orientalia. Commentarii Periodici Pontificii Instituti Biblici*. Rome.
OS	*Orientalia Suecana*. Stockholm.
PAL	*Perspectives in Arabic Linguistics*. I, ed. Mushira Eid. Amsterdam and Philadelphia: J. Benjamins, 1990; II, ed. Mushira Eid and John McCarthy. Amsterdam and Philadelphia: J. Benjamins, 1990; III, ed. Bernard Comrie and Mushira Eid. Amsterdam and Philadelphia: J. Benjamins, 1991; IV, ed. Ellen Broselow, Mushira Eid and John McCarthy. Amsterdam and Philadelphia: J. Benjamins, 1992.
PCALL	*Proceedings of the Colloquium on Arabic Lexicology and Lexicography, Budapest, 1–7 September 1993*, ed. Kinga Dévényi, Tamás Iványi and Avihai Shivtiel. Budapest: Eötvös Loránd University.
PS	*Palestinskij Sbornik*. Moscow and Leningrad.
Q	*Qur'ān*.
REI	*Revue des Etudes Islamiques*. Paris.
RO	*Rocznik Orientalistyczny*. Warsaw.

SbBAW	*Sitzungsberichte der philosophisch-philologischen Classe der kaiserlichen bayerischen Akademie der Wissenschaften*. Munich.
SGA	*Sprache und Geschichte in Afrika*. Cologne.
SHAG I	*Studies in the History of Arabic Grammar. Proceedings of the First Symposium on the History of Arabic Grammar held at Nijmegen 16th–19th April 1984*, ed. Hartmut Bobzin and Kees Versteegh (= *ZAL* 15). Wiesbaden: O. Harrassowitz, 1985.
SI	*Studia Islamica*. Paris.
Théorie Analyses	*Travaux Vincennois. Etudes Arabes. Théorie Analyses*. Paris [a.k.a. *Analyses Théorie*].
TJ	*Travaux et Jours*. Beirut.
WdI	*Die Welt des Islams*. Leiden.
WKAS	*Wörterbuch der klassischen arabischen Sprache*. Wiesbaden: O. Harrassowitz, 1957–.
Word	*Word. Journal of the International Linguistics Association*. New York.
WZKM	*Wiener Zeitschrift für die Kunde des Morgenlandes*. Vienna.
ZAL	*Zeitschrift für arabische Linguistik*. Wiesbaden.
ZDMG	*Zeitschrift der deutschen morgenländischen Gesellschaft*. Leipzig and Wiesbaden.
ZDPV	*Zeitschrift des deutschen Palästina-Vereins*. Leipzig and Wiesbaden.

INDEX